The History of Mental Retardation

Volume 2

THE HISTORY
OF
MENTAL
RETARDATION

Collected Papers

Edited by
Marvin Rosen, Ph.D.
Director of Psychology
Elwyn Institute

Gerald R. Clark, M. D.
Professor of Psychiatry and of Pediatrics
University of Pennsylvania Medical School;
President, Elwyn Institute

Marvin S. Kivitz, Ph.D.
Director of Programs
Elwyn Institute

University Park Press
Baltimore · London · Tokyo

UNIVERSITY PARK PRESS
International Publishers in Science and Medicine
Chamber of Commerce Building
Baltimore, Maryland 21202

Typeset by The Composing Room of Michigan, Inc.
Manufactured in the United States of America by Universal Lithographers,
Inc. and The Maple Press Co.

Library of Congress Cataloging in Publication Data
Main entry under title:

The History of mental retardation.

　　Includes bibliographical references and indexes.
　　1. Mentally handicapped—History—Addresses, essays,
lectures. 2. Mental retardation services—History—
Addresses, essays, lectures. I. Rosen, Marvin.
II. Clark, Gerald Robert, 1918–　　III. Kivitz,
Marvin S. [DNLM: 1. Mental retardation—History—U.S.—
Collected works. 2. United States. WM11 AA1 H6]
HV3004.H57　　　362.3'09　　　75-30670
ISBN 0-8391-0827-3

VOLUME 2

Contents

SECTION EIGHT The Impact of Genetics

SECTION NINE Light on the Horizon

SECTION TEN   The 1960's and 1970's

PREFACE

This is the second volume of a two part series of collected papers dealing with the history of mental retardation. The papers presented in Volume 1 trace the origins of the mental retardation movement as a humanitarian concern, linked closely to the philosophical tenets of British and French Associationism. Descriptions of the first schools in Europe and the United States are presented and the physiological method of Edouard Seguin is set forth in Seguin's own words. The volume also illustrates early scientific concerns over classification of subtypes of mental retardation which led to finer diagnostic distinctions among clinical syndromes.

The era following the American Civil War was one of a rising wave of disillusionment. It was characterized by a growing concern about the mentally retarded as a social menace and the growth of institutions as a solution to these problems. The volume ends with a description of the mental testing movement and the manner in which intelligence tests were used to reinforce pessimistic attitudes about the irreversibility of mental retardation.

Volume 2 picks up the story early in the twentieth century. It identifies the first signs of changing attitudes in the research of a few progressive thinking educators and scientists. It documents the very slow acceptance of these findings as a basis for change in programs or policy until finally, in the last two decades, growing public concern about the rights of the mentally retarded and the burgeoning awareness of their capabilities have led to a major revolution in the philosophy and direction of service delivery systems.

SECTION SIX

Research
Laboratories
and
Clinics

Research in the field of mental retardation has grown so rapidly that it is difficult to recall a time when only a handful of research laboratories was actively pursuing knowledge about the mentally handicapped. Today, mental retardation research papers appear regularly in the journals of psychology, education, social work, rehabilitation, genetics, clinical medicine, and all the basic experimental sciences. Research reports appear not only in the two journals of the American Association on Mental Deficiency, but also in numerous foreign journals and the proceedings of innumerable research conferences. Two prestigious research compilations published in the 1950's and 1960's (Stevens and Heber, 1964; Ellis, 1963) provide impetus for burgeoning research efforts. These efforts have mushroomed sufficiently, even with recent cut-backs in federal funding, to justify two annual reviews of mental retardation (Ellis; Wortis) and a comprehensive Mental Retardation Abstracts (Department of Health, Education, and Welfare) updated several times a year. The scope of research activity is gleaned from Wortis' recently published Sixth Annual Review in Mental Retardation and Developmental Disability, which includes articles dealing with clinical medicine, genetics and intelligence, congenital malformations, developmental biochemistry, federal funding policy, sociology, education, sexual behavior, physical education, employment, language development, and volunteers.

The turn of the century witnessed the beginning of psychoeducational research, initially associated more with schools and clinics in the community than within the institution, and often directed by persons not well accepted by the influential medical superintendents. By 1901, Bancroft in New Jersey was advocating special training in the public schools for those with sensory or motor defects and restorative training in small schools for retarded with underdeveloped "faculties."

At the University of Pennsylvania, in 1896, Lightner Witmer established the first psychological clinic in the United States. This clinic was in continuous operation for the next sixty years. Witmer, never fully accepted by his profession during his lifetime, is today regarded as a pioneer (Gardner, 1968). The first to use the term "clinical psychology," Witmer had an enduring interest in studying the problems of mental retardation. His was the first clinic to treat the retarded and served as a model for other clinics at universities and school systems throughout the country.

Witmer was a student of Wundt in Leipzig, along with Titchner, Kulpe, Angell, and others. Before this he had been a psychology assistant to James McKeen Cattell. After receiving his doctorate, he succeeded Cattell as director of the Laboratory of Psychology when Cattell moved to Columbia. The journal, *The Psychological Clinic,* which he founded and edited, provided a forum for his interests in individual diagnosis, distinctions between psychosis and mental retardation, and the effects of environmental and emotional deprivation. Witmer founded the first university course in mental retardation. He is summarily dismissed in one paragraph by Roback (1964) as "too critical of his more recognized colleagues," as not bothering with systems, and uninfluenced by psychoanalysis and dynamic concepts, yet he is grudgingly described as influential in the fields of vocational guidance, remedial speech, and education.

The method of diagnostic teaching was implemented by E. E. Farrell in her work as director of ungraded classes in New York City. Farrell had studied in Germany and Belgium. Later, she worked with Witmer at the University of Pennsylvania. Taking her degree at Columbia, where she was influenced by both Thorndike and Dewey, she developed methods of educational diagnosis and prescriptive teaching far ahead of her time.

The influence of Goddard in shaping official attitudes and opinions concerning the value of intelligence testing and irreversibility of mental retardation has already been presented in Volume 1. His extensive publications and elaborate descriptions of "psychological work among the feeble-minded" (1907) are unparalleled in the influence they exerted. The laboratory he directed at the Vineland Training School was considered a center for mental deficiency research for decades after his resignation in 1918.

Records of the Vineland Training School trace the origins of Goddard's laboratory to the formation of the "Feeble-minded Club" in March 1902, to discuss problems of mental retardation. E. R. Johnstone, director of the Training School, was committed to the idea that public institutions should be considered as human laboratories where problems of human growth and development could be studied under controlled conditions. In his annual report in 1906, Johnstone recommended the establishment of a scientific laboratory. Financial support was obtained including that provided by Mr. Samuel S. Fels.

Goddard had studied under G. Stanley Hall, illustrious president of Clark University, editor of four psychological journals, first president of the American Psychological Association, and pioneer in the study of developmental psychology. Hall had as students a prestigious list of psychologists including

James McKeen Cattell, Joseph Jastrow, E. C. Sanford, Lewis Terman, Frederick Kuhlmann, Arnold Gesell, and John Dewey. It was Hall who recommended Goddard for the position of director of the new laboratory at Vineland.

Goddard's early pedagogical studies and experiments with psychomotor tests stimulated his interest in the 1905 Binet scale which was translated by Elizabeth Kite, his assistant and field worker. His standardization of the scale on 2000 Vineland Public School children, his classification of 400 feeble-minded children, and his conclusions from these studies are well known. By 1912, Goddard had established three divisions in the research department to study biochemistry, neuropathology, and clinical psychology, and was involved in the field studies of the Kallikak family.

After Goddard resigned, S. D. Porteus was appointed Director of Research (1919) and continued the Goddard tradition with studies of temperament and disposition. During this period he also developed the Porteus Maze Test. When Porteus resigned in 1925 to be professor of clinical psychology at the University of Hawaii, Edgar A. Doll was appointed director of research. Doll had worked as a psychologist under Goddard. Like Witmer, he opposed the sole use of the IQ test in diagnosis. He distinguished oligophrenia from intellectual subnormality as diagnostic categories and developed six criteria for diagnosis of mental deficiency. Doll is best known for his development of the Vineland Social Maturity Scale, designed to measure social competence in persons of low IQ.

In addition to Goddard, credit for development of the psychoeducational clinic, as it is known today, is generally given to J. E. Wallace Wallin. Another of G. Stanley Hall's students, Wallin had a varied experience as teacher, researcher, and educational administrator. From 1914 to 1921, he was director of a psychoeducational clinic for the St. Louis Public Schools, one of the earliest clinics of its kind. As Wallin describes it (1955), his responsibility was the administration of psychoclinical examinations, special classes, and the training of special class teachers. While Goddard laid the foundations of prescriptive teaching by describing the mental age as indicative of instructional level, Wallin expanded the diagnostic procedure to include other factors such as the case history. Wallin made distinctions in diagnosis and programming between the mentally subnormal and the pedagogically retarded; he provided for the admission of trainables to public instruction; and he outlined the essentials of vocational evaluation, training, and follow-up. Wallin was a controversial but productive clinical psychologist and educator. Far ahead of his time, he understood the importance of community involvement and responsibility for the mentally retarded.

Two other laboratories deserve mention. During the 1930's and 1940's, Harold M. Skeels, Harold B. Dye, Beth Wellman, Marie Skodak, and others conducted research at the Child Welfare Research Station and the Institution for Feeble-minded Children at Glenwood, Iowa, which challenged prevailing attitudes concerning the constancy of the IQ. The impact of these Iowa studies is treated in a later section.

While the Iowa studies were being reported, another research group had been assembled at the Wayne County Training Center in Northville, Michigan. During his tenure, Robert H. Haskell, superintendent at the Training School, developed a spirit of research that attracted and held such men as Samuel

Kirk, Newell Kephart, Boyd McCandless, Alfred Strauss, Thorleif Hegge, Heinz Werner, M. H. Ainsworth, Z. P. Hoakley, and Sydney Bijou. At the Training School, Kirk developed a "Self Determining Cottage," Kirk and Hegge experimented with the value of preschool educational programs for the retarded, and Hoakley published reports on the variability of the IQ as early as 1933. While at the Training School, Strauss, a child psychiatrist trained in the Gestalt approach, and Werner, an experimental psychologist, developed the concept of the brain-injured child. Kephart, trained by the Iowa group, succeeded Kirk at the "Self Determining Cottage," and, with Strauss, co-authored the second volume of "The Brain Injured Child." Kephart was succeeded by McCandless who was followed by Bijou. The graduates of the Training School form an illustrious group of researchers in psychology, mental retardation, and education.

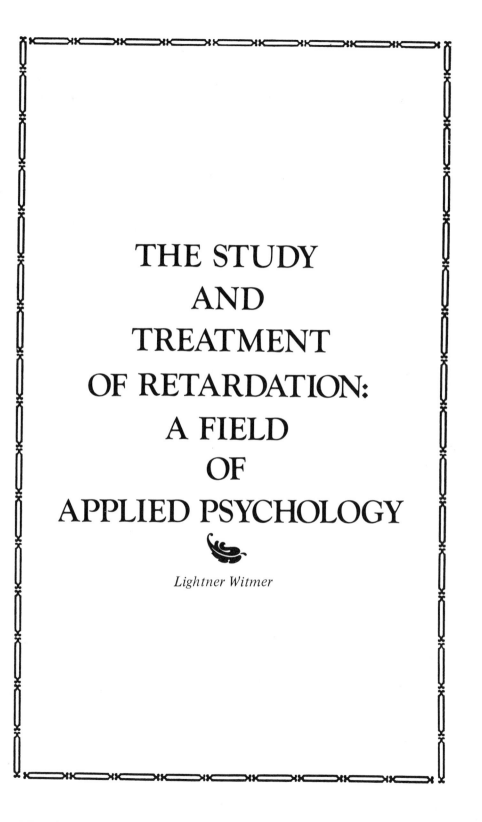

THE STUDY
AND
TREATMENT
OF RETARDATION:
A FIELD
OF
APPLIED PSYCHOLOGY

Lightner Witmer

The psychological clinic organized by Witmer at the University of Pennsylvania was in continuous operation until the early 1960's. Witmer describes the development of the Orthogenic School and defines orthogenics as the science "which investigates retardation and deviation and the methods of restoring to normal condition those who are found . . . to be retarded or deviate." Finding a precedent in Seguin, Witmer suggests that "idiotism may be a mental status not resting upon an incurable brain defect," and distinguishes between psychophysiological and pedagogical retardation.

No valid distinction can be made between a pure and an applied science. That "the final test of the value of what is called science is its applicability" is the opinion of a former president of the American Association for the Advancement of Science. This thought impelled me as long ago as the meeting of 1896, to lay before the members of the American Psychological Association an outline of a field of applied psychology. Under the designation of practical work in psychology was included: (1) The direct application of psychological methods to therapeutics and to education, whether by professional psychologists, practicing physicians, or educators. (2) Such psychophysical investigation of mental conditions and processes as may serve to throw light upon the problems presented in the practice of medicine or teaching. (3) Instruction in psychology containing the promise of usefulness to students of medicine and education in their respective professions.

Thus the plan had a view to the professional practice of psychology, to research and to instruction, as these stand related to the two professions of medicine and teaching.

During the twelve years which followed the first announcement of this plan of practical work, the Laboratory of Psychology at the University of Pennsylvania has been engaged in prosecuting original research along these lines, and in training investigators capable of carrying on independent work. Sufficient time has now elapsed to present a statement of what has been accomplished.

In the prospectus to which I have referred, I suggested the necessity of a psychological clinic, or dispensary, which I had recently organized at the University of Pennsylvania, and which has since been continued, receiving children from the public schools, from the juvenile court, charitable organizations, and from physicians. This work has grown year by year until at the present time we are seeing from six to ten new cases each week. In the examination and treatment of cases referred to the psychological clinic, I am assisted by three medical associates and a number of psychological assistants, including Dr. Holmes, who is specializing in the direction of the moral training of adolescents, and Miss Town, who is resident psychologist at the Friends' Asylum for the Insane.

Although the necessity of keeping these children under observation and prolonged training had led me to recommend the establishment of schools or homes for those children needing expert psychological and pedagogical treatment, it was not until July, 1907, that I was able to establish on a satisfactory basis what I originally called a hospital school, but more recently the Orthogenic School. This school is conducted by the Psychological Laboratory, as a medical school conducts a hospital, both for private and free cases.

Psychological Bulletin, 1909, 6(4): 121–126.

Through the psychological clinic, but chiefly in the orthogenic school, a number of cases have been under such prolonged observation and training that it is now possible to present reports which will show the mental and physical status of the child at the time he was received into the school, the methods of training and physical treatment employed, and the results which followed such treatment. Primarily for the purpose of reporting these cases in a satisfactory manner, the publication of a journal called *The Psychological Clinic* was undertaken in March, 1907.

I have recently proposed the word *orthogenics* as the name for that branch of science which investigates retardation and deviation and the methods of restoring to normal condition those who are found for one reason or another to be retarded or deviate. Through the reporting in this journal of our work at the University of Pennsylvania, and of such independent work as that of Dr. Margaret K. Smith, of New Paltz, New York, and of Dr. Sterling, of Baltimore, we believe we are contributing to the establishment of a clinical psychology as a department of orthogenics.

The characteristic features of the clinical method in psychology are:
1. Its concern for the individual, which makes it in effect an individual psychology; and
2. The application of remedial or orthogenic treatment to individual cases of retardation or deviation, and even to the hypothetically normal child.

A comparative psychology may be based upon a study of individuals or upon a study of groups of individuals; that is to say, upon the clinical method primarily or the statistical method primarily. Accomplishments of the statistical method are admirably shown in such investigations as have proceeded from or been inspired by Cattell and Thorndike. But the statistical method is susceptible of great error, as Thorndike has pointed out in his report on elimination. He claims that to settle the question of elimination from the grades, it would be necessary to follow a large number of individual children through the eight grades of the school and through the high school. In other words, he proposes to develop a statistical result on the basis of an individual psychology and from an application of the clinical method. The germ of this method is undoubtedly to be found in the remarkable investigations initiated by Dr. Hall through the employment of a syllabus. At the University of Pennsylvania we realized the necessity for obtaining statistical data through the clinical method as soon as we sought to determine the number of backward children in the public schools. This work has produced results of value and has led to a restatement of the problem of retardation.

It is well known that Séguin was the first to subsume idiocy under the concept of retardation. He defined idiocy as an arrest, or retardation of development. He himself distinguished between idiotism as the mental state and idiocy as the brain defect upon which idiotism might rest, a distinction which suggests the possibility that idiotism may be a mental status not resting upon an incurable brain defect. As soon as a civilized community begins to enforce compulsory education it is discovered that there are a number of children unable to make normal progress through the grades. How many such children are there in the public schools?

This question cannot be answered by a clinical examination alone. It must be solved, in the first instance, by what is essentially the statistical method, as this has been developed by Cattell and Thorndike. I am led, therefore, to distinguish between psychophysiological retardation and pedagogical retardation. Physiological retardation may be defined in two ways, either as a failure of the child to reach the supposed normal level of development for his chronological age, or as a failure of the child to reach the development indicated by his natural endowments. Any child who reaches adult age without having had his brain developed up to the full limit of its capacity has suffered from retardation and will manifest throughout his life an arrest of development. It is possible that the brightest member of a class may be more retarded than the dullest. I believe that these two definitions of retardation should be kept separate, but neither of these is a satisfactory definition with which to approach the problem of retardation in the schools. Our standard of the hypothetical normal child is inadequate and unsatisfactory, and our opinion as to whether a child at a given stage of development is as far along as he ought to be must necessarily be a matter of conjecture. To fix the standard of retardation I undertook to define pedagogical retardation with reference to the number of years that a child was behind the grade for his age. This involved a statistical classification of the children of a public school system by grades and ages.

Superintendent Bryan undertook this investigation for the city of Camden, N.J. He found that 26 per cent were two years or more behind the grade in which their age should have placed them; that 12.7 per cent were three years or more behind the proper grade, and nearly 5 per cent were four years or more behind grade. Indeed, backwardness or retardation, measured in terms of school progress, is manifested by a surprisingly large percentage of children. Thus, Dr. Cornman shows for five cities of the United States, comprising one fifth of the elementary school population, that from 21.6 per cent to 49.6 per cent are one year or more behind the grade in which the school and the public expect these children to be; that from 7.3 per cent to 26.3 per cent are two years behind the proper grade; that from 2.1 per cent in one city to 12.7 per cent in another city are three years or more behind grade; and in one city as high as 5.1 per cent are four years or more behind the grade in which these children should be.

A great deal of confusion exists in the mind of the people, and also in that of our educational authorities, as to exactly what a backward child is.

Just as soon as the discovery is made that some children manifest backward-ness or retardation in their school work, and special classes are formed to facilitate the progress of these children, we find these classes filled up with children who are incurably feeble-minded, who cannot be trained in public day schools and who should be sent for training and care to some special school like that at Elwyn. Thus, I have brought to me at the University of Pennsylvania for examination and suggestion as to educational treatment, children who have been rejected from the Pennsylvania Training School for Feeble-minded Children, because they were below the level of children who could be educated in that school. And yet these children were applying for admission to the public schools, and in some instances were to be found in the grades for normal children.

This failure to recognize that there is a difference between feeble-minded children who cannot be educated in public day schools and other children properly designated backward, who can be trained in day schools and some of whom can be restored to normal condition, results in the calling of many incurably feeble-minded children, 'backward children.' However justifiable this may be to save the sensibilities of the parents, it simply confuses the problem of remedying the backwardness which is found throughout the grades in many of our city schools.

Independently, Dr. Falkner, while Commissioner of Education for Porto Rico, and Mr. Ayres, while Superintendent of Schools at San Juan, came upon this problem from the standpoint of a superintendent. Endeavoring to compare the schools of Porto Rico with those of the United States, they could find no statistics which would enable them to determine whether the pedagogical retardation of children in the Porto Rican schools was greater or less than that prevailing in city school systems in the United States. It was not until they obtained the statistics of Bryan and Cornman that they had the material data for a preliminary statistical comparison and analysis of condi-tions. They are now in the position, Dr. Falkner as statistician for the Immigration Commission, and Mr. Ayres as Director of the Backward Chil-dren Investigation of the Russell Sage Foundation, to contribute results which will be determinative for the schools of this country. Mr. Ayres is employing the clinical method also, in connection with his statistical investi-gation.

Recently, the Russell Sage Foundation persuaded Dr. Gulick also to devote himself to this work, and we look to this Foundation to do as important a piece of work in connection with the problem of retardation in the public schools, as the Rockefeller Institute is expected to accomplish in the study and treatment of disease. In our work and the work of Twitmyer, Bryan, Cornman, Heilman, Thorndike, Gulick, Ayres and Falkner, we see the foundations of a new science. It is strictly an applied psychology. It may be designated also as experimental or scientific pedagogy in the proper sense of that word.

From the cultivation of this field of applied psychology we expect results of value to psychology and education for the following reasons: (1) The investigation of retardation, which measures the amount by which individual children fall short of obtaining a standard public school education, is an approach to the problem of education from the right direction. These investigations will furnish standards of reference which will enable us to determine to what extent we fail to really educate the rising generation in this country. (2) These investigations are demonstrating to educators the necessity of calling upon the psychological expert to assist in solving their peculiar problems. In Philadelphia merely publishing the fact that 12.7 per cent of the children of Philadelphia had been more than two years in grade in June, 1907, reduced the number of such children in June, 1908, to 6.6 per cent. (3) It offers to superintendents, through both the statistical and clinical methods, and to grade teachers, through the clinical method alone, an opportunity to do practical work, as a result of which they may become original contributors to the science of psychology and to education. (4) This will ultimately make the profession of teaching a scientific profession, which it is not at present, because educational practice remains to-day largely a matter of opinion. Medicine is a scientific profession because of the invention of instruments of precision like the thermometer and because of the development of exact methods of observation and report. I look forward to the day when the educator will also be looked up to as a scientific authority whose opinions will either no longer be questioned by a foolish parent or some ignorant member of a school board, or else, if questioned, can be supported by an appeal to unanswerable facts. (5) The development of an applied psychology assures the future of psychology as a pure science, for in the final analysis the progress of psychology as of every other science will be determined by the value and amount of its contributions to the advancement of the human race. Let us hope that we are even now escaped from beneath the pall of such debilitating opinions as the one attributed to William James: "Perhaps you will ask me what are the practical benefits conferred on the world by this interesting science. So far as I am able to discern, absolutely none." (6) Through applied psychology, in training psychological experts for our public school systems as well as for institutions for the insane and the training of feeble-minded children, we shall find another outlet for our students than that which leads them to the gateway of an academic career.

A
PRELIMINARY
REPORT ON
THE CAREERS OF
THREE HUNDRED FIFTY
CHILDREN
WHO HAVE LEFT
UNGRADED CLASSES

Elizabeth E. Farrell

Farrell provides an early follow-up of mentally defective children leaving special classes. This publication precedes Fernald's investigation of persons leaving Waverley by four years.

PROBLEM

The problem, upon which this study[1] seeks to throw some light, is concerned with the careers of children who have left ungraded classes at sixteen years of age. All children in such classes, in the public schools of New York City, have been certified as mentally defective by duly qualified psychologists and physicians, therefore the children whose careers are here presented have been certified as mental defectives. The school attendance law in New York State operates until a child is sixteen years of age, unless he has satisfactorily completed the first half of the seventh year of the school course at his fourteenth birthday or subsequent thereto. This required school attainment is obviously impossible for ungraded class children; they would therefore, be obliged to attend until their sixteenth birthday if it were not for the fact that there is no legal authority at present for compelling the school attendance of children who are mentally defective. The need for this authority is not yet felt to any appreciable degree. The classes are small, the teachers are interested in the children, and the result is that the children do attend school. The average attendance in the ungraded classes in New York is very high.

SCOPE

Reports on the careers of 600 former ungraded class children who have been out of school from one to eight years are available. The first were discharged in 1907, the latest in 1914. The territory covered includes that of the five boroughs of the greater city.

Of the above mentioned records of 600 children, tabulations of 350 are completed to a degree which warrants this presentation.

METHOD

The material here presented was gathered by ungraded class teachers, visiting teachers and by settlement and other social workers. It was secured by (1) visits to the children's home; (2) visits to the employer; (3) visits of parents to the school.

---

[1] Read at the meeting of the American Association for the Study of the Feeble-Minded, Berkeley, California, August, 1915.

Journal of Psycho-Asthenics, 1915, 20 (1) 20–26.

DISTRIBUTION BY BOROUGHS

The records here presented are distributed throughout the boroughs as follows:

	Total
Manhattan	154
The Bronx	43
Brooklyn	122
Queens	22
Richmond	9
Total	350

DISTRIBUTION BY SEX

The records now tabulated show that one girl was discharged for every two boys. The distribution by sex is as follows.

Girls	123
Boys	227
Total	350

REASON FOR DISCHARGE FROM SCHOOL

	Girls	Boys
16 years of age or over	113	
By order of the Court	1	
Other reasons	9	13
Total	123	227
Grand Total		350

PERCENTAGES BASED ON ABOVE

A). Children discharged as 16 years of age or over   92. per cent
B). Children discharged by order of the Court   1.2 per cent
C). Children discharged for other reasons   6. per cent
    Under *B* are included children removed by the Court (improper guardianship, inability to establish age, etc).

    Under *C* are included those whose parents made other provision for them, Private Schools, Parochial Schools, to be tutored, etc.

PRESENT STATUS

The actual status of these children at the time of the last visit in June, 1915, is as follows:

	Girls	Boys	Total
1. Cared for at home	54	32	86
2. Employed for wages	50	142	192
3. Employable, but out of work at present	7	24	31
4. In Penal Institutions		3	3
5. In Institutions for feeble-minded	3	10	13
6. In other institutions	2	3	5
7. Unknown	2	5	7
8. Dead	3	7	10
9. Married	3		3
Total	124	226	350
Grand Total			350

For the purpose of this presentation those employed for wages are put in contra-distinction to those cared for at home. It is not to be understood, however, that all of those cared for at home are without economic value. Reports on this group throw the following light on this: "Keeps house with mother;" "Works in father's candy store;" "Assists mother in making artificial flowers at home;" "Pulls bastings in father's shop," etc. Those employed for wages represent 64 per cent of all cases tabulated. Of this percentage less than 9 per cent were out of employment at the time the report was made. In this connection it is interesting to note that one boy, the only known mental defective in his family, is said to have been the only wage earner during the prolonged period of unemployment during the last winter.

By "other institutions" is meant hospitals, homes for incurables, sanatorium for tuberculosis, etc.

Of the one per cent reported as married, one child, now dead, was the only birth reported. One woman has been deserted by her husband.

OCCUPATIONS

The occupations in which these children are employed group themselves into four large divisions: trades, factories, stores and miscellaneous. The most interesting one is the trades. In this group, six are reported as members of the union organized in connection with the trade in which each is employed.

This tabulation seems to indicate that a small minority of the children are engaged in street trades and in peddling.

Occupations	No. Employed
Misc.—	
Housework	16
Errand boy	13
Driver	12
Newsboy	4
Peddler	4
Nurse maids	4
Farm hands	4
Maids	2
Market	2
Mail carriers (?)	2
Elect. con.	1
Elevator boy	1
Navy yard	1
Gas fixtures	1
Laundry	2
Caddy	1
Mov. Pictures	2
Odd Jobs	4
All Others	6
Unknown	7
Total	89
Factories—	
Biscuit	1
Clothing	8
Ice cream	1
Harness	1
Candy	1
Paper box	1
Lace	1
Necktie	2
Shoe	1
Sugar	1
Macaroni	1
Mattress	1
Feed bag	1
Handkerchiefs	2
Silk Mills	5
Jute	1

Hardware   2
Iron   1
All Others   7
    Total   39

Stores—
Candy   1
Feathers   2
Grocery   7
Stationery   2
    Total   12
Fruit   2
Butcher   2
Bakery   1
Dry Goods   3
Drugs   1
All Others   13
    Total   34

Trades—
Cabinet-Maker (helper)   3
Printer (helper)   5
Machinist   2
Cabinet repair work   2
Plumber   1
Dressmaker   2
Carpenter (union)   2
Bricklayer (union)   1
Cap Maker (union)   1
Tin Smith (union)   3
Blacksmith   1
Tailor   2
Metal Worker   1
Mason   2
    Total   28

Unemployed—
At Home   86
Unknown   9
Out of work   31
Institutions   21
Dead   10
Married   3
    Total 160

Weekly Wage Distribution
$ 1 to 1.99   2
   2 to 2.99   4
   3 to 3.99   13

cont.

cont.

Weekly Wage Distribution

$ 4 to	4.99	26
5 to	5.99	29
6 to	6.99	22
7 to	7.99	18
8 to	8.99	7
9 to	9.99	6
10 to	10.99	—
11 to	11.99	1
12 to	12.99	2
18		1
26.40		3
30		1
Unknown		57
Out of employment		31

Occupations and Weekly Wages of 30 Wage-earning Girls Discharged From Ungraded Classes

Name	Age	Occupation	Weekly Wage
G.H.	19	Milliner's asst.	$6.00
G.M.	19	Artificial flowers	3.50
S.P.	19	Milliner's asst.	5.00
E.S.	19	Artificial flowers	6.00
H.H.	17	Envelope factory	5.00
M.M.	18	Candy factory	4.50
L.M.	17	Factory[2]	5.25
R.B.	19	Nurse maid	$1.00 and bd.
E.D.	17	Packer	4.50
J.M.	20	Feather maker	5.00
R.V.	18	Factory[2]	7.00
E.L.	22	Button maker	5.00
R.S.	21	Paper box maker	5.00
L.S.	21	Saleswoman	5.00
R.A.	17	Shirt-waist factory	4.50
R.G.	18	Sewing dresses	4.00
M.H.	18	Dressmaking	4.00
V.E.	17	Errand girl (Milliner)	4.00
A.S.	17	Working[3]	4.00
M.G.	17	Cork factory	4.37
J.G.	17	Factory[2]	4.00
E.Y.	18	Shirt-waist shop	4.00
E.S.	17	Floor girl	2.50
N.D.	19	Laundry	5.00
C.F.	19	Paraffin works	4.00
C.H.	21	Working[3]	5.00
E.E.	17	Silk factory	4.00

M.H.	. . . . . . .17	Dressmaker	. . . .	3.00
L.Y.	. . . . .18	Suit house	. . . .	4.00
S.L.	. . . . .17	Packer (Dept. Store)	. . . .	4.50

---

[2] Type of factory not reported.
[3] Occupation not reported.

SUMMARY

This study of the careers of 350 children who have left ungraded classes at sixteen years of age shows that:

The ratio of girls to boys is 1 to 2.

92 per cent of the children attended school until their sixteenth birthday.

1 per cent discharged by order of the court.

6 per cent were discharged for other reasons.

25 per cent have never worked out of the home. 65 per cent of this number are girls; 35 per cent of this number are boys.

64 per cent employable out of their own homes, and for wages. 9 per cent of this number were out of employment at the time of the investigation.

1 per cent were in penal institutions. These were boys.

4 per cent were in institutions for the feeble-minded. Less than 1 per cent of these were girls.

1½ per cent were in other institutions.

2 per cent were unknown.

3 per cent are dead.

Less than 1 per cent are married. These are girls.

CONCLUSION

This study will be continued for the purpose of ascertaining the ability of the worker to stick to his job; his ability to seek and to attain promotion in his field of work, and to make a comparative study of the ungraded class product with his more fortunate brother from the regular school course.

CURRENT
PROBLEMS
IN
MENTAL DIAGNOSIS

Edgar A. Doll

Doll identifies himself as a clinical psychologist in the tradition of Goddard and Healy but labels his field as more an art than a science. Calling for greater objectivity in diagnosis, he outlines a clinical syllabus of mental diagnosis which includes developmental and family history as well as direct examination.

It is some time since the study of the feeble-minded shed its first light on the understanding of delinquents. About 12 years ago the pioneer studies by Goddard, applying the methods of clinical psychology to the study of delinquent groups, showed that an unexpectedly large proportion of juvenile delinquents were mentally defective. Many subsequent studies covering the same ground, substantiated Goddard's findings without, however, improving upon the early methods of study and conclusions. An important departure was the work of Healy, begun at about the same time, but reaching fruition nearly five years later. Healy's work was epochal in that it emphasized the individual delinquent, his traits and peculiarities, rather than the delinquent group as a whole. Of course, Goddard's studies had been based upon individuals, but Goddard did not attempt to analyze the causal factors of delinquency as did Healy, except from the point of view of general intelligence and social inadequacy. The early studies of Anderson combined the technique of Goddard with the technique of Healy, and concentrated particularly on the defective delinquent group as a particular social problem lying between the problem of feeble-mindedness and of delinquency.

A survey of the studies on the problem of defective delinquency reveals many scientific short-comings. A severe analysis leaves one with but little confidence in the generalizations in this field, because of the lack of uniformity in the technique of studying delinquents. Thus, the studies of Goddard were limited principally to Binet mental tests, supplemented more or less by supporting tests, and the social history of the individual. The Binet Scale of that day was admittedly imperfect, especially in the upper ranges where the majority of the defective delinquents were found to test. The studies of Healy were largely qualitative, being based principally on personal interpretation of history data and case analyses rather than on standardized tests or differential symptoms. Healy's great contribution lies in his earnest endeavor to analyze the nonintellectual factors in delinquency by means of a method approaching more that of psychiatry than that of psychology. Anderson endeavored to employ the complete clinical syllabus so far as circumstances permitted, but his work also suffered from inadequacy of standards, and uncertainties of clinical method. In all studies, the inadequacies of method of clinical diagnosis were still further complicated, so far as generalizations were concerned regarding the proportion of mental defectives among juvenile delinquents, by the many conditioning circumstances which governed the selection of cases.

Journal of Psycho-Asthenics, 1924, 29: 298–308. Reprinted by permission of Mrs. Edgar Doll and the American Association on Mental Deficiency.

After leaving Vineland, Dr. Doll served as coordinator of research to the Devereux Schools and as consulting psychologist to the Public Schools of the City of Bellingham, Washington. He was consultant to the Vanguard School at his death in October 1968.

In view of the growing importance of the scientific study of delinquents and particularly defective delinquents, it seems apropos to call attention to some of the problems which complicate mental diagnosis in relation to delinquency. The studies mentioned have amply demonstrated the need for a more uniform technique and closer agreement in the application of standards. Such scientific uniformity, both of methodology and of terminology, is essential if there are to be any generalizations or any comparisons between studies made under different conditions or by different authorities. My purpose in this paper is to indicate some of the present inadequacies of clinical psychology, and to indicate those problems which must frankly be faced if our future studies are to have scientific validity.

If we examine the present status of clinical psychology and its ﹐rief history, it must be obvious to the candid student that clinical psychology today is more an art than it is a science. In spite of the very marked improvement in clinical technique, one can not escape the conclusion that mental diagnosis is more subjective than it is objective, and that accuracy of diagnosis is largely a matter of expertness and skill rather than of exact measurement. One of the most important needs of clinical psychology, in view of its wide-spread application and the great social importance of its findings, is greater objectivity. We must free ourselves from the complacency into which we have fallen, and endeavor by critical analysis, research, and experience, to improve our theory, our technique, and our standards.

THE CLINICAL SYLLABUS

The clinical syllabus of mental diagnosis customarily covers about ten fields of inquiry, aiming thereby to make a complete survey of the individual under examination. These fields of inquiry are variously described and variously grouped. They may be arranged under two main headings, (1) The study of the individual on the basis of his previous history, and (2) the study of the individual by direct examination. In the field of history taking, it is customary to consider family history, personal developmental history, social history, school history, and medical history. If the individual is mature, there is also a study of his industrial or occupational history. Some authorities group the histories under two heads; namely, family history, and personal history, the latter comprising the different histories enumerated above. The examinational study of the individual commonly includes a physical or medical examination, usually including a neuro-psychiatric examination, a mental or psychological examination, a scholastic or pedagogical examination, and in the case of adults, an industrial or vocational examination. The psychological examination has several aspects; namely, a study of intelligence, personality traits, special abilities or disabilities, skill, and sensory-motor function.

As a matter of fact in ordinary practice, the clinical syllabus is seldom applied in its entirety, especially in the case of defective delinquents. All too frequently the sources of information bearing on the history of the individual are not at hand, and only such data can be obtained as the subject under examination is able or willing to present. In the case of defective delinquents, such information is obviously both limited and untrustworthy. Similarly the medical and neuro-psychiatric examinations are ordinarily quite perfunctory or superficial, unless the individual under examination presents a fairly obvious physical or psychiatric peculiarity. In the same way, the psychological examination is commonly limited to a study of the intelligence level by means of intelligence tests, more or less frequently verified or supplemented by a battery of tests. The scholastic examination of the individual is quite generally ignored except perhaps with respect to superficial observations regarding reading, writing, and arithmetic. If, however, the complete syllabus has been applied, and if adequate and reliable information has been obtained, nevertheless the interpretation of these data is essentially qualitative or subjective, rather than scientifically exact and certain. Different diagnosticians, of presumably equal professional standing, do not employ the same standards of interpretation and all too frequently fail to present either their standards or their data in such form as to permit re-interpretation.

Avoiding generalizations, let us examine these departments of clinical inquiry in detail, and see just what is their contribution from the point of view of objectivity, or scientific precision.

Family History

All orthodox clinicians endeavor to obtain information regarding the hereditary antecedents of the individual under examination. This is justified on the long accepted principle of family resemblances. These resemblances are probably even much more persistent and definite than is at present understood, but at the present time the laws of their transmission are too little known to yield much reliability for purposes of differential diagnosis. Who of us examining a child suspected of feeble-mindedness and finding one of the parents feeble-minded, would not immediately be heavily prejudiced toward a positive diagnosis by this fact? And yet who of us would take the pains to determine whether such parent's feeble-mindedness had been acquired through illness, accident, disease, or whatnot, rather than being itself of hereditary type? Who of us would attempt or be able to prove that the remaining normal parent was a simplex normal rather than a duplex, since only in the former case could any of the progeny be feeble-minded. And again, who of us could predict that the particular child under examination was bound to be feeble-minded, since normality and deficiency result in equal ratio from such a mating. Family history interpreted on the basis of the Mendelian Law is practically useless for purposes of diagnosis, although to be sure it may have a high presumptive value in accounting for feeble-mindedness previously diagnosed by other methods. It is only when both parents are of the hereditary feeble-minded type and lineage is certain that family history may be used with any certainty for diagnosis. If one parent is known to be of the hereditary feeble-minded type, and the other parent of the simplex normal type, both of these being rather difficult of proof, the chances are only one to one that the offspring will be feeble-minded. If both parents are simplex normal with feeble-mindedness in the family once removed, the diagnostic ratio is only one to three, and such simplexity is practically impossible of proof. Nevertheless, however unreliable family history may be for purposes of diagnosis, we must not discount its value as an etiological factor and particularly as the most important single social problem involved in the eradication of feeble-mindedness. Its value in the study of groups is undoubtedly great, however limited it may be in the diagnosis of individuals.

Personal Developmental History

The facts of ontogenetic development are also of dubious value for diagnosis. In the first place they can seldom be reliably obtained, because the information may be either inaccurate or prejudiced. The fond parent is usually the only source of such information, and his memory, as well as his observation, is unreliable, but here again, assuming that we have exact information, we are greatly limited in our differential norms, so that precise interpretation of such data is a matter of guess-work or individual belief. There are only fragmentary standards regarding the functional development of normal children, and very little in the way of differential standards. Kuhlmann's Tests for the Infant Period give us practically our only means of accurately determining these stages of development. In general, it is known, or at least accepted, that the feeble-minded develop in practically all respects at a retarded rate. Yet this is more a matter of observation than a result of precise investigation. The difficulty of mental diagnosis, is with the borderlines and high-grades, and for them such retardation has not yet been determined with any approach to statistical accuracy.

In the same way we might review the other aspects of historical data of the individual and show their unreliability for purposes of diagnosis, while not failing, however, to give credit to such information as etiological factors or as a means of accounting for a condition otherwise diagnosed. The school history, to be sure, is both more accurate and more significant than any of the other information. The child's progress in school is a direct and objective record of his mental and social adequacy, yet we are now coming to see that failure to progress in school beyond the fifth grade may be a result of specific scholastic deficiency, rather than direct feeble-mindedness in the sense of inability to manage one's affairs with ordinary prudence or to get along independently in society. Again, an appreciable number of high-grade feeble-minded may exceed in their school work the progress made by a fairly large number of socially capable individuals who are scholastically defective.

Perhaps we need not be too much distressed about these limitations of history data, realizing that in practice, the data often are not available or when obtained in sufficient quantity and reliability, are more often used for etiology than for diagnosis. We suspect, however, that many a clinician is subsequently prejudiced by such information when it supports his tentative diagnosis. After all, if the individual can be diagnosed by more direct measures it is reasonable to ignore these indirect and less reliable sources. The history of clinical psychology shows a definite trend away from such a historical study of the individual to the more exact examinational study. The ordinary clinician includes such information as sidelights on the case study.

Direct Examination

The direct examination of the individual is obviously more scientific and more exact than the historical analysis. This does not mean that the historical survey can be eliminated, since the direct examination gives only the status quo of the individual, whereas the histories indicate previous status and may be extremely valuable for prognosis.

Medical Examination

The physical examination is an indispensable pre-requisite to any study of the individual. Such examination, to be effective, however, must be a complete survey seriously conducted and not merely a superficial "once-over" concerning the principal organs, organ systems, external stigmata, and the like. Such examination should indicate the functional status of the organism as a whole as well as its parts. It should both positively and negatively give information regarding all such physical conditions as might inhibit or aggravate mental functioning. It should indicate the degree of physiological as well as physical development of the individual and indicate such conditions as might give rise to temporary rather than permanent retardation or defect. No mental study of the individual can stand without some such assurances regarding the physical soundness of the organism. Unfortunately the most important medical aspects of the individual, such as metabolism and toxemia, require much time and energy for adequate examination. These, together with a complete neurological survey, are all too often left out of consideration, although most clinicians recognize their desirability. Again, while many claims are made concerning the physical or medical correlates of deficiency and delinquency, there is much to be desired in the way of more ample and more adequate study of these problems.

Neuro-psychiatric Examination

In the same way the neuro-psychiatric examination of the individual is theoretically indispensable to an adequate diagnosis. The possibility of neurological disturbances or psychiatric conditions as causes of delinquency, or as pseudo signs of deficiency, is too great to be overlooked, even though the experimental studies have not yet revealed a very large proportion of neuro-psychiatric conditions existing among defective delinquents. Probably this may not be interpreted to mean that such conditions are not present, but rather that the methods of investigation employed up to the present time have failed to reveal factors which may have been present. Here again, an adequate method of examination is both expensive and time-consuming, requiring hospital and laboratory facilities of the highest order, as well as a corp of specially trained technicians. The importance of such conditions has been too clearly demonstrated in individual cases to permit one to say that this field may be eliminated.

Psychological Examination

Perhaps the greatest progress in mental diagnosis relating to defectives and delinquents has been made in the fields of applied psychology. Starting about fifteen years ago with the original Binet Scales, the past decade has witnessed rapid developments not only in the elaboration of the Binet Scale, but especially in the field of group tests, performance tests, and tests of all sorts of mental abilities. It is now possible to employ a battery type of diagnosis where formerly only single tests could be applied. It is also possible to study the individual in many ways beyond the determination of his intelligence level. The technique of mental testing now includes so many different methods as to tax the ability of the clinician to employ them. The development of standards, however, and especially of differential standards, has not kept pace with the development of methods as such. In particular, the various tests available have been standardized in widely different parts of the country, on widely different types of subjects, and under widely different experimental conditions. The mental testing department of clinical psychology is greatly in need of a house-cleaning, or at least of an inventory so that these methods may be set in order, or classified with respect to their greatest usefulness. Psychology has not made such progress as has been demanded of it in the study of personality traits particularly regarding the emotional life or temperament of individuals. We may expect, however, to witness very rapid development in these directions during the next decade. In fact the pioneer studies are already appearing. It may be expected that developments in the field of emotional and personality studies may for a time eclipse the intelligence studies, just as these previously eclipsed the sensory-motor studies. Among the difficulties encountered in the psychological study of deficiency and delinquency, we may enumerate some as follows:

1. There is at present considerable uncertainty as to the age at which the development of general intelligence ceases.

2. We are not agreed as to what is the average mental age of unselected adults.

3. We are not agreed as to how this problem is complicated by differences in nationality and color, and whether such differential mental age averages as were established by the Army studies should be employed in differential diagnosis.

4. We are not agreed as to the methods of calculating and of interpreting intelligence quotients although perhaps no single scientific term is now more glibly and less intelligently used among school people and clinical psychologists, than this much-abused device.

5. We are much confused as to the statistical devices to be employed in the standardization of tests and the interpretation thereof. Tests have been variously standardized on a mental age basis, on a point-scale basis, on medians, on measures of deviation, on percentiles and so on. Undoubtedly, the percentile method is the most satisfactory for purposes of diagnosis, although the use of medians, which has been applicable for group studies, has been widely employed in the clinical field.

6. The significance of unequal standing in a succession of tests, is not at present subject to exact interpretation. Batteries of tests are being employed without knowledge of the correlation and weights for combining test results.

7. Recent work has indicated the great importance of differentiating indi-

viduals as to types of ability, as well as levels, and we are beginning to understand that special talent may socially offset special disability or even general disability.

8. The role of the emotions in relation to the social significance of intelligence is still a matter of opinion rather than knowledge.

These uncertainties need not prevent us from continuing our practical service, but should certainly encourage us to proceed cautiously and with due respect for the rapid progress which is being made in the academic field.

Scholastic Examination

We have said that the school progress of the individual is one of the best measures of his social adaptive capacity, and one of the best indications of his ultimate social success. It is therefore highly desirable that we measure the status quo of the individual by means of objective educational tests, rather than by relying on school progress in general. These tests may also be used to indicate specific causes for success or failure in the psychological tests. Thus a child with special reading disability should not be expected to perform normally in a group verbal intelligence test, or in a test heavily influenced by the language factor. Such verbal deficiency must be reckoned with, even though the individual may have compensating ability in other fields. The studies of delinquency in New Jersey have amply demonstrated the fallacy of relying on verbal tests for mental diagnosis.

Perhaps more distressing than these difficulties of the several parts of the clinical syllabus, is our present impossibility of accurately combining these different aspects of individuality into a composite whole. If a physical disability has been demonstrated by the medical history or by the medical examination, its influence on the mental performance of the individual is at present largely a matter of conjecture. If his environment has been grossly defective, we cannot with any assurance make a numerical allowance therefor. If his educational opportunities have been limited, we do not know definitely how this affects his present mental or social status. Indeed, as has been said, we are even unable to combine by any present statistical advice, supplemented by experimental data, the various results obtained from applying a battery of mental tests. Our greatest problem today is to make a comprehensive clinical survey of a fairly large number of individuals whose social status is definitely recognized, or whose mental diagnosis has been determined by the practical test of life or social adaptation, and see just how these different influences help them.

Meanwhile, we may repeat that we need not sit idly by until all these problems are solved, but on the other hand, we must be careful to avoid complacency and dogmatism in stating the results of our investigations. The presence of these problems should spur us on to further and more exact studies under the realization that uncertainty is one of the most potent causes of progress in science.

Just as the original stimulus toward a scientific method of studying behavior came from the institution, so we must look to their laboratories for help in our present difficulties. A cooperative effort joined in by the laboratories, requested in the association, and by the communities would be a move in the right direction. Let us have a committee of the association on research, and let us join reserves for a solution of our problem.

DISCUSSION

DR. HOWARD W. POTTER: Sometimes I think it is a mistake to use the term mental diagnosis, or physical diagnosis, or neurological diagnosis, because we can never adhere strictly to just those terms in arriving at a diagnosis. To make a proper diagnosis, one as nearly correct as possible, we should consider the individual as a whole coordinated being. There seem to me two things to keep in mind in taking histories: first, to get an idea of the background of the patient and the stuff he is made of; second, to find out with what facility he has met the various demands of his environment, whether mental, intellectual, emotional or physical. The next thing is to take a cross section of the patient when we see him. That includes the physical side, not only a general physical examination but all our various special physical examinations, and probably also some anthropological and anthropometric data, etc.; and review of mental equipment, his intelligence, his affective or emotional condition, his educational attainments, etc.; and then the more technical methods of examination relative to laboratory, chemical, serological and metabolic studies. I think it is very important to keep in mind—I suppose my interest in patients as human beings prevents me from running absolutely true to type as a scientific individual, but I cannot get away from the fact that the human being is a psychobiological organism, and that in addition to all our diagnostic paraphernalia the most important thing is our judgment.

CLASSIFICATION
OF
MENTALLY DEFICIENT
AND
RETARDED CHILDREN
FOR
INSTRUCTION

J. E. Wallace Wallin

Wallin provides a history of special classes and plans for handicapped children in the public schools. He calls for sharper definitions and criteria for acceptance into such classes, pointing out that standards differ from city to city. He suggests a dual system of separate classes for lower and higher grade retarded pupils in special and ungraded classrooms.

TWO BASIC ASSUMPTIONS ACCEPTED AS DEMONSTRATED FACTS

What I have to say regarding methods of differentiating sub-average pupils from the elementary schools for instruction is predicated on the acceptance of two basic assumptions as facts.[1] First, I assume there is substantial unanimity of opinion among competent school men who have had extensive first-hand experience in the investigation of individual children and in the field of elementary education that there is a limited proportion of pupils in the grades who are so mentally deficient or pedagogically retarded as to be unable to meet the requirements of the regular curriculum, or to keep pace with the measured progress of the normal pupils. Second, I assume that there is general acceptance of the thesis that it is desirable and profitable, educationally and socially considered, to supply pupils of this class with special aid and attention, individual instruction, or differentiated training. I shall take it for granted not only that these propositions express the true state of affairs, but also that the assumptions themselves are in harmony with objective fact.

CONTRIBUTION OF MODERN TESTING MOVEMENT
TO THE DISCOVERY AND DIFFERENTIATION
OF EDUCATIONAL DEVIATES, AND TO EDUCATIONAL THERAPY

The recognition of the existence of a high degree of variability or of pronounced individual differences among elementary school children of the same age or the same grade classification, and of the need of differential instruction to meet the requirements of pronounced educational deviates, antedated by decades, the intelligence-test and achievement-test movements. Nevertheless, from the intelligence-testing movement, which had not attained any appreciable momentum before 1910, or from the achievement-testing movement which did not arrive until later, we have derived not only our keenest and truest appreciation of the extent and implications of the problem, but also improved techniques for discovering and differentiating the pupils in need of special instruction. On the other hand, the contribution of the modern testing movement has thus far been of much less significance so far as concerns the elaboration of educational schemes, plans and devices, and

---

[1] Delivered, in substance, before the Department of Special Education of the Ohio State Teachers Association, December 27, 1923, before the section of clinical psychology of The Educational Conference of Ohio State University, April 4, 1924.

This subject is more fully to be published by Houghton Mifflin Co.

Journal of Psycho-Asthenics, 1924, 29: 166–182. Reprinted by permission of the American Association on Mental Deficiency.

the modification of curricula and of educative processes to meet more completely the individual requirements of the pupil material in the schools. The essential elements of most systems of corrective or remedial pedagogy or of instructional plans were elaborated many decades ago: for the deaf child prior to 1620 (manual alphabet) or 1740 (oral method), for the blind child prior to 1786 (embossed line type) or 1825[2] (Braille point type), and for the feeble-minded child during the first half of the last century. The testing movement has not wrought any essential modifications or contributed any basic innovations in the teaching technique or in the methods of adjusting instruction for these primary groups of educational defectives, or for children less gravely deficient in their sensory, motor or intellectual equipment.

Let us review briefly, for the sake of illustrating the truth of the statement just made, and for the sake of securing proper orientation for the recommendations to be made in this paper, a few of the numerous plans which have from time to time enjoyed more or less vogue in the public schools for adjusting the processes of instruction to the needs of children who are sub-average in their sensory, motor and intellectual endowment, or in their educational potentials, or who are pedagogically retarded.

PLANS IN VOGUE IN PUBLIC SCHOOLS
FOR AIDING SUB-AVERAGE PUPILS IN THE GRADES

Apparently the earliest attempt consciously and systematically made by the public schools in this country to adapt the methods and contents of instruction to the special needs of handicapped children was through the establishment of special schools or special classes. Special public schools or classes were first established for the instruction of the deaf in Boston in 1869[3] (the Horace Mann school, an oral method school), for the training and discipline of refractory and truant boys in New York in 1874 and in Cleveland in 1879, for the training of the feeble-minded or mentally defective in Providence November 30, 1896, for the training of crippled children in Chicago in 1899, for the training of the blind in Chicago in 1900[4], and for the training of the partially sighted in Roxbury, Massachusetts, in April, 1913, and in Cleveland in the fall of 1913. Classes for "backward," "dull," or "retarded" pupils were probably organized as parallel classes at about the same time as the classes for

---

[2] 1829, according to Americana. The New York point type was devised in 1868.

[3] A private school using the sign method was established a long time before in 1816, by Thomas Gallaudet.

[4] The schools for the blind started in New York and Boston in 1832 and in Philadelphia in 1833 were privately conducted.

the mentally defective, but the information at hand does not indicate just when or where such classes were first organized in the United States.

Less radical schemes of grouping or segregating pupils have also found favor.

The "Baltimore plan," which was introduced about 1898, aimed to further the progress of normal, bright, and dull children. Different courses were provided for these groups during the first six years. The slow pupils covered less ground than the average or bright. It was also intended, I believe, to give them more oral and concrete instruction and more hand work. The bright pupils were afforded fuller opportunities in the literary branches, and were given more initiative and greater responsibilities. Beyond the sixth grade, instruction was departmentalized, promotion was by subjects, while the bright pupils were permitted to pursue extra subjects. The "Santa Barbara plan" was similar.

The Cambridge, Massachusetts, double-track plan provided, in its 1910 revision, two parallel courses in the elementary grades, one of eight years for the average pupils and one of six years for the gifted pupils. Children were transferred according to individual requirement from the one course to the other at various "transfer points." This arrangement was designed to further the interests of gifted or superior children, who were able to do one-third more work each year. The Le Mars, Iowa, plan was similar to the Cambridge plan.

In the Elizabeth, New Jersey, plan, which also was essentially a scheme for the rapid advancement of bright children, the pupils in the eight grades were divided into three or more sections according to ability, and were permitted to progress as rapidly as possible. Transfers were made from section to section according to the progress made. All sections were taught by the same teacher.

It is evident from these very brief references that there is nothing unique or original about the practice of sectioning children into rapid, average, and slow divisions on the basis of group intelligence tests, which nowadays is vigorously advocated by the makers and users of group tests, nor is there anything ultra-modern in the vigorous, organized propaganda and drives of our own day in behalf of superior or supernormal children.

In the Newton, Massachusetts, plan an unassigned teacher gave special attention to maladjusted pupils either individually or in divisions or in small groups.

In the original "Batavia plan," introduced into the Batavia, N. Y., schools in 1898, and which attracted considerable attention at one time, a second teacher was added to the room to "work-up" by developmental instruction (rather than by mere "coaching") the laggards in order to secure equal progress among all the pupils. Later all the teachers gave half their time to individual instruction and half to class instruction.

Somewhat similar to the revised Batavia plan are the systems of individual aid, instruction, and promotion introduced into the regular grades years ago by Preston I. Search ("the Pueblo plan"), and Frederic Burk (in San Francisco) and more recently by C. W. Wasburn (in Winnetka). In these systems minimum emphasis is placed on group recitations or on "hearing lessons," thus leaving the regular teacher free to give each pupil special aid and instruction. Each pupil is allowed to progress as rapidly as he can, quite independent of the pace of the other pupils.

Other schemes for reaching the individual and reducing retardation in the elementary schools include the promotion of children quarterly or semi-annually instead of annually, so the inefficient child will not have to repeat the whole year's work (the St. Louis plan of quarterly promotions, introduced particularly for the benefit of superior pupils in the early seventies and still in use, stands out conspicuously among short-interval promotion systems); promotion by individual subjects, so that only the subjects which were failed will have to be repeated; the use of effective methods and devices, dynamic incentives, concrete materials, and vital projects and cores of correlation, so that the children, having become properly enthused in their studies will put forth increased effort, in consequence of which many children will respond who now fail in their studies; and the organization of instruction and all school activities in accordance with the requirements of an adequate system of mental hygiene, so that the child's whole personality may be harmoniously developed, so that his instincts and emotions may be properly controlled and sublimated, so that economical and desirable habits of feeling, doing, thinking, and studying may be formed, so that healthy attitudes toward the problems of life may be engendered, so that wholesome interests in objective realities may be developed, so that the child may be freed from auto-erotic, infantile and selfish fixations, and from phobias, misconceptions, superstitions, repressions, conflicts, and inhibitions, to the end that his energies may be released for creative, constructive activities.

Indisputably these plans and schemes and other proposals not mentioned here for adjusting the work to meet the needs of the school laggards possess elements of merit of various kinds, although the disadvantages and drawbacks of some of the plans mentioned are quite obvious. Nevertheless most of the plans formerly used, even those of undoubted merit, seem to have enjoyed merely a temporary vogue. They have had their day and have been abandoned or forgotten except in isolated instances. But this is not true of the system of segregating mentally deficient and backward children in special classes. Very few large school systems have ever abandoned their systems of special classes for mental inferiors, and the number of special classes in existence today is relatively larger than ever before in the history of the American public schools.

REASONS FOR THE PERMANENCE OF SPECIAL CLASSES

The reasons for the unbroken continuity of the special classes for subnormals are fairly obvious. On the one hand, great relief was afforded the normal pupils and the regular grade teachers by the removal of the flotsam and jetsam, the hold backs and drags, who retarded the progress of the class and often created difficult problems of discipline. On the other hand, the deficient pupils themselves began to respond in the special class as they had never responded before, under the influence of individual attention and guidance, differential training adapted to individual needs and the personal touch of a sympathetic, understanding, and properly trained teacher. The present indications are that the special classes have come to stay, at least for a long time, and it therefore behooves us to so organize and administer these classes that the highest interests of every child who has been removed from a regular grade will be properly conserved.

THE NEED OF A CRITICAL CONSIDERATION
OF THE PLANS OF ORGANIZING SPECIAL CLASSES

Over a decade of experience in examining candidates for, and matriculates in, special classes and in investigating the special-class situation in many public school systems, particularly in Pennsylvania, Missouri, and Ohio, and also years of experience in supervising special classes, have convinced the writer that the need is urgent for drawing much sharper definitions and delimitations of the grades or types of subnormals who should be assigned to different kinds of special classes. For, although many school systems maintain classes which are reserved by definite board action or executive promulgation for "feeble-minded" or "mentally defective" children, the standards of what constitutes feeble-mindedness in school children vary greatly from city to city. In some cities the brightest children assigned to such classes cannot do satisfactory third grade work, while in other cities they may reach the sixth grade level. In some cities children of sub-kindergarten attainments are admitted, in others they must reach the kindergarten or first grade level of competency. In some schools the children assigned to the same class vary by two or three grades only, in others by six or seven grades. In some classes the children vary from low grade imbeciles to those who are merely slightly retarded, or who are normal, many of the latter being merely pedagogically retarded or suffering from specific handicaps, such as speech defectiveness, muscular paralysis (of the spastic or flaccid type), impaired audition or vision, visual aphasia, dyslexia, and the like.

RECOMMENDED DIFFERENTIATION
OF PUPILS AND SPECIAL CLASSES

The plea of this address, as well as its excuse, is that there must be a sharper differentiation than has generally hitherto been obtained between grades of deficient or sub-average pupils, that there must be a sharper differentiation of types of special classes to meet the needs of various grades of such pupils, and that the prime consideration in the organization of such classes and in the differential assignment of the pupils must be purely educational.

In harmony with these principles, the specific suggestion which I have to offer is that there must be organized at the minimum two distinct orders or kinds of classes for mentally inefficient and retarded pupils in the grades. One of these types of classes should be reserved for children of very limited mental power or educational potentialities, and the other for children of higher mental and educational ability. I shall in this address refer to the classes for the lower grades as special classes or special schools, and to the classes for the higher grades as ungraded classes. Doubtless there will be differences of opinion as to where to draw the upper and lower boundary lines for each type of class, while certain doubting Thomases may even deny that a definite boundary line can be drawn between these two orders of classes. To these scruples a two-fold answer may be made: first, a line must perforce be drawn somewhere, for no recognized authority on the education of abnormal children, so far as I am aware, has the temerity to defend the practice of assembling in the same class idiots, imbeciles, morons, backward and normal children, and non-mentally defective children with specific defects. The custom of doing this is due purely to inertia, slothfulness, carelessness, or bias, and is without any excuse whatever in any large school system. Second, it is entirely feasible to organize a successful, flexible, dual system of special classes in conformity with the principles enunciated above in any elementary school system with a sufficient enrollment of pupils. These bold statements are made not as plausible hypotheses or as ex-cathedra arm chair dicta, but as demonstrated facts, for I have organized and supervised, directly or indirectly, successful, "going," flexible systems of special classes in harmony with this plan in two large public school systems, and have submitted similar plans of organization to many other school systems which have acted on the recommendations.

CRITERIA FOR DIFFERENTIAL ASSIGNMENT
OF PUPILS TO SPECIAL AND UNGRADED CLASSES

What, then, are the standards which have governed the differential assignment of pupils to these two systems of classes? Stated briefly in terms of the most important criteria (mental and educational capacities), the assignments to the special classes or schools (the classes for the most deficient children) have been limited to pupils whose intelligence quotients (as determined by the Stanford-Binet) have varied from 30 to 65 or 70, whose intelligence age has varied from 3 years to 9 years, and whose educational status has varied from sub-kindergarten capacity to a possible maximum attainment of beginning third grade work (the chronological age at the time of withdrawal being 14). In other words, the brightest pupils in this group will not do satisfactory all-round school work at the age of fourteen beyond the beginning of the third grade, although many may function beyond this level in certain branches in which they possess greater talent. The pupils assigned to the ungraded classes (the classes for the least deficient), on the other hand, will vary from an I.Q. of about 65 to an I.Q. of 85 or 90, and from a potential or eventual educational attainment level of from the third grade to the sixth grade, or even higher. The intelligence age level will vary greatly according to the age of the child at the time of transfer.

This plan of differentiation will require the grouping together of children of as wide a range of mental and educational capacity and level as can be successfully taught in one class, since it amounts to at least 35 I.Q., a half dozen mental age levels, and four or five grade levels. Where a large number of children are congregated in centralized schools, it would be quite possible under this arrangement to group the children for instruction into four or more levels in each kind of class, whether the plan is followed of having a teacher handle a given class or the instruction is departmentalized.

PREREQUISITES FOR SUCCESSFUL OPERATION
OF THIS DUAL SYSTEM OF CLASSES

What are the essential prerequisites for the effective operation of a system of parallel special classes as projected above?

First children who are near the limiting borders or who are of uncertain diagnosis must always be given the benefit of the doubt. This applies both to those who are near the lower entrance limit and to those near the upper limit. This rule practically applied, means that children of low mental power should not be ruthlessly excluded without any probationary tryout whatever in a special class, as is so frequently done in certain school systems—*e.g.,* if the child has an intelligence test age of only three or four years, or proves to be a Mongolian, a cretin, or a hydrocephalic. Let us not forget that under our laws even a low grade child has certain inalienable rights. No educator or school administrator should be precipitate in reaching an adverse decision in regard to any child, nor should he attempt to arrogate to himself autocratic powers over the life and happiness of unfortunate children. The experience of England throws serious doubt upon the soundness of the practice of ruthless exclusion from school. After having for many years debarred by statute all grades of imbeciles from instruction in special public school classes, volunteer associations have demonstrated that these unfortunates, when admitted to their occupation centers (there were 47 in July, 1923) are capable of a considerable amount of improvement in the service they can render to themselves and to others, and in their economic possibilities. Many low grade children admitted to special classes under the writer's direction have gradually reached a higher level of competency than ever could have been surmised from their early school record or initial test findings. As a result of appropriate training many of these children have become far less of a burden to the home or to the community, thus justifying the expense of the training. Of course, low grade pupils who fail to respond to the training should eventually either be excluded from school or be given merely a minimum amount of the teacher's time. Older higher grade pupils could, no doubt, supply the necessary training under direction.

This rule also means that children of an I.Q. of 65 or 70 who seem from a careful consideration of all the data at hand to possess considerable potentials for growth and improvement, should be assigned on probation to the ungraded class (for the higher grade pupils) in preference to the special class. If such children do not make reasonable progress within a year or two they should be re-examined for possible transfer to the special class.

Second, the organization of the classes, and particularly the system of assignments and reassignments must be so flexible that the child can be transferred, after due consideration has been given to his progress and to the results of retests, from one type of class to the other. My experience indicates that if adequate examinations are made and due care taken in making the assignments, not many children will have to be transferred from the special classes to the ungraded classes, for the tendency of the I.Q. of these children is to decline slowly.[5] Mentally deficient children progress in their school work only from one-tenth to one-third of the normal rate, so that they become relatively more backward as they grow older. In view of this fact, it is

---

[5] See J. E. Wallace Wallin, Problems of Subnormality, 1917, 265f. The Value of the Intelligence Quotient for Individual Diagnosis, Journal of Delinquency, 1919, 109–124.

to be expected that more transfers will have to be made from the ungraded classes to the special schools. In the writer's experience this has proved actually to be the case. Again, many children will be assigned to the ungraded classes who are pedagogically backward but mentally normal or almost so. Such children should be restored to grade as soon as possible. No child should be retained in a special class after he can function properly in a regular grade. Of 3,111 children in the St. Louis ungraded classes in 1916–1917, 42% were reported to the writer as restored to grade.

Third, the curriculum must be adapted to the individual requirements of the pupils in both kind of classes. In both there must be a maximum of individual attention and individual diagnosis of cases, and of concrete activities skillfully correlated around vital cores or projects. In the special classes, however, more use must be made of concrete, practical activities and of the oral method of instruction, and less emphasis should be placed on literary instruction than in the ungraded classes. Younger children in the ungraded classes will be given every advantage of skilled instruction in the literary branches until it becomes clearly evident that their literary limitations are irremovable, when they will be given an increasing amount of industrial arts work in correlation with the academic work. Pedagogically retarded children of normal mentality will be given intensive instruction in the regular studies of the curriculum, so that they may cover the ground lost more rapidly and be restored to grade as quickly as possible.

Fourth, the practice of applying the terms "feeble-minded," "mentally defective," "imbecilic," and "moronic" to the children in the special classes of special schools (for the lower grade cases) should be abandoned. Nor should it be assumed that these classes or schools are established for such pupils, although, in point of fact, many of those assigned will prove to be feeble-minded or mentally defective in the properly accepted meaning of those words. In proposing the abandonment of these terms when applied to children who have been differentiated for educational purposes in the public schools, I cannot be accused of harboring a prejudicial attitude in the matter, for I have used these terms for over a decade for purposes of classification and assignment of pupils to special public school classes. But I have gradually become convinced that the words should be no longer connected with our schemes of educational differentiation. This conclusion has been reached for a number of cogent reasons.

1. The words feeble-mindedness and mental defectiveness have by numerous statutory enactments or by definitions or resolutions emanating from technical organizations been given definite and limited social, economic, and legal connotations from which they cannot be reclaimed.

2. The social or legal definition of a feeble-minded child or adult as one who is "incapable, from mental defect existing from birth or from an early age, (a)

of competing on equal terms with his normal fellows, or (b) of managing himself and his affairs with ordinary prudence," is entirely too vague and elastic to serve the purpose of a scientific definition of a criterion for differentiating immature children for purposes of education. A definition that defines a thing in terms which are not defined and which are highly ambiguous is worse than useless. This definition, although it has been very widely but uncritically adopted, is a patent absurdity, a delusion, and a joke. The estimates of the number of feeble-minded in the schools based on this definition have varied from 0.3% to 10%. England, the country from which we derived this concept of feeble-mindedness (the definition originated with the Royal College of Physicians of London) has, fortunately, definitely repudiated the definition in the Mental Deficiency Act of 1913. Nevertheless, the rejected definition is still prolifically quoted.

3. Even the more acceptable revised definition of a feeble-minded person as one who is socially, industrially, or economically dependent or incapable of leading an independent existence, does not constitute a serviceable criterion for differentiating children for purposes of instruction, for the very obvious reason that often we cannot predict with accuracy whether or not a given child will eventually acquire sufficient skill and judgment to earn his livelihood and lead an independent existence. Frequently, we must suspend judgment until the child has been given a chance at various jobs after leaving school. It is, in point of fact, indisputable that thousands of persons who have gone out from special public school classes for the feeble-minded have "made good" socially, morally, industrially, and economically.

4. The more recent attempt to define feeble-mindedness in terms of years of intelligence retardation, or intelligence quotients, or maximal upper limit of intellectual development, as determined by so-called intelligence tests, does not seem to promise any greater success, in view of the pronounced differences of opinion regarding the precise criteria to be adopted. Thus the limit of intellectual development for the highest grades of the feeble-minded, as determined by the Binet-Simon scale, has been variously drawn at a level of twelve years, eleven years, ten years, nine years, and eight years. The writer drew the line at the nine-year level over a decade ago, thereby definitely rejecting the concepts of the middle and high grade morons as equivalent terms for the high grades of feeble-minded persons. During 14 years of constant examination and classification of, and practical work with, mentally and educationally inferior and abnormal children, he has never diagnosed as feeble-minded anyone grading as high as ten years by the 1911 Binet or the Stanford-Binet scales.[6] Many, indeed probably most writers, however, con-

---

[6] The basis for the conclusions reached have been set forth in a discussion of "Who is Feeble-Minded?" in Ungraded, 1916, 105–113, in the Journal of Criminal Law and

tinued to diagnose as feeble-minded older adolescents and adults with mental levels as high as twelve years until the psychological findings in the army, as announced in 1919, demonstrated the utter absurdity of the generally accepted standard.[7] Recently Cyril Burt has gone farther still, having fixed the "provisional limit" at the "age of eight." It is a fact that adults have been tested in the United States who have not developed beyond the Binet-Simon age of VIII, and yet they have been able to support themselves and conform to the legal and conventional requirements of the community. According to Burt, in England individuals below the eight-year level "become almost invariably parasites."

Similarly the upper limit of mental defectiveness in terms of intelligence quotients (based on Binet-Simon age) has been placed at various points. William Stern placed it as high as 80. The dictum that an I.Q. below 70 indicates "definite feeble-mindedness" has been very widely accepted, but even this more conservative standard has been shown by follow-up studies and the investigation of case histories to be quite untenable. Now comes Cyril Burt with the proposal to draw the line at an I.Q. of 50 (based on his eight-year limit and age XVI as the normal adult level). Below 50, he says the case is an "institutional" one, and between 50 and 60 a "supervision" case.

5. Realizing that the intelligence standards for the diagnosis of feeble-mindedness have been drawn entirely too high, it is now proposed to call persons feeble-minded who are emotionally, temperamentally, nervously, morally or volitionally unstable or ill-balanced. To attempt to differentiate

---

Criminology, 1916, 706–716, 56–78, and 222–226, and in Problems of Subnormality, 1917, 110–277. See also The Concept of the Feeble-Minded, Especially the Moron, The Training School Bulletin, 1920, 41–53, and The Achievement of Subnormal Children in Standardized Education Tests, Miami University Bulletin, XX, No. 7, 1922.

[7] Time has brought unexpectedly swift and conclusive vindication and a liberality and catholicity of view which contrast sharply with the whilom dogmatic fixation. It is now deemed not only proper but essential to assume a critical attitude toward the Binet scale or any other scale of tests, and the inferences and conclusions drawn from their use, and the critic of today is not treated with the contemptuous silence, or attempts at personal disparagement or professional ostracism which not infrequently have pursued the very few who a decade or more ago were intrepid enough to undertake the disagreeable task of repudiating the cherished idola theatri or the status quo. Conclusions which everybody now accepts as a matter of course when announced a decade or more ago were lampooned, or evoked derisive laughter, or subjected the writer to vituperative personal attacks for alleged bias, obsessional predilection for "preconceived notions," and impudent temerity. Rather than face the inevitable consequences of the facts in the case, it seemed to some whose opinions had already been firmly crystallized preferable to close their eyes to further arguments or additional evidence, and to ignore or deny the facts. It is notorious that those who were most vociferous in that day in denouncing as extravagant theorizing conclusions which were in conflict with prevailing beliefs, have remained ominously silent since the "intelligence survey" of 94,004 American recruits showed that the average "intelligence age" of the white soldiers was 13.1, and that 47% of the whites and 89% of the colored drafted soldiers had an intelligence level of less than thirteen years.

mentally defective children for instruction on the basis of temperamental or emotional instability would be the height of folly, although emotional poise is of paramount importance for success in any activity of life. We have at present no means whatever of accurately measuring or determining the degree of a child's emotional or temperamental instability. An emotional or temperamental classification in the present stage of science would be purely subjective. But let me be quick to add that no child, no matter how emotionally or temperamentally abnormal he may be can be classed as "feeble-minded" who does not suffer from a radical defect of judgment, understanding, common sense, or intelligence, dating from birth or from early life. Unless we hold fast to the basic elements in the classical, age-old concept of feeble-mindedness (social and industrial dependency due to native or early acquired defect of intelligence), we shall emasculate the concept entirely. This proposed extension of the connotation of the term will serve no useful purpose whatever as an aid in the classification of mentally deficient and retarded children for instruction.

SUMMARY

Let us repeat, therefore, in brief summary form, the conclusions we have reached:

1. The considerations of prime importance for the classification and segregation of mentally subnormal children in the schools are the child's present educational status and educational potentialities, which of course, are vitally affected by his mental capacity—his "intelligence age-level" and "intelligence quotient"—and mental peculiarities.

2. Children who differ very greatly in amount of handicap or deficiency should not be assigned to the same kind of class. The successful operation of a special or ungraded class demands a certain degree of homogeneity in the pupil material.

3. Accordingly it will be necessary to draw a line of demarcation somewhere. The point at which such a line is drawn will, admittedly, be more or less arbitrary. We have suggested above that there must be at least two orders, levels, or kinds of special classes for mentally and educationally retarded children, and have indicated where the line can be successfully drawn between special and ungraded classes. The suggestions made are not based on speculative arm-chair theories of special class organization, but they represent the culmination of many years of actual experience in the organization of different kinds of special classes in public school systems.

4. Children transferred to the special classes should not be assigned for the

reason that they are feeble-minded socially and industrially considered, nor should it be assumed that they are feeble-minded although most of them or all of them may prove to be so. They should be assigned solely because their mental and educational potentials are so limited that they cannot do satisfactory work in all of the regular branches of the curriculum beyond the primary grades (or the beginning of the third grade). Certainly it will be a decided advantage to relieve the educator of the necessity of attempting to determine what children are or are not going to prove to be feeble-minded, or of attempting to solve the apparently insolvable question of where to draw the boundary line between mentally defective or non-mentally defective subnormals. We probably cannot avoid the necessity of applying some term to the children assigned to the special classes for the lower grades. It is very difficult to propose a term that is free from objections. The designations *mentally deficient children* or *mental deficients* will serve if not used as synonyms for feeble-minded or mentally defective children. I submit these recommendations for your serious consideration.

DISCUSSION

MR. G. M. WILSON: It seems to me there has been some criticism of the special class because of the difficulty of putting across adequate vocational training there, training in woodwork, carpentry, etc. To my mind we have missed the point a little because we have a class of children there that can not profit by vocational training in any degree. I always think of special class curriculum as fundamentally an organizing of activities, that through the mediumship of better habits these children can become better citizens. They can not be turned out experts in anything. They are always going to be laborers or the lower type of industrial workers; but we can build up in them habits of citizenship through an organized curriculum of activities by means of which such habits can be fostered. Something was said this morning about so-called parolees from public schools as compared with those from feeble-minded that was a little unfair to special class graduates, showing a larger percentage of special class graduates as having failed in society than of those from institutions. Of course special classes have to parole or graduate everybody. The institutions do not. They can graduate only those they think will succeed. I think also that the special classes attempt many times to handle and train individuals they should not, individuals that are institution cases. If they would distinguish more closely between the type that should be there and the institutional type I think special classes would be more successful. Then if they would more systematically organize their training in habits, or citizenship, thinking of that as the most fundamental thing they can do, and make attempt to check up as they go along with respect to their degree of success as to the stage they have reached, I think it would be beneficial. We have some citizenship habit scales that can be used. They were made for children in regular classes and are particularly adaptable, I think, for those in special classes.

THE DEVELOPMENT
OF
A RESEARCH PROGRAM
IN
MENTAL DEFICIENCY
OVER
A FIFTEEN-YEAR PERIOD

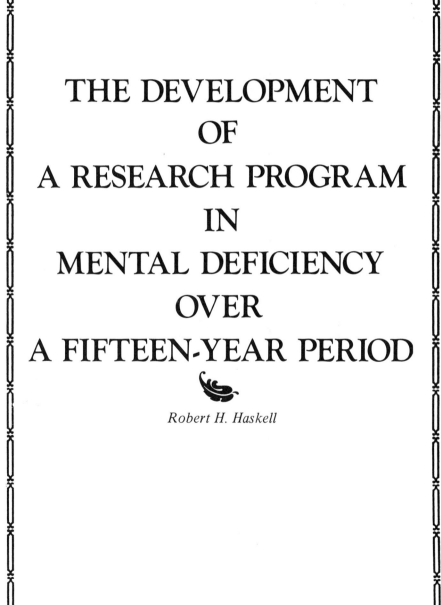

Robert H. Haskell

This paper introduces the three subsequent papers by Kephart, Strauss and Werner, and Lehtinen and Strauss. The author describes the functioning and goals of a research department at the Wayne County Training School from 1926 to 1944. During an era when institutions were largely custodial, this group was challenging the constancy of the I.Q., reporting significant increments in intellectual and social growth as a result of certain educational interventions, and documenting the favorable social adjustment of persons returned to the community.

The Wayne County Training School opened its doors in 1926.[1] Those responsible for its creation had set as its purpose increase in salvage among the higher grade mentally deficient. Institutional treatment and care of the mentally deficient in America had seventy-five years' experience back of its ideas and methods. If the purpose of the establishment of this new institutional venture was to be attained, research for possible better ways became a *conditio sine qua non.*

Research, in whatever field, is a call for the future. It cannot be undertaken otherwise than with a feeling of discontent with the achievements of the past and the hope for a possible improvement in the time to come. There are, however, limitations in research especially under institutional conditions: limitations with regard to the worthwhileness of the research project in respect to time and money required; limitations as to the immediate need; and limitations as to the possibility of practical applicability of the theoretical results. It seemed worthwhile, today, after fifteen years to review and evaluate the results of such a research program, originated admittedly with a selfish purpose solely to help the administration of the institution in the search for a new program, but which has sought none-the-less never to forget the major objectives of science.

Where did we stand in our scientific knowledge on the problems of moron and borderline defectives when the Training School opened in 1926?

Our knowledge on mental deficiency is derived mainly from four different disciplines. They are:
1. Social science, including administration.
2. Psychology including psychopathology.
3. Education, especially special education.
4. Medicine, especially neuropsychiatry.

Let us consider sketchily each field separately and discuss the main problems involved.

The original purpose behind the creation of public institutions for the mentally deficient was ameliorative. At the risk of delaying progress in our theme, I would urge you to read John Greenleaf Whittier's essay in 1848 on

Read at the ninety-ninth meeting of The American Psychiatric Association, Detroit, Mich., May 10–13, 1943.

From the Wayne County Training School, Northville, Mich.

References on this paper are divided into two parts. Reference numbers in parentheses refer to the "Bibliography." Superior reference numbers refer to the "Publications from the Wayne County Training School."—*Ed.*

American Journal of Psychiatry, 1944, 101(1): 73–81. Reprinted with permission of the author and The American Psychiatric Association.

Dr. Haskell is now retired and resides in the Leeward Islands in the West Indies.

Peculiar Institutions of Massachusetts, where his deep religious soul discusses Dr. Samuel G. Howe's first mental hygiene survey on the problem of feeble-mindedness in the Commonwealth. Practical forces, some might say natural, have determined, perhaps too largely, an asylum type of development in this field. It is within our memory that parole was formally recognized in law. And yet, even today, within the classic institution no particular differentiation of program for the higher grade deficient has been evolved to prepare him the better for his attempted return to the community.

If we were to increase salvage among the higher grade deficient, where the community-objectionable characteristics of this type of individual are largely his threatening aggressive behavior, the program could not be satisfied with attempting merely to impart more academic knowledge or increase vocational skills but must be more vitally concerned with helping these individuals in their inter-personal relations, in their development of different emotional attitudes and in their creation of different mores.

Various experiments in the organization of our community life were made in many directions from the very opening of the training school. It may be sad, but it is none-the-less true, that negative aspects seem the easiest patterns for institutions to adopt. Emphasis is much more easily laid upon what these children cannot do and why they shouldn't be permitted to try to do anything outside the narrowest possible circle of prescribed activities, particularly if the doing is the least bit noisy or otherwise disturbs an adult or an adult's viewpoint, rather than focusing on what they might do.

The attempt to develop a democratically self-determining cottage among the boys was made on several occasions, from the second year of operation on, but without continued success. The reasons were various but mainly related to the fact that while self-government was existent, it was existent only up to a point but not beyond that point; it was a form but not a whole substance. In 1935 we established in an area more than half a mile removed from the group of other cottages the Homestead Cottage. Whatever the principles of mental hygiene had taught us should be expected from an experiment in child living, but which we had not achieved in our earlier trials, had been obtained at this self-determining cottage.

The so-called Iowa studies were unknown to us at the time the Homestead Cottage was projected and started. Our gain in administrative relations with this cottage had been enough: so-called disciplinary problems with our older boys had been greatly lessened; the boys were happier; our employees in the other cottages were furnished a laboratory course of instruction constantly at their disposal; actually fewer employees are required in these two cottages (a second cottage had been established a year later). But actually, in addition to social growth, significant acceleration of intellectual growth became even more significant as later certain specifically designed educational ventures were introduced into the cottage program. Kephart[2-5] in particular has reported on these studies.

Still in the realm of the social science discipline, we have made carefully documented studies of all boys and girls discharged from the training school up to a date three years before the beginning of the study so that conclusions could be reached of their social acceptability after at least three years on their own in the community.

Forty-three per cent of all boys from the training school, who had been returned to the community with our approval prior to July 1, 1933 were found in a very carefully conducted personal survey made during the winter of 1937–1938 to be totally self-supporting—even in these depth-of-depression days. Nineteen per cent of this entire number, in addition to supporting themselves, were also aiding in the support of others. An additional 29 per cent were classified as partially self-supporting. Kephart[6] and Ainsworth and Bijou[7] and Ainsworth have reported on these studies.

We are now engaged in testing out a manual on cottage operation written as a teaching device to facilitate the interpretation to cottage workers of the reasons for certain attitudes and methods based upon these investigations: this manual was prepared by Melcher-Patterson and McCandless.[9]

What was the challenge in 1926 from the contribution of psychology to the field of mental deficiency?

Binet's revolutionary attempt to "measure" intelligence had been translated to America by Goddard and further developed by him to fit American conditions. Stern's formula of the intelligence quotient had been adopted to make possible an apparently exact measurement of an individual's mental inventory. The 1916 revision of the Binet scale by Terman had made possible the use of "the test" by any school teacher who could afford to buy the book! For the keen observer, however, a rigidity of thinking about retardation in mental development became more and more apparent.

Was the I.Q. something to be accepted as constant and invariable? Was the currently accepted deterministic viewpoint of low I.Q. as settling all future personal problems of the child so tested to remain unchallenged? Any deviation from that viewpoint was sacrilegious in most educational circles at that time. And yet, if our efforts in the rehabilitation of the mental defective should be sustained in his readjustment to community life, it was necessary to demonstrate that this then general belief was a misconception.

We mention two very significant studies by Hoakley[10,11]: the first in 1932 entitled "Variability of Intelligence Quotients" based on a study of the results of 1469 Stanford-Binet examinations made on 550 different children at intervals varying from six months to twelve years. This study, important as it is in many respects, is most important because of the inescapable evidence it presents that not even sixteen years is the upper age limit for intellectual growth. The other study, published in 1935 and in all respects a continuation of the same fundamental problem, was a "Comparison of the Heinis Personal Constant and the Intelligence Quotient." One of her conclusions from this study, that the P.C. is a more constant and more representative index than the I.Q., would, if adopted generally, serve to answer many of the questions so perplexing where such laboratory terms have to be used in courts and similar situations before laymen where intellectual constants and such "tom-foolery" details are just as much out of place as the details of Wassermann procedure would be.

More than just variability in I.Q. could be shown. Was the institution-alized mental defective condemned to "lower his I.Q.," as had been stated so often, or could proper and adequate training in an institution provide the necessary stimuli for a fuller development of such a child's limited capacities? The studies by Kephart,[5] just mentioned, and several others gave [24, 25] ample proof that, especially in the familial type of mental defectives, the success of such efforts could even be measured by a "heightened" I.Q.

Yearly examination of all children with a broad battery of standardized intelligence tests, non-verbal as well as verbal and collateral educational achievement tests, combined with psychiatric observation focused upon personality reactions and psychogenetic origins, served only to mordant our impressions that knowing more about differences in manner of learning of our children was more important for our purpose than any other question confronting us and that until we could clarify this seemingly perpetual maze of qualitative vs. quantitative differences in our children's mental activities, we were to continue befogged. If we were to make even a step forward in the assignment given us, to increase salvage, research in education was inescap-able.

In 1926, one hundred twenty-five years had passed since Itard's grandiose attack upon the educational possibilities, even of an idiot child, had shaken the pedagogical world. His attempt in spite of its failure—nowadays we may say he did not have the facilities to diagnose this child as severely brain-injured—awakened the educators to explore a hitherto forgotten field. Seguin's efforts contributed much to popularize special education in the United States. But the field remained quite sterile until, at the beginning of this century, Montessori in Italy and Decroly in Belgium, both psychiatrists, opened new avenues of educational approach. Unfortunately both seemed dissatisfied with their success in the field of mental deficiency and turned back to work with normal children. The Montessori method of "sense training" is still in use for the low-grade child; the Decroly method never became popular in the United States because we developed independently the "activity program" and "progressive education." For our purposes neither method seemed to offer promise: the one was too specific and the other too general in its scope.

In 1926 Orton's publications (1) from Iowa on strephosymbolia were attracting considerable attention. They seemed to offer a starting point to learn more about these undoubted differences in manner of learning.

For several years reading disability among our children was the point of attack. The results were fruitful. We discovered that cases of reading disability identical with reading disability of normals existed among our children: that they existed among them in about the same proportion as found among normal children, about 11 per cent; that these disabilities could be overcome; that methods of treating the disabilities of normal children were not applicable to our children; indeed, that the very method perhaps, used today to teach normal children to read might be a prominent factor in producing the disability; that specific methods of treatment could be devised to teach our children whereby spectacular results followed; that children six, seven and eight years in school without learning to accomplish even first grade reading could be taught to read up to their mental age level at a rate two to three times as fast as the normal child learns to read: that a method of prevention was probably possible.

This field of investigation was very fruitful. It stimulated the imagination of many persons important to the support of the total project who had been perhaps lukewarm to the possibility of anything but a relatively barren future. The results of remedial teaching could be measured and described in terms that anyone, not merely an educator or a psychologist, could understand.

An impressive series of publications of original investigations by Hegge and his associates[41-59] resulted from this area of disabilities. The most important book yet written on the teaching of reading to this type of handicapped child grew out of these studies—the book by Kirk (2).

We would call particular attention to the transformation that takes place in the rebellious, anti-socially-headed non-reader child, twelve, thirteen, or fourteen years of age, when he comes to recognize that at last he is going to learn to read.

Perhaps the most important conclusion from our researches in this field was the conviction that reading disability, so far as the higher grade defective was concerned, was largely the result of the attempt to teach the child to read before he was prepared for the experience.

Upon the theory that the most vital educational need for the younger children entering the training school is not more academic drill, but a longer preparation period in which to acquire more of the foundation of unfolded experience with which normal children just naturally start their academic training, we began a few years ago to create an environment which shall meet the younger child's needs and stimulate him to mental activity in accordance with the principles which have been so successfully demonstrated in preschools for very young (normal) children and perhaps kindergartens.[65]

This program has been under the continuing direction of Ruth T. Melcher-Patterson.[66-70] Its results in terms of effect upon intelligence, social maturity and personality adjustment, also later academic achievement, have been fully reported in detail in the literature as well as the details of the organization of the unit and its methods.

You may ask why I have not discussed earlier the contributions and challenges we received from the medical sciences. Isn't Tredgold who wrote the first and still standard book on mental deficiency in English, a physician? Is not his classification of primary and secondary amentia still in use? Is not his concept of social competence of the feeble-minded the most widely used criterion in the circles of lawyers and laymen? No one would, or could, minimize the contributions of Tredgold, or of Fernald in the United States. However, for our special problem—the rehabilitation of the high grade mentally defective—the usual fields of brain pathology, biochemistry, genetics and clinical syndromology offered no prospects. Child psychiatry outside the child guidance movement, which has always had thumbs down on the mental defective, was little known. Homburger's (3) standard work had just been published in Germany. Kanner's (4) outstanding treatise was to follow only many years later.

There should be no wonder that our first studies in the medical field were medical researches pure and simple and not in any sense research in the field of mental deficiency as such.

H. S. Willis[80] and associates reported on sensitization from repeated injection of the new PTP tuberculin, a hitherto unobserved phenomenon turned up in the course of studying the incidence of tuberculosis in our population.

Ferry and associates,[76-79] among a long series of studies in immunology, worked out important developments in the treatment of meningococcic meningitis which were to reduce the mortality of that disease another 50 per cent below the point where Flexner had left it.

Huddelson,[81] and a group of research associates of the Rockefeller Foundation spent several days a week for two years studying the possible presence of brucellosis in our population.

Bunting[84] directed over a period of several years a rather elaborate study on dental caries.

Lewis studied the urine of almost a thousand children with particular interest respecting the presence of phenylpyruvic acid.

Watson and Moehlig investigated the growth pattern in a group of children showing extreme retardation in physical growth as well as endocrine anomalies and then the results of administration of specific growth hormone. These studies are still in progress under Watson and Strauss.[87]

None of these studies touched our essential problem.

The very earliest impressions we gathered of our children were those of extreme heterogeneity. In a group of mental defectives from which all idiots and imbeciles were excluded, to use the descriptive expression of heterogeneity may seem strange but to the clinical psychiatrist no other impression would be possible.

With respect to this early perplexity over the very evident question of qualitative vs. quantitative differences in the learning processes, notwithstanding the tremendous advances in our knowledge of our children from the extensive research I have just sketched so briefly, we still continued, in 1937, perplexed.

The National Research Council through its Committee on Psychiatric Investigation had published in 1934(5) a report on the Problem of Mental Disorder. Feeblemindedness is barely mentioned anywhere in all that exhaustive report of practically four hundred printed pages. Meyerson (6) can be said to have been the only contributor even to mention the subject and I quote from his contribution to "Current Points of View" (7):

". . . . as a matter of fact, there is no such unity as is implied in the term feeblemindedness.

There are, as a matter of fact, groups of individuals who present as part of the syndrome by which they are differentiated from the normal the symptom of lowered intelligence. Thus the cretin, the Mongolian imbecile, the feebleminded with organic brain-disease, brain-injury, post encephalitis, etc., represent groups not at all biologically related to one another, except in the appearance of mental defect.

The quality of the research done in feeblemindedness is on the whole inferior because it has been dominated by the misleading concept that feeblemindedness is some kind of biological unit. Here and there work has been done on the anatomy of the brain of the feebleminded. Very creditable studies have been done on the cretins because this subject linked itself up with the definite subject matter of endocrinology. A few radiographic studies have appeared. Sporadic biochemical papers appear in the literature. Most of the work on feeblemindedness appears in psychological studies, which really only measure the quantitative effect but give us no hint as to causation. Surveys galore have been made at great expense largely to bolster up preconceived ideas. It is a striking commentary on the schools for the feebleminded that very few of them have clinical directors, and one can count on the fingers of one hand the places where pathology, biochemistry and physiology are used in the studies of the hypophrenias. This great problem needs clinical investigation in all its forms. The psychological and sociological studies should go on; but the basic investigations into the nature of the individual who is feebleminded can hardly be said to have started."

In 1937, through the support of the McGregor Fund, research at the training school was greatly expanded by the addition to the research staff of Heinz Werner, experimental psychologist, and Alfred A. Strauss, child psychiatrist. From the collaborative endeavors of these two men and their associates, has come much to answer this persistently perplexing problem of qualitative vs. quantitative differences.

Typology had not hitherto been considered a matter of very great significance beyond the question of expressing etiology. Even Meyerson didn't suggest any importance attaching to the subject beyond differential diagnosis of origin.

Strauss, a pupil of Goldstein, had started in 1930 (8, 9) to apply the findings of brain-neurology in the field of mental deficiency. After years of study in developmental neurology he has succeeded in establishing clinical criteria for differentiation between the brain-injured, exogenous, and the familial, endogenous type of feeblemindedness.[20-26] By evaluating isolated reflex disturbances in brain-injured children, usually overlooked or pushed aside as not significant, he has crystallized an organic behavior syndrome diagnostic even in children where these residual isolated signs were absent.

In collaboration with Werner[27-40] who contributed his vast experience in genetic and experimental psychology, the foundation was laid for a psychopathological analysis of perceptual and conceptual differences between the exogenous and the endogenous type of mental deficiency. Those differences in fundamental aspects of behavior, now confirmed by objective laboratory demonstration, give new and vastly different significance to the old problem of type of defectiveness. The results of Strauss and Werner's investigations are ample proof of the usefulness of Gelb and Goldstein's (10) pioneering approach relative to the psychopathology of brain-injured adults on the basis of Gestalt-psychology.

Several of these researches have been presented before this section: in 1939, "Behavior Differences in Mentally Retarded Children Measured by a new Behavior Rating Scale";[26] in 1940, "The Mental Organization of the Brain-Injured Mentally Defective Child";[32] in 1942, "Comparative Psychopathology of the Brain-Injured Child and the Traumatic Brain-Injured Adult."[36]

Others have been presented before the American Association on Mental Deficiency and psychological groups. We are convinced that these researches meet Meyerson's (11) challenge that "basic investigations into the nature of the individual who is feebleminded can hardly be said to have started." The appearance in the current literature of the terms exogenous and endogenous in the sense developed in these studies, shows how quickly the usefulness of these differentiations has been recognized by workers in the field.

To touch one important implication of this new classification we must turn back to the field of education. The classical system of instruction for mentally defective children is based overpoweringly upon the quantitative concept of mental deficiency. Hollingworth (12) has stated that "feebleminded children differ from ordinary children only in amount of ability, not in the kind of abilities, they possess. No mysterious or unique matter or method is necessarily required in the task of training them. They can learn the same things that other children learn up to the limits of their capacity." Some variety of that formulation governs most educational thinking and practice in this general field even today.

Statistical studies[24,25] in our own school showed that the endogenous, or familial, defective child tended to advance educationally through the school opportunity given him while the brain-injured, or exogenous, defective child tended to lag behind: i.e., the quantitatively defective profited, the qualitatively different child, so far as brain function is concerned, lagged behind.

There was a challenge here that could not be avoided. The results of the applications of methods that Strauss (13) had developed in the education of individual cases earlier as adapted to class situations with brain-injured defective children is just now reaching publication after three years' developmental experimentation.[71-75]

In the field of special education of the feebleminded in general, Werner,[12-19] the experimental psychologist, brought his techniques to bear for the first time and gave us the opportunity to see what functional analysis of psychological processes might contribute to the understanding of differences in learning of mine-run feebleminded children.

I quote from a letter which Allport, professor of psychology at Harvard University, wrote me:

"We all know that the empirical, rough-and-ready devices employed by mental testers have a limited value in disclosing the true nature of mental deficiency. Indeed, these tests are now known to mask important functional disorders that presumably underlie mental handicap. Through their fresh attack upon the subject and through their discovery of some basic patterns of mental handicap, I believe that Werner and Strauss are making significant discoveries that promise eventually to improve our understanding and therefore our methods of treating the different kinds of mental retardation."

I have tried to present to you the high lights of the development of a research program in mental deficiency over a fifteen year period under the conditions as outlined in the beginning. We are well aware of many gaps in its texture; of many existing problems we have not touched. Many ventures I have not even mentioned: excursions into drug and allied therapy,[86-88] speech disorders,[60-64] electroencephalographic studies now under way and some others.

The most important problem of all—which will become still more significant in the future—concerns studies on personality and group relationship. We have utilized, for example, the measurement of interpersonal relationships in groups by the Moreno technique:[2] we have studied group formation under democratic and autocratic leadership according to Lewin's hypotheses;[8] a study on the personality make-up of the brain-injured child[37] is to be published soon. These results all enter into administrative usefulness. The most important problem of the personality of the high grade defective, his reactions and his constitutional deviations, is far from being solved. We see in Sheldon's new books (14, 15) on constitutional psychology one possible approach to it.

Whatever the future will bring we do not know. We have followed and will follow in our research efforts principles which have been so excellently expressed on a similar theme "The World We Want," in the Christian Science Monitor recently, by the great Spanish philosopher and politician, Madariaga (16). He says: to see the way clear, we have:

1. To define what is desirable,
2. To define what is possible at any time within the scheme of what is desirable,
3. To carry out what is possible in the spirit of what is desirable.

BIBLIOGRAPHY

1. Orton, S. T. Wordblindness in school children. Arch. Neurol. Psych., 14: 581, 1925.
2. Kirk, S. A. Teaching reading to slow-learning children. Houghton Mifflin Co., Boston, 1940.
3. Homburger, A. Psychopathologie des Kindesalters. Jul. Springer, Berlin, 1926.
4. Kanner, L.. Child psychiatry. Charles C Thomas, Springfield, Ill., 1935.
5. Bentley, M., and Cowdry, E. V. The problem of mental disorder. Mc-Graw-Hill Book Co., New York, 1934.
6. Myerson, A. Medical psychiatry. L. c.
7. ____. Ibidem, pp. 37 and 38.
8. Strauss, A. Beitraege zur Einteilung, Entstehung und Klinik der schwersten Schwachsinnsformen. Arch. Psychiat., 99: 693, 1933.
9. ____. Heilpaedagogik. Z. f. Kinderf., 41: 445, 1933.
10. Goldstein, K. The organism. Am. Book Co., New York, 1939.
11. Myerson, A., L. c., p. 38.

12. Hollingworth, L. A. The psychology of sub-normal children, p. 91. New York, Macmillan Co., 1920.
13. Strauss, A. Pedagogia terapeutica. Publishers: Editorial Labor, Barcelona, 1936.
14. Sheldon, W. H., Stevens, S. S., and Tucker, W. B. The varieties of human physique. Publishers: Harper and Brothers, New York, 1940.
15. Sheldon, W. H., and Stevens, S. S. The varieties of temperament. Publishers: Harper and Brothers, New York, 1942.
16. de Madariaga, Salvador. The world we want —Series. Article 27. The Christian Science Monitor, Saturday, Oct. 31, 1942, p. 53.

PUBLICATIONS FROM THE WAYNE COUNTY TRAINING SCHOOL

Social Sciences

Administration

1. Haskell, R. H. An organization for the training of the higher grade mental defective. Proceed. Am. Assn. Study Feebleminded, **37**: 252, 1932.

Social Studies in Group Behavior

2. Kephart, N. C. A method of heightening social adjustment in an institutional group. J. Orthopsychiat., **8**: 710, 1938.
3. Kephart, N. C. Group autonomy in a children's institution. Ment. Hyg., **22**: 585, 1938.
4. Kephart, N. C. The effect of a highly specialized institutional program upon the I.Q. in highgrade mentally deficient children. Proceed. Am. Ass. Ment. Def., **44**: 216, 1939.
5. Kephart, N. C. Influencing the rate of mental growth in retarded children through environmental stimulation. 39. Yearbook, Nat. Soc. Study Educ., part 2, p. 223, 1940.
6. Kephart, N. C. and Ainsworth, M. H. A preliminary report of community adjustment of parolees of the Wayne County Training School. Proceed. Am. Ass. Ment. Def., **43**: 161, 1938.
7. Bijou, S. W., Ainsworth, M. H., and Stockey, M. R. The social adjustment of mentally retarded girls paroled from the Wayne County Training School. Am. J. Ment. Def., **47**: 422, 1943.
8. McCandless, Boyd R. Changing relationships between dominance and social acceptability during group democratization. Am. J. Orthopsychiat., **12**: 529, 1942.
9. McCandless, B. R., and Melcher-Patterson, R. Guidance Principles for cottage workers at Wayne County Training School. (Manuscript.)

Psychology

Psychometrics

10. Hoakley, Z. P. The variability of intelligence quotients. Proceed. Am. Ass. Study Feebleminded., **37**: 119, 1932.

11. Hoakley, A. P. Comparison of the Heinis personal constant and the intelligence quotient. Proceed. Am. Ass. Ment. Def., *40:* 403, 1935.

Genetic Psychology and Functional Analysis

12. Strauss, A. A., and Werner, H. Deficiency in the finger schema in relation to arithmetic disability (fingeragnosia and acalculia). Amer. J. Orthopsychiat., **8**: 719, 1938.
13. Werner, H., and Strauss, A. A. Approaches to a functional analysis of mentally handicapped problem children with illustration in the field of arithmetic disability. Proceed. Amer. Ass. Ment. Def., **43**: 105, 1938.
14. Werner, H., and Strauss, A. A. Problems and methods of functional analysis in mentally deficient children. J. Abn. Soc. Psychol., **34**: 37, 1939.
15. Strauss, A. A., and Werner, H. Fingeragnosia in children (with a brief discussion on defect and retardation in mentally handicapped children). Amer. J. Psychiat., **95**: 1215, 1939.
16. Werner, H. Perception of spatial relationship in mentally deficient children. J. Genet. Psychol. **57**: 93, 1940.
17. Werner, H. Psychological approaches investigating deficiencies in learning. Am. J. Ment. Def., **46**: 233, 1941.
18. Werner, H., and Carrison, D. Measurement and development of the finger schema in mentally retarded children; relation of arithmetic achievement to performance in the finger schema test. J. Educ. Psychol., **33**: 252, 1942.
19. Werner, H. Measurement and development of visuomotor performance on the Marble-Board. To be published J. Genet. Psychol. 1943.

The Brain-Injured Mentally Deficient Child

20. Strauss, A. A. Typology in mental deficiency. Proceed. Am. Ass. Mental Def., **44**: 85, 1939.
21. Strauss, A. A. The incidence of central nervous system involvement in higher grade moron children. Am. J. Ment. Def., **45**: 548, 1941.
22. Strauss, A. A. Neurology and mental deficiency. Am. J. Ment. Def., **46**: 192, 1941.
23. Strauss, A. A. Effects of exogenous and endogenous factors on the organism as a whole in mentally deficient children. Proceed. III. Biennial Meet. Soc. Res. Child Devel. p. 93, 1939.
24. Strauss, A. A., and Kephart, N. C. Rate of mental growth in a constant environment among higher grade moron and borderline children. Proceed. Amer. Ass. Ment. Def., **44**: 137, 1939.
25. Kephart, N. C., and Strauss, A. A. A clinical factor influencing variations in intelligence quotient. Amer. J. Orthopsychiat., **10**: 343, 1940.
26. Strauss, A. A., and Kephart, N. C. Behavior differences in mentally retarded children measured by a new behavior rating scale. Amer. J. Psychiat., **96**: 1117, 1940.
27. Werner, H., and Strauss, A. A. Types of visuo-motor activity in their relation to low and high performance ages. Proceed. Amer. Assn. Ment. Def., **44**: 163, 1939.
28. Werner, H., and Strauss, A. A. Causal factors in low performance. Amer. J. Ment. Def., **45**: 213, 1940.

29. Werner, H., and Bowers, M. Auditory-motor organization in two clinical types of mentally deficient children. J. Genet. Psychol., **59**: 85, 1941.
30. Werner, H., and Thuma, B. D. A deficiency in the perception of apparent motion in children with brain-injury. Am. J. Psychol., **55**: 58, 1942.
31. Werner, H., and Thuma, B. D. A study of critical flicker frequency in children with brain-injury. Amer. J. Psychol., **55**: 394, 1942.
32. Strauss, A. A., and Werner, H. The mental organization of the brain-injured mentally defective child (the mentally crippled child). Am. J. Psychiat., **97**: 1194, 1941.
33. Werner, H., and Strauss, A. A. Pathology of figure-background relation in the child. J. Abnorm. Soc. Psychol., **36**: 236, 1941.
34. Strauss, A. A., and Werner, H. Disorders of conceptual thinking in the brain-injured child. J. Neuro. Ment. Dis., **96**: 153, 1942.
35. Werner, H., and Strauss, A. A. Impairment in thought processes of brain-injured children. Am. J. Ment. Def., **47**: 291, 1943.
36. Strauss, A. A., and Werner, H. Comparative psychopathology of the brain-injured child and the traumatic brain-injured adult. Am. J. Psychiat., **99**: 835, 1943.
37. Strauss, A. A. Ways of thinking of brain-crippled deficient children. To be published Am. J. Psychiat., 1943.
38. Strauss, A. A., and Werner, H. Experimental analysis of the clinical symptom "Perseveration" in mentally retarded children. Am. J. Ment. Def., **47**: 185, 1942.
39. Werner, H., and Carrison, D. Animistic thinking in brain-injured mentally deficient children. To be published Am. J. Ment. Def., 1943.
40. Werner, H., and Carrison, D. Animistic thinking in brain-injured mentally deficient children. J. Abn. Soc. Psychol., **39**: 43, 1944.

Education

Reading Disability

41. Hegge, Th. G. Effects of remedial reading in supposedly feebleminded children. Studder Tillagnade Ef. Liljequist, Lund, 2: 151. 1930.
42. Hegge, Th. G. Reading cases in an institution for mentally retarded problem children. Proceed. Am. Ass. Ment. Def., 37: 149, 1932.
43. Hegge, Th. G. Special reading disability with particular reference to the mentally deficient. Proceed. Am. Ass. Ment. Def., *39:* 297, 1934.
44. Hegge, Th. G. A method for teaching mentally deficient reading cases. Proceed. Am. Ass. Ment. Def., **40**: 476, 1935.
45. Hegge, Th. G., and Ward, Lewis B. Remedial reading methods. Am. J. Orthopsychiat., **6**: 421, 1936.
46. Hegge, Th. G., Kirk, S. A., and Kirk, Winifred D. Remedial reading drills. With a manual of directions by Samuel A. Kirk, Ann Arbor, Mich. George Wahr, Publishers, 1936.
47. Hegge, Th. G. The significance of special reading disability in mentally handicapped problem children. Am. J. Psychiat., **94**: 77, 1937.
48. Hegge, Th. G. Remedial approaches to reading difficulties in the mentally handicapped. Elementary English Rev., **15**: 293, 1938.
49. Hegge, Th. G. Results of remedial reading at the middle moron level: a case study. J. Juv. Res., **19**: 128, 1935.

50. Hegge, Th. G. Kor varig er lesedugleiken hos evnefatige born med Lesevanskar? (Retention of rapidly acquired reading abilities). Norsk pedag. tidskrift, **9: 1**, 1939.

51. Kirk, S. A. The Influence of manual tracing on the learning of simple words in the case of subnormal boys. J. Ed. Psychol, **24**: 525, 1933.

52. Kirk, S. A. The effects of remedial reading on the educational program and personality adjustment of high grade mentally deficient problem children: ten case studies. J. Juv. Research, **18**: 140, 1934.

53. Kirk, S. A. A study of the relation of ocular and manual preference to mirror reading. J. Genet. Psychol., **44**: 192, 1934.

54. Kirk, S. A., and Kirk, Winifred D. The influence of the teacher's handedness on children's reversal tendencies in writing. J. Genet. Psychol., **47**: 473, 1935.

55. Sears, Richard. Measurements of associative learning in mentally defective cases of reading disability. J. Genet. Psychol., **46**: 391, 1935.

56. Sears, Richard. Characteristics and trainability of a case of special reading disability at the moron level. J. Juv. Res., **19**: 1, 1935.

57. Vaughn, Charles L., and Hubbs, L. Teaching reading vocabulary to lower grade morons. Proceed. Am. Ass. Ment. Def., **42**: 68, 1937.

58. Vaughn, Charles L. Classroom behavior problems encountered in attempting to teach illiterate defective boys how to read. J. Ed. Psychol., **32**: 393, 1941.

59. Martinson, Betty. Post training progress of mentally handicapped children given intensive remedial reading lessons. Am. J. Ment. Def., **45**: 408, 1941.

Speech Training

60. Kennedy, Lou. Studies in the speech of the feebleminded. Doctor-Diss. Univ. of Wis., 1930.

61. Muyskens, John H. Speech as emergent specificity. Am. J. Psychiat., **93**: 857, 1937.

62. Rossettie, Thomas. Speech re-education of the mentally retarded. Proceed. Am. Ass. Ment. Def., **42**: 191, 1937.

63. Meader, Mary H. Emergent specificity in the child as affected by interference with the developmental processes, with special reference to speech deviations and mental deficiency. Doctor-Diss., Univ. of Mich., Ann Arbor, 1938.

64. Heide, B. V. Systematics of classification relative to speech deviants on the basis of etiology especially introducing the syndromes of dyssynergotalia and hypotonotalia. Doctor Diss., Univ. of Mich., Ann Arbor, 1943.

Pre-Academic Training

65. Hegge, Th. G. The problem of reading deficiency in the mentally handicapped. J. Except. Childr., **4**: 121, 1938.

66. Melcher, Ruth T. A program of prolonged pre-academic training for the young mentally handicapped child. Am. J. Ment. Def., **44**: 202, 1939.

67. Melcher, Ruth T. Developmental progress in young mentally handicapped children who receive prolonged pre-academic training. Am. J. Ment. Def., **45**: 265, 1940.
68. Patterson, R. Melcher. Organization of a residence unit for preacademic training of mentally deficient children. Am. J. Ment. Def., **48**: 174, 1943.
69. Curtis, Louise E. Working toward academic readiness in mentally deficient children. Am. J. Ment. Def., **48**: 183, 1943.
70. Etz, Elizabeth. Pre-academic activities to challenge the mentally deficient child from five to eight years of mental age. Am. J. Ment. Def., **48**: 179, 1943.

Education of the Brain-Injured Child

71. Strauss, A. A. Principios de la educación del miño oligofrénico con lesión cerebral. Bull. I. Congr. Am. Enseñanza Especial, Montevideo, Uruguay, p. 74.
72. Strauss, A. A. Principles of the education of brain-injured mentally defective children. Bull. Forest Sanitarium, Des Plaines, Ill., **1**: 54, 1942.
73. Strauss, A. A. Diagnosis and education of cripple-brained, deficient child. J. Except. Child., **9**: 163, 1943.
74. Martinson, B., and Strauss, A. A. Education and treatment of an imbecile boy of the exogenous type. Am. J. Ment. Def., **45**: 274, 1940.
75. Lehtinen, L. E., and Strauss, A. A. A new approach in educational methods of brain-crippled deficient children. To be published, Am. J. Ment. Def., **48**, No. 3, 1944.

Medicine

76. Ferry, N. S. et al. Clinical results with measles, streptococcus, toxin and antitoxin. J.A.M.A., **91**: 1277, 1928.
77. Ferry, N. S., and Clark, L. T. Studies of the properties of bouillon filtrates of the gonococcus. J. Immun., **21**: 233, 1931.
78. Ferry, N. S., and Norton, J. F. Studies of the properties of bouillon filtrates of the meningococcus: Production of a soluble toxin. J. Immun., **21**: 293, 1931.
79. Ferry, N. S. Active immunization with meningococcus toxin. J.A.M.A., **104**: 983, 1935.
80. Willis, H. S. The application of the newer purified tuberculin products by the Pirquet method. Int. Med. Digest, **32**: 40, 1938.
81. Huddleson, F. Studies in Brucella infection: I. Techn. Bull., Agric. Exp. Station, Mich. St. Coll., No. 149, 1936.
82. Steele, A. H. Nocturnal enuresis. J. Mich. St. Med. Soc., **33**: 455, 1934.
83. Steele, A. H. A study of nocturnal enuresis in an institution. Proceed. Am. Ass. Ment. Def., **40**: 234, 1935.
84. Bunting, R. W., and Jay, P. Studies on Dental Caries. Child. Fund of Mich. Pub.
85. Dowling, Harvey E. An analysis of the visual findings in subnormal individuals. Proceed. Am. Ass. Ment. Def., **42**: 169, 1936.

86. Cutler, M., Little, J. W., and Strauss, A. A. The effect of benzedrine on mentally deficient children. Am. J. Ment. Def., **45**: 59, 1940.
87. Strauss, A. A., and Watson, H. Evaluation of hormone treatment. J. of Pediatrics, **23**: 421, 1943.
88. Stevenson, I., and Strauss, A. A. The effects of enriched vitamin B2 (Riboflavin) diet on a group of mentally defective children with retardation in physical growth. Am. J. Ment. Def., **48**: 153, 1943.

THE EFFECT
OF A
HIGHLY SPECIALIZED
PROGRAM
UPON THE I.Q.
IN
HIGH-GRADE
MENTALLY DEFICIENT
BOYS

Newell C. Kephart

Distinctions between exogenous and endogenous mentally deficient children, with I.Q.s between 50 and 80, proved meaningful in terms of their response to environmental change. The more favorable results with the endogenous group were explained in terms of their presumed intact nervous system and educational compensation for previous environmental deprivation.

In a previous publication[1] data have been presented which suggest that in a group of high-grade mentally deficient children (I.Q. range 50 to 80) at least two clinical types of retardation can be distinguished: An exogenous type (showing evidence of physical damage to the nervous system) and an endogenous type (showing no such damage). Groups representative of these types showed a marked difference in their response to a favorable environmental change. The endogenous group, which in the previous environment had shown a marked deceleration of mental growth, in the new environment reversed this trend and now displayed a relative acceleration in mental growth; whereas, the exogenous group continued its decelerated mental growth in spite of the favorable environmental change.

A theoretical hypothesis was presented which would account for this difference. It is considered that children of the endogenous type have an essentially intact nervous system. It is suggested that their retardation is due, in part at least, to an environment so circumscribed that the child is unable to absorb from it the skills, attitudes and knowledges necessary to the development of intelligence. In such a case the effect of a favorable change in environment would be to permit some at least of these skills, attitudes and knowledges, which were missed in the former environment, to be absorbed, and hence to produce a relative acceleration in rate of mental growth.

Strauss[2] and the writer in a paper being read in this meeting present data showing that, in the general environment presented by the Wayne County Training School, children of the endogenous type show a rise in I.Q. during residence and that the magnitude of change is, in the average, 4.0 I.Q. points in 4.4 years or (assuming a constant change) approximately one I.Q. point per year. This represents a marked reversal of the trend in I.Q. change, since the I.Q. shows a tendency toward relatively rapid drop during residence in the child's own home.

If our hypothesis regarding these children is correct, the provision of an environment, within the institution, which is specifically planned to offer additional stimulation to these children, should result in a further rise in I.Q. It is this latter question which the present study is designed to investigate.

Mental stimulation is a result of interaction between the organism and the environment. This presupposes not only that the environment presents the

The writer wishes to express appreciation to Mr. J. G. Genest and Miss Mary E. Haskell for their help with this study.

Journal of Psycho-Asthenics, 1939, 44(1): 216–221. Reprinted by permission of Mrs. Newell Kephart and the American Association on Mental Deficiency.

After leaving the Wayne County Training School, Dr. Kephart was director of the Achievement Center at Purdue University. In 1968, he became director of the Kephart Glen Haven Achievement Center in Fort Collins, Colorado, and remained in this position until his death in 1973.

proper material, but also that the organism is receptive towards the possibilities offered by these materials. A child may be in an optimum physical environment and yet through his unwillingness or unreadiness to respond to that environment not obtain stimulation therefrom. This has sometimes been referred to as "effective" stimulation and sometimes as "psychological" environment. It may possibly be thought of as a motivational factor. It appears in our cases to be influenced by the emotional and personality adjustment of the child and by adequate social presentation of stimuli.

Because of this factor of interaction in mental stimulation any attempt to provide an enriched environment must pay attention to the social situation in which the enrichment is embedded. It is this social situation upon which we depend to make the stimulation effective.

The subjects used in the present study, a group of older boys, were resident in one of the "self-determining" cottages at the Training School. These groups have been more extensively described elsewhere in the literature.[3] It had previously been found possible to mould these children into a closely knit social group wherein the individual feels himself a dynamic part of the social whole. In such a group, willingness to respond can be rather easily created when the group is directed toward some constructive activity, either through suggestion by the leader or through utilization of natural forces within the group itself. The individual is carried along by the motivation of the group and absorbs enthusiasm from the cumulative enthusiasm of those around him. Thus by motivating the group each individual becomes motivated toward the stimulation presented.

The group on which data are presented is composed of 16 boys, ranging in age at the beginning of the experiment from 15 to 18 years (mean age 16 years 6 months). Their initial I.Q.s range from 48 to 80 (mean I.Q. 66.3). Of the total cottage group 7 have been omitted from the present study: 3 who were over 20 years of age, 2 who showed definite signs of brain damage and 2 who left the group too soon after the beginning of the program to make retesting possible.

Limitations of space prohibit a detailed description of the program undertaken. In general, the aim was to stimulate constructive activity with whatever materials might be provided. Social approval was directed toward the recognition of productions, concrete or abstract, which showed ingenuity, initiative and original planning.

Concrete materials, such as wood, light gauge metal, etc., were provided from which the child was set the task of producing some recognizably rational object. Ready made plans or procedures were avoided, but the boys were required to evolve their own plans and methods. In this way the child, from a relatively amorphous material, had to construct something definite through observing and employing rational relationships between concrete materials.

The same type of approach was employed in the field of social relations through requiring the child to work out for himself a rational solution for social problems as they arose. Instead of being told by the adult what to do, the child was required to follow through alternate plans of action and discover their implications. Where help from the adult was necessary, suggestion and discussion were preferred. As far as possible the child was encouraged to solve for himself any problems which arose and to recognize a new situation as a challenge for thinking.

In informal settings abstract problems were presented for solution through the relating of absurdities, stories with illogical parts, etc. Here the child who recognized the illogical element was in the same position as one who sees the point to a joke while others do not. By more carefully concealing these illogical elements the difficulty of such problems could be increased.

The purpose of this program was not merely to provide more opportunity to work with materials. Opportunity for work with a great variety of materials is presented in the school and vocational training facilities offered by the institution. In these more formal situations, however, the child learns prescribed methods of manipulation and specific, already developed, trade processes. The emphasis must be upon the achievement of an end product through the use of specified skills and knowledges. Under such shop conditions rote memory and motor automatization alone can be sufficient for success.

The experimental program, however, places only secondary emphasis upon the finished product. The interest of the experimental program is primarily in the child's own original development of means toward the end. Free choice, both of the end and the means, stimulates ingenuity, spontaneous evaluation of methods and similar qualities. Such a change of emphasis from more external to more internal productivity represents a departure from customary methods of training.

As one method of testing the effectiveness of this program, we compared mental tests given after the beginning of this program of stimulation with earlier tests to learn what changes in I.Q. might have occurred. Since the Training School employs a routine program of retesting, no long gaps between tests occur. In these subjects the test retest interval varied from six months to two years eleven months, the average interval being one year six months. (In all cases the Stanford-Binet test was used.)

The average I.Q. of the experimental group at the beginning of the program was 66.3. The average I.Q. as measured by tests given at the end of this phase of the study was 76.4. The difference between these means is +10.1 I.Q. points. One case only showed negative change (−3). The magnitude of the positive changes ranges from 2 to 22 I.Q. points.

It is often assumed that any I.Q. change of less than five points is not significant. In the present experimental group we find that 81% show an I.Q. increase of 5 or more points, thus meeting this criterion of significance. It is also significant that 50% of this group show an I.Q. increase of 10 or more points and four cases or 25% raise the I.Q. 15 or more points.

It would accordingly appear that the experimental group has shown a significant gain in I.Q. as evidenced both by the average gain (10.1 points) and the percentage of individual cases gaining 5 or more points (81%).

There are certain questions which are raised in connection with these results: (1) Is this change associated with this program or does it occur in any event in the experimental group due to selection of cases or other uncontrolled factors in the general environment? (2) Has there occurred some change in the program and technique of the testing which might account for these changes?

To answer the first of these questions we investigated by the above method changes in I.Q. in the experimental group occurring prior to the further development of the program of this group. It should be mentioned that new boys are admitted to this self-determining cottage only through election by the group itself. This procedure naturally tends toward the addition of the least rigid and most responsive endogenous cases among the population. This method of selection, however, has not changed during the last three years. Since the method of selection remains the same, any change in achievement specific to the period studied must be due to the entrance of a new training factor also specific to this period.

Tests given in the experimental group between January 1, 1937 and August 31, 1937, are taken for comparison. Thirty-three such tests are available. Changes in I.Q. in the experimental group during this period range from −7 to +18, the mean being +2.3. During this period, further, we find that only 36% of the cases showed a gain of 5 or more points, only 9.1% showed a gain of 10 or more points, and only 6% a gain of 15 or more points. These percentages are to be compared with 81, 50 and 25, respectively, for the same group in 1938.

From this we conclude that the present results in the experimental group cannot be explained merely by selection of cases or other factors existing in the general situation; and, further, that these results are specific to the period studied and have not occurred previously without being noticed.

To answer the second question, we investigated by the same method all tests given in 1938 to subjects of similar chronological age in all other boys' groups in the institution aside from the experimental group. Twenty-six such cases are available. In this control group we find that changes in I.Q. vary from −10 to +15, the mean being +1.9. This amount of variation is similar to the mean change in the general Training School population during residence.

Of this control group 23% show a gain of 5 or more points, 11.5% a gain of 10 or more points and 3.8% a gain of 15 or more points. These figures, again, are to be compared with the percentages 81, 50 and 25, respectively, for the experimental group.

Further evidence in this direction is presented by Hoakley,[4] who investigated 1,505 test retest I.Q. comparisons among Training School children over sixteen years of age. She found that 25% of this group gained 5 or more points, 9.5% gained 10 or more points and 3.5% gained 15 or more points. These figures agree rather closely with the present findings for non-experimental groups.

From this we conclude that the present results cannot be explained by a change in the testing methods and that they are specific to the experimental group. The above figures are summarized in Table I.

A similar program, with certain modifications necessitated by differences in chronological age and institutional setting, was attempted with a group of 3 eight-year-old boys in the school situation. At the time of the present study, two of these children had experienced this program for 14 months and the third for 8 months.

On these three children test retest data are available, using four measures of mental ability: The Stanford-Binet, the Terman Merrill Binet, the Goodenough drawing of a man test and performance tests.

For these four measures the average I.Q. (or P.Q.) change in the three subjects was: Stanford-Binet, +7.3 points; Terman Merrill, +8.7 points; Goodenough, +11.0 points; Performance Test, +14.7 points. Although the number of cases is admittedly small and each of the tests used has a greater or less degree of unreliability, it is felt that the consistency of the results throughout all tests strongly suggests that there has been a positive change in the rate of mental growth and that this change is of sufficient magnitude to

Table I. Changes in I.Q. of various groups in various years

	Number	Average change	% changing +5 or more	% changing + 10 or more	% changing + 15 or more
Experimental group (1938) .	16	+10.1	81	50	25
Experimental group (1937) .	33	+ 2.27	36	9.1	6
Other groups (1938)	26	+ 1.90	23.0	11.5	3.8
Hoakley	1505		25	9.5	3.5

be significant. Paralleling this increased rate of mental growth these three children have shown an average advancement in academic achievement from the 17th percentile of the kindergarten norms to the 70th percentile of the first grade norms.

From the data presented in this study we conclude that there is strong evidence to indicate that, with high-grade moron and borderline subjects in an institutional situation, the rate of mental growth can be increased through specific programs of stimulation. This would appear to be true at both the relatively early and relatively late chronological age level.

The present discussion is to be considered as preliminary only. It is not considered that the hypothesis presented is proved. The number of cases are small and the controls are insufficient to insure complete scientific reliability. However, in view of the fact that the majority of previous studies report a declining I.Q. in retarded children, the present data seem more important than would be indicated by the figures alone. Furthermore, our results are in line with those of numerous studies regarding the effect of enriched educational programs under other conditions.

BIBLIOGRAPHY

1. Kephart, Newell C., and Strauss, Alfred A.: A Clinical Factor Influencing Variations in I. Q. Accepted for publication, Amer. J. Orthopsychiat., 1939.
2. Strauss, Alfred A., and Kephart, Newell C.: Rate of Mental Growth in a Constant Environment Among Higher Grade Moron and Borderline Children. Paper read before Amer. Assoc. Ment. Def., 1939.
3. Kephart, Newell C.: Group Autonomy in a Children's Institution: An Experiment in Self-Determined Activity. Mental Hygiene, 1938, 22: 585–590.
   Kephart, Newell C.: A Method of Heightening Social Adjustment in an Institutional Group. Amer. J. Orthopsychiat., 1938, 8, No. 4, 710–717.
4. Hoakley, Z. Pauline: The Variability of Intelligence Quotients. Proc. and Addr. Amer. Assoc. for the Study of the Feebleminded, 1932, 56.

THE
MENTAL ORGANIZATION
OF
THE BRAIN-INJURED
MENTALLY DEFECTIVE
CHILD

Alfred A. Strauss and Heinz Werner

Strauss and Werner distinguish between exogenous and endogenous forms of mental retardation. The description of the exogenous mentally retarded child was later popularized as the model for the Strauss syndrome or brain-damaged child.

The first workers in the field of mental deficiency were chiefly concerned with those abnormalities which are strongly correlated to a physical malformation. Accumulation of subsequent experience has shown that much mental deficiency is not accompanied by any apparent corporal defect. This is particularly true in that type of mental deficiency which has been variously called familial, hereditary or endogenous,[9] and especially among the moron and borderline group. However, it is often still considered that the so-called organic or exogenous type of mental deficiency, in which the amentia is due to a brain lesion, is linked with a visible defect in the motor apparatus. Numerous data contradict this assumption. The number of children belonging to the exogenous group who do not show gross motor disturbances exceeds the number who do show motor defects.

An unselected group of moron and borderline children at the Wayne County Training School has been examined.[11] The diagnosis of exogenous type of mental deficiency was based upon:

1. The developmental history of the child,
2. The absence of mental deficiency in other members of the family,
3. The neuropathological pattern demonstrated by clinical signs.

These data revealed that 20 to 25 per cent of the children examined had evidence of brain lesions, notwithstanding that only 3 to 5 per cent showed evidence of a gross neurological disturbance.

Moron and borderline children of the exogenous type would hardly impress anybody who is dealing with them superficially as being conspicuous within an unselected group of mental defectives of the same I.Q. range. A more intimate knowledge of their response to the environment and a clinical analysis of their mental behavior, however, reveal a personality that is fundamentally different from the personality of the endogenous type.

There are general indications that mentally handicapped children of the exogenous type do not respond readily to environmental stimulation. If we can take an increase in I.Q. as an indication that the child responds positively to our training efforts, a decrease would be an indication of either a deterioration or an imperfect training.

American Journal of Psychiatry, 1941, 97:1194–1203.

Dr. Strauss was research psychiatrist at the Wayne County Training School during this time. He received his training in neuropsychiatry, psychopathology, and special education at the University of Heidelberg, Germany, where he was strongly influenced by Kurt Goldstein. Dr. Strauss was also founder and president of the Cove School in Evanston, Illinois from 1947 to 1957. He died in April 1971. Dr. Werner was research psychologist at the Wayne County Training School from 1937 to 1944. Later he was professor and chairman of the Psychology Department at Clark University. Dr. Werner died in May 1964. The clinical descriptions of the brain-injured child by Dr. Strauss and Dr. Werner are still widely accepted.

In a survey[11] of the first five hundred admissions to the Wayne County Training School it was found that children of the exogenous type as a group showed a decrease of 2.54 points in I.Q. during a residence in the institution of four to five years, whereas children of the endogenous type as a group showed an increase of 4.0 points in I.Q. during a similar period of residence.

In a study of children whose mental growth could be traced through a period before and a period after admission to the institution, differences between endogenous and exogenous groups were again found. Endogenous children showed a cumulative loss in rate of mental growth during the period before admission. The same cumulative loss was characteristic of the exogenous children but in a lesser degree. After admission to the institution, the endogenous group is speeding up its mental growth; whereas in the exogenous group no such change occurs.[6] These data raise the question of what factors make the exogenous child unresponsive to stimulation.

The sensori-motor function is one aspect of the behavior of the organism which permits strict and controllable observation. It is because of this fact that early mental development is measured in terms of motor performance. We have, therefore, attempted to construct tests which permit us to analyze sensori-motor performance.*

One such sensori-motor test deals with performance on a marble board.[18] This board contains ten rows of ten holes each in which marbles can be placed. The examiner constructs a mosaic pattern which the child is requested to copy on a second board. Each move is recorded on a blank. The test consists of six patterns, one of the first showing two interlocked squares and one of the more difficult four adjacent hexagons.

The results point to a striking difference in the manner of performance between endogenous and exogenous groups. Though objectively the patterns made by children of both types may be equally correct, the analysis shows that the endogenous child uses a procedure different from that of the exogenous child. Successes and failures of the endogenous child are very similar to those of normal children of the same mental age. The endogenous child tends to proceed continuously around the outlines of the pattern. His figures, though not always perfect copies of the original patterns, are whole-forms. The exogenous child, on the other hand, constructs his pattern predominantly in an incoherent manner: he jumps from one part of the board to another; he sometimes even starts in the middle of the line. The figures he constructs are frequently disorganized patterns lacking closure, connection of parts, etc.

---

*A previous survey[9] showed that, among children whose performance age was one year or more below the corresponding mental age, more than 60 per cent were diagnosed as exogenous; whereas, among children whose performance age was three years or more above the corresponding mental age, only 5 per cent were diagnosed as exogenous.

Children's drawings of such marble patterns and constructions of three-dimensional "tinker-toy" forms showed similar characteristics.

Are these differences due to a specific visual defect? This pathological variable was controlled by the use of tasks measuring the ability to perceive abstract visual forms. In such tasks no difference in ability was found between endogenous and exogenous groups.

Is this abnormal behavior only present in the visual-motor field or are there similar disturbances in other sensory fields? An attempt has been made to analyze auditory-motor performance.[14] In this test the children were requested to sing a melodic pattern presented to them on the piano. The perfromances of our exogenous and endogenous children were compared with previous results concerning the reaction of normal children to this test.[1, 15] Here again the endogenous group made errors strikingly similar to those of normal children of the same mental age. The exogenous group made errors of a type rarely seen among normal children. Their reproduction lacked melodic-harmonic synthesis, satisfactory endings, or were unrelated to the original pattern, etc.

From these investigations involving two entirely different sensory fields, we conclude that there exists an impairment of rather general nature in the exogenous child.

Head,[2] Goldstein,[4] and other neurologists have presented evidence indicating that the brain-injured organism is much more controlled by outside forces than the normal organism. His attention will be caught and riveted much more rigidly upon those stimuli in the sensory field which are quantitatively distinguished. This may lead to a paradoxical situation; such defective individuals may disregard significant objects because of their smallness in favor of the diffuse background because of its largeness.

In a second formboard small triangular units of holes formed a definitely structured *background*. Against the strong influence of this *background* the child has to copy different *foreground* patterns from the examiner's board. Here it could be definitely observed, that the endogenous children withstood these *background* forces and constructed according to the *foreground* pattern given. Exogenous children, in contrast to this, changed the *foreground* pattern by slipping into the *background* pattern. These exogenous children were helplessly drawn into the *background,* arranging the marbles in lines suggested by its structure.†

This peculiar behavior of the exogenous child was shown still more strikingly by a tachistoscopic experiment.

---

†Detailed report and illustrations in: H. Werner and A. A. Strauss, Pathology of Figure-Background Relation in the Child. Accepted for publication in J. Abnorm. Soc. Psychol.

The test consisted of a series of pictures. These pictures were black and white line drawings of objects such as a hat, a bird, etc., which were embedded in clearly structured homogeneous backgrounds consisting of jagged and wavy lines, squares, crosses, etc. The child was asked, after a short exposure (1/5 sec.), to tell what he saw. The endogenous child predominantly saw the object, mostly without mentioning the background. The exogenous children saw mostly only the background, describing it either vaguely or definitely.

Before going on in the general discussion of our observations we may sum up the statistical results of the various tests.

The evidence gathered from these various tests points to a definite sensori-motor syndrome characterizing the brain-injured mentally defective child.

Sensori-motor activity, however, is only one aspect of mental organization. There is evidence that the brain-injured mentally defective child shows similar peculiarities in verbal intellectual functions.

These verbal intellectual functions of the exogenous children were analyzed, first, by comparing their answers given in the Stanford Binet test with answers of endogenous children of the same mental ages. Although the investigation is still not completed there are definite indications of a qualitative difference.

In many instances these exogenous children impress us by their verbosity, the fluency of speech, the peculiar use of unusual words and an affected

Differential responses of two types of mental defectives in four test situations

Test		No. of individuals	Disorganized pattern, per cent	Organized pattern, per cent
I. Marbleboard I	Exog.	25	70	11
	Endog.	22	6	85
II. Auditory-motor	Exog.	26	61	39
	Endog.	22	11	88
			Background reaction, per cent	Figure reaction, per cent
III. Marbleboard II	Exog.	23	84	. .
	Endog.	20	15	. .
IV. Tachist.	Exog.	25	76	11
	Endog.	25	14	58

style. For example, in defining "what is a balloon?" one child answered: "it goes up to the stratosphere." In response to the question as to what the child learned from the fable of the fox and the crow (in which the fox lured the crow into dropping a piece of meat which she held in her beak by flattering her voice) a child of this type (M.A. 9.5 years, I.Q. 63) answered: "the crow didn't have a sweet tone, the fox just said it to fool her."

Answers of these exogenous children too, are sometimes queer, irrelevant and dyslogical. In detecting absurdities (Stanford-Binet year X) for example, the sentence is given: "A man said—'I know a road from my house to the city which is downhill all the way to the city and downhill all the way back home.' " One exogenous child answered: "the man wasn't talking to anyone." Another answered: "Most anyone would know the road." A striking example that the selection of characteristics in the definition of objects deviates from the kind of selection made by individuals of other types of feeblemindedness may be illustrated by the answers of exogenous children to the question, "What is a balloon?" The answer "goes up in the air" or "filled with air" occurred in 27.5 per cent of the answers given by normal children, in 24.5 per cent of those given by endogenous children, but in 58 per cent of those given by exogenous children.

On the basis of these preliminary results a reasoning test has been devised including definitions, verbal absurdities, a verbal completion test, and a picture completion test. The results of this test so far yield further confirmation of the difference between the exogenous and endogenous child on the verbal intellectual plane.

Finally, there are personality characteristics of the brain-injured child. The results of recent psychiatric studies by Hohmann,[3] Kasanin,[5] Schroeder[8] and others point to a specific so-called "organic" behavior in these children. Strauss and Kephart presented last year at the annual meeting of this association a paper dealing with the behavior differences of these two groups, measured by a new behavior rating scale.[12] The scale shows the exogenous group to be erratic, uncoordinated, uncontrolled, disinhibited and socially unaccepted. The study suggests that behavior problems occurring in endogenous retarded children are completely apart from the commonly accepted picture of organic behavior.

On the basis of these observed differences—and it is highly probable that further investigations will confirm and extend our findings—it is concluded that the exogenous mentally defective children deviate in a number of important aspects of mental organization from the great mass of other types of feebleminded children.

To distinguish this organic syndrome of mental deficiency from the mine-run of feeblemindedness we suggest to characterize these exogenous children as mentally crippled. This term may also imply that these children are damaged in the mental sphere during development in a similar way as the crippled children in the physical.

What do these findings mean for the problem of educating the exogenous child? We have already demonstrated that in an institution with an educational environment most favorable for the total class of the feebleminded child the exogenous child does not respond satisfactorily. We can now interpret, at least partially, such an educational failure.

Children with a definite lack of sensori-motor organization will lag behind the other children in any work which demands the coordination of motor and sensory functions, particularly in certain vocational activities. Because of specific intellectual impairment academic achievement will be more or less impeded. Because of a particular behavior deviation difficulties in group adjustment may arise.

Have we, then, to be contented with the little educational improvement the children might gain, or to be resigned to permitting the children to deteriorate? Or can we hope to offer this defective organism educational means more adequate for overcoming his difficulty?

Nine years experience with the training of mentally crippled children has demonstrated that through the use of special methods and special material there is often a much better educational prognosis than is ordinarily supposed.[10] Time does not permit a description of the special means used in vocational and academic training or in the educational and medical treatment of the behavior disturbance.

As a demonstration of the effectiveness of such methods, we may refer to one imbecile boy, now sixteen years old, trained for the past eighteen months as a test case in the Wayne County Training School. This boy had suffered in early infancy from an inflammatory disease of the brain. In the last four years before special training was started, a gain of only eight months of mental age had been achieved. As a result of one hour of academic training daily and a specially devised general program in the group, this boy gained 14 months in mental age during the next 18 months period. This case was particularly chosen because of the unfavorable prognosis given him by the psychiatrist. Most significant is the fact that the speed of mental growth in this boy during the experimental period surpassed the average for the children in the institution.[7]

The mentally crippled child presents to the child neuropsychiatrist a problem analogous to that of the brain-injured adult. Research furthering the knowledge of the mentally crippled child is greatly needed for the improvement of our diagnostic methods, our understanding of the relation between the brain-injured adult and the mentally crippled child, and especially for the devising of necessary and adequate training methods.

BIBLIOGRAPHY

1. Brehmer, Fritz: Die melodische Begabung des Kindes. Zschr. angew. Psychol., 1925, Suppl. 36.
2. Head, Henry: Studies in neurology. London, 1920.
3. Hohmann, L. B.: Postencephalitic behavior disorders in children. Johns Hopkins Hospital Bull., 33: 372, 1922.
4. Goldstein, Kurt: The organism. American Book Company, New York, 1939.
5. Kasanin, J.: Personality changes in children following cerebral trauma. J. Nerv. Ment. Dis., 69: 385, 1929.
6. Kephart, N. C., and Strauss, A. A.: A clinical factor influencing variations in I.Q. Am. J. Orthopsych., 10: 343, 1940.
7. Martinson, B., and Strauss, A. A.: The education and treatment of an imbecile boy of the exogenous type. To be published. Am. J. Mental Deficiency, 1940.
8. Schroeder, P. L.: Behavior difficulties in children associated with the results of birth trauma. J. Amer. Med. Assoc., 92: 110, 1929.
9. Strauss, A. A.: Typology in mental deficiency. Proc. Amer. Ass'n Mental Def., 44: 85, 1939.
10. Strauss, A. A.: Pedagogia terepéutica. Barcelona, 1936.
11. Strauss, A. A., and Kephart, N. C.: Rate of mental growth in a constant environment among higher grade moron and borderline children. Proc. Amer. Assoc. Mental Def., 44: 137, 1939.
12. Strauss, A. A., and Kephart, N. C.: Behavior differences in mentally retarded children measured by a new behavior rating scale. Am. J. Psychiat., 96: 1117, 1940.
13. Werner, H., and Strauss, A. A.: Types of visuo-motor activity in their relation to low and high performance ages. Proc. Am. Assoc Mental Def., 44: 163, 1939.
14. Werner, H.: Auditory-motor organization in two clinical types of mentally deficient children. To be published. J. Genet. Psychol., 1940.
15. Werner, H: Comparative developmental psychology. Harper and Brothers, New York, 1940.

DISCUSSION

DR. LAUREN H. SMITH (Philadelphia): It would seem that the exogenous type, in reception and response to training, is somewhat blocked, that the experiences of life are not received well in comparison with the endogenous type. This is similar to our experience with the post-encephalitic children.

I would like to ask a question pertaining to the experience of the authors in the training programs. Is it not true that through separation of endogenous from exogenous cases better results for the former would be accomplished?

DR. LOUIS H. GOLD (Hartford, Conn.): I should like to ask if the tests that

Dr. Strauss devised showed any correlation with any of the tests of Goldstein and Gelb.

DR. SAMUEL BECK (Chicago, Ill.):   An interesting question may be raised with reference to the Rorschach test and its possibilities of differentiating in these two groups of feebleminded children.

DR. LEO KANNER (Baltimore, Md.):   It has been refreshing to note in recent years the efforts made in various centers to get away from too generalized a consideration of feebleminded persons. Psychometric tests have made possible a quantitative gradation of intellectual inadequacy. But the idiots, imbeciles and morons were still dealt with in the main as if they were homogeneous groups with identical or very similar group characteristics. Feeblemindedness was, and often still is, spoken of in a fashion reminiscent of the undifferentiated use of the terms lunacy and insanity in the olden days.

In the last two decades, quantitative evaluation has been extended to the degree of social maturation of feebleminded children. Psychologists and sociologists alike have begun to pay attention to factors expressed in terms of communal adjustment values, stability, type of occupational usefulness intramurally or in free circulation. Psychiatrists have begun to interest themselves in studies of individual performances as well as smaller or larger groups presenting distinguishable features.

The paper by Drs. Strauss and Werner is a further valuable contribution in the direction of breaking down the erroneous conception of the feebleminded of any I.Q. range as a homogeneous mass to be dealt with in generalities. One may perhaps at first thought wonder about the three criteria upon which the diagnosis of exogenous type of mental deficiency has been based. On the other hand, the sensori-motor and verbal intellectual differences obtained by the authors and the personality differences described by others are so marked that a selection on the grounds of those criteria is justified by the results of the reported investigations. I believe that this study is definitely a solid first step towards the separation of a group of retarded children who, be they referred to as mentally crippled or by any other name, deserve specialized attention from a highly practical point of view. Those who, as this discussant, are conversant with the caution and great reliability of the work of Drs. Strauss and Werner, will be gratified to have offered to them a workable series of differentiating tests. Beyond this, there certainly is a crying need for greater individualization in the study of the feebleminded, and the paper under discussion goes a long way towards supplying this need.

It would be helpful to know what the authors consider as "evidence of brain lesions" in 20–25 per cent of the children examined. It would also be of interest to know whether electroencephalographic investigations have been carried out and, if so, whether the group of mentally crippled children shows any departure from the rest of the retarded children considered in the study.

DR. ALFRED A. STRAUSS (Northville, Mich.):   We are very grateful for the comments the discussors gave to our paper.

We did not use the electroencephalographic method as the necessary equipment was not available, but I believe that electroencephalographic studies would be very useful. The percentage of organic or exogenous cases goes from 15 per cent in the borderline to 40 per cent in idiots.

As far as the psychological diagnosis is concerned, we have not made the Rorschach tests. Eight or nine years ago we tried to use the Rorschach test. At that time we did not succeed. I think the Rorschach has developed so far now that we should try again to use it.

There was a question about the Goldstein psychological test. In the course of our experience with it we were led to develop, for these exogenous children, tests with which we hoped to reach further than the Goldstein tests.

We are convinced that, in the work of training, isolation of the exogenous children is necessary.

A
NEW APPROACH
IN
EDUCATIONAL METHODS
FOR
BRAIN-CRIPPLED
DEFICIENT
CHILDREN

Laura E. Lehtinen and Alfred A. Strauss

This paper is one of the earliest describing specific educational methods to deal with the cognitive and perceptual deficits of the brain-damaged child.

Recent research has contributed much to change the concept of mental deficiency (Kanner).[3] With the exception of very specific clinical types such as mongolism, cretinism, etc., the term "mental deficiency" formerly signified a homogenous group of individuals characterized by mental retardation measured in terms of I.Q. Tredgold's classification into primary and secondary amentia is an outstanding example of this earlier concept. Within the group of secondary amentia brain-injury was mentioned as an external factor; it was assumed, however, that this type of mental deficiency appeared commonly with defects of the neuro-motor system (Doll,[1] Tredgold[8]). Strauss[4] called attention to the brain-injured mental defective without gross motor disturbances. Strauss and Werner have presented before this Association a number of papers demonstrating that this exogenous type of mental deficiency differs in fundamental aspects—behavior, perception, concept formation—from the endogenous type of feeble-mindedness.[7, 9, 10, 11]

For many years Strauss[5] has emphasized that this particular mental organization of the brain-injured mentally defective child (the brain-crippled deficient child) must be taken into consideration if efficient educational methods for these children are to be developed. He has demonstrated that his methods have proved successful in individual cases.

In January, 1941 the Wayne County Training School opened an experimental class where these methods for brain-crippled children are applied in a group setting. The present paper will describe the setting and some of the material and methods used in academic training.

Strauss and Kephart[6] presented data before this association in 1938 demonstrating that the exogenous children exposed to a training program designed for the endogenous children do not respond to educational stimulation. If we assume that the lowering of the I.Q. as opposed to a rise in I.Q., indicates a lack of response to training, the investigation showed that the endogenous children as a group tend to increase in I.Q. during their residence in the Training School whereas the exogenous children tend to decrease in I.Q.

Why does the brain-crippled child not respond to the classical special education program? Through every phase of the education of the mentally deficient child, emphasis by educators is placed upon the normal rather than the pathological aspects of his mental organization. Abilities and capacities of

American Journal of Mental Deficiency, 1944, 48(3): 283–287. Reprinted by permission of Dr. Laura Lehtinen Rogan and the American Association on Mental Deficiency.

Dr. Rogan was teaching fellow at the Wayne County Training School from 1944 to 1946. She later received her doctorate in psychology from Northwestern University. In 1947, she became clinical director of the Cove School in Evanston, Illinois, a position which she still holds.

mentally deficient children are conceived of with reference to the position these children occupy (in terms of I.Q.) on a continuous curve of intelligence or capacity to learn. From this follows naturally the generalization that the mentally deficient child learns in the same manner as the normal child of the same mental age, only more slowly; that he learns the same amount and the same kind of subject matter as a normal child of the same age, only more slowly. In accordance, therefore, with the generally acknowledged similarities between the mentally deficient child and the normal child, the psychological and pedagogical principles underlying their education are the same. Hollingworth writes that "feebleminded children differ from ordinary children only in amount of ability not in the kind of abilities which they possess. No mysterious or unique matter or method is necessarily required in the task of training them. They can learn the same things that other children learn up to the limits of their capacity."[2]

If we consider the fundamental differences in the mental make-up of the endogenous and the exogenous child, a difference for which we have ample material of clinical observations and psychological experiments, we need not wonder why the exogenous child does not profit from the routine educational stimulation. Who would think of training a physically crippled child in his defects—may he be spastic or athetotic or ataxic—by offering him dancing lessons or gymnastics intended for the training of the normal child?

The deficiencies of the exogenous child, the brain-crippled deficient child, are manifold. There are general disturbances, like hyperactivity, distractibility, hypervigilance, forced responsiveness to stimuli, pathological perseveration, and many specific defects in reading, arithmetic, writing and speech. With reference to education three conclusions have to be drawn.

1. The brain-crippled deficient child does not profit from methods derived from the concept that the mentally retarded child is a slow-learning child with normal abilities in lessened degree.

2. The brain-crippled deficient child, in addition to materials for the acquisition of special skills, needs training which takes into account his general disturbance.

3. The brain-crippled deficient child should be trained in the acquisition of special skills on the basis of his pathological mental organization which is the result partly of general disturbances and partly of specific deficiencies.

To develop such a program the Training School has established an experimental unit which consists of three rooms, one designed for academic teaching and the two others for manual training.

The academic room is a large sized room where twelve children can be comfortably placed, each one seated at a large table by himself. There are no decorations on the wall and the lower halves of the windows are painted translucent. Having eliminated external stimulation as far as possible, the child has less opportunity to become distracted. At the beginning of the school year a plan of instructions is worked out for each child after an observation period of at least four weeks. The results of previous achievement tests are considered but the results of the observations in the teaching situation give a more accurate picture of the method to be followed and the material to be constructed for each child. The material is constructed as self-tutoring and is changed frequently if interest and motivation decrease. Change is also necessary as long as the child because of his general deficiencies in perception and comprehension is prone to become distracted or to perseverate. Much varied and different material must be available so that distractibility may be overcome and perseveration broken when either occurs. The more knowledge the child acquires, the less apparent become the general disturbances.

There is no group work as it is known in the average school—no class recitations or drills. The child recites individually to the teacher. It therefore happens that each child may have a different lesson from every other child in the class or he may employ a method which is tailor-made for him. The range in one class may be from the pre-primer level to the fifth grade in certain subjects. The academic training consists of instruction in the tool subjects—reading, arithmetic, writing, and spelling. Enrichment of the child's program is obtained by supplementary work after he has completed the basic training requirements. The child usually stays in the experimental group until he has reached an even achievement level of the third grade. He is then transferred to the general school in the institution.

One viewpoint stressed is that commercially prepared material as far as possible is avoided; the child prepares his own material from material familiar to him in his daily living. For example, he may build simple sentences from familiar words cut from magazines, he may cut out a picture and compose a story about it, or he may illustrate his own work with pictures or numbers found in magazines or newspapers.

In turning now briefly to a discussion of the methods used let us recall that this new approach for the education of brain-crippled children is intended to develop first: methods and material for the improvement of general disturbances, second: methods and material for the remedial training of specific defects, and third: material primarily self-tutoring in its use.

The following is given as an example of material used in overcoming a general disturbance like distractibility. Robert is a brain-crippled deficient child, eleven years of age, I.Q. 64. During the years he has been in school he has acquired certain rudiments of knowledge and academic skills. His number concept is elementary, but he can, with considerable skill, arrive at the answers to simple problems in addition by counting silently to himself. Addition problems orally given and orally answered present no difficulty. When Robert was given a lesson in which the answers must be written below problems printed on a page, he failed—not in his ability to arrive at the answer, or in his ability to form the written number, but in his ability to put the answer on the page in the place provided for it. One could find the answer at the bottom of the page, in the margin or under a different problem. The difficulty confronting the teacher was how Robert could learn to write the answer where it belonged. Discussion with his former teacher revealed that in spite of many attempts she had never been able to get him to answer written arithmetic problems in an understandable way. To tell him where his answer should be placed was of no use. He was given then a device which consisted of two cardboards 8' × 10' between which the arithmetic page was placed. In the upper cardboard was a small opening which exposed one printed line at a time. Over the opening in the cardboard was a slide with a window, permitting one problem after another to be exposed. By moving the slide from one side to the other and the page inside from the top to the bottom all the problems could be seen alone one after another. Robert worked his next arithmetic lesson using this device and produced naturally a perfect paper with the answers all in their proper places. On the following day he was given a page of similar examples to be worked without the aid of the device. On this day his paper was as correct as it had been on the previous day with the aid of the device. From then on there was no regression to the earlier behavior. A similar device is used when there is distractibility in reading.

Space does not permit further explanation of many more of these devices or those for overcoming perseveration. A description of the training methods used in overcoming perseveration may be found in a paper discussed last year by Strauss and Werner.[7]

The material in general is very concrete and distinctive for the step which it illustrates. Color cues are widely used. One example of their use is in writing. Although writing paper in which the relative heights of the letters are provided for with lines of varying width is used, this is sometimes not enough for a child with a severe handicap in the perception of spatial relationship. He may need to have the lines marked with a colored crayon as a cue to force attention to the differences of space. Having learned to discriminate in this way, the color cue is then removed but the lines are still drawn heavily in black ink. Finally this cue is taken away and the child uses the paper as it is.

As an example of specific deficiency we present the following case. Gerald is a thirteen year old boy with an I.Q. of 45. He could count orally to 10, could match a group of blocks with other blocks, but was unable to recognize the written number. That is, he suffered from a number blindness. We observed that he confused the numbers because of some similarities inherent in parts of the written numbers. For example, the upper part of the number two—the half circle—is similar to the upper part of the number three;

the lower part of the number three is similar to the lower part of the number five, the vertical line in the number four is similar to the number one and so on. The boy was given small cards on which the similar parts of the numbers which brought about his confusion were drawn in varying colors. After he had studied these cards and copied them, he was able to recognize the numbers if drawn in black; he learned to copy them and to make them correctly himself. He could then advance to solving written number work. The learning of arithmetic in this case was halted, not by a deficient memory, or lack of number understanding, but by a disturbance of form perception in written numbers.

DISCUSSION

We have attempted to acquaint you with a new method for the academic training of the brain-crippled deficient child. For many years these methods have proved successful in individual cases; their application to larger groups is now in process. Space does not permit presentation of more than a few illustrative features. We may, therefore, add a remark concerning the methodology. To one not familiar with it, the method may appear to consist of a series of devices, *i.e.,* material-aids or crutches. Although it is true that mechanical aids are widely employed, especially in the retraining of general disturbances and on the lower achievement levels, these aids form a plan of successive steps which are followed until the brain-crippled child reaches a level where he is able to profit from the routine educational procedure. The devices are so constructed that they either illustrate an analytical principle or express a step in the process by some visuo-motor activity. Insofar as it is applicable, the method for normal children is the basis of the program. It is analyzed and supplemented and reshaped to meet the educational demands of the brain-crippled child and his particular mental organization. If it is possible to develop methods for the retraining of conceptual disturbances, as we hope in the future, then brain-crippled children beyond the beginning school grades will find a more adequate academic program.

REFERENCES

1. Doll, E. A., Phelps, W. M., Melcher, R. T. Mental Deficiency Due to Birth Injuries. New York: Macmillan, 1932.
2. Hollingworth, L. A. The Psychology of Subnormal Children. New York: Macmillan, 1920.

3. Kanner, L. Child Psychiatry. Mental Deficiency. (Review of Psychiatric Progress, 1941.) *Am. J. Psychiat.*, 98:595, 1942.

4. Strauss, A. A. Typology in Mental Deficiency. Proc. Am. Ass. Ment. Def., 44:85, 1939.

5. Strauss, A. A. Pedagogia Terapeutica. Barcelona, pub. Editorial Labor, 1936.

6. Strauss, A. A., and Kephart, N. C. Rate of Mental Growth in a Constant Environment among Higher Grade Moron and Borderline Children. Proc. Am. Ass. Ment. Def., 44:137, 1939.

7. Strauss, A. A., and Werner, H. Experimental Analysis of the Clinical Symptom "Perseveration" in Mentally Retarded Children. *Am. J. Ment. Def.*, 47:185, 1942.

8. Tredgold, A. F. A Textbook of Mental Deficiency. 6th ed. Baltimore: W. Wood Co., 1937.

9. Werner, H., and Strauss, A. A. Types of Visuo-Motor Activity in Their Relation to Low and High Performance Ages. Proc. Am. Ass. Ment. Def., 44:163, 1939.

10. Werner, H., and Strauss, A. A. Causal Factors in Low Performance. *Am. J. Ment. Def.*, 45:213, 1940.

11. Werner, H., and Strauss, A. A. Impairment in Thought Processes of Brain-Injured Children. *Am. J. Ment. Def.*, 47:291, 1943.

SECTION SEVEN

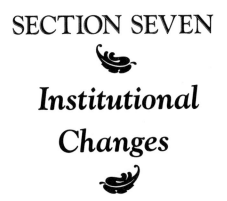

Institutional Changes

By the turn of the century, asylum and custodial departments were an integral part of many institutions, and the period of pessimism had taken firm hold. Martin Barr set the tone for the next few decades in his 1902 address to the American Association on Mental Deficiency. Public school programs for backward children had been initiated, but the public schools made it clear that they did not want "untrainables." Neither did the institutions, who saw these children as further drains upon staff time and energies, and as largely noncontributory to the maintenance of the institution. Barr called for separate asylums for idiots which could be run on a more economical basis than could be accomplished within the institution. He also suggested the use of the farm colony, a concept which was pioneered by Fernald in Massachusetts, where workers trained at the institution could maintain themselves productively and relieve the overcrowding of the institution. Barr's "imperative call" also renewed the plea for rigid segregation of the sexes and asexualization, procedures he saw as necessary to maintain the role of the institution as a protector of society.

According to a report in October 1918, by the New York Committee on Feeble-Mindedness, the first extra-institutional colony was developed by the Indiana School for Feeble-Minded Youth in 1893, on land which was later purchased by the state for use as a farm. However, as early as 1881, land was purchased by the Massachusetts School for this purpose, partly in the town of Medfield and partly in the town of Dover. Fifteen boys stayed at "Howe Farm at Medfield" in 1883, but the farm was sold in 1889.

Despite these early beginnings, credit for the first farm colony is generally given to Fernald, who established Templeton Colony in 1900. Occupied by 47 boys, the farm was three miles long and a mile wide. The Trustees' Report for 1903 stated: "A few years since, finding that there were no suitable places to which many of our boys graduating from the school department could be sent, we founded our colony at Templeton for big boys and men, a repetition on an extensive scale of our former experiment at the Howe farm." The

Superintendent's Report in 1912 stated: "The farm colony at Templeton continues to demonstrate the desirability and feasibility of housing able-bodied male imbeciles in simple, low-cost dwellings, and of providing health-ful, profitable utilization of their labor in the clearing of wild land and the raising of crops." An early farm colony was also established at Vineland (Menantico) in 1913. Colonies for the insane at Gheel, Belgium, and for epileptics in Germany, were also functioning at this time.

The intent of Fernald and others in establishing the farm colonies may have included the best humanitarian concerns for the happiness and welfare of the students selected for these programs. However, it is difficult to contradict the accusations of recent critics of the farm system (see Wolfensberger, 1969, pp. 119—121) that the need to maintain economical productive farms became paramount, with minimal expenditure provided even for necessities such as heating and medical care.

Maintenance and control of large numbers of retarded persons seem to have been the prime concerns of the superintendents during the first half of this century. Johnstone's (1903) paper concerning discipline expressed a humanitarian, progressive approach based upon incentives rather than corporal punishment. The discussion which followed his paper, however, clearly reflects the feeling of other superintendents that corporal punishment is necessary and effective for children judged responsible.

The use of the parole system gained acceptance during the 1920's. However, it is clear from Potter's (1926) paper that parole of the mentally retarded individual to the community was a serious concern which implied a great deal of supervision and continuing control.

"It is seldom that we find a patient's home in which there is a suitable environment for him and in which he will receive the necessary supervision. . . . (The) comparatively small number of paroles reflects the conservatism of the institutional administration in regard to the parole problem and is also explained by the fact that the parole material has been limited by the small inmate population of the past several years" (pp. 166—168).

This conservative attitude was clearly the official position of the American Association on Mental Deficiency. The 1939 issue of the official publication of the Association includes among its stated objectives: "The construction of institutions for the feebleminded; a complete census and registration of all mentally deficient children of school age; the segregation of mentally deficient persons in institutional care and training with a permanent segregation of those who cannot make satisfactory social adjustments in the community; parole for all suitable institutionally trained mentally defective persons; extra-institutional supervision of all defectives in the community."

THE
IMPERATIVE CALL
OF
OUR PRESENT
TO OUR FUTURE

Martin W. Barr

This paper sets the tone for the pessimism of the early part of this century. It calls for honest recognition and expression of the need for lifelong maintenance of the "imbecile" in order to safeguard society from a "pernicious element." Furthermore, it urges exclusion of "untrainables" from the training school, where they are a burden to staff, and the establishment of "separate asylums for idiots which could be run on a much more economical basis."

In this year of 1902 we pass the new century threshold of our work, and looking backward through the maze of time since first Itard led his "Victor" before the world of science, we mark in each decade a continuous advance in all lands; an advance in which America has been by no means a laggard.

Without pausing to review historical detail, in itself a most interesting chapter, it behooves us here in conference to consider what are the urgent demands which the experience of the past coupled with the needs of the present, makes of our future.

While not forgetting that we owe the position of to-day to the struggle of both nations and individuals separated and detached from one another in the past century, let us not fail to accept "Togetherness" as the watchword of the coming century. Indeed, did not the very creation of this association embody such a thought? And surely we have grown in twenty-six years to such maturity as to warrant the propriety of calling to our confreres to come and help us. Numerous communications received from these lead me to consider more and more how in the multitude of counsellors there may be wisdom, and to arrive at the conviction that could we here unite in, and give out to the world, an authoritative statement and opinion as to the paramount needs of our work, we might evoke a similar expression from other countries, and thus materially accelerate a second advance along new lines.

As one by one our institutions become patriarchal, having received successive generations of defectives, we find growing upon the pages of their reports a clearly implied interrogation: "We have trained, for—what?"

Without formal expression emanating from our association as a body there is yet, I believe, a consensus that abandons the hope long cherished of a return of the imbecile to the world.

Now if this conviction arrived at through long experience and much disappointment involves principles affecting the progress of our work and the welfare of children and of society, ought we to be backward in declaring it? And in failing to do so do we not rather underestimate the value of our association to science and to the world at large? If we do not speak authoritatively upon the subject, who shall? And how, then, are legislators and others to be enlightened as to the futility of hopes which the very progress of our work has tended to foster? Indeed, I think we need to write it very large, in characters that he who runs may read, to convince the world that by permanent separation only is the imbecile to be safe-guarded from certain deterioration and society from depredation, contamination and increase of a pernicious element.

Journal of Psycho-Asthenics, 1902, 7 (1): 5–8.

Dr. Barr was Chief Physician of The Pennsylvania Training School from 1893 until 1930. He wrote the first American textbook on mental retardation in 1904.

That men are ready to hear, ready to heed, is evidenced by the repeated calls upon all of us for information and for expert opinion, but the opinion of one man certainly goes farther when sustained and endorsed by his colleagues.

To affirm this, therefore, as a fact touching most intimately the welfare of society, the defective, and our relations toward each, I claim to be our first care and obligation, nor should we neglect any opportunity to urge this result of our experience upon the notice of any and every properly constituted authority.

The establishment by the public school system of special classes for backward children is yet another proof that the time is ripe for concerted action.

Our work—a silent object lesson—has taught the necessity of special methods tested and proven a success, and the educational world is in this simply following our indications.

Already from these classes comes a sifting out, which sends to us a class needing prolonged training, firmer control and regular occupation under insistent supervision; at the same time the pressure for the admission of untrainables is increasing rather than diminishing.

Here is our second call to stand and declare. A training school should not be called upon any longer to accept untrainables.

Our methods, advancing from those adapted only to the improvement and self-help of the idiot, have established industries which provide not only the needed occupation for this new class coming to us, but which may, if properly protected, aid largely in maintenance. But this protection to be effectual should include two vital points: a release from the burden of untrainables, whose care heretofore an object now absorbs much valuable time of both employes and trained pupils, which might bring in a better return, while separate asylums for idiots could be run on a much more economical basis. This on one hand—on the other hand, the industries themselves demand the protection of a certain form of apprenticeship preventing the withdrawal of one set of trained workers until at least another set be ready to carry them forward. Not only for the industry, but for the child is this protection essential. When we consider how large a proportion of children in the primary schools drop out for work before reaching the grammar school, we can readily understand how parents and guardians fail to realize that the period required for the training of an abnormal is four times that for a normal child; and this ignorance, joined to the pressing necessity of contributing to the support of the family, often withdraws a child who has just entered upon what can prove his life work only after years of persistent compelling force, without which disappointment to the home, to the child and to the work is inevitable.

Various charitable associations are likewise eager to exchange and refill their quota from the many crowding their lists, so that hardly is an industry well started before it suffers from loss of operatives.

As this is an experience common to all, it surely requires consultation, co-operation and united action in formulating and outlining some plan for the common good.

Might not a long apprenticeship coupled with increased privileges upon attaining a certain standard tend to adjust naturally the question of permanent sequestration?

Once settled and interested in his work with a little more freedom than the children of the school, the imbecile is satisfied and contented—a certain self-hood is attained and the institution becomes his home; indeed, we have had many pathetic appeals for return from those withdrawn. Without this there is an ever-ruling spirit of discontent—or may we not better recognize it as a natural longing for the beyond—different from the *wander lust* in our run-aways? which reveals itself in our trained boys and girls who seek to leave us in a legitimate way to make their own way in the world.

I presume in this all have the same discouraging experience. The few succeed where carefully placed under the regular surveillance and rule to which they have been accustomed. A young fellow in military service, a young girl as nurse in the hospital are with us notable exceptions in a long list of more than failures, where vice, crime, and marriage or illicit connections fast swell the census roll of abnormality. Still to all of us who are in touch with young life the gratification of this normal yearning becomes a serious and ever present problem:—a problem that is sure to become more perplexing in the future should the supply of trained workers begin to exceed the demands of the institution.

The separation of the sexes is another problem which experience is slowly defining. At Elwyn teachers are a unit in declaring there is nothing gained in co-education, even in convenience, while nerve strain in disciplining is greatly increased, and a re-arrangement of classes according to sex rather than grade is already deemed advisable.

From the fact that such separation has become a necessity in school, custodial and cottage systems, superseded only by eternal vigilance in those industrial departments where the sexes are brought together, and statistics showing a steady increase of defective element, there has come to be a growing conviction in many minds that "diseases desperate grown by desperate appliances are relieved or not at all," and that the whole matter might be simplified and the nervous atmosphere relieved by early invoking the aid of surgical interference to secure at once safety to society, less tension to community life, and greater liberty, therefore greater happiness, to the individual. This has taken distinct form in an effort on the part of several members of my own Board (whom I accompanied to Harrisburg last winter) to seek legislative authorization for the asexualization upon admission to institutions of those adjudged mentally and morally defective. The bill, which passed both houses, was finally lost through the timidity of the Governor. We feel, however, that the step is a gain in that the attention of legislators has been called to the need of some measures to check the alarming increase of imbecility, and later the need may become more strongly evidenced in the development and evolution of the colony system, the foundation of which has been the culminating work of our nineteenth century history.

This the natural outcome of the work must form the only natural relief from the overcrowded conditions; and, in satisfying the craving for change of environment, it would offer greater variety and stimulus in maintaining the standard attained during the period of training.

In this Massachusetts holds her own, Waltham celebrating most fittingly its half century by entering upon a new endeavor in establishing a colony for her trained children. While this is an example challenging our emulation, again recurs the suggestion that united effort for a common end might accomplish more. The States may not be ready to respond to calls for many colonies, nor the institutions yet ready to supply them, but the national government might heed a proposition from us for one which would serve as an outlet for all.

An ideal spot might be found—either on one of the newly acquired islands, the unoccupied lands of the Atlantic seaboard, or the far West which, under proper regulations, could be made a true haven of irresponsibility, and deriving its population as it would from the trained workers from the institutions throughout the country, might become in time almost if not entirely self-sustaining.

The new century finds us then at a parting of ways where new fields open before us. Cutting loose from early traditions, we need to build upon the experience which has demonstrated the impossibility of training for the idiot by claiming from society immunity from that burden, while untrammeled we employ our energies to getting best results in building up a self-sustaining factor out of the improvable imbecile, and address ourselves to the task of weeding the garden of humanity from the tares which a highly nervous age has sown broadcast. Not only weeding out, but garnering so safely that no untoward accident or chance may scatter seed that can produce only imperfection and ill.

Some definition of our position and of our obligations as guardians for defectives and defenders of society which they threaten, would, it seems to me, come with singular appropriateness just at this juncture. Forming an authoritative basis for private judgment and expert opinion as also solid grounds for appeals for legislative aid, it would discharge at once our obligation to the past and also the future, in preparing the way for those who shall enter into our labors for continuous advance on new lines.

DISCIPLINE

Edward R. Johnstone

Johnstone tries to deal with the question of "How do you punish your children?"

When we remember the number of things parents fear when they bring children to our institutions the wonder is that so many are brought. Only the strong pressure of circumstances, the inability to care for them in the home, etc., forces many reluctantly to the point of bringing the child. The fear is great that this little child who has probably had the greater share of the mother's tenderest love and for whom every member of the family has sacrificed will now be among a lot of young ruffians who will abuse him and otherwise mistreat him, or that he will be placed with a lot of children of much lower grade. Almost without exception parents are sure that their child is brighter than any they see in its group. But the thing that is most feared is the methods of discipline that will be used. It is surprising how many intelligent people there are who associate tortures, dungeons and brutal restraints and punishments with the word institution, even at this late day, and the sensational press tends to foster this idea. "How do you punish your children?" is one of the first questions not only by the parent but by the visitor. Even on the application blanks in reply to the question,—What methods of discipline have been used? the few who say "whipping" are sure to add, "with poor results" or "it always makes him worse," so great is the fear of bodily harm to the child.

Even we, who see so much of it, can hardly appreciate how solicitous the parents of these stricken children are regarding this question of discipline, but the loving devotion which has kept the child at home altho the burden is almost impossible to bear, excites our deepest sympathy and because our discipline is founded on the most humane principles we welcome the question, knowing that a thorough explanation of our methods will relieve many anxious hearts.

The State of New Jersey in framing the new School Law this year has inserted a clause prohibiting corporal punishment and extending the powers of the law so as to include also all State and Private educational and charitable institutions. While I believe that there are certain rare cases when such punishment administered coolly and without anger is as efficacious as a dose of medicine given by the physician for certain forms of disease, still I think the law good, for in most institutions the power of corporal punishment is restricted to the Superintendent; in his absence he must delegate it to some assistant upon whose judgment, perhaps, he cannot always rely as upon his own. In institutions for the feeble-minded there are but few vicious children. It has been said with much wisdom, "If we knew all we would forgive all."

Journal of Psycho-Asthenics, 1920, 7 (2): 38–46.
Dr. Johnstone was principal and director of the Vineland Training School from 1901 to 1943. He was responsible for the creation of the research department at Vineland and appointed Goddard as its first research director.

In considering the question it is well for us to glance for a moment at the way our employes view the matter of punishment.

A). Some are not beyond the ancient idea that punishment is for revenge, getting even. The person injured is to be satisfied without regard to the one who has done the wrong. He must be paid back in full.

B). A second class of employes hold the idea that a child is to be punished so that he shall not repeat the offence and that others will also be driven to good behavior by fear of like punishment if they do wrong. Many of our present laws are based on this idea. "We shall make this a lesson to him and to others," they say. I am reminded of Mark Twain's story of the boy who climbed on a high roof and fell and so injured himself that he was a helpless cripple the balance of his life, and people said, "That will be a lesson to him." The deterrent effect on others might be some good but the value to the individual is nil and after all it is the wrong-doer himself whom we must reach. In the minds of this second class then the one who does the wrong and the person wronged are secondary to the desire to protect others. The doctrine of eternal punishment is based upon this idea, also the idea of capital punishment.

C). There is still another class of our employes, however, who realize that wrong doing is the result of disease or ignorance. The wrong doer himself is the one to be primarily considered and he is to be trained or cured. Herbert Spencer says that, "Punishment can be justified only in so far as it is educative, and to be educative it must never be arbitrary, but must be a natural reaction growing out of the wrong that has been committed." The indeterminate sentence laws which with the growing intelligence of the world are becoming more common, are based upon this idea that disease or ignorance are the causes of violation of law. The chief aim in all discipline should be to correct harm. Unfortunately this is too often not considered at all.

So much for the employe, let us look for a moment at the child's attitude toward punishments. Most of our children assume the same attitude as the first class of employes mentioned. "He hit me. I want to hit him back." "An eye for an eye." In nearly every case the aggrieved one must be satisfied not by having the wrong righted but by causing a like wrong to the guilty party. Studies upon a large number of children, conducted by Earl Barnes and Estella Darrah, give the following conclusion. "Young children under twelve ignore law, therefore rules should not exist in the discipline of the school. Each infraction of the law of right and each act of disobedience should be treated on its individual merits."*

---

*Studies in Education, Earl Barnes, Stanford University, 1897.

Our discipline must be based upon the law of loving kindness. Perhaps the most effective way to keep good discipline is to provide occupation. A busy child interested in his work needs no punishment.

The institution life should be full of special privileges. If this idea can be firmly grasped by the employes to the extent that everything that a child is ever called upon to do is a privilege, means of discipline are always at hand. It is only a matter of depriving the child of one of these privileges. The child who doesn't make a bed nicely is not permitted to make another. Tommy gets that privilege now and if Willie "doesn't care" he is not permitted to make any to-morrow, but sits idle while the other boys do his work. It is this idleness that hurts. I have yet to find the child who has sense enough to make a bed who doesn't want to do it, if he finds all of the others doing it and he is constantly reminded that he cannot do it. Nothing so rouses the desire to do as to be told that we cannot do. With new attendants it is often hard to make them appreciate this fact but it simply becomes a question of who will hold out the longest, the child or the employe, and I have never yet known it to fail when the attendant persists. As this idea gradually worked out I often thought I had reached its limitations, but it still expands. It is no longer a mere theory, but the most practical method of discipline I have found.

The merry-go-round, the trip to the Zoo, the ride in the donkey wagon, entertainments, parties, club meetings, skating, etc. all form excellent means of discipline.

The Superintendent who makes it a point to speak to every child who addresses him can help the discipline a great deal by saying, "I cannot say good-morning to you to-day because you have done (or neglected to do) certain things," etc. We have several groups in which children of a certain grade may live only so long as they live up to a standard of behavior. Attendance at band or various of the shops or classes is only permitted while behavior is especially good and work in other departments well done.

Sometime ago there was presented to the Iowa Board of Control a paper on paying inmates of institutions and many plans were given. At that time our system was in its infancy. Since then, however, we have found it admirable and it may be of interest to outline it here. It is not meant to be payment for services rendered, but rather as a method of discipline and we find that not only are children working cheerfully, well behaved, but also that well behaved children usually do good work. We pay a number of our children each week, amounts varying from one to five cents. Each child brings from every department in which he lives or works, a credit slip which signifies that he has worked well or behaved well for the week. No slips of discredit are given—the lack of a slip signifies that the child has not been good, etc. He is not told that he gets no slip because he was bad, but because he was not good. There is a vast difference in the two ways of putting it.

If A. works in the Laundry and Shoe-Shop and also milks, he must bring four slips, one from each of the above, and one from his attendant. If his allowance is three cents per week and he comes with only three slips, then he gets three-fourths of three cents (two and one-fourth cents). We can use fractions of a cent because candies, nuts, etc., are sold so many for a cent.

Each Saturday night in one of the rooms a table is tastefully arranged with candies, nuts, ribbons, etc., etc., and the children come in groups to buy. This, coming as it does once each week, keeps the training idea constantly before them. The children's interest does not seem to lag. The whole thing is an excellent means of breaking up small habits and helps general discipline wonderfully.

Encouragement must be at the bottom of all lessons. Our employes must learn not to say "don't" if they will succeed in their discipline. Down through the years, mankind lived under the rule, "Thou shalt not" until Christ preached the Gospel of encouragement when he said, "Thou shalt." The successes of a child must be noted rather than the failures. Let the blue pencil and the colored chalk mark in all lessons be the correct thing and then instead of finding their pages marked with failures, each mark dragging the discouraged little soul deeper in the mire of dissatisfaction, they will bristle with approbation and encouragement and brighter faces and happier dispositions will result. It is scarcely realized how much wrong doing on the part of the child is really caused by a headache or an attack of indigestion on the part of an employe. A quiet voice, an even temper, pretty and clean surroundings, good ventilation, encouragement, employment, everything a special privilege, these are the requisites for good discipline.

I am sorry I cannot recall the name of the author of the following lines, but if the spirit contained therein is kept in the hearts of those who have to do with feeble-minded children, they will not go astray.

"My little son who looks from thoughtful eyes,
And moves and speaks in serious, grown up wise,
Having my law the seventh time disobeyed,
I struck him and dismissed
With harsh words and unkissed;
(His mother, who was patient, being dead.)
Then fearing lest his grief should hinder sleep
I visited his bed
And found his lashes yet
With his late sobbing, wet.
Then I, with moan,
Kissing away his tears, left others of my own,
For on a table, drawn
Beside his bed, he had placed within his reach
A box of counters and a red-veined stone,
A piece of glass abraided by the beach

And six or seven shells,
A bottle of blue bells
And four French coins, ranged there with careful art
To comfort his sad heart.
So when that night I prayed
To God, I wept, and said,
'Ah, when we lie at last with trance'd breath,
Not vexing thee in death
And Thou rememberest
The toys
That made our joys,'
Then, fatherly not less than I
Who am moulded out of clay,
Thou'lt leave Thy wrath and say,
'I will be sorry for their childishness.' "

DISCUSSION

DR. ROGERS: I think this is a valuable paper and the spirit is excellent. It is always a delicate matter to discuss this subject of corporal punishment, we are so liable to be misunderstood. That corporal punishment is sometimes necessary is a point upon which we will all agree, yet, as a general statement, I do not believe in corporal punishment. I have found cases in my experience where I believed it was absolutely necessary. I do not allow any person to strike a child. If I know that it is done I discharge the employee unless it is done in self-defense. I do not recall more than two cases of the latter kind, both being cases of attack upon the attendant by boys with articles of furniture. I believe there should be rigid rules for the protection of the management and they should be understood. The first is that if there is to be any punishment it should be given by the superintendent and by no one else. I carry that out rigidly. I know there has been much trouble in some institutions that has resulted from delegating that power to others. Another point is that if a case is reported where severe discipline is needed it is important that it shall not be administered at once. It can always be postponed twenty-four hours. It is an interesting fact that we may view the situation very differently after a few hours reflection. In that time the child may be honestly repentant and need no punishment. I think the public should understand these rules. The only real trouble I ever had over severe discipline was when I whipped a boy and neglected to inform his parents. The boy informed the parents himself. I believe I did the proper thing for the boy, but I should have told them. He was a great strong boy physically, and had simply domineered over his associates—farm boys—and his attendants, who were forbidden by me to punish him, until the limit of forbearance was reached. His mother insisted upon taking him home. I said that I would like to have the boy taken before the board of trustees and let them see what had been done and hear the reason and then if she cared to take him home it was all right. This was done and the boy went home. A week later I had a letter in which she said she would like to return him under certain conditions. I replied that he could not be returned under any conditions except to be treated as I thought best. Within a month she sent him back under my conditions and he has been a splendid boy ever since. That is a typical case where I believe punishment was required. He came from a home where there was no control. In fact, I understand, he pounded his mother during the time she had him home after my punishment and I presume this treatment was a powerful argument with her in my favor. It is an extremely rare case where corporal punishment is required. Mr. Johnstone expresses the proper spirit in relation to our children.

MR. JOHNSTONE: The general public would not approve of whipping a feeble-minded child.

DR. WILMARTH: We should never whip a boy unless we are sure it will be for the child's good. It is not a question of defying public opinion. I do not think we should ever whip a child.

QUESTION: Do you think you should always notify the parents in advance?

DR. ROGERS: If I could not do it before I would do it at once. I should notify any parent who took any interest in his child. I believe frankness is due to the public and to the friends. It may make resentment for a while, but the community will see the justice of it and that establishes confidence in the institution.

MR. JOHNSON: I think as a matter of policy it is a great mistake for a superintendent to do it himself.

DR. ROGERS: I believe it is a responsibility the superintendent should take. I believe no one else should do it. It is the most disagreeable thing and the very fact that he takes the responsibility will make it a thing of seldom occurrence. It is the most disagreeable thing I ever did in my life.

MR. JOHNSON: I think he should delegate it.

MR. JOHNSTONE: I ordered it done once by a person in whom I had confidence and I found afterwards two other punishments by the same employee under circumstances he thought justifiable.

DR. ROGERS: I had the same experience where I deputed minor punishment.

MR. JOHNSON: One has to be careful in delegating punishment of course. I once had occasion to tell an attendant to punish a boy who had strayed away by giving him a bath and putting him to bed. It was Thursday. On Sunday he asked if the boy were to go to Sunday school. Inquiry showed that the boy was still in bed. His only excuse was that I had told him to put the boy to bed and had not told him to take him out.

DR. KEATING: When a child is brought to me for admission I make it understood that I am to have authority over the child. If I see fit to give corporal punishment I must give it, and I have yet to find the slightest opposition on the part of the parent. I am opposed to corporal punishment, but I reserve the right to administer it. I do not recall but one case where I ever resorted to it. That was a runaway. He told the neighbors that if he were caught I would give him a thrashing, and I told him that if he ran away again I *would*. The boy did not go for six months. I thought he had forgotten what I said, but when he was brought back I asked if he recollected. He replied, "Yes, you said you would whip me." I said, "I am very sorry to do it, but I am a man of my word," and I got a switch and whipped the boy and he has never run away since. While I am opposed to it, if it must be given it should be given only by the head of the institution. If an employe or any subordinate officer administered punishment without my permission his resignation would be immediately asked.

DR. ROGERS: I do not believe that a person can administer corporal punishment without injury to himself. It is a matter of history that one who is placed where he is obliged to administer corporal punishment feels that it has a thoroughly demoralizing effect upon himself. Prison managers admit this.

DR. POLGLASE: I never thought of it in that way.

DR. ROGERS: He can not do it without injuring his moral nature. I think this consciousness would deter a man many times.

MR. JOHNSTONE: My first experience in corporal punishment was in a reform school where we all used a strip of rubber about the size of my thumb. The first time it shocked me. I was pretty young at that time. At the end of two months I woke to the fact that it did not mean anything to me to whip those boys. I was no longer shocked. I feel pretty strongly now and I would not like ever to get into that condition again. The demoralizing effect on myself was something awful.

DR. POLGLASE: I think the times for corporal punishment are very few. The longer we live with these children the more we distinguish certain types. There are the children who are cruel and bloodthirsty and when a boy attempts to burn up a building or do some cruel thing I think a dose of his own medicine is all right for him. Dr. Keating has spoken of runaways. I do not think whipping is a deterrent for them. If a boy has assumed a false dignity among his fellows and falls from his high estate and does something deserving of punishment I should put him at some manual labor that he dislikes. Every boy should feel that you are sorry to administer punishment. I have one boy who runs away and no punishment would have any effect upon him. It is an impulse that he can not control. I think nothing would stop him unless he were tied. So I keep him constantly in dresses. He will not run away with a girl's dress on.

DR. ROGERS: Another point to be considered in handling young people is that there is a period in the boy's life when he assumes a spirit of bravado. That is as true among feeble-minded boys as among strong-minded. It is an age habit. The boy if wisely treated will outgrow that.

MR. JOHNSTONE: I do not think our discipline should consider the idea of punishing for the offence committed but to prevent its being done the next time. Do not let there be a next time. Whatever is done should be with the idea of making the boy better, so that there will be no repetition of the offence. Whipping for the offence lasts only as long as the smarting lasts.

DR. POLGLASE: We had a boy whom we trusted to do many things and he ran away. We gave him some slight discipline, deprived him of dessert or something of that kind. He ran away a second time. He had a great aversion to working inside the low grade buildings and had a contempt for that class of children. He was told that if he would do such things he must mingle with them and I put him there to work. I do not think there was ever a more humble individual. He begged time and again to be taken out and after I thought the dose was heavy enough I let him out and put him to work. He may run away again; I cannot tell anything about it, but in the meantime I trust him. When I trust I trust fully.

DR. KEATING: If you punish a child by giving him a disagreeable task and he refuses to do it what punishment would you give for that?

DR. POLGLASE: I do not know that I have ever had such a case. I should not force him to do it at once.

MR. JOHNSTONE: Hasn't it a bad effect on the boys who do that work regularly to have their employment looked upon as a punishment? Why should not they say, "Why must I do this every day when I am good, if it is a punishment for a bad boy?"

DR. POLGLASE: It would have a bad effect unless you made an explanation.

MR. JOHNSON: We say to a boy that he has proved by his conduct that he is not in the right place for him; that he belongs in division "Six" and so in he goes. If I want to be very forcible I have his clothes marked "6."

DR. FERNALD: Is not that the best way, simply to transfer them to a low grade department without any words? Let them draw their own inference. That takes the bravado out quicker than anything else. In regard to punishing feeble-minded boys I never could see why we had any moral right to administer punishment to a feeble-minded boy more than to an insane person. In no country in the world would corporal punishment be tolerated for the insane. Presumably the mistakes of the feeble-minded are due to mental irresponsibility and is it not unfair to punish them for that? It is a short cut, there is no question about that, but I never have been able to see the difference between them and the insane in that respect.

DR. WILMARTH: If punishment is to improve the child why should you not punish him as you would your own children?

DR. FERNALD: That would apply to adults.

DR. WILMARTH: It is to strengthen the child's will. When it is done in a kindly spirit, a just spirit, a spirit of love toward the child and solely for its good and the child so recognizes it then it strikes me that punishment is justifiable.

DR. ROGERS: There is all the difference in the world between the adult and the adolescent. Penologists have agreed that with very rare exceptions it never pays to whip an adult, while it might be beneficial to whip a child. When we speak of an insane person we refer to an adult.

DR. FERNALD: Nothing hurts an institution more than to whip an inmate.

DR. KEATING: The errors committed by the insane are from delusions. I do not think the infraction of rules by boys is from delusion; it is usually from *cussedness*. Why should you not punish a *boy who knows* that he is doing wrong? In the case of the boy I whipped it hurt me more than the boy and I think that impressed him. I did it only as a last resort.

DR. SIMCOE: My observation has been that there is as much whipping in insane asylums as in feeble-minded institutions. The employes do it. I have had four years' experience in a State asylum for the insane and I dare say that there is more punishment going on in insane asylums that the superintendent knows nothing about than ever was in a feeble-minded institution.

MR. JOHNSTONE: You may not know how much is going on in the institution of which you are superintendent.

DR. SIMCOE: I am a firm believer in not letting institutions get too big, for a superintendent *cannot* know what is going on in a big institution. I was raised in an insane asylum town and I knew what was going on when I was growing up.

DR. ROGERS: After all I think we agree on the essential points. An *irresponsible* person, be it child or adult, should certainly *never be whipped.* It is only in those rare cases in our work where we recognize responsibility, and then only as a last resort, that it should ever be employed. In the case I mentioned there had been months of patient effort, and a variety of minor methods of discipline employed without avail before the dose was administered.

FARM COLONY
IN
MASSACHUSETTS

Walter E. Fernald

Fernald justifies the use of the farm colony on the basis of the work training provided and the economics of operation.

At the time of our meeting in New York we had just bought land for our farm colony—about two thousand acres of wild land in western Massachusetts, partly hilly, partly valleys. The best and most fertile farms in that part of Massachusetts are on the hill-tops. The valleys are corroded by the glaciers and stripped of the soil, which is covered with gravel and drift, but the hill-tops are covered with strong, fertile soil. So we included three or four hills in our purchase. We were compelled to go a long distance—sixty-one miles—from our home institution because we could not buy cheap land, which was also good land, nearer. That seemed like an objection at first, but we felt the essential thing was to get fertile land and enough of it, along with wood and water. We found all we needed, water, wood, clay for bricks, gravel and sand, and stone in addition to the fertile land.

Two years ago at about this time we began our work by sending to the farm the first group of fifty boys. They were sent up in charge of people employed at the school. We fitted up some rough sheds in the rear of one of the old farm houses and covered them with tarred paper. We made quite extensive temporary provision for the colony. One building was for a dining room, one for a clothing room, and in addition we had a sitting room, and the boys lived in the camp until the first of January, before we had our first permanent group of dormitories built. Our first work was the water supply. We discarded the old wells and dug new ones. We tore down the old sheds and excavated basements and built in the rear of the old New England farm house a building for sleeping rooms. Each of the two sleeping rooms accommodates twenty-five boys. They are connected by a corridor with a building containing the water closets and the toilet arrangements. This building is one hundred and fifty feet from the frame house and is occupied only as sleeping rooms. In the day time the sleeping rooms are not occupied. The sitting room has a huge fire-place. The room is decorated with pictures and they have their games there. To my mind it is the most attractive room in our institution. The original farm house is used for living rooms for the matron and farmer, and the people who take care of these boys. This constitutes a group. In the rear we built a first-class new kitchen detached from the house with every convenience, pantries, store-rooms, etc. The other buildings which we are about to open are similar. We have some 25,000 acres in wood. It grows rapidly and we burn it in place of coal; we use no coal on the place. The dormitories, which are rectangular, 20 x 50 feet, have large fireplaces in the centre and we use the fire-places for heating and ventilating in the fall and

Journal of Psycho-Asthenics, 1903, 7 (4): 74–80. Photographs have not been reprinted.

Dr. Fernald was superintendent of the Massachusetts School for the Feeble-Minded from 1887 to 1924. His leadership as an educator, administrator, and scientist during this tenure was unequaled.

spring. In the winter we put in a huge heater in the fire-place, a cylindrical wood stove that stands four feet high and is two and a half in diameter. The heating of the dormitories is done with this stove. The flue goes up through the centre of the fire-place flue. The flue is two feet square, and we get excellent ventilation. There is no waste in the fuel because the fire is not kindled until about half an hour before the boys go to bed. The ventilation is the best of any dormitory in our institution. The climate is very severe, like Wisconsin, or Minnesota. We are twelve hundred feet above the sea. That fire at night, when the stove is filled with wood and shut off so that it burns slowly, warms the room sufficiently, and in the morning a boy opens the stove before the others get up and it is comfortably warm for dressing.

Conditions there are absolutely primitive. We have no electric light plant, but use kerosene lamps made of very strong metal; and, unless there were a wanton destruction of the lamp, I hardly see how any accident could happen. The falling of the lamp could do no damage.

The first group has been in operation since a year ago last January. We have learned a good many things about farm colonies. I had to change my notion about the number of people to be employed. In our state it is not feasible to suggest that a man who is attendant on the boys all day, or who goes and works in the fields with them, should stay with them until nine at night; and we have gradually increased the number of people caring for them until now we have a matron, a cook who is a woman, and two female attendants, who have charge of the dormitory work and who will relieve the matron and cook. If it were not for the necessity of recreation we might have a smaller number of attendants. We employ three men where we could get on with two men. When we observed the physically nervous condition that our men would get into from working long hours with feeble-minded boys and successfully keeping them employed, we decided to add a third man.

Those boys have worked every day since they went to the colony, and they put in long days' work. We have not done much farm work yet, but we have put in our mains and sewers and done a large amount of that sort of work.

As soon as we got the first group of the colony in we began preparations for the second. And there is a large amount of work where you have a separate water supply and sewage disposal. The first two are two miles apart. The second colony is practically like the first. We took an old farm house and made a boys' dining room. We now have one hundred inmates at the colony and before fall we expect to add about eighty more. The supplies are all bought and furnished from Waverley just as at our farm house there. The monthly requisitions cover the principal wants. Groceries are ordered as for the school and sent direct. Broken packages are sent out first to the local buildings. We have not found the slightest difficulty in doing this. The marketing is done a certain day and certain things are sent by express. We found the express charges very small. We receive from the colony every morning an itemized report, and from the matron and foreman one every twenty-four hours.

The cost I am not able to tell. I have ostentatiously avoided being able to tell the cost up to this time. In our state it would not be desirable to prove that you could run a colony too cheaply. I have no doubt that our expectations have been more than realized, but we know this: I requested the builder to make an estimate of the cost of the work which they have done at the colony and his estimate was—and we have every reason to believe that it is correct—that the cost of maintaining those fifty boys for the period they had been there is less than it would have cost to have paid for the labor they have done. That is a way of getting at the market value of what the boys have done. This year we are beginning to farm on a large scale and we shall be able to tell in a year or two something about the cost. That is a question we are not anxious about because we have demonstrated to our satisfaction that the colony scheme is not going to be an expensive way of maintaining the boys and that it will be much less than at the parent institution.

A second test of the value of the colony was whether we could keep those boys who were accustomed to institution entertainments and the life of the institution on the top of a mountain in the country with only boys like themselves, happy and content. Some of our good friends thought that we were making a great mistake, and I had some doubt myself and that is where I found I had to have a little larger staff than I had anticipated. Each evening one assistant is detailed to help in this and we take pains that he shall not be worn out by a long day's work. Preferably we choose a woman to have care of the entertainment for the boys in the evening. We have selected perhaps fifty or seventy-five volumes of boys' stories and from the beginning every evening a woman has read aloud a certain number of chapters. They have read book after book through, and it is a settled thing now. I think these continued readings have had a great deal to do with the content of the boys. We have an organ and several other musical instruments, and every evening there is a half hour of song. After the songs it is a settled policy to play games, cards, dominoes, checkers. It is easy to keep the work up, but the matron's report shows that it has not lapsed there. Our report every morning provides against that. Unless you have a plan like that the tendency is after awhile to drop such things. The best boys we have ever had are the boys in the colony and none of them would go back to the parent institution if they were given a chance. They are happier than any boys of that age and class that I have had in the institution.

Another bug-bear I had anticipated was difficulty in getting employes. The colony is three miles from the railway station and two miles of the way there are no houses. It is all up hill, a long sandy road. I have, however, no difficulty in getting employes. The fact is that the colony is the popular branch of the institution for the employes. There is only one grade of employes there. None of the delicate questions of rank come in. There is a wholesome atmosphere which reacts on the children and makes possible an amount of zeal and effectiveness in dealing with them which the machinery of the large institution is apt, perhaps, to cover up. We have selected from the parent institution the very best of our employes to go there, and we have made it an unwritten law that they must have served at the home school before they go to the colony. We admit no boys directly to the colony; they must go by way of the school and have had a variety of discipline and training before going there because the conditions of life are so simple. They have no restrictions, except that they must stay on our own land. They must not go down on the main road nor leave our territory, but, provided they obey this rule, there is no objection to going where they choose. It has a great charm for the boys,—the freedom which they feel.

DISCUSSION

DR. LAWLOR: What number of the children of the parent institution are eligible to go to the colony? How long are they required to stay in the parent institution before going? We have three hundred and twenty-one boys at our institution and I do not think we could have more than thirty-five that we could trust to make this attempt.

DR. FERNALD: We carry out the industrial principle at Waverley. We build the institution there.

QUESTION: From how many boys in the parent institution did you call those?

DR. FERNALD: We had three hundred and seventy-five boys. We do not care to rob the parent institution of all the workers, but we expect to transfer from fifty to seventy-five next spring.

QUESTION: When your land is cleared how many boys can you keep there?

DR. FERNALD: We believe that two thousand acres will care for from twelve to fifteen hundred boys.

QUESTION: Of what grade?

DR. FERNALD: The first group was made up of twenty-five of the brighter boys and twenty-five of our low grade. The second group were boys who had never been able to read or write, but who had managed to get an industrial training. We have made it a point for many years of having the teachers go out with lower grade boys and teach them the simplest forms of manual labor. The simplest exercise is to get those boys in a row with a piece of scantling in front of them to keep them in line and give each of them a grub hoe, a very primitive implement, and teach them how to use it.

MR. ALEXANDER JOHNSON: That is the kind "The Man With the Hoe" used.

QUESTION: What is the scantling for?

DR. FERNALD: To keep them in line; if you don't have it in thirty seconds they will go in every direction.

DR. LAWLOR: Do you have any objection to this sort of work on the part of the parents? It would raise a howl of indignation in California to ask these boys to do manual work.

DR. FERNALD: There was great prejudice when we moved into the country. In our reports we explained to the parents and to the public the necessity for that sort of thing. If you wish to really reach the feeble-minded boys you must do it through work, for you can do it no other way. We have a public sentiment now which thoroughly backs us up. I have not heard a word of complaint from a parent for years. We wondered how it would be in sending them to the colony, but we found that the parents of the children were perfectly content with the work they are doing there, and they do good work. I believe our hundred boys will do as much work as one hundred laboring men that we could hire in that country community. It is not as intelligent and it can be easily wasted and diverted, but when it comes to actual work units I believe they are capable of as much work as we are able to hire in a Massachusetts village. That is a qualified statement, because the laboring man means to do very little—the unskilled laboring man.

We found that if those boys had to do that kind of work then we had to re-consider the question of diet. With a breakfast of cereals and bread and butter and coffee there was not enough to keep him at work from 7:30 to 12:00 o'clock, and we had to provide for more nourishing food than the average institution affords. When you consider the extra amount of food that a feeble-minded boy eats, anyway, it means quite a difference in the provision you have to make. But it is a very necessary thing. The institution dietaries are generally based on the needs of a person who leads a quiet life.

DR. ROGERS: Have you any definite data in mind with regard to meat? How much meat per capita do you give them?

DR. FERNALD: They have a beef stew, for instance, and for fifty boys fifty pounds of beef go into that stew. I have not been able to convince the matron that that can be kept down.

DR. POLGLASE: Our boys doing heavy work have meat twice a day.

DR. LAWLOR: We do the same.

DR. FERNALD: It seems as though these boys required more fuel to make them go. It is marvellous the amount of food they eat, digest, and assimilate.

DR. LAWLOR: The thing that strikes me as remarkable is the number of boys who can do that kind of work. Most of our boys cannot pick up an apple. They cannot pick it from the tree. If they try to help in picking fruit they have to have a corps of people with them or they will destroy more than they will pick. You must have a different class of boys in Massachusetts.

DR. FERNALD: I think we have a lower grade of boys than any other American institution. The brighter imbeciles do not come to us. They go to the house of the Good Shepherd or to the Lyman School.

DR. LAWLOR: We have no non-residents in our institution, but from three hundred and twenty-one boys we could not get more than forty-five or fifty who would do that kind of work.

MR. JOHNSON: In a few years you will change your mind. Nothing is more gratifying than to see how much work can be got out of the lower grade children. It has been a constant surprise. We have girls ironing today who several years ago could not do anything but pull a floor rubber, and now they are competent to do good work.

DR. FERNALD: I have always been interested in the employment of the imbecile, and I have personally put a good deal of time and work into it. You have got to begin with them when they are young. Our stone piles at Waverley are pretty nearly the first steps to industrial work. We have two circles of stones about thirty feet apart. We fill one of these circles full of stones about as big as a man's head. Then all the stones of one circle are carried to the other side. And the boys get a lunch and go home. We begin with many cases so low that the teacher has to put the stone into the boy's hand and hold his hand on it to keep him from dropping it and urge him to drop it in the right place. It is surprising how few catch on to the idea of carrying these stones. That is the primary lesson in our industrial training—that stone pile. But you must realize that that is not to be done long, and the sooner you graduate him into doing work with some purpose the better for the boy and the more interest he will have in it. At least fifty of the hundred at the colony began their training at those stone piles. The boys at the colony who are now putting in a good day's work began with our stone piles ten or twelve years ago, and but for that training we should not have been able to teach them the many things they have been able to learn. They would have been typical almshouse idiots and would have sat on the benches all day moving only to their meals. It is owing to work alone that their physical condition has been improved and their untidy habits have disappeared.

Our colony has grown very slowly. We have felt that it was an experiment, and that we could not afford to have it fail. And we have resisted the temptation to push the development too fast. We expect eventually to have six or seven hundred in the colony.

QUESTION: Do you put high grade inmates into your colony?

DR. FERNALD: A few of them.

QUESTION: Do they disturb it?

DR. FERNALD: I have transferred one boy back, and one boy I have sent home as unsuitable for institution life. We tried him in Waverley. He was a troublesome fellow. Our high grade boys have been contented at the colony. They are not tempted by seeing people from the town or a large number of visitors. They have practically everything that is to be had in the community. Their life fills their wants more than one would think.

In a country village when boys get to the period of adolescence the normal boy likes to show off before his young lady friends. I have learned that these boys in that period of development show their restlessness in attempts to run away as a bit of bravado,—they like to show off before the girls in the institution. They are much more simple and natural in the colony, and that desire to show off is entirely absent. That is very striking.

MR. JOHNSON: We have twenty boys in our colony, in a farm house with rooms upstairs. It is a little domestic place with a man and wife in charge. They have a chicken farm and are raising tomatoes, cabbages, and other garden things. The cooking is done in an old-fashioned way on the cooking stove. The boys are of different grades. I should prefer to put them in a brick house on account of fire, and we could build one as we make our own brick. We have only about one-seventh of the land that Dr. Fernald has.

DR. FERNALD: What is your experience in the matter of help?

MR. JOHNSON: We have about one to six. We could get on with fewer if our boys did not work.

DR. FERNALD: Yes, if you have boys to work and keep them up you have to have about that number of assistants.

DR. ROGERS: Do you try a man and wife at any time?

DR. FERNALD: I never employ a man and wife.

DR. ROGERS: Why?

DR. FERNALD: I should modify that. Sometimes people marry each other who are employes. We have now a man and wife who came back to us in that way. But if you employ both man and wife, and get into trouble you have two people instead of one to deal with. If you would like to dispense with the services of one you must lose both. It leads to complications.

MR. JOHNSON: So does every arrangement. The better your arrangement the more complex it is; just as it is with machinery. The machinery of the man and wife is more complex and it takes more oil to keep the bearings smooth. But there are advantages which seem to me to outweigh the difficulties.

DR. POLGLASE: If you have a young man and a young woman in your colony without any head official I should thing there might be a tendency to immorality.

DR. FERNALD: I employ as matron a settled woman who is equal to the supervision. I have had no trouble in that direction. The standard of behavior has been as high as at the school. A bill has gone through the house which provides that eight hours shall constitute a day's work for any employe in any state institution. If that becomes a law it will increase the number of our assistants.

DR. LAWLOR: We have the same law in California.

DR. FERNALD: That will add to our per capita cost. It will not pass this year, but it is probably bound to come.

A RESUME
OF
PAROLE WORK
AT
LETCHWORTH
VILLAGE

Howard W. Potter and Crystal L. McCollister

This paper describes a program of extra-institutional living used with more capable students at Letchworth Village during the era. Parole to the home of family or employer involved strict rules of supervision by the institution. Only a small percentage of parolees earned discharge from the institution because of satisfactory adjustment in the community.

Letchworth Village, a state institution for mental defectives at Thiells, N.Y., was first opened for the admission of children on July 11, 1911. It is designed to receive and care for all types of cases of mental deficiency and is especially adapted to the care, training, and development of those who can be benefited by the numerous facilities which are available. In the institution at the present time there are about two thousand patients varying in level of intelligence from the idiot to the high grade moron, with chronological ages ranging from six to fifty years. The majority of the patients admitted to Letchworth Village are from the Metropolitan District and the southeastern part of the state; the number of commitments from the other sections of New York State are distributed about equally. Patients are usually admitted through the courts, schools, and social agencies.

Each patient admitted to the institution is intensively studied and classi- fied and treated to meet his individual needs. Various kinds of physical, mental, laboratory and educational examinations are given each patient on admission. During his stay in the institution he receives medical, surgical, scholastic, industrial, social and mental treatment as may be required.

Our boys and girls have been paroled from the institution either to their own homes or to those of employers, and occasionally are allowed home on trial for three months and then if their behavior has been such as to warrant their remaining at home they may be paroled. Relative to those children paroled to their own homes either the relatives have made application for their return to the community or the application has come from some judge, lawyer or other interested person. When such an application is received the Parole Agent makes an investigation of the home. The findings are reported to the doctor in charge of the patient who decides whether or not the patient may go home or the case may be brought before the Staff which in turn makes a decision. It is seldom that we find a patient's home in which there is a suitable environment for him and in which he will receive the necessary supervision.

Selection of patients for parole to working homes is made by the doctor in charge of the patient or by the Staff. In considering whether or not a patient is ready for parole his chronological age, mental age, school training, industrial training and efficiency, personality, and his behavior and history before and after admission to Letchworth Village are considered.

In making an investigation of a working home the following points are considered—the location of the home; the surrounding environment, personal- ity of supervisor; number, occupation, and personality of other members of

Journal of Psycho-Asthenics, 1926, 31:165–188. Reprint by permission of Dr. Potter and the American Association on Mental Deficiency. For the sake of brevity tables have been omitted from this paper.

Dr. Potter was director of research at Letchworth Village from 1921 to 1929. He is now emeritus professor of psychiatry at The State University of New York and resides in Fredonia, New York. Crystal McCollister was parole agent at Letchworth Village.

the family; amount of supervision patient would receive; the kind of room patient would occupy; the work expected of patient; and the recreation for patient. The paroling of patients in working homes is more nearly ideal as far as environment is concerned than the paroling of patients to their own homes because the home as well as the patient is carefully selected. We attempt to place our paroles in homes which are morally good, with people who are fairly successful economically and socially, with those who are kind, sympathetic, and who will understand mental defectives sufficiently to give them the necessary supervision.

The Parole Agent visits the majority of patients at least once a month. Some patients are visited as often as two or three times a month and others only once or twice a year. When the agent can not visit a patient each month a letter is written to the home and to the patient asking for a report in regard to patient's health, behavior, recreation, type of work he is doing, and whether or not he is happy and contented. In some communities remote from the Institution the workers of other agencies assist in the supervision of paroles.

Our paroles are under no absolute rules or regulations as we found that we had to consider each individual case separately. We can allow some patients more privileges than others. Others have to be held down to very strict rules and regulations. The type of patient, the kind of parole home, the community environment, the supervision and the length of time on parole all have to be considered in determining what limitations are to be set for any particular patient. We do insist, however, on general principles, that no girl be permitted out after dark unaccompanied by a responsible person, that her mail be supervised, and that she is to receive no mail or attention from male friends or acquaintances.

Patients are returned to the institution from their parole for various reasons. These are set forth in Table V and will be dealt with later on.

Patients are discharged from parole for a number of reasons. Ideally we did not intend to discharge any patient unless he or she had completed a three year parole period satisfactorily. Practically this was not carried out in nearly half of those discharged on account of broader administrative policies which were concerned with the relation of the institution to the communities, courts, and newspapers. The reasons given for discharge are detailed in Table VI and will be analysed later in this paper.

CLINICAL DATA—GENERAL STATISTICS

This study includes two hundred seventy-eight paroles; one hundred seven were males and one hundred seventy-one females. The actual number of patients involved is two hundred fifty-five; one hundred seven males and one hundred forty-eight females. Some of the females were paroled more than once thus the total number of paroles is in excess of the actual number of patients.

Table I shows the total number of paroles of each sex to homes of relatives and working homes, the number returned to the institution (L. V.), the number discharged from parole, and the number remaining on parole March 1, 1925. The figures cover a five-year period preceding March 1, 1925 which is the length of time parole work has been carried on at the institution. This comparatively small number of paroles reflects the conservatism of the institutional administration in regard to the parole problem and is also explained by the fact that the parole material available has been limited by the small inmate population of the past several years.

DEFINITION

From general psychiatric experience we felt that certain general and specific factors may have some bearing on the kind of adaption which the mentally deficient boy or girl makes in the community after having spent a more or less prolonged period in an institution. In general these factors relate to the patient, to the family stock, and to the environment. Therefore, we have statistically dealt with the following clinical data.

FAMILY STOCK

We roughly classified the various stocks met with under four headings as follows:

Socially Good Non-defective Stock

Cases with a definitely good ancestry, socially and economically competent and free from definite mental or nervous instability or incompetency.

Socially Good Mentally Deficient Stock

Cases with a history pointing to one or more mentally deficient ancestors, yet who on the whole were free from delinquent, criminal or other antisocial tendencies. Economically some were self-supporting, some on the borderline of dependency and some actually dependent on public charity.

Socially Bad Mentally Deficient Stock

Patients who came from families characterized not only by mental deficiency but in addition by immorality, delinquency, criminality or any sort of antisocial behavior.

Psychopathic Unstable Stock

Patients having an ancestry compromised by psychopathic personalities, epilepsy, or frank psychoses of a non-organic type.

EARLY ENVIRONMENT

Good Influences

This heading is essentially self-explanatory. It includes those patients who had parents that were at least not below the average in their methods of bringing up a family. The general atmosphere of the home was good, the various members of the family lived harmoniously on the average and there was nothing of importance environmentally so far as could be determined which would warp the child's personality.

Inadequate Training

Cases who came from homes where the children like Topsy "just grew." The members of the family were not particularly vicious or bad. They set no examples of a distinctly detrimental flavor but on the other hand they were by no means the ideal type of parent or other relative for bringing up a family or as a pattern for the growing child to copy.

Bad Influence

Patients who came from homes which were colored by a distinctly unfavorable behavior or attitude. These were homes in which drunkenness and immorality were rife, where petty criminality was common and where the chief consideration obtained by the child was the manifestations of the "hitting and slapping disease."

Institutional

A certain group of our patients had lived practically all their lives in an institution of one sort or another. From infancy they had been brought up in various kinds of orphanages, homes, etc.

EARLY BEHAVIOR

Social

Patients whose early behavior showed no outstanding abnormalities. They were committed to the institution as a result of failure in school or as a means of temporarily meeting a situation of dependency following the death of one or both parents.

Anti-social Behavior Exclusive of Sex Irregularities

Patients who had been given to petty thieving, truancy, vagrancy, incorrigibility, etc., but who had not had, so far as we could determine, any gross heterosexual experiences.

Anti-social Behavior Inclusive of Sex Irregularities

Patients who in addition to the anti-social behavior outlined in the above section had had gross heterosexual experiences.

AGE ON ADMISSION TO LETCHWORTH VILLAGE

We divided our cases into four different age periods which correspond roughly to physiological periods of development. The first period, that of preadolescence, included all cases below twelve. The second period, that of adolescence, included patients between the ages of twelve and fifteen inclusive. The third period, that of post-adolescence, included cases from sixteen to nineteen years inclusive. The fourth period, that of adult life, included patients who were twenty years of age or over.

LENGTH OF TIME IN LETCHWORTH VILLAGE

We grouped our patients according to the length of time they had been in the institution under four headings: less than one year; one year and over but less than two years; two years and over but less than three years; and three years and over.

AGE WHEN PAROLED FROM LETCHWORTH VILLAGE

We made four groups: those below sixteen years of age, those sixteen or seventeen years of age, those eighteen or nineteen years of age and those twenty years of age or over. Such a grouping was made to determine statistically whether or not the so-called physiological instability of adolescence had any bearing on social adaptability.

MENTAL TEST LEVEL WHEN PAROLED

We have grouped the patients in this study as being below the six year mental level or low grade imbeciles and idiots; high grade imbeciles from the six year level to seven years, eleven months; low grade morons from eight year level to eight years eleven months; middle grade morons from the nine year level to nine years eleven months; and high grade morons from the ten year level to ten years eleven months. Two further groups from the eleven year level to eleven years, eleven months and twelve year level and over were also formed, which include individuals who may not have been strictly mentally deficient.

PERSONALITY MAKE-UP

We met with many handicaps under this topic because there were quite a few who had not been studied at all and many of them had only superficially studied as regards their personality. Despite this, however, we have attempted to make the best of the situation and from the data at hand made the following subheadings.

No Outstanding Maladaptive Traits

Patients who appeared to have no very definite habits of reaction of characteristics which could be considered specifically detrimental. It must be understood at the start, however, that all mental defectives commonly have the characteristics of being more or less at the disposal of environmental influences whether these influences be of a personal or an impersonal nature.

Labile Type

Patients who had no very definite established forms of reactions which were distinctly unfavorable but yet on the other hand seemed to be possessed with an unusual amount of suggestibility. They represent the rather typical "chameleon" type of mental defective who changes his reactions with so much facility and ease that he readily takes on the coloring of the environment, favorable or unfavorable as it might be.

Emotional Unstable Type

Individuals who seemed to be inherently unstable. They are so constituted that their emotions are dominant and control almost exclusively the situation.

Defensive Reaction Type

Patients who had acquired the facility for projecting their difficulties and shortcomings onto conditions or factors which they relegated beyond their control. This sort of reaction not only served to excuse them from the point of view of the outsider but also tended to repress their own self-criticism. Some of these individuals possessed a mild shut-in or schizoid sort of make-up.

Egocentric Reaction Type

Patients who as a result of an inferiority complex attempted to compensate for rather than defend their inferiority. They were mostly of the rather positive, egotistic, self-centered, self-satisfied, smug sort of individuals. Many of this type seemed to be activated by an inherent urge for antisocial behavior. They were the type that very readily hunted for trouble and were usually successful in finding it.

Tables II, III, and IV series present in detail the statistics of the clinical make-up of the total group paroled, the group returned from parole, and the group discharged from parole. Tables V and VI set forth the conditions covering the return and discharge of patients from parole.

CLINICAL MAKE-UP OF TOTAL PAROLES

The clinical make-up of the total paroles as a group is as follows. Nearly half came from a socially bad mentally deficient stock, a negligible number from an absolutely good stock, and a fifth from psychopathic or socially good defective stock.

Nearly two-thirds of the group had a neutral sort of early environment—not particularly bad but poorer than the average.

More than three-quarters of them began early to show anti-social tendencies.

About one-half were below sixteen years of age when admitted to Letchworth Village and one-fifth were twenty years old or over.

Half of them had been in the institution for three years or more before they were paroled.

About two-thirds of the group were over eighteen years of age when they were paroled.

One-fifth were below the moron level, two-thirds were morons, and the remainder borderline types.

One-third of the group had rather favorable personalities while the remainder had personalities that were not well balanced.

For details see Table II series.

GENERAL ADAPTABILITY OF MALES AND FEMALES ON PAROLE

Table I shows very definitely that males are far more successful in extra-institutional adaptation than are females. The statistics in Table I cannot be used to indicate the relative merits of relative's homes and working homes as factors in the adaptation of our patients because many of the patients that are paroled to homes of relatives are only nominally under our supervision and direction. It is quite the usual thing for relatives to take matters in their own hands and refuse to abide by the advice of the parole agent. Their refusal to permit a patient's return to the institution even in the face of a situation that plainly requires such a step, is a common occurrence. The institution has learned by experience that it is useless to assert its rights in such a situation because eventually the courts will uphold the relatives in their stand, by sustaining the usually ensuing writ of habeas corpus.

The better success of the males in extra-institutional adaptation can be explained by a combination of facts. Referring to Table II series it will be noted that the male parole material had a definite advantage over the female parole material in that it is, almost point for point, made of better stuff. We find that proportionally less than a third of the males as against nearly two-thirds of the females come from anti-social feeble-minded stock. Many more of the females than the males came from homes where the influences were decidedly bad. The males had a decided edge on the females for good early behavior while sex delinquency had been present in nearly two-thirds of the girls and was seven times more common than among the boys. In the matter of personality make-up the boys had an enormous lead; over half of them were well adjusted and only small fractions were handicapped by one or the other of the more or less unhealthy types of reactions; the girls present an almost perfect opposite.

Furthermore there are certain general considerations which combined with the above differences in clinical make-up tend to explain why our boys are more easily adjusted in an extra-institutional environment. The girl has problems to meet which do not commonly confront the boy. The girl is occupied in-doors at work which affords but little outlet to her emotions. The boy works out-of-doors at labor requiring the use of large muscle groups which provides a safe outlet for fundamental emotional urges. The end of the day finds the girl in a state of nervous tension, not particularly physically tired, and craving some sort of excitement as a relief. The boy is physically tired, experiences no nervous tension, and his chief craving is a comfortable bed.

At times of relaxed supervision the girl is the easy prey of unscrupulous persons and, pursued, falls a ready victim to sex delinquencies. The boy, belonging to the aggressive sex, because of his dull wit, cannot successfully compete with his more normal brethren in the game of procreation.

PATIENTS RETURNED FROM PAROLE

Ninety-eight patients, fourteen males and eighty-four females were returned from parole (Table I) for the various reasons shown in Table V. Generally speaking males and females were not returned for the same reasons (Table V). Of the total returned half of the boys and only one-seventeenth of the girls were generally incorrigible. Over two-fifths of the girls and only one boy showed tendencies or actual expressions of sex delinquency. None of the boys and one-seventh of the girls returned had proved industrially incompetent. The girl is usually called on to do a rather higher type of work than the boy.

During the first year the largest number of failures occurred. (See Table V.) Nine out of fourteen male failures and fifty-eight out of eighty-four female failures occurred before the end of the first year on parole. During the third year only three of each sex had to have their parole cancelled. This study seems to indicate that the majority of the failures may be expected to occur in the first two years of extra-institutional life.

Nine of our girls have borne illegitimate children. In terms of percentage then five per cent of all females paroled or ten percent of those returned from parole, became pregnant while on parole and gave birth to illegitimate children.

Despite the fact that all of the failures were not returned, some being discharged as a matter of administrative policy, the group of patients returned from parole may be regarded as examples of unsuccessful extra-institutional adaptation.

PATIENTS DISCHARGED FROM PAROLE

Nineteen boys and twenty-seven girls, forty-six in all, were discharged from parole. The length of time each had been on parole and the reason for discharge are shown in detail in Table VI. Ten of the males and fifteen of the females had proved entirely satisfactory during the time they had been on parole. None of the remainder may be regarded as having adjusted completely to extra-institutional life during the time they were under observation.

The group discharged from parole cannot be considered as necessarily representative of the types making for good extra-institutional adaptation because nearly half of them were discharged as a matter of policy rather than because of successful adaptation. In addition satisfactory adaptation on parole of any patient is by no means a guarantee of continued successful adaptation.

CLINICAL TYPES AND MALADAPTATION

Because we have no instances in which we are certain that the adaptation is genuine and permanent we may use the clinical data in this study only indirectly by inference to suggest the relationship of clinical findings to satisfactory extra-institutional adaptation. We have many instances of un-doubted failure in adaptation. We have many instances of undoubted failure in adaptation in the group returned from parole and by comparing the clinical data in this group with the total group paroled, we may find some suggestion of the relation of clinical types to unsuccessful extra-institutional adaptation.

Family Stock

Nearly two-thirds of those returned from parole came from socially bad mentally deficient stock as against one-half of the total group. Whether this is a matter of biological heredity or whether it is a result of social heredity and therefore one of environment is a debatable question. The writers hold to the latter point of view.

Environment

Our statistics give us no definite information concerning the relation which early environment bears to faulty adaptation on parole except as is suggested in the preceding paragraph. The proportion having been exposed to definitely bad influences in early life is only slightly higher in the returned group than in the total group.

Behavior

The relation of early behavior to unsuccessful adaptation on parole is quite definite. Nearly ninety per cent of those returned had been anti-social in their early behavior as compared to three quarters of the total group showing the same tendencies. The total group had six per cent who were not early anti-social but the returned group had less than one per cent, only one patient, whose early behavior was satisfactory.

Age

There are no striking comparisons in the ages on admission or length of time spent in the institution between either the returned or paroled groups. Those who spent between one and two years in the institution are present in a much smaller proportion in the return group than in the total group. This is probably due to the fact that those patients who remained such a comparatively short time were paroled to homes of relatives, and their return even when indicated was not sanctioned. The most appreciable difference in the various age levels when paroled between the two groups is found in the proportion of those who were twenty years old or over. Forty-three per cent of the total group were twenty-years old or over as against fifty-nine per cent of the returned group. Again this is explained by the fact that practically all of our younger patients were paroled to their own homes and were not returned when they failed on account of the antagnostic attitude of the family. This naturally raises the proportion of the older patients in the returned group.

Mental Test Level

We find no appreciable difference between the proportions of the various mental test levels of either group except in the higher grade moron levels. Of those having a level of ten and eleven, there were twenty-eight per cent in the total group and thirty-seven per cent in the returned group. This would indicate that the high grade moron level has the greatest potentiality for social maladaptation.

Personality

The relation of personality make-up to maladaptation is very pointed. Thirty-four per cent of the total group had reasonably good personalities as compared to nine per cent of the returned group. Suggestible types, emotionally unstable make-ups, and defensive or egocentric trends were far more common in proportion in the returned group than in the total group.

SUMMARY

1. This study is a review of two hundred seventy-eight paroles (one hundred seven males and one hundred seventy-one females) of mentally deficient

patients from an institution for mental defectives. The patients were paroled to homes of relatives and to working homes.

2. The clinical data concerning each patient was compiled and evaluated so as to include an estimation of the patient, the family stock and environment.

3. Males were more successful than females; the ratio being three and one-half to one.

4. The relative merits of relative's homes and working homes cannot be evaluated on the basis of this study owing to peculiar local conditions.

5. The patients paroled had, as a group, a generally compromised family stock; an indifferent, poorer than average, early environment, and a history of anti-social behavior prior to admission. Half were in adolescence or preadolescence when admitted and two-thirds were in early adult life when paroled. Half spent more than three years in the institution. Four-fifths were of a moron or borderline level of intelligence and only one-third had definitely good personalities.

6. The males were, almost point for point, of better material than the females.

7. The character of the work required of the patients while on parole was such that it favored more satisfactory sublimations for the boys while the general constitution of society gave more opportunities for anti-social behavior especially sex delinquency, on the part of the girls.

8. Thirty-five per cent of the total paroled were returned to the institution. Considering the sexes separately, thirteen per cent of the males and forty-nine per cent of the females were returned. These figures do not represent all parole failures because several were not returned on account of administrative difficulties.

9. The males were returned mainly on account of general incorrigibility and the girls principally for tendencies or actual expressions of sex delinquency.

10. Nine females gave birth to illegitimate children. This is an illegitimacy of five per cent for all females paroled. From statistics furnished by the New York State Department of Health it is estimated that one per cent of all the females between the ages of 15 and 45 in the year 1923 gave birth to illegitimate children.

11. Seventeen per cent of the total number paroled were discharged. Only a trifle more than half of this number can be regarded as having proved entirely satisfactory in their adaptation from our point of view.

12. Comparing the clinical make-up of the total parole group with the group returned from parole it is found that a socially bad mentally defective stock was more commonly found in the group returned from parole than in the total group paroled. The various kinds of early environment were present in the same proportion in each group. Nearly all of the returned group had shown anti-social behavior prior to admission as against seventy-five per cent

of the total group. No significant comparisons were apparent relative to age on admission, age when paroled and length of residence in the institution. A rather higher percentage of morons were present in the returned group and compromised types of personality were far more common among those returned from parole.

COMMENT

It is probably unwise to generalize on the basis of statistics where the problem is such a human one as this study represents. From the bare facts as presented here it would seem that we have a rather unpromising problem on our hands when we try to reinstate defectives into the community. It must be remembered, however, that our choice of material is limited to those patients who have been committed because of their failure to meet and adjust themselves to the demands of the community. Thus the institution is working with defectives whose personality, habits, and reactions have been warped and conditioned by long continued misunderstanding and mismanagement on the part of the home, the school, and the community at large. Such "damaged goods" the institution has to select from for its parole material and after a period of retraining, attempt to readjust in the community.

A second point to be considered is the attitude the institution takes as to what constitutes a satisfactory community adaptation. It must be indicated that our attitude has been distinctly colored by a eugenical point of view. Many of our paroles would have been considered as having made a satisfactory extra-institutional adjustment if we had disregarded what one might term a normal interest in the opposite sex. It should be emphasized that the patients we placed on parole but rarely indulged promiscuously in sex activities. They reacted to an instinctive urge for procreation which is resident in every living thing and the matter of eugenics has made us regard even the rather normal flirtations of our patients with the opposite sex as a sufficient reason for cancelling their parole. In other words if we had put our "eugenical pride" in our pocket we would have had a far greater percentage of successes on parole.

How much weight must be really given to eugenics as a part of the program in the parole of the feeble-minded? Are we yet sufficiently clear in our knowledge of the heredity of mental deficiency to justify a definite stand for or against the inclusion of eugenics in the consideration of this problem? It would seem that our knowledge on this subject is still in a speculative state and therefore difficult of application, except as a secondary consideration, in the face of so many important practical situations which can be met in no other way at present without utilizing community care for the great majority of the higher grade mental defectives who are committed to our institutions.

This study has proved at least to the writers, that good behavior of a mental defective within the institution is no index of a future satisfactory extra-institutional adaptation. In fact no one factor by itself, family, environment, mental age level, or personality make-up is a criterion on which to base a social prognosis. The patient must be considered as a whole after a careful analysis of his own individual assets and liabilities in relation to specific environmental situations.

Meanwhile the fact remains that extra-institutional adaptation of the mental defect is the contemporary and imperative challenge to social psychiatry.

DISCUSSION

DR. WALLACE: "We cannot listen to this admirable paper of Dr. Potter's without it making us at least very thoughtful. At Wrentham since 1914 we have been experimenting with the parole problem. We sometimes think we are successful and sometimes that we are failures. We sometimes know we are failures with individual problems on parole. We sometimes wonder whether the whole problem of parole is a success or a failure. Dr. Potter has very clearly outlined the basic fundamental principles entering into our parole problem, and after listening to him it makes us a little more doubtful than ever. Dr. Potter's failures have been larger than ours. I wonder, however, whether he has not considered some things failures that we have considered successes. For instance, we have not always considered it a failure when a girl that has been out on parole has married someone of her own social status, or even sometimes as they do, of a higher social status. We have really been optimistic enough to consider that—I do not like to say it—a success, and the reason we have considered it a success is because after all this whole social problem that we are dealing with, is simply a comparative problem. If we realize mental deficiency basically is a condition rather than a disease, we know very well that they will measure up intellectually, socially and practically in the things that they can do, that perhaps an eighth of the population can do, in the district from whence they came. After all it makes us wonder whether those are not special problems that have been consigned to our care and whether we are not to some extent shifting responsibility because we all know very well that no feeble-minded person should be granted parenthood, from the heredity side that has been so stressed, but that is all important—we cannot get away from it.

"It makes me believe that we have these last few years been a little too pleased to find an easy way out from our responsibilities. Now I am an optimist in regard to parole. We were amongst the first to start it. We were forced into it, but after all, are we emphasizing enough the need of institutional care and institutional provision for the feeble-minded? It seems to me that there has been a great let down these last five years since we have been exploiting—and I say exploiting—I have done my share of it, the idea of this community care. We are over-stretching it, it is becoming general talk, and we are defeating the very thing we are trying to do. We need to get back and talk a little more heredity—talk a little more about the prevention of that class having children.

"I just want to leave one other thought. That the community idea should be more properly directed. Dr. Potter says that you do not know after your children come to the institution, and you have no criterion, as to whether they are going to be fit subjects for parole. We do, but it takes us too long. We do it empirically. We have to study these boys and girls for years."

DR. LITTLE: "Regarding sterilization, these girls who have gone out from our institution and have come back as failures would have been successes if they had been sterilized. A girl has not any chance anyway; when she goes out on parole she goes into a home to be sure but when she is through her work is through. She may possibly be allowed to sit around with the family and possibly not. She may possibly be taken to the movies once a week; she may go to church with some of the family on Sunday, but she has many hours in which there is nothing to do. She is not particularly interested in reading and what chance has a girl? The iceman comes along and talks to her the first time, the second time, but the third time he says come out tonight and go for a little walk, and it would be the end of any normal person to be out in the same position. They are successes—they have good personalities, but from our standard and the standards of the social workers they are failures. They cannot go out year after year and keep absolutely straight."

SECTION EIGHT

The
Impact
of Genetics

Concern with the moral imbecile, introduced by Kerlin, was revived by Fernald, Goddard, Barr, and others in the early 1900's even though it is clear that less than five per cent of the retarded persons living in institutions could be so classified. The atavistic theories of Lombroso (1911) were generally accepted. Criminals were born to be criminals and can be identified by "stigmata of degeneracy." The prevailing opinion included the acceptance of a close relationship between mental retardation and delinquency, and a genetic basis for the two conditions. Alcoholism, tuberculosis, paralysis, prostitution, and crime were felt to have their roots in mental deficiency. Popular concern about the social menace of the mentally retarded was marshaled by Goddard's "Kallikak Family." Caught up in this scare, Fernald wrote in the Journal of Psycho-Asthenics (1913, volume 70):

> "The feebleminded are a parasitic predatory class never capable of self-support or of managing their own affairs. They cause unutterable sorrow at home and are a menace and danger to the community. Feeble-minded women are almost invariably immoral and if at large usually become carriers of veneral [*sic*] disease or give birth to children who are as defective as themselves. . . . Every feebleminded person, especially the high grade, is a potential criminal needing only the proper environment and opportunity for the development and expression of his criminal tendencies."

Flame was added to the fire by a re-publication of the Jukes study by Arthur H. Estabrook in 1915. While Dugdale had reported only one case of idiocy and had attributed the generations of criminal behavior to bad environmental factors, Estabrook re-analyzed the Dugdale data and concluded that one half of the Jukes were feeble-minded and all of the Jukes criminals were feeble-minded. As Royfe (1971) pointed out: "Thus, what was regarded in

1877 as primarily a problem in criminal degeneracy, became in 1915, mainly a problem of mental deficiency" (p. 206).

The eugenic alarm was at high pitch. The reaction of civilized society, threatened by the intrusion of virulent genetically defective strains, was hostile and repressive: larger institutions to corral the offending classes for life-long periods of care; restrictive immigration laws to bar offensive foreign hordes of inferior stock from American shores; and sterilization laws to curtail further procreation of the socially and mentally unfit. Davies (1930) reports that the number of mentally retarded persons within institutions increased from 14,000 in 1910 to close to 43,000 in 1923.

The intensity of the feeling against the mentally retarded can be judged from the paper by Rev. Karl Schwartz, a prominent church rector in Syracuse, New York:

"The author holds that it is not a pessimistic view of life to wish to see a man get out of the world, who is not fit for it, and who has little or no chance of ever becoming so. To one who anticipates the general upward trend of human life, it is evident that the occasional removal by society of an individual, or even of many individuals, may be necessary to the welfare of the social group" (p. 74).

Indiana passed the first sterilization law in 1907. By the time of Haskell's review of a hundred-year history of mental deficiency (1944), the law had been upheld by the United States Supreme Court, some thirty states permitted the operation, and wide scale eugenic sterilizations were performed in California.

Even during the height of the eugenic scare, a few stalwart souls attempted to apply some reason to the problem. Fernald's 1909 paper acknowledges that genetic tendencies toward moral imbecility may be modified by suitable environment and training (p. 19). Goddard, in the ensuing discussion, attacks the notion that immoral behavior can be inherited, classifying it as "belonging to the middle ages of sociology and ethics" (p. 37).

Fifteen years later (Fernald, 1924), Fernald was willing to admit the exaggeration of previous judgments of the extent of the influence of heredity upon mental deficiency. Studies at the Wrentham State School (Myerson, 1926) and at Letchworth Village (Potter, 1922), showing that more than half their residents had parents who were not mentally deficient, put the finishing touch upon the eugenic alarm. Clinical studies demonstrated the significance of other sources of mental retardation such as infection, trauma, and endocrine disturbances. Wallin's scholarly review of the literature (1956) debunked as artifacts of poor experimental design the presumed association between crime and mental retardation, and the "fecundity" of the mentally retarded population. Although Whitney was calling for sterilization laws in Pennsylvania as late as the 1930's, the issue of sterilization for *eugenic* purposes had lost its impact.

NATURE'S CORRECTIVE PRINCIPLE IN SOCIAL EVOLUTION

Rev. Karl Schwartz

Nature's principle of "survival of the fittest" is interpreted by this writer to mean rejection of the unfit, the incompetent, and the nonproductive who represent a "drag upon humanity's progress." Legal restrictions on marriage, asexualization, and segregation are methods considered as ethical mandates to aid nature in her process of elimination. This paper is of interest for what is implied but left unsaid.

In presenting this thesis, the author realizes that he will be exposed to the criticism of those whose philanthropic natures find expression in the formation of societies and institutions for the excavation of the "submerged tenth." To these so called philanthropists there is but one law—the law of love. They profess to believe that all men are equally worthy of survival; and that those who, unassisted, are 'unable to survive should be made special objects of fostering care, even though they be attached as a drag to the car of human progress. The author holds that it is not a pessimistic view of life to wish to see a man get out of the world, who is not fit for it, and who has little or no chance of ever becoming so. To one who anticipates the general upward trend of human life, it is evident that the occasional removal by society of an individual, or even of many individuals, may be necessary to the welfare of the social group.

Much has been said and written concerning the hypothesis of natural selection; how the keenest, the fleetest, the most cunning, choosing others of their kind and quality, beget offspring that are yet more keen, more fleet, more cunning. This hypothesis has, by common consent been applied to the human race, and men, seeing the inevitable fate awaiting those individuals that are not chosen, are busy with their philanthropies and their societies and organizations for social betterment, trying to prepare the inferior members of the human race, those who stand far below the average of their fellows in morals, in intelligence, and in physical endurance, for entrance into the class where they may acquire or develop powers which may enable them to survive in the struggle for existence. There is another class, a class that seems to be below the reach of any social uplift, a class of individuals whose lack of endurance—the result of crime, dissipation, or inheritance—entirely unfits them for the race with the strong. What becomes of the individuals of this class? Are they permitted to remain a drag upon humanity's progress? To maintain an idle, inefficient, and vicious class would sap the strength of the strong. Does nature fold her hands and permit this economic waste to go on? But far more important than a consideration of any economic question is the question of whether or not nature permits the continued existence of this class, being, as such a class must always be, a standing menace to the race, making possible the transmission, through the individuals of this class, to unborn generations, habits of viciousness, immorality, and incompetence.

It seems evident to the observing mind that the old dictum, "All men are born and created free and equal," admits only of an academic interpretation,

Journal of Psycho-Asthenics, 1908, 13:74–90.

Rev. Schwartz was rector of the Church of the Savior, Syracuse, New York, and was nationally known as an author, inventor, sportsman, and preacher. He was author of several books including *Inherited Criminal Tendencies and How Nature Deals with Them*, which was also the subject of his doctoral dissertation.

and it is one of the purposes comprehended within the limits of this thesis, to prove that, considering the widely differing degrees of ability possessed by different individuals to apply themselves to any remunerative work, any mental employment or any moral development, we may say, without much fear or hesitation, that there is very little freedom in the world and nothing like equality in the gifts which nature bestows; that every child is born with mental, physical, moral, and temperamental qualities for which he is not wholly responsible, and which fix, most rigorously, the range of his possible achievement.

The nature and the quality and the length of a human life appear to depend very largely upon heredity. So plainly may heredity be proven to be a determining factor in the general estimation of a child's possibilities, that the direct effects of pre-natal influences are looked for and expected with the confidence of a settled and incontrovertible law; honesty and virtue and health are expected in the offspring of honest and virtuous and healthy parents; dishonesty, lack of virtue, and disease are likewise expected in the offspring of dishonest and dissolute parents. This expectation is so generally fulfilled that when the contrary condition pertains it is cause for much surprise. But this is not all; there is yet a higher law, the resultant of an external force which is forever interfering with this known and acknowledged law of heredity, and which regulates production and determines multiplication. It is the power which nature gives to all organisms by which those organisms become capable of ejecting waste and harmful material, applied and made effective in the social composition.

Abnormal individuals are not only valueless but are generally harmful to society; for, beside being nonproducers, they absorb the energies and the productive power of others. Hence, in the development of a people it becomes necessary that the lifetime of these abnormal individuals should be shortened. But, though death may be shown to be a beneficial occurrence, yet we do not attempt to account for it on grounds of utility. There is a law higher than this and more general; it is the law of the "survival of the fittest." But while in the field of biology the law of the survival of the fittest appears to be broad enough to include all organic evolution, yet in the consideration of the question of social evolution where the psychic phenomenon of conscious choice makes itself felt as an ever varying factor, indeed a factor of such varying value as to render it impossible to lay down this law as universally binding, we may consider independently and without unjustified encroachment upon the field already occupied by biology, this particular phase of the law of the survival of the fittest which we shall call the rejection of the unfit.

That crime breeds disease and that disease brings death is one of the most hopeful signs for human development. It is the disease that proves fatal that becomes the greatest agency in the maintenance and the progression of the race. To the elimination of the weak and the unfit, much of the physical and moral strength of the race is due. To increase the speed and the efficiency of a train of cars it is as necessary to let off the brakes as to open the throttle. To make satisfactory social progress it is no less necessary to relieve society of its drag than it is to give it added impetus. If this is not possible then it is of no use to apply added power. How is this drag removed? How is society relieved from its burden of crimes and entailed disease which like a dead weight would retard and even prevent its progress and development? This is the problem stated in terms of social dynamics.

It may be shown that as human society develops, nature assists in that development; that the ability to survive comes as much by subtraction as by addition; that progress is made by elimination quite as much as by preservation; that human development comes by the rejection of the weak and the unfit, and thus through the survival only of the strong, in spite of human processes and philanthropies which tend to the equalization of human powers and the reduction of mental and physical grades to a common level. It may be shown that a correct answer to the question as to how and by what process the human race may be empowered to advance would be by the utility of death—the death of the unfit.

SYNCHRONISM OF CRIME AND DISEASE

Is there a close analogy between an abnormal and defective mind and an abnormal and defective body? Does the one necessarily induce the other? If so, then nature will work out this problem of itself and according to her own methods. To answer these questions we must ascertain how physical maladies originate and how they are more general and more destructive in the cases of degenerates, than in the cases of persons possessing a normal morality. The physician whose patients are those afflicted with nervous and mental maladies, discovers two phases of degeneration and neurasthenia. These two conditions or phases of disease frequently occur in the same patient. It is often easier and more effective to treat these two phases of abnormality in the patient as one condition expressing itself in two ways, than to treat each separately.

Morel[1] gives us his definition of degeneracy which, it will be observed, is also a partial definition of neurasthenia. "The best idea we can form of degeneracy is to classify it as a morbid deviation from a normal type. This

---

[1] Traite des degenerescences physiques, intellectuelles et Morales de l'espece humaine et des causes qui produisent ces varietes maladives, p. 5.

deviation, though in the beginning it is trifling, possesses transmissible qualities of such a nature that the one bearing them gradually becomes incapable of fulfilling the natural functions of life."

Degeneracy expresses itself in the human race in certain marked physical characteristics which are denominated "stigmata." These stigmata consist of malformations indicating arrested or abnormal development of certain organs of the human body.

Lombroso[2] gives us a partial list of the anatomical abnormalities of degeneracy such as irregularities of the teeth in form and position; hare-lips; enormous ears; squint eyes; the unequal development of the two sides of the face; and while all these physical irregularities of the degenerate are of interest to us as indicating a necessary connection between the abnormal mind and the abnormal body, yet it is to be especially noticed that Lombroso, in the work from which we just quoted (p. 147) as does also Dr. Ch. Fere[3] calls particular attention to the significant fact that one of the anatomical stigmata most frequent in degenerates is an unequal development of the two sides of the cranium. This fact, above all others, would indicate the unbalanced mental condition and the anatomical abnormalities of the individual as synchronistic and this synchronism to be the necessary consequent of the practice of crime either in the individual or his forbears since both are the acknowledged result of the same or similar causes.

Science has also discovered that with these anatomical stigmata there is a concurrence of others of a mental order no less manifest and not less related to the practice of crime.[4] The anatomical peculiarities of the degenerate find their counterpart in the mental peculiarities of the same individual. The asymmetry of the cranium is matched by the abnormal mental faculties; there is an absence of a sense of morality and a lack of a proper appreciation of the rights or the persons of other individuals. Another expression of degeneracy of mind is a marked slowing of vital activities together with a lessened power to resist noxious influences. There is an increasing tendency of the whole organism toward physical and psychical infirmity. G. Nacke is authority for the statement[5] that degeneration may readily pass over into actual disease; in fact, disease and weakness appear with remarkable frequency in the persons whom we call degenerates. Under similar circumstances one man will contract a fatal disease while another will not. This susceptibility to disease is ascribed to an absence of resisting powers which absence indicates an imperfect physical organism. Such is the physical condition of a

---

[2] L'uomo delinguente in rapporto all'Anthropologia, Giurisprudenza e alle Discipline carcerarie, 3rd edition, p. 147.

[3] La Famille nevropathique, p. 176 et seq.

[4] Compare Nordau, Degeneration, p. 17.

[5] Quoted in American Journal of Sociology, Vol. V, No. 1, p. 128.

greater number of degenerates—abnormal in body as in mind—they become easy victims of disease and death. Dr. Bruce Thompson, whose eighteen years of experience as surgeon of the general prison of Scotland would entitle any statement that he might make upon the co-existence of tendencies to crime and to disease in the same individual to receive much consideration, has declared[6] that he had never witnessed in any post-mortem which he had attended upon the body of any non-criminal, such an accumulation of morbid appearances as he witnessed upon the post-mortem examinations of the prisoners that died in the institution of which he was surgeon. Scarcely one of them, as he goes on to tell us, could be said to have died of one malady for almost every organ of the body he found to be more or less diseased. He declared that their physical frames seemed about on a par with their moral natures. Out of fifty autopsies on the bodies of degenerates, Flesch[7] found the liver normal in six cases only. McKim[8] declares that as a rule criminals are physically defective. Dugdale[9] puts himself on record as a believer in the close relation between the abnormal, or diseased mind and the abnormal, or diseased body, when he says: "It has been said that whatever is physiologically right is morally right; and we have a confirmation of that saying by its acknowledged converse that whatever is physiologically unsound is morally rotten." Lincoln[10] declares that crime, insanity, idiocy, epilepsy, and hysteria are close kindred. The relation between crime and disease is by no means a recent discovery. It has been a recognized fact for centuries. Herodotus, born 484, B. C., tells of the Persian king Cambyses who was afflicted with epilepsy and who was outrageously cruel as was shown by his murder of his own brother and wife. Associating the crime with the disease, Herodotus declared[11] it was not surprising that with so diseased a body his mind should not be sound.

In the preceding discussion one principle has been involved. It is the principle that immoral and defective mental phenomena and abnormal and diseased physical organisms are generally either synchronous, or else bear to each other in the same organism the relation of cause and effect. It is not necessary that we should undertake to ascertain which is the cause and which the effect; it is sufficient for our purpose if we have proved that the manifestation of a phenomenon in one field involves and warrants us to look for some expression of it in the other. If we have proved this parallelism then we are able to classify, under the same heads, the phenomena of the two

---

[6] Hereditary Nature of Crime, in Journal of Mental Science, Vol. XV, p. 487.
[7] See McDonald, Criminology, p. 68.
[8] Heredity and Human Progress, p. 159.
[9] The Jukes, p. 87.
[10] Sanity of Mind, p. 32.
[11] Herodotus Bk. III, p. 33: Teubner, Leipsic, 1894.

fields. An abnormal moral condition must correspond to, and be in a sense an expression of an abnormal physical condition. So, too, for each physical abnormality there is likely to be some corresponding mental condition. Morel[12] admits that causes influencing health produce deviations from the normal characteristics to the extent that they become types capable of indefinite transmission until sterility and extinction follow. Criminals form a distinct variety of the human family. A degenerate character expresses itself in a low type of physique. A comparison of the juvenile criminals in houses of correction and reformatories, with the children of the public schools, shows the comparatively low physical condition of the former.[13] They are sickly, scrofulous, and with malformation of the cranium; they are sluggish, stupid, and defective in vital energy. They are usually repulsive in appearance and are afflicted with unhealthy bodies. They are especially subject to tubercular diseases and to derangement of the nervous system.

In a vast majority of the cases they are the victims of an inherited tendency to commit crime as well as an inherited tendency to disease, which would prove our hypothesis of a close relation between crime and bodily defect.

That children resemble their parents is a matter of common observation. It is also a matter of common observation that while the child may favor either parent, yet it is most likely that the characteristics of both parents are combined in the offspring. But while heredity may include the family resemblances in color of skin, eyes, hair, in stature and physique, it also extends far beyond these physical likenesses. It includes the size and shape of the head, the condition of the nerves and digestive organs, the richness or poverty of the blood, as also the diseases which we call constitutional. In this category longevity and shortness of life must be included; medical science, to-day, justifies the witty aphorism of Dr. Holmes that the proper time to begin the treatment of some diseases is a hundred years before birth. It was Heine who wisely remarked that a man ought to be very careful in the selection of his parents.

With these physical peculiarities and defects, heredity is deeply concerned. This similarity seldom ends with physical resemblance, since modern science has established, without a doubt, the transmission by heredity of mental and moral qualities. This phase of heredity is difficult to prove. This hypothesis has encountered most hostile prejudice and its battles are by no means all won. The line of demarkation between physical and moral characteristics is one exceedingly difficult to draw; and although science has not yet succeeded in assigning mental phenomena to physical causes, yet it has done much in

[12] Traite des Degenerescences Physiques, p. 3.
[13] E. S. Talbot, Degeneracy, Its Causes, Signs and Results, p. 18.

this direction and our knowledge is widening with our experience. One might prove examples of an hereditary tendency to crime, and to attendant physical weakness, from the pages of history. The vices, the avarice, the insolence, the physical weakness of royal families, descending from father to son through many generations, is a fact of history. The same might be said of many conspicuous families.

HEREDITY AND ENVIRONMENT

We are not altogether wise in our generation, for we go on multiplying agencies and institutions for social betterment seemingly attributing the results of vicious character in individuals solely to the causes of environment, apparently working on the theory that the only agency needed for social uplift of the degenerate individual is a change of surroundings and associations. And while these agencies in the formation of character are powerful, yet we must not lose sight of the fact that there is an influence deeper than environment, and that the kind of child or man which is to meet and to be moulded by environment, has been inexorably determined by the character of his forbears.

The writer during a residence in New York City took occasion to study the inmates of police courts and the Tombs. Of the 200 prisoners that came directly under his observation, seventy per cent. of them were found to be descended from dissolute or criminal parents. Their appearance confirmed their statements of an inherited mental, moral, and physical underdevelopment. Their bodies, their mental capacity, and their moral turpitude bore evidence of an inheritance from a degenerate ancestor or ancestors; and that their unsocial and vicious natures as well as their pinched brains and diseased bodies were defects for which they could not be held altogether responsible.

A consideration of the element of heredity must of necessity include the vice of intemperance. While intemperance itself may not be transmissible, yet is is impossible not to see that the physical condition that makes intemperance easy, and, if circumstances favor almost inevitable, is transmitted from parent to offspring. And while there is an insistent tendency to transmit like habits and identical vices from parent to offspring, yet the vice of intemperance is likely to express itself in the impaired health, morals, and intelligence of the progeny of its votaries. The children of intemperate parents are likely to come into the world without having either the moral or physical strength to struggle against their temptations. They are victims of tyranny—the tyranny of weakened constitutions. So early was the law of hereditary intemperance understood and so fully were the baneful influences of the dissipation of parents upon unborn children appreciated, that the ancient Carthaginians

promulgated a law forbidding all drinks but water on days of marital intercourse.[14]

We are compelled to face the awful law that vice and crime, with all their
attendant consequences of disease and incompetency, are hereditary; that
every parent who disregards morality and temperance is helping to form the
vicious characters and the impaired constitutions of his unfortunate children;
that the excesses of one generation are likely to be the curses of the next
generation, that streams of tendency, hot with passion and lust and lurid with
disease, flow from generation to generation; and that every individual is, in a
marked degree, a product of the past.

The degenerate is no rival for the healthy normal man, with his good
judgment, his strong will, and his logical thought. The moral and physical
weakling, degenerated by vice and weakened by disease, both inherited and
acquired, is driven from the good things of the earth and consigned, with
contemptuous pity, to the slums, the hospitals, the asylums and the prisons.
Nature is aided in her task of eliminating the unfit by the men with clear
heads, hearty stomachs and hard muscles. An age-long contest for food and
honor has trained selected men against whom the degenerate can not compete. With arrested development, with great susceptibility to disease, with a
sub-normal nervous system, millions of these degenerates perish in infancy, or
at the first stress of life. The tendency of the unfit is toward extinction. The
law of the rejection of the unfit is nature's protest against many of our
philanthropies which are being misguided and misruled by the too generous
impulses of human nature. The reaction from those old social distinctions
which were once so fundamental and were the result of social gradations
made by unnatural social forces, has carried us quite as far in another
direction. Elated by our success in overthrowing those artificial and unnatural
grades we have disregarded the fundamental and natural grades. The hypothesis that individuals are virtually equal or ever can become equal in terms
of social value, leads to the most monumental follies. It has created an
hysterical philanthropy that would rob the honest citizen of his rights of
protection and security to bestow upon those who are unworthy of freedom
and are dangerous to the welfare of society, an unmerited paternalism that
would prolong their days and augment their vitality and thus increase their
possibilities for social detriment and expose society to dangers from which
nature, if unopposed, would effect a permanent relief.

It is no true wisdom that would influence society to perpetuate and to
vitalize forces that are detrimental to it. It is no true philanthropy that would

---

[14] Gustafson, The Foundation of Death, p. 171: Heath and Co., Boston, 5th edition.

foster and vitalize individuals whose very presence in a community is a standing menace to that community; neither is it charitable to the individual whom nature has marked as unworthy of survival to prolong his days and to increase the radius of his polluting influence.

A misguided philanthropy is persuading us to expend vast sums of money that have been earned by the capable and worthy in the care and perpetuation of those classes which neither our reason nor our judgment would pronounce to be fitted to survive. We are directing our philanthropies towards a perpetuation of the unfit and the multiplication of their numbers. We train a portion of the feeble-minded to become able to marry and to beget their kind, and permit them to do so. We open our asylum doors and release every year twenty thousand persons who have been committed for insanity and permit them to contract marriage. We maintain free dispensaries, conveniently located, where little or no effort is made to discriminate between those who need medical attention because of misfortune and those who desire it because of a weakened physical condition through degeneracy and dissipation—all are treated alike and at the expense of industry and thrift. We take the inebriate out of the gutter where he belongs by his own choice, doctor him up until he is able to procreate his kind, and then send him back to his wife and family. We care for the pauper through the winter and allow him to run at large for the rest of the year. We employ an indiscriminate out-of-doors charity that keeps the lazy, shiftless, intemperate, and diseased husband and wife together that the class to which they have willingly assigned themselves may not become extinct. We hedge the degenerate around by all kinds of legal devices to preserve for him a freedom which is dangerous and harmful. The element of protection that enters into the conduct of the court when passing sentence upon the criminal degenerate effects a protection that is immediate only and not prospective since it does not primarily provide against the perpetuation of the criminal degenerate in the persons of a progeny with like inclinations. If a criminal degenerate is brought before the bar of justice in any civilized land, to-day, these considerations enter into and chiefly affect the sentence of the court: First, what sort of punishment and of how long duration will be commensurate with the crime; second, what should be the nature of the punishment that it may in some degree work a reclamation—seeking chiefly to prepare the criminal degenerate for as speedy a return to liberty as the nature of the crime and the dignity of the law will permit, overlooking the fact that with that liberty goes also the possibility of procreating children with like tendencies. Nor is this all, for a maudlin sentimentality often leads honest and healthy people to marry with these social and moral outcasts. Women often marry those whom they know to be moral lepers for the purpose, as they declare, of "reforming them."

LEGAL RESTRICTIONS ON MARRIAGE

An examination of the laws of 1906 in reference to the causes for which marriage is prohibited, void, voidable, and criminal, shows that of the fifty-three states and territories, forty-five, representing a population of 66,554,359 (census 1900), or nearly eighty-seven per cent. of the entire population of the United States, have placed no restrictions on marriage for the cause of insanity or degeneracy in any of its forms; that in forty-two states and territories, representing a population of 62,688,641, or over eight-two per cent. of the entire population of the United States, a marriage is not legally void by reason of one or both parties being degenerate or insane; that in thirty states and territories, representing a population of 46,960,996, or sixty-four per cent. of the entire population, a marriage is not rendered legally voidable by reason of one or both parties being adjudged degenerate or insane; and that in forty-nine states and territories, representing a population of 69,338,922, or nearly ninety per cent. of the population, a marriage is not considered criminal even when it unites individuals one or both of whom are adjudged degenerate or insane.

It is plain that society's attitude toward the degenerate must be changed. An effort should be made towards a systematic education of the social mind and a systematic training of public sentiment until society shall fully comprehend the danger to which it is exposed through many of its present methods of dealing with the degenerate class. Having fully appreciated its danger, society would then surely turn towards the erection of suitable safeguards by which it would be enabled to protect itself. The voice of the people would demand the enactment of laws providing for permanent public or private custody of all degenerates. This would be followed by legal enactment making it mandatory to commit by indeterminate or life sentences, to institutions provided for the purpose, all degenerates coming within the cognizance of the legal authorities of communities. It seems evident that any community or nation might be vastly improved if, instead of bending its energies to defeat nature, it would direct those energies toward assisting nature in her positive working toward social evolution. The civilization of the twentieth century should face these problems of degeneracy with a definite and fixed purpose to aid nature in her efforts for their removal. Christian ethics teach us to regard these unfortunates as our wards. Social science teaches us to regard them as unfit and with no rational basis for a claim to the rights of liberty. What general course shall be adopted for their disposal? It is hardly necessary to discuss the attempts that have been made for the improvement of the degenerate farther than to state that an increasing experience is proving that the best planned and most scientifically conducted experiments have failed utterly to restore defectives to a normal condition.

To attempt to train them to a point where they may be self-supporting and then to release them from institutions of detention is to permit them to propagate and perpetuate their kind, and thus to multiply the evils of our social structure. A growing sentiment among students of the problems of degeneracy is declaring itself in a demand for the asexualization of the members of the degenerate class. This is certainly a radical measure but serves to show the growing appreciation of the ghastly evils which the misinterpretation of the laws of ethics has assisted to grow up in our midst. (The asexualization of degenerates is provided for by law in the state of Indiana.)

With regard to the essentially unimprovable character of the degenerate, the community at large is but poorly instructed. Public sentiment is continually declaring itself for a better training of the degenerate, and for an improved environment in institutions provided and maintained by the state. All this is wise, charitable, and just. But public sentiment must be taught more seriously to comprehend the awful consequences of permitting a consummation of the marriage contract among the members of this submerged class. It is plainly the duty of society, if it would protect itself, to assert its right to prevent the degenerate from reproducing himself. Society should understand that the law of heredity is immutable in its operation; that the character of the child that is begotten of degenerate parents is fixed by the character of its forbears. It is plain that society's remedy for degeneracy is society's control of the source of degeneracy. There are two ways by which this control could be made effective and at the same time kept entirely within the strict interpretations of the laws of Christian ethics. First, it is possible to establish a better and a broader system of instruction among the younger generations concerning the hereditary transmission of traits and peculiarities. The youth of this and succeeding generations might wisely be taught that marriage entered into by individuals who are imbecile or epileptic, or the weak consumers of nervines and stimulants or opium or intoxicants, or by individuals whose lives show erratic tendencies and peculiarities, become a standing menace to the social interests of future generations. It is the first duty of the state to teach the youth of the public schools that a marriage between those who are unfit is not to secure happiness but untold misery for themselves and for those to whom in after years they may bear the relation of parents. The young man should be brought to understand that the silly, neurasthenic, untruthful girl will make both an irresponsible wife and will bear him a progeny of like-minded children. The young woman should be taught that there is but little hope that her lawless, thriftless, drinking lover will reform himself after marriage, because these habits, which possibly she may admire, are but the outward expressions of innate vice.

But what is the plain duty of the state towards the degenerate or the insane person who, surrendered by the parents or guardians or committed by a sentence of the court, comes under the state's custodial care? In the treatment of these cases there is one fact that should be considered seriously by all legislators, social workers, and moral reformers and it is this: that any treatment of the degenerate that has for its primary object the reconciliation of the degenerate to society and the consequent extending of the radius of freedom, is a course of action that if effected will, in almost every instance, insure the infusion of an element into the population that will not be conducive to social prosperity, honesty, safety, or intelligence. It is plain, therefore, that society should be protected from such harmful influence.

"An ounce of prevention is worth a pound of cure." A very large part of the wretchedness, of the effects of crime that we see about us is avertable by a wise and proper control of the source of degeneracy. With reference to the wide-spread army of degenerates, a fraction only of whom are regarded by the state as her wards, and which is annually adding to the general plethora of degeneracy, it is plain that public morals, the protection of future generations, and the prevention of the inheritance of degeneracy demand a permanent segregation of the entire list of degenerates, and especially would it be wise for the state to assume a guardianship over every degenerate or feeble-minded girl or woman of child-bearing age.

CONTROL OF THE SOURCES OF DEGENERACY

Legislation during the year of 1907 in the states of New York, Pennsylvania, and Indiana, in regard to the treatment of the criminal degenerate, indicates the beginning of an awakening of legislators to the necessity of the proper control of the sources of degeneracy. Section 688-a of the New York penal code makes it obligatory upon the presiding judge to impose a life sentence upon the individual who has been four times convicted of felony. The penal code of Pennsylvania makes the third conviction sufficient for life imprisonment. An act of the Indiana legislature (H. C. Sharp, M. D., The Sterilization of Degenerates, Jeffersonville, Ind.) makes it obligatory upon the institutional physicians to perform such operation as will prevent procreation, upon such individuals coming under the care of the state institutions as shall be adjudged undesirable procreators.

The writer recently addressed to the secretary of the state boards of charities or kindred departments of all the states and territories of the United States, the following communication:

"Will you kindly inform me whether or not you consider advisable any legislation that may have for its object the prevention of the degenerate from becoming a parent; and if so, will you please state what method (whether permanent custodial care or asexualization) is in your judgment best for that end, taking into consideration the rights of all parties concerned—society, the degenerate, and the unborn child? Please state whether or not your commonwealth has taken any legislative action upon this matter."

In reply to this request forty-one carefully prepared answers were received, thirty-four of which advise permanent custodial care, and seven, asexualization. What would be the effect upon the general morals of the people of this country if we were to remove the degenerate from society, deprive him of liberty and house him in some institution where he could do no harm? The effect could only be salutary. The degenerate contributes nothing that is beneficial to the public morality, while on the contrary he tends by direct act, by example and by bequeathment to lower the standard of public morals more nearly to his own level. As the segregation of the degenerate would effect an advance in the moral standards of society, so would it result in a distinct elevation of our code of ethics since we would then learn to interpret it in terms not of individual but of social freedom. Ethics are rightly applied only when the social interest is made paramount. To deal with the unfit by methods that may aid nature in her task of elimination is not opposed to the highest code of ethical law. Indeed, the best interpretation of Christian ethics already recognizes the absolute necessity of such action in some extreme cases of degeneracy. Commitment for long periods, indeterminate sentences, life imprisonment in penal institutions, even death by hanging or electrocution are legal requirements which are clearly recognized as necessary measures for the protection of human society in all lands and among all people where Christian ethics form the very basis of all law.

It would be a distinct improvement of our present method of interpretation and application of ethical law if we were to direct our philanthropies towards the moral and physical uplift of society in such a way as would assist nature in her effort to remove the unfit, even though that assistance should compel a restriction of liberty for that class whose liberty can result only in a prolongation of the process of social evolution, and whose fostering by a misdirected charity and a misguided philanthropy, is removing the social millennium farther and farther into the future.

The segregation of the degenerate would also be a means of preventing a great economic waste. The degenerate, when permitted his liberty, becomes an enormously expensive individual. The greater part of the expense for the maintenance of our criminal courts, our city police, our prisons and penitentiaries is directly chargeable to the degenerate. And while we shall never be able to express in figures this enormous cost, yet we do know that in our country alone several hundred millions of dollars are annually diverted from the proceeds of economy, thrift and industry for the maintenance and control of this class. Mr. Eugene Smith (Proceedings of National Prison Association, 1900, House document No. 491, 56th congress, 2d session) estimates that there are 250,000 persons in the United States who make their living, at least in some degree, by the practice of crime and begging. Their annual income, he estimates, averages about $1,600 each, or $400,000,000. Taxation caused by crime in the United States may be safely estimated at $200,000,000 besides the expenses for steel safes, safe deposit values, burglar alarms, etc. It is safe to say that the criminal element alone costs the people of the United States $600,000,000 annually; add to this the 3,000,000 abnormal dependents in the United States at an annual expense of $200,000,000 (Compare Special Reports of the Census Office, 1900) and we have the conservative estimate of an annual cost to the nation for the maintenance of the degenerate element, of $800,000,000. This is more than one-third of the total wage income of all the manufacturing establishments in the land (Compare 12th census report, U. S., parts III and IV). Massachusetts pays for her charities and corrections the sum of $23.59 annually for every family in the state. For Connecticut the expense is $28.00 per family. For New York it is $18.00 per family—$4,000,000 greater than that of all the city schools of the state. In Pennsylvania the capital involved is more than $500,000,000 or more than half the value of all the farming property of the state, one-third of all the manufacturing capital and fifteen times the value of the public property invested in the public schools. The degenerate is an expensive individual.

There is a further reason why the segregation of the degenerate would be the shutting off of a great economic waste. In most cases of sequestration the degenerate may be trained to become in part self-supporting. This is true even of the epileptics and the feeble-minded. Dr. T. C. Fitzsimmons, a member of the Pennsylvania State Commission for Epileptics and Feeble-minded, in a report says that while he fully realizes that few, if any, of the epileptics and feeble-minded can ever be cured, yet he believes that their condition may be greatly improved by a life confinement in institutions where they may be trained to become largely self-supporting.

An objection might very naturally be raised to the incurrence of an additional expense for the first cost of the necessary farm land and institutional buildings for the proper housing of the committed individuals of this class; but for the greater good and with the purpose of eventually, through industrial training of the inmates so that they may become self-supporting, removing the entire burden for maintenance which now lies so heavily upon society, this temporary tax-rate might well be endured.

With these facts before us, it is difficult to see why our moralists, our ethicists and our economists do not unite in insisting upon a plan of treatment of all the degenerates who come within the cognizance of our legal and medical authorities, that shall conserve the best and highest interests of society and at the same time co-operate with nature in a speedy, effective, and painless removal of that class of individuals which public morality, Christian ethics, economics, and nature as well, have marked as unfit to survive.

But the elimination of the unfit is not the work of a man, or of men; it is a world's work. It is not the work of a generation or an age; it is a work of time.

THE
IMBECILE WITH
CRIMINAL
INSTINCTS

Walter E. Fernald

Fernald uses the term imbecile to refer to mild forms of mental retardation. He generalizes about their moral insensibilities and believes all imbeciles to be potential criminals. However, these tendencies may be "suppressed" by suitable environmental conditions. He seems to embrace the concept of moral imbecility but believes such persons are cases of "true imbecility" with intellectual impairment as well as moral degeneracy.

In this paper,* I shall briefly consider the class of imbeciles who as a part of their life history present certain persistent tendencies or repeated acts of a criminal nature. I use the term "imbecile" advisedly as an adequate synonym for the many different expressions used to describe various degrees of lesser mental defect, resulting from causes operating before birth or in early childhood, as contrasted with mental impairment or disease developed later in the life of the individual, like dementia praecox, epilepsy, etc. Cases of actual idiocy are also excluded from this discussion.

The term imbecility was formerly applied only to a class of persons presenting simple, obvious intellectual shortcomings. The field of mental defect has been gradually extended and widened so that the time-honored definitions and classifications have become incomplete and obsolete. To-day institutions for defectives are often expected to receive patients where the intellectual defect is apparently only moderate, and the principal reason for institution treatment is the failure to harmonize with the environment as shown by low tastes and associates. In other cases the prominent symptoms are general incorrigibility, purposeless and needless lying, a quarrelsome disposition, a tendency to petty stealing, a propensity for setting fires, aimless destruction of property, a tendency to run away and lead a life of vagrancy, sexual precocity or perversions—these may be the symptoms which impress the parent or the physician.

The recognition and understanding of these and other less obvious phases of defect are largely due to the correlation of the results of the modern scientific study of normal psychology, pedagogy, degeneracy, criminology and sociology.

A brief review of the ordinary phenomena and symptoms of imbecility is necessary for the proper interpretation of the cases to be described. From a biological standpoint the imbecile is an inferior human being. If the mental defect is due to direct heredity or to developmental abnormalities of the central nervous system having their genesis in the ovule or in foetal life, the various anatomical, physiological and psychical stigmata of degeneracy are usually present. Indeed, in no other class of human beings are these various stigmata found so constantly, so frequently and so well-marked as in the congenital imbecile. If the mental defect is caused by traumatism, or acute local disease, or other causes operating at birth or soon after birth, the physical stigmata of degeneracy are often absent.

---

*Read by title at the sixty-fourth annual meeting of the American Medico-Psychological Association, Cincinnati, Ohio, May 12–15, 1908. Also at the meeting of the association at Chippewa Falls, Wis., June 21, 1909.

Journal of Psycho-Asthenics, 1909, 14(1):16–38.

Some of the physical evidences of mental defect are as follows: abnormalities in the size and shape of the skull and cranium; in the size, shape and weight of the brain; variations in the size, shape and relative position of the ears, abnormalities in the form, situation, and structure of the teeth; protruding lower jaw; congenital deformities of the hard palate; pallor of the skin; scant beard, etc.

Imbeciles of all grades exhibit in varying degrees certain well-marked mental characteristics. In mere memory exercises they may excel. They have weak will-power. The power of judgment is defective and uncertain and often determined by chance ideas, not by the outcome of past experience. They are unable to grasp and utilize the experiences of life.

Pronounced backwardness in ordinary school studies is, of course, a constant feature of the uncomplicated cases. At the end of his school life, at the age of 15 or 16 years, the imbecile may be able to read in the third reader, to do simple addition and subtraction, and easy multiplication. Division is not often achieved.

Imbeciles are childish even in adult life. They make friends quickly and are cheerful and voluble. They are boastful, ungenerous, ungrateful. Notwithstanding their stupidity, they are cunning in attaining their own ends. They seem to have but little sympathy with distress or suffering. They are often cruel, especially to small children or weaker persons. They seem to take special delight in stirring up trouble and are often fond of tale-bearing.

They are vain in dress and love bright and gaudy colors. They like to be well dressed, and are indifferent to cleanliness of body.

In actions and conversation their own personality always comes into prominence. They manifest unbounded egotism, leading to marked selfishness. Their whole life revolves around their own personal well-being and the possession of things desired.

They are prone to lie without reason and often lie unhesitatingly when truth would be to their own interest. They are inclined to steal.

They are morally insensible. As a rule, they are able to carefully differentiate in the abstract between what is right and what is wrong as applied to their personal environment, but in practice their ability to make these distinctions bears no relation to their actions and conduct.

They seldom show embarrassment or shame when detected in wrongdoing. I have never known an imbecile to exhibit traits of remorse. Correction or punishment is of little effect.

They revel in mawkish sentiment. They are susceptible to the emotional phase of religious expression. They are very apt to choose intimate companions very much younger than themselves, or persons very much beneath them socially or below them in the scale of intelligence. They are generally cowardly in the presence of actual physical danger. They are very susceptible to suggestion and are easily led.

They show marked physical insensibility. Galton says, "To the imbecile pain comes as a welcome surprise."

Few imbeciles have been seen to blush. They show an early craving for tobacco and alcohol. They are proverbially lazy and fond of idleness. They seem incapable of forethought.

Imbeciles of both sexes usually show active sexual propensities and perversions at an early age.

There are two traits common to all imbeciles with few exceptions. One is that they will cheerfully risk severe punishment for the sake of some slight gain which appeals to their personal desires. The other is that they seem unable to apply themselves continuously in any one direction. The imbecile often becomes skilled in some one line, perhaps in some branch of a mechanical trade, but unless under the closest supervision, he will not apply himself to the work which he is perfectly capable of doing well.

The above generalizations apply to a very large number of the imbecile class. Many of these symptoms and tendencies may be appreciably modified or suppressed by suitable environment and training. The expression of these tendencies is varied according to sex, age, state of physical vigor, opportunity, etc.

The cases to be reported were selected from the 1236 patients now in the Massachusetts School for the Feeble-Minded. They include various degrees and types of defect, from cases bordering on actual idiocy to so-called "borderline" cases, where the mental impairment is slight compared with the moral and social deficiencies. Some of these cases now in adult life have been in the school continuously since early childhood. Other cases, at large in the community until the time of puberty, were then sentenced to the reform school by the criminal court and thence transferred to this school. Others were referred to the school from the community without an actual criminal court record.

In many cases repeated acts of a criminal nature have been committed in the community. In other cases the persistent criminal tendencies have been expressed only as modified by institution conditions, but I have no hesitancy in classifiying these "criminals who have actually committed no crime" in this group.

The tendency to promiscuous and precocious sexual vice, common to all types and degrees of imbecility, is considered only as incidental and corroborative evidence.

Case I. F. M., female. Age when admitted, 18 years. Personal history very meagre and nothing known of ancestry. It is known that this patient has been a prisoner at the State Industrial School, at Sherborn prison, and in various jails and houses of correction. She was a state ward and was placed out in families several times, but always absconded after the theft of money and other articles. The experienced court officer who brought her to the school stated that in her language and in the freedom with which she discussed her various escapades, she was "the most brazen and depraved human being he had ever seen." She gloried in her misdeeds and unblushingly related stories of her various adventures. At times she shamelessly revealed her sexual propensities. She stole everything she could get her hands on. She was wantonly destructive of property. Even attempted violence toward her attendants. Showed ability as an organizer and as an inciter of rebellion and mischief.

Degenerative stigmata Supra-orbital ridges prominent. Zygoma prominent.

Present age 22 years. Reads in 4th reader. Is fond of books and magazines. Expresses herself fluently and well. Adds and substracts slowly to 20. Cannot multiply 4×5. No division. Patient is childish in her ideas and tastes. Conceited and egotistical. Sly and cunning in small things, but shows lack of caution in concealing her serious lapses in conduct. Kind to children. At several periods has shown a marked infatuation for patients much her inferior mentally, and who were, in fact, of a very low grade of mentality. She has never chosen as her particular chums, patients of her own grade. Easily influenced by people of whom she is fond, and is scrupulously loyal to her special chums. She is selfish and ungrateful. She is always in sympathy with any evidences of rebellion or insubordination. At first was quite slovenly and careless in her work. Of late, she has become more particular, and to-day, with close supervision, is quite the equal of the average seamstress. Without supervision the quality of her work at once becomes poor.

Case II. J. C., female. Age at admission, 17 years. Paternal grandfather and grandmother both insane. Father and mother not up to the standard mentally. Mother had convulsions to age of six years. Patient dishonest, untruthful, destructive. Could not apply herself in school work. Liked to play with younger children. Had convulsions in early childhood. Wet bed until 14 years old. Showed no remorse when detected in theft. Would tell lies without any apparent reason. Was at "George Junior Republic" for a while. Says she was "in jail" there almost continuously for lying, stealing and general incorrigibility.

Degenerative stigmata High, perpendicular forehead. Receding chin. Small mouth. Ears badly made, with adherent lobules. Teeth badly placed. Face markedly asymmetrical.

Can read in 4th reader. Likes to read story-books and magazines. Penmanship good. Uses language intelligently. Adds and substracts by hundreds, and multiplies by two or three figures. No division. Patient is childish, deceitful, boastful. Likes to tell stories of her connection with men and boys, although her family say these stories have no foundation in fact. Likes to change from one thing to another, but does fairly good work under supervision. Likes to be well-dressed, but has to be forced to wash neck and ears. Forms violent attachments towards other patients. Chooses very defective patients for her chums. Indolent, untidy. No affection for relatives. Gloats over her misdeeds. No shame or remorse. Shows absence of motive by stealing things for which she has no use.

Case III. F. S., female. Age when admitted, 16 years. Colored. Committed to State Industrial School when 14 for stubbornness and violence towards brothers and sisters. In a fit of jealousy tried to kill baby brother. Mother was ugly tempered and quarrelsome. Girl wet bed until 16 years old. Had attacks of irritability and violence during which she walked about aimlessly. Always incorrigible. Ordered out of public school at age of 12.

Degenerative stigmata Prominent zygoma. Face asymmetrical. Ears gross, with adherent lobules and exaggerated details.

Present age 22. Reads easily in 4th reader. Likes to read newspapers, books and magazines. Slow of speech but expresses herself well. Handwriting admirable. In number work can add slowly to ten, but not above that. Can tell time by five-minute intervals. Patient is vain, fond of dress and of ornament. Selfish. Exceedingly proud of whatever she does herself. Disobliging, stubborn, often sulky and rebellious. Shows no affection for relatives. Has attacked other patients and attendants in fits of temper, brought on by failure to get her own way. Can do beautiful laundry and other work, but will not do it unless very closely supervised. Sexual pervert. Her indecent actions with other patients are carried on regardless of the presence of others.

Case IV. M. B., female. Age at admission, 15. Mother intemperate. Father in prison on charge of assault and sexual connection with this girl and an older sister. Persistent thief and liar. Sexually precocious.

Degenerative stigmata Deep orbits. Face asymmetrical. Ears asymmetrical, with adherent lobules. Palate high-vaulted. Teeth badly placed.

Present age 17. Reads in 3rd reader. Likes to read storybooks. Uses language expressively and fluently. Adds and subtracts sums in three figures and multiplies by two or three figures. No division. Can tell time by five-minute intervals. This patient is selfish, conceited, egotistic, indolent. Lies habitually with no motive. Sly and cunning in attaining her own ends. Selfish and grasping. Very ungrateful in every way. Has been taught to do work under supervision. Will not work if not watched. Deceitful, unreliable. Silly and childish in her behavior and actions. No modesty. Steals things for which she has no use. An inciter of mischief and insubordination. Loves to talk of crimes and criminals. Referred to school by criminal court after persistent habits of thieving, etc.

Case V. K. N., male. Age when admitted, 11. No family history. No personal history previous to admission.

Degenerative stigmata Bushy eyebrows, meet in center. Heavy supraorbital ridges. Deep orbits. Ears crinkled and dissimilar in shape and position. Face asymmetrical. Palate high-arched. Very deaf.

Present age 21. This patient was in school classes from the time of his admission until he was 18 years old. He is now able to read fairly well in 3rd reader. Reads newspapers and magazines intelligently. Has a good vocabulary and uses language understandingly. Can add numbers to 10 accurately, but cannot subtract these numbers. Cannot subtract or multiply. Patient is vain and boastful. Excels in athletics and likes to exploit his athletic prowess. He is contemptuous in his comparisons of his own doings with those of his companions. Very egotistical. Profane and obscene. Lies unblushingly in securing his own desires. A cruel practical joker. Is wantonly cruel to smaller boys and to his associates. Steals anything he may desire. Shows good intelligence in many directions. Absolute disregard for the rights of others. Greedily reads the newspaper accounts of crime and criminals and boasts of the crimes he would commit against property and persons if he were at large. Is an inciter of mischief. Industrious and capable in all forms of ordinary work under close supervision.

Case IV. C. X., female. Age when admitted, 16 years. Was abandoned by parents at an early age. Says mother was intemperate. Patient had an illegitimate child when she was 14 years old. Committed by criminal court to State Industrial School for theft and incorrigibility.

Degenerative stigmata Very high cheek bones. Deep orbits. Face markedly asymmetrical. Ears asymmetrical, with adherent lobules.

Present age 24. Reads well in 3rd reader. Good command of language. Adds and ʾsubtracts in hundreds; multiplies numbers of two figures. No division. This patient can do first-class table-waiting and other forms of domestic work when closely supervised. If not supervised does very poor work. Has keen sexual propensities. Forms violent friendships for girls much less intelligent. Chatters and giggles endlessly in a simple way. Very deep and cunning in carrying out her own schemes. Is tyrannical to weaker people. Cruel to animals. Harsh to young children. Very neat in dress and person. Very vain, ungrateful, selfish. Lies unblushingly. Will run the risk of losing some much-desired pleasure for some small gain. Never shows signs of remorse for wrong-doing. Skims through the paper each day for accounts of crimes and murders. Her general behavior is that of a child of 11 or 12.

Case VII. N. C., female. Age when admitted, 20. Father intemperate: mother epileptic. As a small child, patient was untidy, played with children younger than herself, was cruel to animals. When 13 years of age was committed to State Industrial School for fornication and assault. Had been incorrigible previously.

Degenerative stigmata Ears large and gross, with adherent lobules. Astigmatism. Prominent supra-orbital ridges. Deep orbits, prominent zygoma. Face asymmetrical.

Present age 27. Reads well in 4th reader; handwriting legible; adds and subtracts slowly to 20. No multiplication or division. Can tell time by five-minute intervals. Patient is loud and assertive in manner. Always puts herself forward. Has a great opinion of her own ability. Sly and cunning. Fond of dress and jewelry. Domineering and overbearing towards others. Shows no affection towards relatives. Quick tempered and violent at slight provocation. Can do good work but will not stick to it unless closely supervised. Masturbates. Sexually perverted. "Oversexed." Becomes sexually excited when men are around. In the institution environment these propensities are usually kept under control, with occasional outbreaks of temper and sexual disturbance. She unwillingly does under supervision the work of a rather inefficient domestic.

Case VIII. X. E., male. Age at admission, 16. Colored. Committed here at instance of criminal court. Has record of having been before the court repeatedly for incorrigibility, destructiveness, stealing of money, etc. Rachitic and undersized.

Degenerative stigmata Receding forehead. Prominent supra-orbital ridges. Prominent zygoma. Ears small, dissimilar and with indistinct details.

Present age 21. Patient reads well in 4th reader. Enjoys reading magazines, etc. Handwriting is admirable. Adds correctly to 20, but is uncertain in adding numbers above 20. No subtraction, multiplication or division. This patient is a vain, bombastic egotist. Has a great opinion of everything he has or does. Is neat and tidy in dress. Sly and cunning. Lies without hesitation. Steals. He is a trouble-maker and inciter of mischief. Polite and courteous in his manner and use of language. Has learned to do excellent work as a house painter, but if not closely supervised is very careless and slovenly about his work. Will not work continuously without supervision.

Case IX. S. U., female. Age when admitted, 17. Father intemperate; has prison record. Patient illegitimate, although father still lives with mother of girl. Neither father nor mother can read or write. At age of 14, patient was committed to State Industrial School for theft and incorrigibility. In court, she testified that the father had committed incest with her, and accused the mother of venally using her for lewd practices. She was placed out from the Industrial School repeatedly, but always with the history of sexual irregularities and theft at each place.

Degenerative stigmata Has deep orbits; prominent zygoma; ears asymmetrical and poorly proportioned with adherent lobules.

Present age 33. Can read in 3rd reader. Reads simple storybooks but shows poor understanding of what she reads. Cannot spell. Uses language intelligently. In number work, can add a little under ten; no subtraction or multiplication. Can tell time by five-minute intervals. Patient is childish, selfish, disobedient. Fond of dress but careless about her personal cleanliness. Fond of music and dancing. Sly and cunning. Is an habitual liar and thief. Is inclined to be stubborn and sulky. Can do beautiful laundry work if closely supervised, but if supervision is withdrawn, does very poor work. Chooses younger and less intelligent companions.

Case X. K. I., male. Age when admitted, 7 years. No family history. Illegitimate. When admitted could not read nor write. Wet bed. Mischievous and sly.

Degenerative stigmata Skull asymmetrical. Forehead lined with heavy transverse wrinkles. Face asymmetrical. Ears show adherent lobules.

Was in school continuously from time of admission until 18 years old. Now 32 years old. Is an omnivorous reader. Reads newspapers, magazines, books and literature of all kinds. Reads scientific reports, agricultural hand-books, etc. Has not a very clear appreciation of what he reads. Expresses himself well. Can add, subtract, and multiply up to 100. Can divide mentally with an easy divisor. Has a vast fund of miscellaneous information. Has a good memory for facts and events, and is especially good at remembering the exact dates of important events at the school in his time. He is an inveterate liar. In an apparently innocent way tells malicious falsehoods which he knows will make trouble. He is boastful and likes to be prominent. He loves to stir up trouble and mischief. Will tell a new patient that he heard the doctor say that the boy's father is dead, etc. He has been detected in perverted sexual actions with other patients. Occasionally runs away and leads a vagrant life for a week or ten days, when he returns to the school of his own accord. He is never in sympathy with the officers who have him in charge. Once attacked an attendent with a knife. Urges other patients to attack officers. Is always sly and cunning in his mischief-making, and always seems prejudiced against the constituted authorities as a matter of general principle.

Case XI. F. Q., female. Age when admitted, 16 years. No bad heredity. Unhappy home conditions. Patient always high-tempered, jealous and hard to get on with. Always desirous of attracting attention. Untrustworthy. Lied about everything. An inveterate thief. Stole money and small articles repeatedly. When accused, lied glibly, and when detected in falsehood or theft showed no signs of sorrow or shame. Would repeat theft at next opportunity. Cruel to little children. Was precocious sexually and had no reserve about exposing her person or in her language or behavior with men or boys.

Degenerative stigmata Face asymmetrical. Ears asymmetrical in shape and size. Adherent lobules.

Age now 17. Reads in 4th reader. Fond of novels, magazines, etc. Handwriting good. Uses language intelligently. Adds and subtracts slowly to 20 only. No multiplication or division. Patient shows about the same characteristics as noted at time of admission. She lies and is deceitful. Fond of dress, boastful and indolent. Will do good work if closely supervised, but if not supervised is very careless.

Case XII. N. M., female. Age when admitted, 18 years. Father intemperate. Mother 48 when patient was born. Patient committed from State Industrial School. Had court record of fornication, street-walking and repeated thefts. Had been repeatedly placed out from the Industrial School with the invariable history of promiscuous sexual intercourse, frequent running away, and several arrests for street-walking. Was a chronic thief, often stealing things for which she had no use.

Degenerative stigmata Prominent supra-orbital ridges. Prominent zygoma. Deep orbits. Prominent chin. Good ears, but with adherent lobules. Face asymmetrical.

Present age 24. Reads easily in 3rd reader. Fond of reading and likes magazines and story-books. Uses language easily and well. Can add and subtract in hundreds. No multiplication or division. Patient is childish and easily led. Noisy and boisterous in daily life. Obliging and anxious to please. Marked sexual propensities and unable to control herself when men are around. Masturbates and has perverted sexual relations with other patients. Sly and cunning, but shows little real foresight. Capable of doing good work, but is slovenly and careless unless closely supervised. Was formerly a great inciter of mischief and a trouble-maker, but during the last year has "settled down" and grown much more tractable and industrious.

Case XIII. T. Q., male. Age when admitted (October, 1907), 16 years. Parents Russian Jews. No bad heredity. Patient was committed here as an alternative to being sentenced in police court for stealing money from his employer. States that he has stolen money repeatedly in places where he was employed. At time of his commitment here, there was a warrant out for his arrest for rape committed on a young girl. He claims that this rape was committed as the result of a "dare" by some of his associates.

Degenerative stigmata Skull asymmetrical. Hair grows low on forehead. Eyebrows bushy and meet in center. Heavy supra-orbital ridges. Ears asymmetrical and unevenly placed. Teeth dark, discolored and crowded in jaw. Teeth at irregular angles, cuspids parallel with bicuspids. Face asymmetrical.

Reads fluently in 3d reader. Spells well. Good handwriting. Can add to 20, but cannot subtract, multiply or divide. Can tell time by hours but not by minutes. This patient is frank about his escapades and describes them freely. Says he found it very hard to do school work. Rather stupid and heavy but with fair understanding of ordinary affairs. Memory as to times and places very uncertain. Apparently an uncomplicated case of imbecility.

Case XIV. X. E., male. Age when admitted, 18 years. Mother feeble-minded. Father unknown. Boy illegitimate. Was committed to the school as an alternative to being sentenced for rape committed on a young girl. This was the third time this boy had committed rape. Had repeatedly stolen money and other articles, and had committed assaults on boys who bothered him.

Degenerative stigmata Hair low on forehead. Heavy supra-orbital ridges. Eyebrows bushy and meet in center. Deep orbits. Ears asymmetrical and badly made. High-arched palate. Face asymmetrical.

Present age 21. Patient had been in public school continuously up to time of his admission here, but is able to read only simple books like the primer. Cannot spell simple words; can write a little; knows nothing of number. Cannot tell time. In using language is able to express himself well. Has a large fund of general information. This patient is extremely talkative; very pompous in manner and language. Vain of his personal appearance. Neat in dress and person. Is a persistent and senseless liar. Is rebellious and contrary with new attendants. Has attacked several attendants without provocation. On general principles is opposed to those in power. Masturbates, but is not a sexual pervert.

Case XV. N. T., female. Age at admission, 16 years. Father moral pervert in every sense. Mother confesses to having lived with many different men. Brother of patient has a history of incorrigibility and multiple court record. Patient had fits of temper as a child. Learned to talk late. Wet bed. Stubborn, willful, passionate, and "could not tell right from wrong." Liked to play with younger children. Cruel to other children. Immediate occasion for commitment was result of being brought into court for incest with father. While patient was with mother on vacation two years ago, she became pregnant and gave birth to a child.

Degenerative stigmata Large supra-orbital ridges. Receding chin. Receding forehead. Prominent zygoma. Palate very high and narrow. Ears asymmetrical.

Present age 21. Reads easily in 3d reader. Writes good hand. Can add in hundreds; subtract slowly under ten; no multiplication. Can tell time.

Expresses herself fluently and intelligently. Patient is indolent, cunning; has no sense of shame. Quarrelsome. Exceedingly crafty in gaining her own ends. Has attacked other patients and attendants with knife without provocation. Had no love for her baby and manifested no real grief when it died. Becomes sexually excited when men are around.

Case XVI. O. L., female. Age when admitted, 14 years. Father and mother both intemperate and degenerate, and always on the verge of pauperism. Patient admitted here from Tewksbury almhouse, with history of incorrigibility. Cruel to animals, etc. Had put a cat on a red-hot stove. Had thrown knives and stones at playmates. Said she would like to have a small baby to strike and kick. Very untruthful and chronic thief.

Degenerative stigmata Eyebrows bushy. Zygoma prominent. Face asymmetrical. Nose small and rudimentary. Ears badly shaped, with adherent lobules. High palate. Teeth crowded, and placed on different planes. Low forehead. Body small and undersized.

Present age 16. Reads in 4th reader. Uses language easily. Can add a little under 5. Can tell time. This patient is sly and cunning. Vain and boastful. Fond of teasing. Has fits of temper when she screams, tears clothing and pulls out her hair. Likes to attract attention and is very vain of her personal appearance. Is in a state of chronic rebellion against the constituted authorities, a trouble-maker and inciter of mischief. About two years ago this patient, with another patient, drowned a fellow patient in a bath tub.

Case XVII. K. I., male. Age when admitted, 17. Irish-American. Family history unknown. Patient walked at 18 months, did not talk until 7, could not learn in school. Had convulsions in first year. Began use of tobacco at age of 8. Referred to the school from the criminal court where he was held on a charge of rape committed on a young girl. Had worked for several years in a factory where he carried goods from one part of the factory to another.

Degenerative stigmata Very prominent supra-orbital ridges. Face asymmetrical. High palate. Ears prominent and outstanding.

Present age 18 years. Reads easily in 4th reader. Poor speller. Adds to 10, but cannot subtract. Typical imbecile of medium grade. Happy-go-lucky fellow. High tempered. Works well under supervision; idle otherwise.

Case XVIII. Q. K., male. Age when admitted, 9. No family history. Peculiar from early infancy. Has always been nervous.

Degenerative stigmata Face asymmetrical. Eyeballs protruding. Eyes widely spaced. Deep orbits.

Present age 11 years. Beginning to read easy sentences in primer. Cannot spell, except 3-letter words. Can add to 5 fairly well. Cannot tell time. Patient very troublesome and incorrigible. Has a bright, knowing and intelligent manner. Has a fund of general information, and seems brighter than he really is. Talkative. Has used tobacco since an early age. Very cruel to smaller children. Has ungovernable temper. Is a malicious liar. A very successful inciter of discontent and rebellion among the other patients. Is most ingenious and convincing in his falsehoods. Inveterate thief. No appreciable motive for his bad behavior.

Case XIX. J. E., male. Age when admitted, 13 years. Parents of Irish decent. Father not very strong mentally. Patient eighth child in a family of 14. Seven children have died, 3 still-born, 1 hydrocephalic. Patient committed to the school after being before the local court repeatedly for incorrigibility, theft, destruction of property, etc.

Degenerative stigmata Skull of microcephalic type and asymmetrical. Ears dissimilar. Nasal septum deviated. Palate high-arched.

Present age 15 years. Reads well in 2d reader. Spells simple words. Can add to 15 slowly and rather uncertainly. Cannot subtract or multiply. This patient is one of the most incorrigible boys I have ever known. He lies persistently, purposelessly and maliciously. He is a great thief. Very impatient of control. Wantonly destructive. Cruel to other children. Vain, conceited, quick-tempered, insolent. Very fond of tobacco which he has used since he was 8 years old. Absence of motive characterizes many of his actions. Works well under supervision.

In every case with a court record, and in the cases from the reform schools, the offense for which the patient was originally committed was not a first offense, but was the climax of a long series of petty misdeeds which finally became unbearable. Probably all this group were committed by the police courts without question as to their mental condition. In several cases it was only after the patient had been "placed out" to service several times, from the reform school, and had repeatedly failed to respond favorably to good environment that it was realized that mental defect was the underlying cause of the delinquency.

A large proportion of the cases described well represents the class of cases who formerly would have been considered merely as criminals, with no thought of mental defect.

By reason of early incorrigibility or bad home surroundings many of these cases had few school advantages in childhood. In court their mental deficiency was probably mistaken for ignorance from bad inheritance or lack of opportunity.

Nearly every case shows either no family history obtainable—which in the case of a child usually means a dubious heredity—or a positive history of bad inheritance.

Nearly every case presents various physical stigmata of degeneracy in skull, ears, face, teeth, palate or physiognomy. All of the cases described are in the period of adolescence or early adult life, and yet only a few present the usual comeliness of feature and physical attractiveness usually shown at this period of life.

All of these patients boast of their evil acts and eagerly discuss the criminal experiences of a new-comer. They gloat over newspaper stories of crime and shame. They delight in "yellow journalism." They reveled in the exploits of Tracy the desperado and of Thaw the assassin.

Of the cases described, none seem able to apply themselves continuously in any one direction, even for a greatly desired reward. Even the brightest were unable to master more than the merest rudiments of arithmetic.

The patients described vary greatly in general intelligence, and in the amount of definite knowledge which they have acquired, but they greatly resemble each other in their childish tastes, excessive vanity, unreliability, aggressive boastful egotism, selfishness, moral insensibility, fondness for malicious mischief and trouble-making; indolence, willingness to run great risk for the sake of some small gain, untruthfulness, lack of shame and remorse, lack of sympathy, etc.

The cases described fairly represent the criminal imbecile type. I have no doubt as to the actual imbecility and the resulting moral irresponsibility of every one of these cases. As a group, the female cases especially well illustrate the so-called "high-grade imbecile." In fact, the physical and psychical stigmata exhibited by the group of imbeciles, selected because of their criminal tendencies and acts, are merely the usual signs and symptoms found in the ordinary case of imbecility, modified only in degree and not in kind.

This class of borderline cases with criminal tendencies now constitutes a troublesome and puzzling factor in our institutions for the feeble-minded. They are often malicious, deceitful and inciters of mischief and insubordination. They have a wonderful power of suggestion over their simple-minded fellow-patients. They are generally committed to the institution against the wishes of their parents. The efforts of their friends to obtain their release are constant and perplexing. If a case of this description is taken before the Supreme Court on a writ of habeas corpus it is more than likely that the patient will be released. Indeed, it is not difficult to find reputable medical men who would testify that the case "is by no means a fool," and that he ought not to be deprived of his liberty. It is evident that clinical types and shadings of mental deficiency have become familiar to the alienist which have not been so definitely formulated and classified as to be readily recognized by the profession generally. It is equally true that the legal definitions and precedents pertaining to ordinary cases of imbecility are inadequate when applied to these high-grade imbeciles. We have, therefore, to face the anomalous fact that it is easy to have a class of patients committed to our institutions who are promptly discharged by the higher courts because these lesser types of deficiency have neither been adequately formulated medically nor recognized legally.

The diagnosis of borderline cases of imbecility is simplified if it is possible to obtain the family history and the personal history of the patient, with special reference to the period of infancy and early childhood. Even in the cases with very slight mental defect there is usually a history of delayed dentition, late walking, delayed speech, relatively long continuance of untidy habits, and very likely a history of convulsions as part of the history of the first few years of life.

The public school history of the patient is almost always illuminating. As a rule these cases do not compare at all favorably in their school work with the average child. It is seldom these cases are carried beyond the standard of third-grade work. Difficulty in understanding simple arithmetical abstractions is very significant. The presence or absence of various degenerative stigmata is significant.

Selfishness, moral insensibility, willingness to run great risks for slight possible gain, childish tastes, lack of affection for relatives—all these are significant symptoms. A very constant symptom is inability on the part of the patient to apply himself continuously either in school work or in any other occupation without constant supervision. In some cases with only slight intellectual defect, the inability to "make good" socially will be a deciding factor in the diagnosis. In a given case the age, sex, social condition, physical health, school advantages, etc., have a distinct bearing on the interpretation of the case.

Some of the cases reported were considered as typical cases of so-called "moral imbecility" without intellectual defect, until long observation and close analysis demonstrated that they were cases of true imbecility, where the anti-social tendencies of the ordinary imbecile were exaggerated to such an extent as to overshadow the presence of intellectual impairment, and the existence of the characteristic physical, mental and moral signs of congenital mental defect.

I have never happened to see a well-marked case of so-called "congenital moral imbecility" which did not exhibit many, or indeed most, of the significant stigmata of true imbecility.

With the moral imbecile the stock of showy and superficial knowledge, the confident and boastful manner, the glibness of tongue, the spurious brightness, the cunning and carefully planned schemes—all these serve to mask the significance of the supreme selfishness, the lack of shame and remorse, the unbounded egotism, the absence of adequate motive, the cruelty, the lack of fear of consequences, the lack of judgment, the love of notoriety, the failure to keep a situation, the failure to respect the feelings of relatives, the abnormal social reactions, the idleness and tendency to early vice, which are so apt to characterize this type of defective.

Kraeplin admirably describes the modern conception of "moral imbecility" as follows:

"Moral imbecility represents a form of mental weakness which includes chiefly the realm of the feelings. It is characterized by the absence or weakness of those feelings which inhibit the development of marked selfishness. The intellect, as regards matters of practical life, is moderately developed; patients apprehend well; they are able to accumulate more or less knowledge, which they use more or less for their own advantage; possess a good memory and show no defects in the process of thought. They do, however, lack the ability to obtain general viewpoints, to perform any work of high grade, and to form an adequate conception of life in the outer world.

Morally, their lack of sympathy is manifested from youth up in their cruelty towards animals, their tendency to tease and roughly use play-mates, and an inaccessibility to moral influences. They develop the most pronounced selfishness, lack of sense of honor and of affection for parents and relatives. It is impossible to train them because of the absence of love and ambition. They tell falsehoods, become crafty, deceitful and stubborn. The egotism becomes more and more evident in their great conceit, bragging and wilfulness, their inordinate desire for enjoyment, their violence and dissipation."

They are incapable of resisting temptation and give way to sudden impulses and emotional outbursts, while the susceptibility to alcohol is especially prominent.

So-called "moral imbeciles" frequently commit the most heinous and revolting crimes. The boy Pomeroy was a high-grade imbecile who had been accepted for admission to the Massachusetts School for the Feeble-Minded when he committed his notorious crimes.

Every imbecile, especially the high-grade imbecile, is a potential ciriminal, needing only the proper environment and opportunity for the development and expression of his criminal tendencies. The unrecognized imbecile is a most dangerous element in the community. The fact that the high-grade imbecile often excels in one or more lines—music, painting, some limited branch of mechanics—is misleading. Maliciously mischievous children, runa-ways and vagrants, the incorrigibles, disorderly and ungovernable children, are often of the imbecile type. Lighter grades of imbecility often fail of recogni-tion in early childhood, but as soon as some unusual situation arises demand-ing discretion and decision of action, and self-control, the mental, moral and social incapacity becomes evident. The mental incapacity becomes more evident in youth and adolescence as contrasted with the rapid mental devel-opment of their playmates.

The juvenile expression of this slight degree of imbecility, especially in children watched and guarded in good homes, is trivial and harmless. The reaction of these patients to the temptations of adolescent and adult life is another matter.

The life history of the case put under permanent protection and training at an early age is very different from that of the cases which grow up at large in a modern urban or town community. Nearly all of the cases trained from childhood or youth may be taught habits of industry and comparatively good behavior, and at from 25 to 30 years of age a large proportion of them "settle down" to a condition of inhibition of the anti-social traits, and indeed to a condition of ostentatious pride in the virtues which they unwillingly practice.

Constant occupation at congenial work, with strict but kindly discipline, and with proper recreation, is the basis of the treatment required.

Butler of Indiana says:

"In the country and local jails we have frequent cause to note the relationship between feeble-mindedness and crime. Boys and young men mentally weak are often found being held for trial or serving a jail sentence for rape, or attempted rape, incendiarism, or other crime.

Many of the children whose cases are brought before the juvenile courts are mentally weak or come from homes where, because of the weak wills of the parents, they were not given proper training or direction.

The last resort of the juvenile courts is the State Reform Schools. In these institutions are many children of this class of mental defectives.

Mental defectives are frequently committed to the reformatories for adults. From studies made at the New York State Reformatory it is stated that this class constitutes about one-fifth of the population of that institution. A far larger proportion is reported as being incapable of controlling their powers of co-ordinating their faculties, and are termed 'control defectives.' The superintendent of the schools at the Indiana Reformatory states that about 21 per cent. of those received are mentally defective on admission.

In the state prisons are also to be found those who are feeble-minded. Some of these were nuisances in their respective communities; some were sent here because there appeared to be no other place to send them, others for the commission of offences for which they were not really responsible.

In both reformatories and prisons these defectives are the most troublesome class of prisoners. Irrational, irritable, their weak minds led by their impulses, they interfere with discipline and their management requires the highest skill. Their presence at times leads to disturbances and sometimes to serious, if not fatal assaults upon officers and inmates."

The literature of criminology teems with references to the close analogy between the imbecile and the instinctive criminal. They have a common heredity, and criminal anthropology proves that the evidences of degeneration—anatomical, physiological and physical—are identical in the two groups.

Is there not more than a close resemblance between the imbecile and the instinctive criminal? Is not the typical instinctive criminal of Lombroso a typical adult imbecile of middle or high grade, plus opportunity and experience in the community?

We have only begun to study the relationship between imbecility and crime. The criminal tendencies of the epileptic are fairly well-known. The insane criminal is being studied from many points of view. There are many crimes committed by imbeciles for every one committed by an insane person. The average prison population includes more imbeciles than lunatics.

We shall eventually apply our knowledge of imbecility to the study and management of juvenile incorrigibles and adult criminals. The ultimate application of that knowledge will materially modify the action of the courts and the methods of treatment and management of prisoners.

Cases of imbecility with criminal propensities—"criminals who have committed no crime"—will be recognized at an early age before they have acquired facility in crime, and permanently taken out of the community and given life-long care and supervision in special institutions, combining the educational and developmental methods of a school for the feeble-minded with the industry and security of a modern penal institution. Such provision would be only a rational extension of the principle of indeterminate sentence, and if safe-guarded by careful and repeated expert examination and observation could do no injustice and would greatly diminish crime in the immediate future. Adult criminal imbeciles, or instinctive criminals, would be committed to an institution under the same conditions. Similar cases developing in institutions for ordinary imbeciles would be permanently transferred to the special institution.

DISCUSSION

DR. SMITH BAKER: With reference to caring for cases at the earlier stage I wish to quote a case briefly: A boy five years old was brought to me with the complaint that he could not learn to read, and that in consequence he was becoming a truant, was rapidly learning the little vices of childhood, and was becoming a nuisance in the school and in the neighborhood. Under the care of an older sister, whom I endeavored properly to instruct, within only about three years the boy learned to read as rapidly and as much as any boy of his age, had gotten off of the street, and had become a respectable boy, and is to-day a respectable man. The family had unwittingly provided him with all the tendencies necessary to make a vicious criminal of him later on. The defect in reading had thrown him into such a miserable sort of contact with the rest of the school and the community, that he was naturally urged on in all such vicious directions, very rapidly. Getting him interested in the right kind of studies under the right kind of direction, in the right kind of environment, resulted in what I have told you—a respectable boy, a respectable young man.

DR. MURDOCH: The point that appeals to me in the presentation of these cases is that they were almost without exception cases that entered the institution when they were past 14 or 16 years of age, some of them, I believe, 18 or 19 years. Most of them had come in contact with a vicious environment before coming into the institution. I would like to know if any of the institution children of this class have been under institution training from very early years. I believe if we can have the imbecile under training in proper institutions during early years that these vicious tendencies will not develop. I think it is largely a question of environment and the lack of appropriate training. In my experience in our own institution, I know, while we are not old, that has been our observation, that these children who have come to us early have not developed these vicious tendencies in the institution, but we do see it in those children who have come to see us too late, after they have been exposed to street life and evil association in the outside world. This is not only so of the imbecile, but I believe it is true of normal boys and girls; if they are protected from evils during early years the liability of generating or acquiring evil habits, alcoholism, etc., is not likely to occur.

DR. WILMARTH: The point that appeals most to me is the absence of true remorse. A girl released from the industrial school in Milwaukee murdered her illegitmate infant. The murder was discovered and she was brought before the justice, and the thing that strongly attracted his attention was her entire lack of remorse over her crime and her inability to appreciate its gravity. It strikes me that the lack of remorse signifies a lack of knowledge or appreciation of the gravity of the offence, and that lack indicates surely a lack of judgment. The lack of judgment, or the lack of will power, which is prominent in these cases certainly indicates the lack of a true mental formation or growth, and, therefore, indicates, in itself, an imbecility or feeble-mindedness. It does not seem to me that the term "moral imbecility" is misplaced, if used in that connection.

DR. GODDARD: I have been through the literature on moral imbecility, and I feel like saying that, in my opinion, the papers we have heard this afternoon on that subject are the first real contribution we have had to the understanding of moral imbecility. There is no place in modern sociology or modern ethics for moral imbecility as it is found in the older writings on that subject. The notion that a child may be born with his natural faculties all right and his moral faculties all wrong is a notion that belongs to the middle ages of sociology and ethics as well. I think this marks the beginning of a new era in which we can get down to the point and study the imbecile, and find out, if you please, why, in imbeciles, some tendencies predominate over others. It would be foolish to anticpate the results of those studies, and yet, sometimes we must have certain impressions which will lead us in the right direction, and I have the impression that the moral imbecile, so called, is the best answer to the argument that we heard last evening, that this whole thing is a mere matter of heredity, and if we stop that, the problem is solved. I believe the imbecility may be hereditary, but the moral part is a question of environment, and it is the child's revolt, or nature's revolt and reaction against a crude and ridiculous educational and training system for that kind of a child. As I said before, these three papers especially appeal to me as a tremendous contribution to this little understood subject.

PROF. JOHNSTONE: I do not know that I can add anything to this discussion, but it seems to me there has been one word that has cried out all through this day, and that word is "ignorance." It seems to me this whole question is in our hands, it lies in the hollow of the hands of this association, and I think it is time for us to let people know. I think we ought to take some definite action to let people understand more of our work and its relationship to ordinary life.

WHAT
IT MEANS

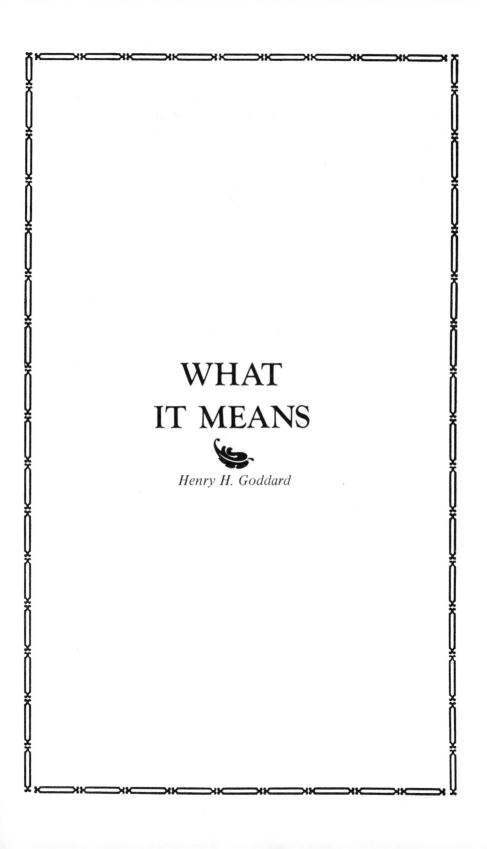

Henry H. Goddard

The influence of heredity upon mental deficiency is described in terms of "bad blood" perpetuating the tainted traits of ancestral stock. Goddard's concern stems from his belief in the strong relationship between feeble-mindedness and criminality, estimating that as many as fifty per cent of the inmates of penal institutions are mentally deficient.

The foregoing charts and text tell a story as instructive as it is amazing. We have here a family of good English blood of the middle class, settling upon the original land purchased from the proprietors of the state in Colonial times, and throughout four generations maintaining a reputation for honor and respectability of which they are justly proud. Then a scion of this family, in an unguarded moment, steps aside from the paths of rectitude and with the help of a feeble-minded girl, starts a line of mental defectives that is truly appalling. After this mistake, he returns to the traditions of his family, marries a woman of his own quality, and through her carries on a line of respectability equal to that of his ancestors.

We thus have two series from two different mothers but the same father. These extend for six generations. Both lines live out their lives in practically the same region and in the same environment, except in so far as they themselves, because of their different characters, changed that environment. Indeed, so close are they that in one case, a defective man on the bad side of the family was found in the employ of a family on the normal side and, although they are of the same name, neither suspects any relationship.

We thus have a natural experiment of remarkable value to the sociologist and the student of heredity. That we are dealing with a problem of true heredity, no one can doubt, for, although of the descendants of Martin Kallikak Jr. many married into feeble-minded families and thus brought in more bad blood, yet Martin Jr. himself married a normal woman, thus demonstrating that the defect is transmitted through the father, at least in this generation. Moreover, the Kallikak family traits appear continually even down to the present generation, and there are many qualities that are alike in both the good and the bad families, thus showing the strength and persistence of the ancestral stock.

The reader will recall the famous story of the Jukes family published by Richard L. Dugdale in 1877, a startling array of criminals, paupers, and diseased persons, more or less related to each other and extending over seven generations.

Dr. Winship has undertaken to compare this family with the descendants of Jonathan Edwards, and from this comparison to draw certain conclusions. It is a striking comparison, but unfortunately not as conclusive as we need in these days. The two families were utterly independent, of different ancestral stock, reared in different communities, even in different States, and under utterly different environment.

Goddard, H. H. *The Kallikak family: A study in the heredity of feeble-mindedness.* New York: Macmillan, 1914, chapter 3. The charts have been omitted for the sake of brevity.

Dr. Goddard was director of research of the Vineland Laboratory from 1906 to 1918.

The one, starting from a strong, religious, and highly educated ancestor, has maintained those traits and traditions down to the present day and with remarkable results; the other, starting without any of these advantages, and under an entirely different environment, has resulted in the opposite kind of descendants.

It is not possible to convince the euthenist (who holds that environment is the sole factor) that, had the children of Jonathan Edwards and the children of "Old Max" changed places, the results would not have been such as to show that it was a question of environment and not of heredity. And he cites to us the fact that many children of highly developed parents degenerate and become paupers and criminals, while on the other hand, some children born of lowly and even criminal parents take the opposite course and become respectable and useful citizens.

In as far as the children of "Old Max" were of normal mentality, it is not possible to say what might not have become of them, had they had good training and environment.

Fortunately for the cause of science, the Kallikak family, in the persons of Martin Kallikak Jr. and his descendants, are not open to this argument. They were feeble-minded, and no amount of education or good environment can change a feeble-minded individual into a normal one, any more than it can change a red-haired stock into a black-haired stock. The striking fact of the enormous proportion of feeble-minded individuals in the descendants of Martin Kallikak Jr. and the total absence of such in the descendants of his half brothers and sisters is conclusive on this point. Clearly it was not environment that has made that good family. They made their environment; and their own good blood, with the good blood in the families into which they married, told.

So far as the Jukes family is concerned, there is nothing that proves the hereditary character of any of the crime, pauperism, or prostitution that was found. The most that one can say is that if such a family is allowed to go on and develop in its own way unmolested, it is pretty certain not to improve, but rather to propagate its own kind and fill the world with degenerates of one form or another. The formerly much discussed question of the hereditary character of crime received no solution from the Jukes family, but in the light of present-day knowledge of the sciences of criminology and biology, there is every reason to conclude that criminals are made and not born. The best material out of which to make criminals, and perhaps the material from which they are most frequently made, is feeble-mindedness.

The reader must remember that the type of feeble-mindedness of which we are speaking is the one to which Deborah belongs, that is, to the high grade, or moron. All the facts go to show that this type of people makes up a large percentage of our criminals. We may argue *a priori* that such would be the case. Here we have a group who, when children in school, cannot learn the things that are given them to learn, because through their mental defect, they are incapable of mastering abstractions. They never learn to read sufficiently well to make reading pleasurable or of practical use to them. The same is true of number work. Under our compulsory school system and our present courses of study, we compel these children to go to school, and attempt to teach them the three R's, and even higher subjects. Thus they worry along through a few grades until they are fourteen years old and then leave school, not having learned anything of value or that can help them to make even a meager living in the world. They are then turned out inevitably dependent upon others. A few have relatives who take care of them, see that they learn to do something which perhaps will help in their support, and then these relatives supplement this with enough to insure them a living.

A great majority, however, having no such interested or capable relatives, become at once a direct burden upon society. These divide according to temperament into two groups. Those who are phlegmatic, sluggish, indolent, simply lie down and would starve to death, if some one did not help them. When they come to the attention of our charitable organizations, they are picked up and sent to the almshouse, if they cannot be made to work. The other type is of the nervous, excitable, irritable kind who try to make a living, and not being able to do it by a fair day's work and honest wages, attempt to succeed through dishonest methods. "Fraud is the force of weak natures." These become the criminal type. The kind of criminality into which they fall seems to depend largely upon their environment. If they are associated with vicious but intelligent people, they become the dupes for carrying out any of the hazardous schemes that their more intelligent associates plan for them. Because of their stupidity, they are very apt to be caught quickly and sent to the reformatory or prison. If they are girls, one of the easiest things for them to fall into is a life of prostitution, because they have natural instincts with no power of control and no intelligence to understand the wiles and schemes of the white slaver, the cadet, or the individual seducer. All this, we say, is what is to be expected. These are the people of good outward appearance, but of low intelligence, who pass through school without acquiring any efficiency, then go out into the world and must inevitably fall into some such life as we have pictured.

Let us now turn to our public institutions. These have not yet been sufficiently investigated, nor have we adequate statistics to show what percentage of their inmates is actually feeble-minded. But even casual observation of our almshouse population shows the majority to be of decidedly low mentality, while careful tests would undoubtedly increase this percentage very materially.

In our insane hospitals may also be found a group of people who the physicians will tell you are only partially demented. The fact is they properly belong in an institution for feeble-minded, rather than in one for the insane, and have gotten into the latter because an unenlightened public does not recognize the difference between a person who has lost his mind and one who never had one.

In regard to criminality, we now have enough studies to make us certain that at least 25 per cent of this class is feeble-minded. One hundred admissions to the Rahway Reformatory, taken in order of admission, show at least 26 per cent of them distinctly feeble-minded, with the certainty that the percentage would be much higher if we included the border-line cases.

An investigation of one hundred of the Juvenile Court children in the Detention Home of the City of Newark showed that 67 per cent of them were distinctly feeble-minded. From this estimate are excluded children who are yet too young for us to know definitely whether the case is one of arrested development. This point once determined would unquestionably swell the percentage of defect.

An examination of fifty-six girls from a Massachusetts reformatory, but out on probation, showed that fifty-two of them were distinctly feeble-minded. This was partially a selected group, the basis being their troublesomeness; they were girls who could not be made to stay in the homes that were found for them, nor to do reasonable and sensible things in those homes, which fact, of itself, pointed toward feeble-mindedness.

The foregoing are figures based on actual test examinations as to mental capacity. If we accept the estimates of the mental condition of the inmates made by the superintendents of reformatories and penal institutions, we get sometimes a vastly higher percentage; e.g., the Superintendent of the Elmira Reformatory estimates that at least 40 per cent of his inmates are mental defectives.

Indeed, it would not be surprising if careful examination of the inmates of these institutions should show that even 50 per cent of them are distinctly feeble-minded.

In regard to prostitutes, we have no reliable figures. The groups of delinquent girls to which we have already referred included among the numbers several that were already known as prostitutes. A simple observation of persons who are leading this sort of life will satisfy any one who is familiar with feeble-mindedness that a large percentage of them actually are defective mentally. So we have, as is claimed, partly from statistical studies and partly from careful observation, abundant evidence of the truth of our claim that criminality is often made out of feeble-mindedness.

Mr. Winship in his comparison of the Jukes and Edwards families has strengthened our claim in this respect. In all environments and under all conditions, he shows the latter family blossoming out into distinguished citizens, not primarily through anything from without but through the imperious force within. Since we may conclude that none of the Edwards family, who are described by Dr. Winship, were feeble-minded, therefore none of them became criminals or prostitutes. But here again his argument is inconclusive becasue he does not tell us of all the descendants.

With equal safety it may be surmised that many of the Jukes family (perhaps the original stock, indeed) were feeble-minded and therefore easily lapsed into the kind of lives that they are said to have lived.

In the good branch of the Kallikak family there were no criminals. There were not many in the other side, but there were some, and, had their environment been different, no one who is familiar with feeble-minded persons, their characteristics and tendencies, would doubt that a large percentage of them might have become criminal. Lombroso's famous criminal types, in so far as they were types, may have been types of feeble-mindedness on which criminality was grafted by the circumstances of their environment.

Such facts as those revealed by the Kallikak family drive us almost irresistibly to the conclusion that before we can settle our problems of criminality and pauperism and all the rest of the social problems that are taxing our time and money, the first and fundamental step should be to decide upon the mental capacity of the persons who make up these groups. We must separate, as sharply as possible, those persons who are weak-minded, and therefore irresponsible, from intelligent criminals. Both our method of treatment and our attitude towards crime will be changed when we discover what part of this delinquency is due to irresponsibility.

If the Jukes family were of normal intelligence, a change of environment would have worked wonders and would have saved society from the horrible blot. But if they were feeble-minded, then no amount of good environment could have made them anything else than feeble-minded. Schools and colleges were not for them, rather a segregation which would have prevented them from falling into evil and from procreating their kind, so avoiding the transmitting of their defects and delinquencies to succeeding generations.

Thus where the Jukes-Edwards comparison is weak and the argument inconclusive, the twofold Kallikak family is strong and the argument convincing.

Environment does indeed receive some support from three cases in our chart. On Chart II, two children of Martin Jr. and Rhoda were normal, while all the rest were feeble-minded. It is true that here one parent was normal, and we have the right to expect some normal children. At the same time, these were the two children that were adopted into good families and brought up under good surroundings. They proved to be normal and their descendants normal. Again, on Chart IX-a, we have one child of two feeble-minded parents who proves to be normal—the only one among the children. This child was also taken into a good family and brought up carefully. Another sister (Chart IX-b) was also taken into a good family and, while not determined, yet "showed none of the traits that are usually indicative of feeble-mindedness." It may be claimed that environment is responsible for this good result. It is certainly significant that the only children in these families that were normal, or at least better than the rest, were brought up in good families.

However, it would seem to be rather dangerous to base any very positive hope on environment in the light of these charts, taken as a whole. There are too many other possible explanations of the anomaly, e.g., these cases may have been high-grade morons, who, to the untrained person, would seem so nearly normal, that at this late day it would be impossible to find anyone who would remember their traits well enough to enable us to classify them as morons.

We must not forget that, on Chart IX-e, we also have the daughter of Justin taken into a good family and carefully brought up, but in spite of all that, she proved to be feeble-minded. The same is probably true of Deborah's half brother.

We have claimed that criminality resulting from feeble-mindedness is mainly a matter of environment, yet it must be acknowledged that there are wide differences in temperament and that, while this one branch of the Kallikak family was mentally defective, there was no strong tendency in it towards that which our laws recognize as criminality. In other families there is, without doubt, a much greater tendency to crime, so that the lack of criminals in this particular case, far from detracting from our argument, really strengthens it. It must be recognized that there is much more liability of criminals resulting from mental defectiveness in certain families than in others, probably because of difference in the strength of some instincts.

This difference in temperament is perhaps nowhere better brought out than in the grandparents of Deborah. The grandfather belonging to the Kallikak family had the temperament and characteristics of that family, which, while they did not lead him into positive criminality of high degree, nevertheless did make him a bad man of a positive type, a drunkard, a sex pervert, and all that goes to make up a bad character.

On the other hand, his wife and her family were simply stupid, with none of the pronounced tendencies to evil that were shown in the Kallikak family. They were not vicious, nor given over to bad practices of any sort. But they were inefficient, without power to get on in the world, and they transmitted these qualities to their descendants.

Thus, of the children of this pair, the grandparents of Deborah, the sons have been active and positive in their lives, the one being a horse thief, the other a sexual pervert, having the alcoholic tendency of his father, while the daughters are quieter and more passive. Their dullness, however, does not amount to imbecility. Deborah's mother herself was of a high type of moron, with a certain quality which carried with it an element of refinement. Her sister was the passive victim of her father's incestuous practice and later married a normal man. Another sister was twice married, the first time through the agency of the good woman who attended to the legalizing of Deborah's mother's alliances, the last time, the man, being normal, attended to this himself. He was old and only wanted a housekeeper, and this woman, having been strictly raised in an excellent family, was famous as a cook, so this arrangment seemed to him best. None of these sisters ever objected to the marriage ceremony when the matter was attended to for them, but they never seem to have thought of it as necessary when living with any man.

The stupid helplessness of Deborah's mother in regard to her own impulses is shown by the facts of her life. Her first child had for its father a farm hand; the father of the second and third (twins) was a common laborer on the railroad. Deborah's father was a young fellow, normal indeed, but loose in his morals, who, along with others, kept company with the mother while she was out at service. After Deborah's birth in the almshouse, the mother had been taken with her child into a good family. Even in this guarded position, she was sought out by a feeble-minded man of low habits. Every possible means was employed to separate the pair, but without effect. Her mistress then insisted that they marry, and herself attended to all the details. After Deborah's mother had borne this man two children, the pair went to live on the farm of an unmarried man possessing some property, but little intelligence. The husband was an imbecile who had never provided for his wife. She was still pretty, almost girlish—the farmer was good-looking, and soon the two were openly living together and the husband had left. As the facts became known, there was considerable protest in the neighborhood, but no active steps were taken until two or three children had been born. Finally, a number of leading citizens, headed by the good woman before alluded to, took the matter up in earnest. They found the husband and persuaded him to allow them to get him a divorce. Then they compelled the farmer to marry the woman. He agreed, on condition that the children which were not his should be sent away. It was at this juncture that Deborah was brought to the Training School.

In visiting the mother in her present home and in talking with her over different phases of her past life, several things are evident; there has been no malice in her life nor voluntary reaction against social order, but simply a blind following of impulse which never rose to objective consciousness. Her life has utterly lacked coördination—there has been no reasoning from cause to effect, no learning of any lesson. She has never known shame; in a word, she has never struggled and never suffered. Her husband is a selfish, sullen, penurious person who gives his wife but little money, so that she often resorts to selling soap and other things among her neighbors to have something to spend. At times she works hard in the field as a farm hand, so that it cannot be wondered at that her house is neglected and her children unkempt. Her philosophy of life is the philosophy of the animal. There is no complaining, no irritation at the inequalities of fate. Sickness, pain, childbirth, death—she accepts them all with the same equanimity as she accepts the opportunity of putting a new dress and a gay ribbon on herself and children and going to a Sunday School picnic. There is no rising to the comprehension of the possibilities which life offers or of directing circumstances to a definite, higher end. She has a certain fondness for her children, but is incapable of real solicitude for them. She speaks of those who were placed in homes and is glad to see their pictures, and has a sense of their belonging to her, but it is faint, remote, and in no way bound up with her life. She is utterly helpless to protect her older daughters, now on the verge of womanhood, from the dangers that beset them, or to inculcate in them any ideas which would lead to self-control or to the directing of their lives in an orderly manner.

The same lack is strikingly shown, if we turn our attention to the question of alcoholism in this family. We learn from a responsible member of the good branch of the family that the appetite for alcoholic stimulants has been strong in the past in this family and that several members in recent generations have been more or less addicted to its use. Only two have actually allowed it to get the better of them to the extent that they became incapacitated. Both were physicians. In the other branch, however, with the weakened mentality, we find twenty-four victims of this habit so pronounced that they were public nuisances. We have taken no account of the much larger number who were also addicted to its use, but who did not become so bad as to be considered alcoholic in our category.

Thus we see that the normal mentality of the good branch of the family was able to cope successfully with this intense thirst, while the weakened mentality on the other side was unable to escape, and many fell victims to this appalling habit.

It is such facts as these, taken as we find them, not only in this family but in many of the other families whose records we are soon to publish, that lead us to the conclusion that drunkenness is, to a certain extent at least, the result of feeble-mindedness and that one way to reduce drunkenness is first to determine the mentally defective people, and save them from the environment which would lead them into this abuse.

Again, eight of the descendants of the degenerate Kallikak branch were keepers of houses of ill fame, and that in spite of the fact that they mostly lived in a rural community where such places do not flourish as they do in large cities.

In short, whereas in the Jukes-Edwards comparison we have no sound basis for argument, because the families were utterly different and separate, in the Kallikak family the conclusion seems thoroughly logical. We have, as it were, a natural experiment with a normal branch with which to compare our defective side. We have the one ancestor giving us a line of normal people that shows thoroughly good all the way down the generations, with the exception of the one man who was sexually loose and the two who gave way to the appetite for strong drink.

This is our norm, our standard, our demonstration of what the Kallikak blood is when kept pure, or mingled with blood as good as its own.

Over against this we have the bad side, the blood of the same ancestor contaminated by that of the nameless feeble-minded girl.

From this comparison the conclusion is inevitable that all this degeneracy has come as the result of the defective mentality and bad blood having been brought into the normal family of good blood, first from the nameless feeble-minded girl and later by additional contaminations from other sources.

The biologist could hardly plan and carry out a more rigid experiment or one from which the conclusions would follow more inevitably.

THE
CONTROL OF
FEEBLE-MINDEDNESS

E. Arthur Whitney

The author argues for the legalization of eugenic sterilization to achieve "race betterment" by the elimination of the "unfit."

Ours is a complex civizilation that grows in complexities with each rising generation. To cope with these ever deepening mazes requires an ever ready mind capable of meeting any emergency. It is the duty of the present generation to strive to produce healthy minds in the next, in so far as is possible. One of the most essential factors in accomplishing this end is the elimination of feeble-mindedness. The feeble-minded alone number 656,000 according to the census of 1920. Popenoe estimates the total to be 1,200,000. Probably the discrepancy between these figures is accounted for by those not classified as feeble-minded as such but who will be listed as criminals, defective delinquents, moral imbeciles, social misfits and insane. Fairly conservative estimates state that 38 per cent of the criminals, 80 per cent of the defective delinquents, 50 per cent of the moral imbeciles and nearly 10 per cent of the insane are feeble-minded.

The biological process which we term heredity functions according to, and with the guidance of, certain well defined laws. One of the most fundamental laws of this biological process is, "Like begets like." This indisputable law we have at our command. It is up to us to use it wisely by preventing the feeble-minded from begetting more feeble-minded.

It has been said that there is nothing inconsistent between the care of the feeble-minded hitherto accepted as the kindest and most effective, and the eugenical point of view. It seems to me that eugenical sterilization may be said to be in the broadest sense the kindest and most effective way of aiding the feeble-minded.

Horticulturists and animal breeders know and use the laws of heredity. One of the outstanding examples is found in the story of the late Luther Burbank. During his life time, by exercising the properly controlled power of heredity, he evolved myriads of new plants and flowers for our joy and mutual benefit. If we but apply the principles of heredity to human beings, then we may evolve a superior race and in so doing, eliminate the social menace of those who are the feeble-minded.

The union of two feeble-minded individuals can only result in feeble-minded offspring. Examples without number can be related to verify this statement. Unions in which one member alone is feeble-minded will result in at least 50 per cent of the issue being feeble-minded. In a recent study of 5,000 cases of feeble-minded, parental feeble-mindedness was found in over 65 per cent of these cases.

Untold millions are spent yearly in the care of the dependent feeble-minded individuals. Taxation of the fit has to be the means of support of

Eugenics, May, 1929. Reprinted with permission of Mrs. E. A. Whitney.

Dr. Whitney was superintendent of the Elwyn Training School from 1930 until 1959. He died in April 1966.

those unfit. If we could but eliminate the unfit, known to be so through heredity, the burden of taxation on the fit would in one generation be reduced at least 65 per cent.

Eugenical sterilization is the only means whereby we may be sure of eliminating hereditary feeble-mindedness. However, at the present time there are only twenty-three states that have legalized eugenical sterilization. In these states but about 7,000 sterizilations have been performed. We know that there are 656,000 avowed feeble-minded. The sterilization of all these should be our goal—a large order to be sure, but one well worth fulfilling.

The ways and means to be used in accomplishing this end are too numerous to mention in a short paper. Paramount in the attempt is the education of public opinion. "Money talks" is a truism that cannot be questioned. We must make the American people realize that the annual expenditure for the care and maintenance of the mentally unfit can be reduced 65 per cent if we can but control that biological process of heredity.

Of the twenty-three states having legislation permitting sterilization, the actual enforcement of the law in these states is woefully lacking. In Pennsylvania there is no statute authorizing eugenical sterilization. However, a number of these operations have been performed in this state at the request of parents or guardians. In the Elwyn Training School alone, 262 inmates have been asexualized, 133 males and 129 females. We expect legislation in favor of eugenical sterilization in the next meeting of the state legislature.

Nearly every state is caring for large numbers of these mentally unfit in state and private institutions. The state receives these unfortunates and conscientiously cares for them as a duty, but that duty will remain not fully discharged so long as there remains the possibility and, in all too many instances, the probability of many of these reproducing their kind.

It is up to the medical profession as well as to the social welfare organizations in those states having legalized sterilization, to act. In acting, the profession will become a humanitarian profession in the broadest sense of the word; and if there is an obligation to action upon the medical profession and social organizations of the several states in which sterilization is legalized, so much the more is it the duty of the medical profession and social welfare organizations to get behind or instigate legislation in commonwealths without such laws.

Let us face the problems of race betterment with a clear vision. Let us give to the laboratory of nature the best materials with which to work by eliminating the mentally unfit, and we can expect from that laboratory a healthy and sound mind in future generations.

SOME RESULTS
OF
SELECTIVE
STERILIZATION

E. Arthur Whitney and Mary McD. Shick

Sterilization is described as most necessary for the "high-grade to the border-line case in which there is unquestionably hereditary mental deficiency" so as to facilitate parole and release procedures. It is also recommended for the "low-grade imbecile" for improvement of obscene habits and general mental condition.

In any attempt to remove a burden on society, it is the dictate of wisdom to select those agencies which are most likely to bring about the greatest results with the least labor or sacrifice of means. It is far better to dig up and destroy evil roots than to only lop off the branches. An untold amount of time, labor and cost are consumed in dealing with the *effects* of the evil of mental deficiency while little is done towards reducing or removing sources and primary causes.

It is not our idea that mental deficiency can be entirely prevented or eradicated through selective sterilization, but that this measure is a step in the right direction.

This Society has had papers presented to it covering a period of nearly 40 years for and against sterilization. The first to urge such a measure was one of the founders, Dr. Isaac Kerlin. In his address as President of this Association in 1892, Dr. Kerlin said: "While considering the help that advanced surgery is to give to us, I will refer to a conviction I have had that life-long salutary results to many of our boys and girls would be realized if before adolescence their procreative organs were removed. My experience extends to only a single case to confirm this conviction; but when I consider the great benefit that this young woman has received, the entire arrest of an epileptic tendency as well as the removal of inordinate desires which made her an offense to the Community; when I see the tranquil well ordered life she is leading, her industry and usefulness in the circle in which she moves, and know that surgery has been her salvation from vice and degradation, I am deeply thankful to the benevolent lady whose loyalty to science and comprehensive charity made this operation possible. I hope the time will come when popular sentiment will not stand opposed, as it now is, to the radical reliefs and helps which may come to the defective and criminal classes by the introduction of this kind of palliative surgery."—"Whose State shall be the first to legalize oophorectomy and orchotomia for the relief and cure of radical depravity."

Following these remarks of Dr. Kerlin's, there were for some years rather frequent discussions on the subject of sterilization, culminating in Pennsylvania's attempt at a law in 1905. This bill was vetoed and hence it was not until 1907 that Dr. Kerlin's question was answered and Indiana became the first to legalize this measure.

It is not our purpose to review the history and literature on sterilization in detail. Suffice it to state that for forty years the subject has been discussed in this association, and the chances are it will continue to be discussed. Public opinion is not yet ready to accept this idea. This association as a whole has

Journal of Psycho-Asthenics, 1931, 36, 330–338. Reprinted by permission of Mrs. E. A. Whitney and the American Association on Mental Deficiency.

Dr. Shick was staff physician at Elwyn Institute.

not been ready to accept it. However, Dr. Watkin's excellent paper of a year ago, together with his ability as a (may we say) "salesman" has done much towards arousing sentiment here in favor of the procedure.

Many are the terms that have been used and *are* used to designate selective sterilization. Castration was probably the first general term utilized; next we find asexualization and desexualization in the literature. Later such expressions as human sterilization and sterilization came into vogue. However, we feel that "selective sterilization" is better for descriptive purposes. All feebleminded do not need to be sterilized, but in certain *selective* instances sterilization should be a part of our therapeutics in dealing with the mentally handicapped.

To every member of this organization the word sterilization alone would suffice to express the meaning intended, but in order to convey to others what we mean, some descriptive term must be added.

In general we feel that we can select two distinct groups for sterilization and for two distinct reasons. The first, and by far the most important group, is that of the high-grade to the borderline case in which there is unquestionably hereditary mental deficiency. This group needs selective sterilization to prevent further propagation of their kind. More of this type of individual are outside than within our institutions. However, if those who are institutionalized could be rendered sterile, release or parole would be safer for the individual and for the community.

The second group, which is entirely an institutional type, is the low-grade imbecile of obscene habits. We have found that sterilization has a definite value with these. We do not advocate it to prevent their propagating their kind because they are permanently segregated and in nearly every case are physiologically incapable of reproduction.

We do not consider it within the province of this paper to deal with objections that have been raised to selective sterilization. We would like to point out that more women have been sterilized, without the same objections, for heart, kidney, lung and local pelvic diseases than have been for selective sterilization of the insane or feebleminded. We feel that this measure is just as ethical a procedure for the mentally deficient as it is for any other reason.

In the past thirty-nine years since Dr. Kerlin had the first operation done at Elwyn, approximately 270 of our patients have been sterilized. The results of most of these have been published in previous papers. In this paper we wish to summarize only those results noted in the past 10 years. During this period 98 operations were done—59 males and 39 females. Of these, 58 were of the middle and high-grade groups.

The first group of 58, consists of 38 males and 20 females. From the operative standpoint these cases made uneventful recoveries. There were no

complications and recovery was prompt and complete. No marked physio-
logic changes were noted in cases where sex glands were removed. However,
in a number of these individuals, we did note changes for the better in habits,
mentality and temperament. Habit changes in this type of case are less
marked than in the lower-grade group. Most of them "brighten up" considerably mentally and the majority seem more easily managed and less temperamental.

(CASE HISTORY OF E. M. TO ILLUSTRATE)

E. M. was born June 3rd, 1905. High-grade imbecile. Representative
notes taken from our School Progress records, we feel, will illustrate the
results in this case.

April 1920:—Chief Physician reports E. M. as a sexual pervert, sexually exaggerated and constantly in trouble. Fond of tale bearing.

Jan. 1921:—Teacher reports E. M. as constantly getting others into
trouble. A writer of vile messages in school, careless of tools—indolent.

June 1922:—Teacher reports him as lazy and careless. He was dismissed from the band but later was given another chance. Conduct and
application decidedly poor.

Jan. 1924:—Instructor reports him as giving unlimited trouble every-
where; disobedient, insolent, lazy, and refuses to be influenced by kindness.

Operation March 14th, 1924—Vasectomy.

June 1925:—Teacher reports him as still lazy and careless in band
room. In carpenter shop he is applying himself fairly well if left alone.

March 1927:—Instructors report him as willing to do anything and
everything, but really doing nothing well. He is improving in the band and
is more reliable.

June 1928:—Matron reports him as having settled down quite a bit.
However, he still has stubborn spells when he is quite hard to manage. He
does his best work when given a little responsibility. In the printing office
he has been found to be a steady, reliable and good worker.

July 1930:—Instructor reports that he has become a valuable asset to
the band. After the death of a former band librarian he was given the
position and is doing very well. No evidences now of sexual perversion.

This case we feel illustrates well the slow but steady improvement in
habits and mental development following selective sterilization.

The group illustrated by the above case shows the following statistics:

	Operations	Improvement of habits	Improvement mentally
Females ...	20	14 or 70%	7—35%
Males	38	30 or 78.9%	16—42%

Thus we had for the group 74½% improvement in habits. Improvement in habits includes not only sexual habits but habits of life and dress and of general conduct. The improvement in mentality, as illustrated by the better work done in school and in institutional tasks, is less marked than that in habits, but we have found that 38½% of our cases showed definite changes in their mental attitude and aptitude. We believe these improvements are largely due to the psychic effect on the personality of the individual who has been so treated. Many of this high-grade group realize the physiological meaning of the operation. Those who have shown excessive sex interests have a definite tendency to turn their thoughts to other channels.

Next we want to consider briefly the second group to which little reference is found in the literature. This is the low-grade type, 40 of whom we have sterilized. Most of these have had the organs of sex removed. Little or no untoward effects have been noted by us in removing the testicles or ovaries in these individuals. This group consists of 21 males and 19 females. We will illustrate this type also by reciting two case histories.

Case 1. R. A. Female, born February 25th, 1908. A low-grade excitable deaf mute.

April 1924:—Matron reports R. A. as going down hill mentally. Runs through dormitory nude, kicks other girls, beats her body, is restless and noisy at night. Retrogression dates from onset of menses. Habits are disgustingly obscene and worse during menstrual cycle.

Operation June 1928.

At operation only one ovary, the right, was found and removed. Left could not be located. The appendix was also removed. There was a short menstrual period in July but none since. Evidently a case of congenital unilateral ovary.

July 1930:—Matron reports R. A. as considerably better behaved. Masturbation has ceased, general appearance improved and she is less excitable.

Case 2. E. H. Female, born August 26th, 1910. A low-grade excitable idio-imbecile.

E. H. was frequently reported by matrons and teachers as being untrainable, difficult to manage, obscene in habits, a chronic masturbator herself and with other children. Often she was cruel to smaller and younger children.

Operation December 1927. Double oophorectomy.

June 1928:—Matron reports E. H. as much quieter; will dry scrub and aid about dormitory.

May 1929:—Matron reports marked improvement, especially in habits and in conduct towards other children.

Sept. 1930:—Matron reports bad habits have ceased. She is doing household tasks, is quiet, tractable and kindly towards other children in the ward.

In this group as a whole we find the following results:—

	Cases Operated	Habit Improvement
Male	21	18 85.7% ⎫
		⎬ 82.3%
Females	19	15 78.9% ⎭

We mention only habit improvements in these cases as that in each case was what was most desired. All were of such low mentality that one could expect little, if any, mental improvement. However, some did seem to "brighten up" for a time following the operation. To obtain improvement in the habits alone in 82 per cent of these cases is to us a justification of the operation.

In conclusion we want to stress one point. We have in selective sterilization one factor applicable to the care and development of the defective individual; not a *panacea* but a *proposition* that should be a part of our therapeutics in handling mental deficiency.

DISCUSSION

DR. BUTLER: I want to commend the doctor's paper, for the great work he is doing at Elwyn. His two main points, improvement on the lower grade type and on the higher grade type, especially the improvement of the lower is very commendable. The majority of the cases in our institution have been among the higher grade type, only sterilizing the lower grade type, chiefly the female, whom we are permitting to go on parole. We all know that there are even the lowest grade type of women of whom men will take advantage in their own home or in the community, whereas with the lower grade male, they do not, nor do they know what sex really means. Consequently, they do not get into trouble in the community as compared with the female.

I was interested to know the result that they are obtaining with the lower grade type. We have not made any special survey of the lower grade type along that line, but we have for our group as a whole, and found that sterilization had improved their general condition in many ways, in at least 37 percent, as well as making them more easily controlled. They seem to concentrate better, especially those we call the hypersexual type, of which we have many, as we have in our institutions, unfortunately, defective delinquents of both sexes.

We have at the present time in California, sterilized nearly 8000 since 1909. The majority of these were done since 1918. In our institution alone, among feebleminded and epileptics we have sterilized a little over 2000, the vast majority of whom are female, for the reasons mentioned before.

We have had no ill effects of any kind with the exception of one case where there might be an ill effect, in that before he was sterilized and while on parole he had no sex tendencies. After sterilization, again on parole, he did start to expose himself and had to be returned to the institution for that reason. That might have been a coincidence. However, it might have been on account of the fact that sterilization had increased his sex desire.

Some people get the idea that sterilization increases promiscuity and venereal diseases. Our survey, or a survey made by the Human Betterment Foundation in Pasadena, which some of you know, headed by Mr. Gosney and Dr. Popenoe, who made a survey of all our institutions where sterilization was practiced found no ill effects in their various papers covering the various points.

We feel, with this result, and the result that the doctor has mentioned here, that sterilization is on a good foundation. There are now 23 states in the Union having valid laws and four foreign countries. And other foreign countries are trying to secure legislation along that line.

The hereditary type of individuals—we used to consider first. In the last few years, it has been brought home to us so much that we have reached the point where we practically disregard whether they are of the hereditary or non-hereditary type, for the reason that rarely is it possible for a feeble-minded mother to care for children properly. I know it is manifested in our State. We have dozens of mothers in our institution with children in the community whom they were not able to care for. Some of them have as high as 11 children, all defective. But the saddest part of all, in my estimation, is a feebleminded mother trying to care for normal, or so-called normal children. As brought out by Dr. Vanuxem, the feebleminded parents beget the feeble-minded children. Out of her 40 some children, I think it was 8 or 10 who came in the normal class, but on the other side of the sheet it showed that the parent or the father, usually of the higher grade type or normal individual, consequently brought that person's intelligence up to the higher level.

We have in our institution several males and females whom we have permitted to marry, who became acquainted in the institution, who are out now maintaining their own homes, very happy indeed. Some of them own their own property. Had it not been for sterilization, it would not have been possible for these individuals to live as you and I desire to live, and as these patients are living today. In this group, as I stated a while ago, of 165 who were married, we have only had very few failures as compared to marriages among normal persons. Of course there is a reason for this, first, before we permit them to marry, all of them are sterilized. Our social service department makes a thorough investigation of the mate, including if necessary a Wassermann test to see if they have any venereal disease or anything in the family history. I believe this is done more than the average parent does, and we keep them on parole for about two years as a minimum after marriage, because the first two years is the most difficult period. We find in ours it is especially true. When we first permitted marriage I gave some of our patients a discharge as a wedding present, to my regret afterwards. Some we do discharge in 6 months, some who have been on parole for many years when we know they are successful, we know that their mate comes from a good family, although a ne'er-do-well class, most of them, or in the defective class, and as a result, we are able with supervision to keep them adjusted and going along nicely.

I hope the time will come when every State will have a law permitting sterilization, and every foreign country. How important it is that this be spread over the world was manifested last year at the International Congress of Mental Hygiene at Washington. Talking with many of the foreign delegates on this particular point from some of the more remote countries of the world, they are thinking along this very line.

On the West Coast we get the misfits from many of the Eastern states, coming to California, thinking they can get not only physical health but mental health by sunshine and fresh air.

We tried to get a law through the legislature this year permitting sterilization outside of institutions. We did not get it by but we are not stopping. We all know that the mentally unfit are coming into the world very fast for those who cannot reach State institutions. As a result of the White House Conference on Child Health and Protection, their survey shows in this direction that mentally handicapped children are 2 per cent of the people in the United States. From the type called undesirable, if you take 2 per cent, the majority of whom might bring defectives into the world you can see what it is going to mean. It means 50,000 in California alone, while we have only 3000 in our institution. The rest of the group are going ahead and propagating very, very rapidly. I hope the time will come when this organization will see fit to officially endorse sterilization.

About three years ago I was asked by a cablegram from a foreign country, to obtain the endorsement of all our State organizations and send it to them as quickly as possible for legislative purposes, and especially they wanted one from the State Medical Society. I got it from every other organization including the Governor's but did not get it from the State Medical Society because it hadn't worked up to that point and given enough thought to get their endorsement. I hope we can, along with the medical minds, think along that line and with organizations such as this kind, which are on a medical basis, we would get further results.

DR. SHICK: May I say just a word with regard to the low-grade patient. Those who take care of low-grade girls in institutions know what an awful charge it is at the menstrual period. It is hard to get attendants to do the work. Now if we could prevent the menstrual period, that alone would make the work with the low-grade girls in the institutions simpler and give better results.

DR. WHITNEY: We are all glad to hear from California because that State is the outstanding one in this particular work. I am glad that Dr. Butler concurs with us in the improvement in habits and concentration on these cases. Dr. Butler spoke of normal children of feebleminded mothers, and the care that the feebleminded mothers can give to a normal child. We have a shining example of that at Elwyn; a rather low-grade feebleminded woman who had an illegitimate child. That child was cared for by a foster family and later found out that his mother was at Elwyn. He came and wanted to see his mother. Dr. Barr took him to one of our custodial buildings where this mother lived and told him to stand in the doorway and he would go over and say something to his mother, which he did. When Dr. Barr came back, the man said, "Is that my mother?" Dr. Barr said "yes,"—he left immediately and we have never heard from him since.

SECTION NINE

Light on the Horizon

The follow-up study of persons previously diagnosed as mentally retarded and currently living in the community as adults has made an important contribution to the mental retardation literature. Dating from the prototype report of Fernald in 1919, through later studies of Fairbanks (1933), Baller (1936), Charles (1953), Wolfson (1956), Dinger (1961), Miller (1965), and Kennedy (1966), investigators have been consistent in revealing satisfactory adjustment of many previously identified retarded individuals.

Fernald's original investigation studied the adjustment of 1,537 former residents of the Waverley State School during the twenty-five-year period from 1890 to 1914. His techniques of locating and gathering information about these persons established a methodology imitated in many subsequent follow-up investigations. Fifty-one per cent of the females located still remained in the community at the time of investigation, and the majority of these had no record of legal difficulty. Sixty-four per cent of the males had remained out of the institution but they were less likely than the females to be married or self-supporting.

Although Fernald was extremely cautious in generalizing from his results, it is apparent that the findings were unexpected and were an important influence in changing attitudes about the need for life-long segregation for the retarded.

Since Fernald's study, numerous follow-up investigations have been conducted for populations of mentally retarded persons discharged from institutions as well as those identified in special classes in the public schools. The more recent studies have improved their methodology, using appropriate control populations matched according to social and economic backgrounds and status (e.g., Kennedy, 1962).

The results of these studies have been uniformly optimistic. There is now little doubt that retarded graduates of special classes in the public schools, and those discharged from institutions, are often able to adjust in the community without drawing undue attention to themselves as social, legal, or occupational misfits. After reviewing twenty-five longitudinal follow-up studies, Tizard (1958) concludes:

"It is apparent from what has been said that, even during the depression years, substantial numbers of mentally retarded subnormal children were able, upon leaving school, to find jobs for themselves and live as self-supporting, socially competent members of society. . . . In the postwar years, during which full employment has come to be accepted as something more than a mere temporary phenomenon, the proportion of mentally subnormal persons who are socially competent has, of course, increased markedly" (p. 447).

More recently major reviews of adjustment outcomes and prognosis have been supplied by Windle (1962), Goldstein (1964), Eagle (1967), and McCarver and Craig (in press).

In 1969, Arthur Jensen revived the age-old, nature-nurture controversy by attempting to answer the question of the relative contribution of genetic and environmental components to the variance of the I.Q. His conclusions concerning the high contribution of genetic factors (heritability), the relative ineffectiveness of early educational attempts with deprived populations, and genetic racial differences, evoked a volley of reaction still reverberating in the psychological and educational journals.

That one of the oldest issues in developmental psychology is still capable of generating such controversy attests to its perceived importance to psychology as a science and to the philosophy underlying educational practice. The heated battles, scientific and otherwise, ensuing from the Jensen thesis are reminiscent of a similar controversy aroused in the 1930's when the research investigations which came to be known as the "Iowa Studies" were being published.

After receiving his Ph.D. at the Iowa Child Welfare Research Station in 1932, Harold Manville Skeels held joint appointments for the next decade at the Research Station and the Iowa Board of Control of State Institutions. Although originally trained in animal husbandry with a firm foundation in genetics, Skeels, along with a productive group of scientists including Harold B. Dye, Marie Skodak Crissey, George Stoddard, and Beth Wellman, became interested in the possibility that environmental stimulation and early intervention could influence the development of mental traits previously thought to be entirely hereditary.

Marie Skodak Crissey, collaborator in this research, described the reaction to this research, in a necrology for Dr. Skeels which appeared in the American Journal of Mental Deficiency in 1970:

"As results of the studies appeared in the journals, beginning in the mid-thirties, an avalanche of criticism was hurled at the 'Iowa group.' As the one responsible for the most dramatic of these studies—the placement of retarded infants in institutions for the retarded with their subsequent normalcy and placement in adoptive homes—Harold Skeels was particularly singled out for attack. It is difficult now to understand the vehemence these studies provoked. Among the most corrosive attacks was the one at the annual meeting of the American Association on Mental Deficiency, in Chicago in 1939, where Skeels reported the findings with particular reference to mental retardation. On the 27th anniversary of this paper, in 1966 in Chicago, he presented a follow-up study of the same children, who as adults showed dramatically the long-term results of differences in childhood opportunities. . . ."

Crissey also reports events in 1968 when prevailing opinion had completely reversed itself. Skeels received recognition (along with Crissey) from the Joseph P. Kennedy Jr. Foundation as recipient of the Joseph P. Kennedy International Award for Research in Mental Retardation. "The stirring presentation ceremonies on April 28, 1968, reached their dramatic climax when Senator Edward Kennedy turned the Steuben crystal trophy to Louis Branca for presentation. In a moving speech, the poised young man identified himself as one of the children in Dr. Skeels' landmark study."

The research laboratory at Vineland started by Goddard continued its programs under the leadership of Edgar A. Doll, director of research from 1925 to 1949. Doll was an important contributor to the field, actively advocating the concept of parole and community care of the mentally deficient. He is best known for his efforts to develop criteria of social functioning to supplement the intelligence test in diagnosing mental deficiency. The Vineland Social Maturity Scale, developed under his direction, was an early precursor of present-day attempts to assess adaptive behavior, and is still a widely used instrument.

Another glimmer of light, visible in the 1920's and 1930's, was the growing recognition of the importance of public school education for the mentally retarded and the need for a close working relationship between public schools and institutions in dealing with the social rehabilitation of the mentally retarded person. Howe had seen the institution as "a link in the chain of common schools." During the period of public alarm about the "menace" of retardation, there were many who argued against the use of the public schools for the education of retarded children. A few stalwart individuals such as Wallin and Davies maintained a constant appeal for involvement of the schools in identification, educational diagnosis and prescription, enforcement of compulsory education laws for *all* children, development of pre-school programs, and provision of training facilities for children who can be maintained in the community, even those functioning below educable levels of instruction. Davies' insistence that "the determination of cases for institutional care should be made on a social rather than on an intellectual basis" was far ahead of his time.

All of the ideas and concepts which so characterized the improvements in programming during the 1960's and 1970's had already surfaced during the first half of this century. Only the climate remained to be altered to catalyze these changes.

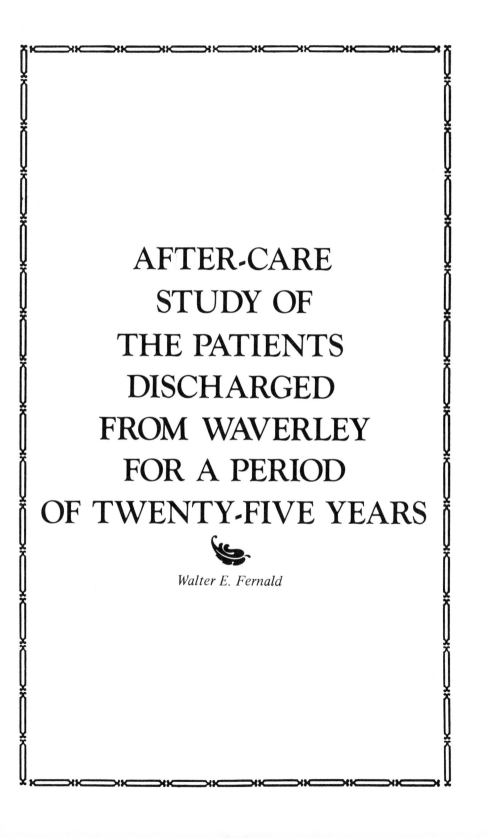

AFTER-CARE
STUDY OF
THE PATIENTS
DISCHARGED
FROM WAVERLEY
FOR A PERIOD
OF TWENTY-FIVE YEARS

Walter E. Fernald

The author reports a study of 646 males and females discharged from the state school at Waverley, Massachusetts, over a twenty-five-year period. The generally favorable adjustment of over half these persons, who "constituted no serious menace to the community," was unexpected by Fernald. "There was a surprisingly small amount of criminality and sex offense, and expecially of illegitimacy." The author is drawn reluctantly to the conclusion that "a few defectives do not need or deserve lifelong segregation."

Early in 1916 the following circular letter was sent to the friends of all patients discharged into the community from Waverley during the twenty-five years 1890–1914 inclusive:

"We are reviewing the last twenty-five years' work of the School and are especially studying the influence of the School upon the boys and girls who have been with us during the period in the hope that our future work may be of more help to the boys and girls who come to us.

For this reason we are anxious to know all that we can of our former pupils,—whether they are now living, where they are now living, how they have occupied themselves, whether they have been useful and helpful at home, or are able to wholly or partially support themselves by work at home, or for wages, whether they have been able to look out for themselves, their problems, trials, experiences, etc.

We especially want to know whether their stay at the School was of benefit to them, and as to what part of their training was most beneficial, whether the school work, the manual training, etc., and especially as to how they might have been better fitted to take care of themselves.

We should very much appreciate a little note from you telling us these facts in regard to. . . . Perhaps you would be willing that we should call upon you some day to talk about these matters. I need not tell you that we should be very glad to be of service to our former pupils in any way. I am enclosing a stamped, addressed envelope, and shall be grateful for a reply."

This letter elicited a cordial and friendly reply from the relatives of a majority of the living and accessible patients. Those who did not reply were evidently pleased at the attention, and graciously welcomed the social worker who visited them a few days after the letter was received. This visitor talked with the family, the pastor, local officials, the police, etc. The information obtained was checked up from several sources in each case.

The total number of discharges for the period was 1537. Of this number 891 were not considered in this inquiry for the following reasons:

187 were directly transferred to other institutions for the feeble-minded,

153 were directly transferred to hospitals for the insane,

89 were directly transferred to hospitals for epileptics,

8 were directly transferred to other custodial institutions,

175 from other states had been sent to those states,

279 could not be located.

This left 646, 470 males and 176 females, whose history in the community could be obtained. Of this number 54 males and 24 females had died, and 68 males and 33 females had been re-admitted to the School.

The relatively small number of discharges for so long a period, with an average number present ranging from 640 in 1890 to 1660 in 1914, shows

Ungraded, 1919, 5(2):25–31. Obtained through the courtesy of the School of Pedagogy Library, New York University.

that the policy of long-continued segregation was consistently followed during the entire period. We honestly believed that nearly all of these people should remain in the institution indefinitely. Some were allowed to go because they seemed to have no vicious tendencies, and their friends were intelligent and able to look out for them, but the majority were dismissed under protest. Not a few of the males took matters into their own hands, and ran away. Those who could not be located were largely the children of recently arrived immigrants in the large cities.

Of the 176 female cases where the history could be obtained, 27 had married, and there were 50 children; 17 children had died and 33 were living. The social worker saw nearly all of these children, and was not sure that any of them were defective. Seven of the married women had no children. Nearly all of the women had married men whose social status was rather above that of their own parents.

Eleven married women were living useful and blameless lives; had neat and attractive homes, bore good reputations in the community, went to church, and apparently were making good in every way. All but one of the married women were morons. One was an imbecile, and her marriage had, of course, turned out badly. These 11 women had 34 children, all of whom seemed normal. Of the 11 successfully married home-makers, 3 were discharged without protest, at the request of responsible relatives; 8 of the group seemed so unpromising that they were not allowed to go from the School until their discharge was ordered by the Supreme Court on a writ of habeas corpus; all of the group of 11 were apparently definitely feeble-minded. All had been immoral before admission, and at first, after their admission to the School, were troublesome on account of their active sex interest. After their discharge and previous to their marriages, they had apparently behaved themselves and had earned their own living.

Of the 16 married women who are behaving badly, every one was discharged against our judgment, and only after a long contest and the use of powerful political influence; in 9 cases, the Courts ordered the discharge. In these 16 unsuccessful marriages, the women turned out about as we had predicted, with a record of sex promiscuity, alcoholism, thievery, etc. Four women had syphilis. None of them conducted a decent home. In all they had 24 children,—one woman had 10 children; one married moron, who had 2 children, and 1, who had 6 children, were subsequently returned to the School. Both had been taken away from the School by town authorities, under strong protest.

There were 11 unmarried mothers among the 176 discharges, and there were 13 illegitimate children in all. Of these mothers, 8 were morons and 3 were imbeciles. Eight of these women were returned to the School after child-birth. Every one of these women was exceedingly troublesome while at the School, and all were discharged only after a long contest. Not one of them had relatives with sufficient intelligence to give any assurance that they would be able to protect the defective daughter or sister, and none were closely supervised.

There were 48 females with a history of known sex immorality after discharge, including 16 married women, 11 unmarried mothers, and 14 subsequently committed to other institutions. Five girls were promptly returned to the School because of immorality. Three women were known to be occasional prostitutes for hire before commitment to other institutions. Three women were known to have syphilis, all in the married group. We did not find any record of other venereal disease. Apparently the discharged female patients have not contributed largely to the sex and venereal problem. Patients with active sex proclivities or with unsuitable relatives were not willingly discharged. The discharged cases had received years of habit-training and education, and the relatives themselves had come to realize the possible sex proclivities of the patients. Apparently the women who had friends capable of understanding them, and of properly protecting them, did not have illegitimate children, and did not become sex offenders.

Twenty-nine women drifted into other institutions after discharge,—4 to hospitals for epileptics, 10 to hospitals for the insane, 1 to prison, and 3 to girls' reformatories. In 25 years only 4 out of 176 women had been sentenced to penal institutions.

As to the economic status of the 176 women, aside from the 11 successfully married women, only 8 were fully and independently supporting and maintaining themselves in the way of getting their own jobs and paying their own bills as ordinary working women do. Of these 8, 1 was earning $6 per week as a nurse maid, and had been four years in the position; 1 was earning from $3 to $7 per week, and had been out 15 years; 1 received $4 per week in a candy factory, another $5 per week in a candy factory, 1 $9 in a cotton mill, and another $20 per month and living in housework. All of them were morons.

There were 32, helping with the housework and not being a burden, although not earning regular wages away from home, but capable of doing ordinary housework at home or for neighbors; some earning wages but not a living wage, carrying a share of the burden of the home. One was in the illegitimacy group, and had two illegitimate children, 3 had active sex tendencies, and 8 were disobedient and troublesome, but 20 had splendid records, and there was no reason why they should not continue to live at home. They were of the low moron and high imbecile group, as a rule. These cases had friends able and willing to protect and care for them.

There were 23 cases of the imbecile and idiot group grade at home, not capable of self support, or of doing anything but the most simple housework;

2 were unmarried mothers; 2 were troublesome sexually; 6 were noisy and troublesome; but the others seemed to be well cared for and protected by their relatives, without annoyance to the neighbors or the family. The character of the home and the intelligence of the family largely determined the result.

To sum up, for 176 discharged female patients, we have the following report:

Married (11 doing well) 27
Self-supporting and self-controlling, unmarried 8
Working at home under supervision 32
Living at home, not able to do much work 23
Committed to other institutions 29
Died 24
Re-admitted to Waverley 33

    Total 176

Of the 90 discharged females now at liberty, 52 are apparently giving no trouble, viz:

Married, living at home 11
Self-supporting 8
Of those working at home 20
Of those living at home 13

In the following tables, some persons are counted in more than one classification, so the totals apparently do not check,—viz: some of the unmarried mothers are in the immoral group, illegitimacy cases in the re-admitted group, etc. The following groups have behaved badly, viz.:

Married women, sex offenses 16
Unmarried mothers 11
Sex offenders not included above 21
Sent to other institutions 29
Of those working at home 12
Of those living at home 10
Re-admitted to Waverley 33

Of the 470 males, 28 were earning a good living, without supervision. All of these were morons. Their stay in the School had varied from 1 month to 20 years. They had been away from the School from 2 to 23 years. Eight ran away from the School. Others went on trial because they seemed useful and harmless, and were very desirous of their liberty. Few seemed capable of self-support while at the School. Their weekly wages ran from $8 to $36. They were working as teamster, elevator man, city laborer, factory worker, farm laborer, soda clerk, tinsmith, carpenter, painter, chauffeur, machinist, etc. One is in business for himself as a sign-painter, a trade he learned at the School. In fact, many are following occupations they learned at the School. One had saved $2000; another had bought a house. Eleven of the group had married, and of these marriages there were 9 children. These 28 men seemed to have a blameless record in their community. They are good citizens, regarded as simple-minded men and recognized as such by their employers, and by their wives, for where they had married normal women (as they nearly all did), the wives spoke very kindly of the mental limitations of their husbands.

Thirteen men in all had married. As before stated, 11 were well behaved and industrious. Two married men were able to support themselves, but had been sentenced to the Reformatory for larceny. There were twelve children altogether,—6 had no children, 1 had 3 children, 3 had 2 each and 3 had 1 each. The investigator saw all the children, and none of them seemed abnormal. The children were clean and well-behaved, and the homes were neat and well-kept. The two men with a criminal record earned $1.50 a day; the other 11 earned from $12 to $18 per week.

Eighty-six were steadily working for regular wages, living at home, closely supervised by their relatives. Nearly every one was a moron, although there were a few high imbeciles. A few were receiving as low as $3 or $4 per week, but the majority received from $7 to $16 weekly. The average wage was $9.60 per week. They were employed in 39 different occupations, 13 in factories, painter, baker, laborer, printing pressman, freight handler, railroad brakeman, machinist, barber, etc. Only a few were doing simple manual labor. None of these boys or men had been troublesome sexually or shown criminal tendencies. They seemed contented and happy. These cases had been away from the School for an average of 9 years. They were at the School for varying periods. In no case would the relatives consider a return to the institution, although nearly all expressed gratitude for the training received there. This group shows the influence of a good home in modifying the after-life of institutionally trained defectives without innate character defects. The good home presupposes the absence of hereditary criminal or anti-social tendencies.

A group of 77 males of low moron and high imbecile grade and of various ages were able to do more or less work at home, but received no wages. Some were quite young, and have much of their lives yet to be lived out. Eight were attending public school, not keeping up, but learning a little slowly. These persons all seemed to be harmless and inoffensive. No record of sex offense could be ascertained. The males of this degree of mentality who had proved troublesome at home had evidently been returned to the institution. Where the members of this group lived on a farm or in a small village, they were evidently happier and did better in every way than those who lived in the cities. In this group also the lack of serious character defect and the fact that they were closely supervised were important factors in their good behavior.

Fifty-nine males of idiot and imbecile grade, unable to do any work, were living at home, and the families seemed able and desirous of continuing the home care of their permanently infantile offspring. No serious obnoxiousness was reported by the families or by the neighbors or by the police. As in the preceding group, evidently those of the group who had proved troublesome had already been sent back to the institution. Favorable home conditions and the absence of disagreeable traits in the patients made home care possible.

Thirty-two males are known to have been committed to penal or reformatory institutions subsequent to their discharge. Of this number 22 adult morons and 2 adult imbeciles were sent to penal institutions. Their average stay at the School was less than 1 year. Eleven ran away from the School, 9 were taken away by parents, and 4 were discharged as unsuitable for the institution. Without exception, they were voluble, plausible, incorrigible, and apparently inherently criminalistic from early childhood. The crimes for which they were sentences were as follows, viz.: 12 for larceny, 2 each for alcoholism, assault, and burglary, and 1 each for homicide, lewdness, sodomy, criminal assault, vagrancy, and highway robbery. Eight young boys were committed to juvenile reformatories for various offenses.

Twenty-three males had been arrested for crimes or misdemeanors, but had not been sentenced to penal institutions. Of this number 16 were morons and 7 imbeciles. One of them had been at the School for 10 years, five for 4 years each, and the rest for short periods only. Two ran away and the others were taken away by their parents. They were arrested for the following offenses,—viz.: 5 for larceny, 5 for breaking and entering, 3 for drunkenness, 2 each for felonious assault, danger to young girls, assault and battery and sodomy and 1 each for setting fires and incorrigibility. This group also showed distinct character defects from early childhood, and, as well as the preceding group, should never have been released except under strict parole. Both groups were typical "defective delinquents," and could not be adequately cared for or restrained in a school for the feebleminded.

Seventy-five of the males were committed to other institutions after their discharge, viz.: 8 to juvenile reformatories, 24 to penal institutions, 26 to hospitals for the insane, 8 to hospitals for epileptics, 4 to schools for the feebleminded, and 5 to various institutions. Few of these persons were discharged without a protest and often a contest. Many were taken away because of proposed transfer to the very institution to which they were eventually sent. Nearly every one was incorrigible and troublesome at home. This group well illustrates the necessity of frequent reclassification of the wards of the State. This clearing-house function should be exercised in the institutions and not in the community.

Sixty-eight males were re-admitted to the School. The time at home varied from less than 1 month to 18 years. Seven were idiots, 42 were imbeciles and 19 were morons. None of these cases had been arrested or in serious trouble, but they did not get on well, or were a burden at home, or were not easily controlled.

Fifty-four died after they were discharged.

To sum up, for 470 discharged male patients we have the following report:

Earning a living without supervision	28
Working for wages, supervised at home	86
Working at home, no wages	77
Living at home, not able to work	59
Arrested but not sentenced	23
Sentenced to penal institutions	32
Committed to other institutions	43
Re-admitted to Waverley	68
Died	54
Total	470

Apparently the cases represented in the first four groups in the above table a total of 250, constituted no serious menace to the community at the time of the investigation.

The results of this survey should be interpreted with great caution. As a rule, the most promising cases are allowed to go home. They have received careful training. The parents have been properly instructed. Still many unpromising cases did well. There was a surprisingly small amount of criminality and sex offense, and especially of illegitimacy. We may hope for a much better record when we have extra-institutional visitation and supervision of all discharged cases. Those with definite character defects, especially those with bad homes, should be discharged with great caution. The survey shows that there are bad defectives and good defectives. It also shows that even some apparently bad do "settle down." And it shows much justice in the plea of the well-behaved adult defective to be given a "trial outside" for apparently a few defectives do not need or deserve life-long segregation. It is most important that the limited facilities for segregation should be used for the many who can be protected in no other way.

THE
INSTITUTION
IN RELATION TO
THE
SCHOOL SYSTEM

Stanley P. Davies

Howe had stated that the early institutions were to become "a link in the chain of common schools." Davies argues that public schools must assume a greater role in the identification and education of the mentally defective child and that "no child should be separated from his home and his parents until every other resource has been exhausted." He emphasizes the importance of teaching social skills rather than merely providing intellectual and vocational training. The ensuing discussion reveals the poor reception by a representative of the public schools of ideas presented fifty years ahead of their time.

The first organized agency of any kind in this country to deal scientifically with the mentally deficient was, as we well know, the institution. From 1848 when the first State institution for mental defectives in American opened its doors in South Boston, until the first special classes began to be organized in the public schools in the nineties, the institution alone offered special care and training to the mentally defective.

There are doubtless members of the American Association for the Study of the Feebleminded here present who can remember the time when this Association was composed almost entirely of those who were connected with institutions. This fact reveals that not only the care of the mentally defective, but such study and research into the problems of mental deficiency as was carried on in those days rested entirely, if not wholly, upon the men and women who devoted their lives to institutional work. In proof of that, we need only to recall the names of the outstanding leaders in the mental deficiency movement of the last 75 years. If, today, the public school looms up as the agency upon which primary responsibility for the training of the mentally deficient must fall, we must not lose sight of the work of the institution in the progress which has been made to date in the mental deficiency movement.

The institution in this country has passed through three main stages of development. The first institutions under the leadership of men like Howe, Wilbur, and Brown were established frankly as schools as "a link in the chain of common schools—the last indeed, but still a necessary link in order to embrace all the children of the State" as Dr. Howe expressed it. These early institutions were in a sense a branch of the public school system, boarding schools having for their purpose the education of the mentally defective according to the special methods devised by Seguin, and organized in the expectation that by means of this training, the pupils could be so improved intellectually that they could be graduated into community life more or less capable of self-support and self-guidance.

When these early education methods proved less fruitful than had been anticipated in the intellectual rehabilitation of the mentally defective, the institutions, without entirely giving up their education ideals, were forced to face reality in the demands made upon them for the custodial care of many relatively unimprovable cases, and they entered upon that second and familiar stage in which custodial care and segregation were most prominent. This second stage coincided generally with the spread of public alarm about the

Journal of Psycho-Asthenics, 1925, 30:210–226. Reprinted by permission of the author and the American Association on Mental Deficiency.

Dr. Davies was the author of *Social Control of the Mentally Deficient,* an important textbook published in 1930. He was formerly associated with the department of mental hygiene in New York State and is now retired, residing in White Plains, New York.

mentally defective as a growing menace to social life. Boys and girls, men and women, were committed to the institutions not so much for training so that they could be restored to community life, but rather with the idea of keeping them safely stowed away until at least they had passed the child-bearing period. This was the stage, also, when so many earnest endeavors were made in various States to increase institutional provision to such an extent that it would be possible to segregate all the mentally defective. It was only after the application of the intelligence tests on a wide scale revealed the enormity of the mental deficiency problem that the aim of institutionalizing all mental defectives was reluctantly abandoned.

It is again to the credit of the institution that after patiently holding the corral for the community round-up of mental defectives so eagerly participated in, it refused to let its original educational purpose remain submerged, and of its own initiative under the leadership of Dr. Fernald and others, reasserted its ability and its right to return a certain proportion of its inmates to community life, sufficiently trained, socially and industrially, to be safe and useful members of the community. It is the institution of this third and present stage, the institution as a center of *social* rehabilitation, that has been described to you in the preceding papers this afternoon. It is this last type of institution to which reference is made in this discussion.

Given then, these two agencies for the training of the mentally defective, the modern institution on the one hand, and the public school with its special or ungraded classes on the other hand, both of which have the educational purpose uppermost, how shall society best utilize them in meeting this problem, and what should be the relation of the one to the other?

As has been repeatedly emphasized in the outlining of various mental deficiency programs, the first and most obvious task is the identification of the mentally defective at as early an age as possible. At present no State begins to know who and where its mentally defective are. This task of identification is one that the public school, given the proper facilities, is uniquely fitted to perform. By means of the compulsory education laws, which should be enforced to the extent of excusing no child from school attendance until he has had at least an examination, the school can bring under its observation every child in the community as he reaches the age of six. If by means of kindergarten attendence, habit clinics, and other agencies, mental retardation can be detected in the pre-school period and suitable training measures instituted, a great deal, of course, can be gained thereby. The importance of pushing further and further back toward infancy the time when retardation and faulty habits are discovered and appropriate training undertaken, is now generally recognized. If the public school is on the job, no case of mental deficiency should in any event get beyond the age of six undetected, unless to be sure the condition is not yet observable at that age.

Identification is, however, only the beginning. The next step is to determine the sort of training best suited to the particular child. This again is a responsibility that clearly must rest on the public school, and it is apparent that to fulfill this responsibility properly, the school must be able to avail itself of adequate psychiatric, psychological and social services. In this task of selection, I believe, the school should proceed on the general principle that no mentally defective child should be sent to an institution who can be suitably cared for at home and receive training in a special class. The axiom upon which modern child welfare work is based, that no child should be separated from his home and his parents until every other resource has been exhausted, applies equally to the mentally defective child. Home care and special class instruction are always to be preferred to institutional care where they are adequate to meet the needs of the situation. It is significant that Dr. Fernald in a paper written as long ago as 1906, before special classes were developed to any extent, said with reference to this question:

> "It is a great hardship to the child and parents to send a child of tender years away from home to a distant institution to be cared for by strangers. In spite of the great advantages to be obtained in the institution, the child is deprived of the normal home life, the moral and social influence of the mother, and the wholesome relations with the community. Philanthropic workers realize from time to time the great responsibility which society assumes when it removes young children from their natural guardians, not only for the child but for the parents."

Without further enlarging upon this point, the chief reasons why home care with special class training should take precedence wherever possible over institutional care, may be summed up as follows:

1. There is no substitute for good, average home care, and the love and individual attention which the child receives in the normal relationship between parent and child. In the past it may have been assumed that because the child was mentally defective, the parents were probably mentally defective also, and therefore unfit guardians for the child, but with the latest evidence as to the heredity of mental deficiency indicating that much mental deficiency is of the non-hereditary type, it is apparent that many mentally defective children may have entirely normal and intelligent parents. Doubtless, all of you are familiar with home situations of this kind.

2. The institution at best is an artificial environment. Since the aim of the work with the mentally defective is to train as many as possible for social life, they can, other things being equal, best learn how to adjust themselves to community life and best insure their later success by remaining in the community during their formative years.

3. It is not reasonable to expect the taxpayers of the State to support expensive institutions for those who can be as well, or better, cared for at

home. Nor should parents be relieved of their rightful responsibility for the support of their children, unless separation from the home is altogether imperative. Comparison of the per capita cost of institutional care with the per capita cost of operating special classes in New York State shows that, entirely aside from overhead, institutional care is at least twice as expensive as special class provision.

After all the above reasons have been noted, there remains the further practical consideration that institutional provision, even if preferable, is at present insufficient in any state to take care of but a small fraction of the mentally defective in the population, and there is no prospect that there will ever be institutional beds to take care of more than a small proportion of such persons. It is therefore all the more important that such institutional provision as does exist, should be reserved for those cases most seriously needing that type of care.

To look at this problem in terms of concrete figures, the New York State institutions including those in colonies and on parole made provision at the end of the last fiscal year for 6,900 cases. Conservatively estimating the number of intellectually defective children of school age at 2% of the school population, the number of such children in the public schools of New York State would be 35,000 not counting the large number of mental defective below and above school age. Deducting the number of children of school age now in institutions, this would mean that there are at least 30,000 and probably many more intellectually defective children for whom special provision must be made in the schools. As a start toward this the special classes in New York City have a total enrollment of 6,250 pupils and those in the State outside the city, a total enrollment of approximately 2,500.

Because of the failure of the public school as yet to make sufficient provision for all of these retarded children, the institution is at present called upon to receive children who really should not have to be committed to institutional care. It is also true that many children who should be in special classes drift along as failures and as over-age children in the regular grades until through disgust and discouragement they fall into truancy with its easy transition into delinquency. Here again the institution is called upon to receive as delinquents, unless the reformatory gets them, cases which might very well have remained in the community without causing difficulty if the school had made suitable provision for them. Any program, therefore, that may be mapped out as to the relation of the institution to the school system falls down at present because the school has not yet measured up to its plain duty of providing sufficient training facilities for the retarded child as well as for the normal or exceptional child.

It may be useful, nevertheless, to consider the relation of the institution to the public school on the assumption that school provision is adequate. In that case the school, after determining the mental level and personality of all children entering at the age of six, will be in a position to lay out a course of training for various groups of children ranging from the most exceptional to the most backward in accordance with what seem to be the several capacities of these groups. At this time there will, of course, be discovered at least in the larger centers of population, a certain number of idiots for whom any kind of public school provision is totally out of the question, and for whom there remains only the alternative of more or less nursing care at home or in the institution. On the other hand, in my opinion, the duty of the public school is not fulfilled if it provides special or ungraded classes only for the higher-grade type of mental defective.

The standard of admission to special classes outlined by the New York State Department of Education seems to follow the generally accepted practice. According to this standard, children having mental ages below 5 or intelligence quotients less than 50, if under 13 years chronological age, should be excluded from special classes. In this connection the official publication of the New York State Department reads: "Children with mental ages below 5 years are not able to do work which public schools are in a position ordinarily to offer. . . . Schools willing to make special provision for the lower mental ages will probably handle them successfully, but in a majority of cases, the placing of them in special classes tends to jeopardize the whole movement."

The plea here made is not that these lower-grade children now excluded from most schools be placed in the special classes provided for those with an I.Q. ranging from 50 to 75, but that another graduation of special classes with the instruction leveled down to an even lower grade of intelligence, be organized for them. It may be questioned whether the schools as an educational agency should be burdened with these relatively uneducable children, but, on the other hand, what happens to them if the school does not provide for them?

The Department of Ungraded Classes of the New York City public schools which has requested, but has not yet received appropriations enabling the Department to organize training classes for these lower-grade children, finds that there are now 1,000 children of this type with intelligence quotients of 50 or less, who are now deprived of school training and are merely living at home. Since the school will not take them, the institution is the only other possible training center and in the case of these 1,000 children, the parents have been either unwilling to commit them or the State institutions have been too overcrowded to receive them. It is neither fair to these children, to their families, nor to the community to deny them such training and leave them merely to degenerate through lack of stimulation. These children are definitely capable of improvement as institutional experience has shown. It is true that they cannot be educated to any great extent in the narrow academic meaning of the word, but they can profit by motor training, sense training, habit training, and character training, so that they will be definitely more amenable to social life, less a burden to their families, and less a menace to the community. They do not need to spend their school years in an institution at great expense to the taxpayers to get that sort of training, the school can provide it if it will. The mere possession of a low intelligence quotient should not mean that a child is automatically excluded from school and recommended for institutional care. The training classes for this type of child perhaps do not belong in the regular school building, but might be more suitably housed in special centers elsewhere under school auspices.

Some of our school systems are already leading the way in providing for these lower-grade children. In Dayton, Ohio, for example, special class pupils are divided into two groups, the mentally deficient and the ungraded. The mentally deficient group takes care of children having mental ages ranging from 3 to 9 years and intelligence quotients ranging from about 30 to 65. The potentiality of this group is from kindergarten through the third grade. The ungraded classes admit children having intelligence quotients ranging from 65 to 90. These children may be expected to cover the school work ranging from the third to the sixth or seventh grades.

If, in accordance with this proposal the public schools would make provision for children with mental ages as low as three years, would this then mean that the institutions would become mere nurseries for helpless idiots? The answer to that question brings me to the point that I would especially emphasize. *The determination of cases for institutional care should be made on a social rather than on an intellectual basis.* This position is taken in the belief that the primary function of the school for both normal and backward children should be to give training for social life, rather than mere intellectual training, or even specific vocational training. If the school cannot be instru-mental above all in developing its students to become good members of the social order, it has failed of its mission. Consequently, the school far from having nothing to offer the child of low-grade intelligence who can get little or nothing out of the three R's, who may not even be capable of much vocational training, has everything to offer that child if it can develop in him habits and characteristics that will make him a reasonably acceptable member of the community instead of a social menace or an undue social burden.

The institution should be left free to provide for those who are too troublesome and too dangerous to remain outside, or those whose home conditions are such as to be unfit for the child, regardless of whether the child's I.Q. is low or high. In such a capacity the institution can be of inestimable service to school and society, and as we are well aware, it will not lack for plenty of work to do, in our generation at least. With its careful discipline, its regularity of regime, its facilities for intensive medical, psychological and psychiatric work, its vocational training courses, its ability to gradually restore patients to the community on trial through the parole and colony systems, the institution is especially equipped to work on the reconstruction of these more difficult types of mental deficiency, and it should be left free to concentrate its energies upon that important work. Let us not clog our expensively constructed and equipped institutions, precious as the bed space in them is, with the dull, harmless type.

It is most important, however, that between the school and the institution there should not be a great gulf of separation with only a one-way bridge leading in the direction of the institution. The institution must cease to be regarded as some far-off place to which a person is sent for life; rather the institution should be regarded as Dr. Howe put it as "a link in the chain of common schools," a close working auxiliary to the special class. The relation between the school and the institution should be such that cases can be readily sent from the school to the institution for special periods of training, and as readily returned to the special class. In many instances a few months or at most a year in the institution with its controlled environment, twenty-four hour supervision and intensive care may result in sufficient improvement so that the child can, at the end of that time, be reinstated in the special class and the community. In other cases where the failure is less in the child himself than in his environment, a brief interval of institutional care may give time in which to make a satisfactory readjustment of the home situation. Both the school and the institution stand to benefit by this very close degree of cooperation.

The public school should strive to prevent institutional commitments by doing all that it can to overcome those two valid reasons for institutional care, unacceptable social behavior in the child, or improper home environment. As we well know, more often than not, the former is but a reflection of the latter, and the improvement of the environment is frequently the key to the improvement of the child's behavior. All this means that if the public school is to fulfill its complete duty toward these mentally handicapped children, it must provide not only an adequate number of special classes and special class teachers, but also an adequate number of psychiatrists and psychologists for the diagnosis, understanding and treatment of the personality and behavior difficulties of the child, and, of not the least importance, a well organized corps of visiting teachers, trained case-workers with the psychiatric point of view. What a visiting teacher service of the right kind can accomplish in improving the out-of-school environment of the child and thereby improving the behavior of the child himself has been shown in such places as Rochester where the school authorities have given this work some adequate recognition. Many institutional commitments are doubtless avoided through this kind of service. The lack of a sufficient staff of psychiatrists, psychologists and visiting teachers is a serious handicap to the work which most of our school systems are trying to do for the backward child.

How few personality and social problems are presented to the special class and visiting teacher where the children come from a reasonably good environment, and how many and complex these problems become in a more unfavorable home and community background is shown in the surveys made by visiting teachers of the Ungraded Department of the New York City schools of two districts in which special classes are located.

Both of these districts were distinctly working class communities. In the first, a district in upper Manhattan, the entire neighborhood makes an impression of cleanliness and thrift. The parents of the children in the special class with two exceptions were foreign born. The occupations of the father include that of painter, janitor, tailor, street-peddler, and chief steward at a prominent hotel. Their wages ranged from $25 to $75 weekly. In only two of the homes, however, was it necessary for the visiting teacher to employ an interpreter. Practically all the homes were neat and clean, and the families were getting along very well. There was only one home where the father was out of work. In most cases both the parents were living. The parents showed a special interest in the welfare of their children and a remarkable desire to cooperate with the teacher and the Ungraded Class Department. In almost every home the mother would voluntarily speak of the special class teacher as "a fine person" or "a very nice lady." There was not one complaint. The physical condition of the children in the class was very good, and in instances where the special class teacher had recommended medical treatment, excellent cooperation had been secured from the parents. When asked by the visiting teacher for special or difficult cases needing adjustment, the special class teacher said she had none to recommend.

The second district situated in down town Brooklyn has been described in the periodical "Ungraded" by Miss Mary H. Comstock, the visiting teacher who made the study. The parents in this district were not only foreign born as in the first, but there is a distinct unAmerican atmosphere to the whole community. Barber shops and candy stores serve as rendezvous for bootleggers and gamblers. Bootlegging seems to be prevalent and in the grape season the side streets are so covered with grape mash as to make passage difficult. The boys and young men find their chief recreation in numerous pool-rooms which are nothing more than dens of immorality where liquor is dispensed and trouble brewed. One of these places was reported to the police as a menace to the morals of two of the girls in an ungraded class. Several of the notorious characters featured in the daily papers had been residents of the district and former pupils of the school.

The parents of the special class children had made little effort to learn English, or to adapt themselves to American ways. The fathers are junk dealers, laborers, fruit peddlers, who are often without employment for weeks at a time. Some of the mothers work in factories or do knitting at home. The children also are frequently employed at home-work such as knitting and thus are deprived of proper recreation after school hours. In all the homes from which the special class pupils come, living conditions were found to be inadequate. The parents seem to be little concerned with the physical ailments of their children or their diet. Mothers take the attitude that "it is bad luck to visit a doctor unless you are really sick."

In a community like this, the problems confronting the special class teachers have been multiplied. All kinds of misunderstanding arise between home and school. The parents are especially prejudiced against the ungraded classes and only with the greatest difficulty can be made to appreciate the purpose of these classes.

Immediately the survey was begun, four particularly troublesome cases were presented which required action at once. One was that of a girl who presented a sex problem; another was that of a family where the mother was dead and the father left the responsibility of the care of his two little girls to a neighbor who exploited them; another was that of two sisters who were being exploited by their own family with the older of the two girls getting into sex difficulties; another of the cases was one urgently demanding physical treatment which had been neglected by the family and had led to social shortcomings on the part of the girl.

During the survey there developed ten cases requiring physical examination and correction of physical defects. Four of these needed general physical examination because of malnutrition; two presenting nervous symptoms were referred to neurological clinics; three were referred to an eye clinic, and one to a nose and throat clinic. Four families were referred to the Social Service Exchange; four families were referred to the Bureau of Charities for supervision and advice; two other children had to be taken to clinics by the teacher because the mothers were not able to go. In a community like this second one, there is ample work for the psychiatrist and visiting teacher and despite their best efforts, there will doubtless arise from time to time cases which by reason of social failure will require institutional care for shorter or longer periods.

In addition to its function as an auxiliary to the school in affording special training and care for those children who are too socially troublesome to remain in the community and in the special class during the school age, the institution may also be called upon to serve as a post-graduate training center for those boys and girls who at the age of sixteen have received all the training that the special class can offer them, but who have not sufficiently profited by this training to be able to get along in the outside world. It is conceivable that a year or two of the more intensive training which the institution can give these boys and girls after they leave the public school will enable them after that time to return to the community equipped at least partially to support themselves and so stabilized in good habits that they can be expected, with the help of such supervision as family or friends can give them, to keep out of social difficulty. On the other hand, some of these special class graduates may never be able to adjust themselves to community life, and may need to remain in the institution indefinitely.

In summary, the public school as an educational agency for all children, and not merely for those above a given I.Q., should assume the complete responsibility for the identification of all the mentally defective of the coming generation at the age of six, or such later age as the deficiency may manifest itself. Upon the school also, should fall the task of studying all these backward children with the aid of specialists employed for the purpose, and of determining the type of training best adapted to the needs of the particular child. The school must, itself, make provision for the special training of the large majority of mentally handicapped children including many of an intellectual level lower than those now received in the usual special or ungraded class. Behind the school, however, should stand the institution as a close working ally, ready to receive those children who, more by reason of social shortcomings than intellectual, need for shorter or longer periods, the controlled environment, close supervision, and intensive training in socialization that the institution is especially equipped to give.

Sooner or later, public school authorities must recognize that they have no right to deprive a child of educational advantages merely because he is found on one of the lower levels of the intelligence curve. At the same time more and more emphasis must be put upon training for social life rather than the mere acquisition of knowledge. When this time comes, and our public schools have provided an adequate number of special, ungraded or training classes with competent teachers, together with sufficient psychological, psychiatric and visiting teacher personnnel for the study and guidance of these children, then, with a reasonable increase in institutional accommodations, we can be assured that the mentally defective need no longer be left to drift, to become social burdens, and social menaces, but that the potentialities of each will be raised by means of training suited to his capacities and his needs to the highest power of social usefulness. That day should not be far off.

DISCUSSION

MISS ETHEL CORNELL: It is true, I suppose, that we all tend to see our own problems so large that others lose their proper perspective. It should be fruitful therefore, for those whose problem is the school and those whose problem is the institution to come together for discussion, in order to bridge the gulf that Dr. Davies has mentioned. We shall surely get better cooperation if we realize each other's problems. Dr. Davies has presented a brief for the institution, admirably. I wish I might do as well for the school.

The gulf is caused partly by a difference of opinion as to what the proper function of the school versus the institution is in regard to the low grade defective. It looks as if we were both trying to "pass the buck" with regard to this problem. Dr. Davies implies that the school should be the dumping ground. The school is apt to think that these children are scarcely educable and naturally prefers to make the institution the dumping ground. Perhaps the best solution—at least the simplest—would be that of the queen in *"Alice In Wonderland,"* who would dispatch the matter by saying "Off with their heads." However, since we cannot dispose of it that way on this side of the Looking Glass, I merely want to offer it to you as a general question—Where, ideally, should the responsibility rest for the training of low grade children? Can the school, in the five or six hours out of the twenty-four that it has the children make an appreciable impression in the habit training that they require? Or, if all day habit clinics are conceived to be part of the public school system, with the necessary corps of social workers to carry the training into the home, how large a community must it be that can afford this?

Dr. Davies is not sure that these children are educable but, he says, "What happens to them if the school does not provide for them?" Let us consider what happens to them if the school should try to provide for them. Dr. Davies agrees with the statement that they should not be placed in classes with children of higher grade, but he believes that another type of special class should be provided,—presumably a sort of habit clinic.

Let us consider what would happen in a hypothetical community of 20,000. This is a typical small city in New York State and probably represents a small city in other states as well. This community will have about 15% of its population in the public schools. This will make its school enrollment about 3,000. If 2% of these children are feebleminded, there will be 60 feebleminded children in the schools. Of these, a certain number will be of the imbecile grade that we are discussing, or in general terms will have intelligence quotients below 50. How many such children there will be, can be determined statistically on the basis of the distribution of intelligence. Statistically, it can be shown that about .3 of 1% of the children in school will be in this group. In a community of 20,000, having a school enrollment of 3,000, there will therefore be 9 children belonging to the low grade of defect that the New York State Education Department has considered not proper subjects for school instruction. Dr. Davies has said that of these low grade children only those whose home environment is suitable should be retained in the community, and he has estimated that about half of these children may have normally intelligent parents. This would make the school problem of our hypothetical community a problem of providing adequate facilities to care for 4 or 5 children. It is almost unquestionable that even some of these would be a social menace because of their personal unfitness, aside from whether they had suitable homes. Probably a total of 3 children would be the maximum of the imbecile grade for whom such a community could be expected to provide training in school. Of course this is an impossible situation. No school system can provide a class with special facilities for 3 children, especially when the returns to the community are so nearly negligible as they are in such circumstances. It would take a community four times this size, therefore, to have enough children of this type to make even one class possible. This would mean a city of 80,000.

There are in New York State 8 cities of 80,000 or more. The school enrollment of these 8 cities is 1,306,000. The total school enrollment of the state is 1,900,000, which leaves 594,000 children living in communities too small to permit special classes for children of very low grade. If .3% of these are of the imbecile grade, there are, therefore, 1,782 imbecile children of school age in New York for whom the public schools could not possibly provide. New York probably has a larger proportion of its people living in large cities than any other state, and the situation is therefore milder in this state than elsewhere, as far as proportions are concerned.

It is very easy when one is not in actual contact with the problems of school administration in the smaller communities to overlook the difficulty that is created when schools attempt to meet such a situation. The unwisdom of trying to take care of these children in classes with the higher grade defectives is apparent to all who have tried the experiment. I am glad Dr. Davies did not suggest this possibility. This is a phase of the situation which I cannot go into here, but it is one which needs emphasizing.

Even in providing adequate special class instruction for children of higher grade,—those who can be expected to make some return to the community when they leave school, there are difficulties that cannot be met in all communities. For, example, it may be assumed that communities which have fewer than 15 defective children cannot provide adequate facilities for them in the public schools. Fifteen is 2% of 750. This means that communities whose school enrollment is less than 750 are too small to support special classes. A school enrollment of 750 represents a population of 5,000. It requires a community of 5,000 therefore, to support even one special class. In New York State, the total school enrollment of cities and villages with a population of 5,000 or over is 1,436,400. The total school enrollment of the state being 1,900,000, there are therefore 463,600 children enrolled in schools too small to support special classes even for the higher grade defectives. If 2% of these children are feebleminded, there are over 9,000 feebleminded children in communities too small to provide special class instruction for them. There are therefore, 11,000 feebleminded children in New York State whom Dr. Davies has left totally unprovided for, however willing the school may be to take low grade cases, merely because they do not exist in large enough numbers in any one community to make it possible. It would seem that these children should be considered the responsibility of the state and not of the local public school.

Please do not think that I am arguing for the segregation of all the feebleminded in institutions. On the contrary, I am vitally concerned with getting special classes established for their training. Nor do I wish to imply that I think the schools have done their full duty. I only wish to emphasize that even if every community of 5,000 or over had enough special classes for all its morons, and if every city of 80,000 established habit clinics for its imbeciles, there would still be a large number of defective children left over, who need to be added to the calculations of those who are building the institution of tomorrow. Institutions are overcrowded now, yet they have not attempted to touch this problem. I think it is not unfair to say that they have not even recognized it. They have passed it on to the schools. If the schools were to assume it, it is clear that the per capita cost for special classes would be more than doubled. Dr. Davies mentioned that the per capita cost of special classes now is about half the per capita cost of maintaining children in institutions. If it should exceed the institution cost, the community might well pause to consider its assets.

A STUDY
OF THE EFFECTS
OF
DIFFERENTIAL
STIMULATION
ON MENTALLY
RETARDED CHILDREN

Harold M. Skeels and Harold B. Dye

This paper is the controversial report to the American Association on Mental Deficiency, challenging the stability of the I.Q. in children transferred from an orphanage nursery to a school for the feeble-minded, where they were cared for by older, brighter girls. The notion that intelligence was modifiable was a direct contradiction of the accepted dogma first established by Goddard, twenty-six years earlier.

The study of nature of intelligence challenges the interest of psychologists and educators not only because of the theoretical concepts involved, but also because of the implications relating to child care and education.[1] If, on the one hand, intelligence is static, a fixed entity and relatively unmodifiable by changes in environmental impact, then changes in living conditions and amount and kind of education can be expected to have little influence on the mental level of individuals.

On the other hand, if intelligence shows change in relation to shifts in environmental influence, then our concept must include modifiability, and the implications for child welfare become more challenging.

This latter concept was postulated by Alfred Binet. In his significant book entitled, *Les Idées Modernes Sur Les Enfants* (1), published in 1911, Binet devotes an enlightening chapter to the topic, *Intelligence: Its Measurement and Education.* He is surprised and concerned at the prejudice against the concept of modifiability of intelligence.

To quote: "Some recent philosophers appear to have given their moral support to the deplorable verdict that the intelligence of an individual is a fixed quantity, a quantity which cannot be augmented. We must protest and act against this brutal pessimism. We shall endeavor to show that it has no foundation whatsoever" (p. 141).

Binet goes on to cite observations and situations relating to the teaching of subnormal children, summarizing as follows: "A child's mind is like a field for which an expert farmer has advised a change in the method of cultivating, with the result that in place of desert land, we now have a harvest. It is in this

[1] This paper was presented at the annual convention of the American Association on Mental Deficiency, Chicago, Illinois, Section 2, Saturday afternoon, May 6, 1939.

The writers wish to express their appreciation to Senator Harry C. White, Senator F. M. Stevens, and Mr. E. H. Felton, members of the Iowa Board of Control of State Institutions, for approving this rather unusual venture; to Mr. Syl McCauley, Superintendent of the Iowa Soldiers' Orphans' Home, who has at all times co-operated in making possible research studies of wards in that institution; and to Mrs. Ethel Nichols, Secretary of the Children's Division of the Board of Control, for her co-operation and encouragement.

Journal of Psycho-Asthenics, 1939, 44(1): 114–136. Reprinted by permission of Dr. Dye and the American Association on Mental Deficiency.

The Iowa research studies were interrupted by World War II. Dr. Skeels served as Captain and then Major in the Unites States Army Air Force. After the war, he returned briefly to the Iowa Research Station, then served with the Veterans' Administration and the United States Public Health Service until his retirement in 1965. Dr. Skeels died in March 1970. Dr. Dye began working in the State Institution in Iowa in 1930 and was appointed superintendent in 1935. After leaving the institution in 1939, he served as medical director for Nothrop Aircraft and then TWA. He was administrator of a hospital in California until 1968, when he began a full-time private practice. He retired in 1971 and currently resides in San Francisco, California.

particular sense, the only one which is significant, that we say that the intelligence of children may be increased. One increases that which constitutes the intelligence of a school child; namely, the capacity to learn, to improve with instruction."

STATEMENT OF THE PROBLEM

The purpose of this study was to determine the effects on mental growth of a radical shift in institutional environment to one providing superior stimulation, introduced into the lives of mentally retarded children of early preschool ages. These children were placed singly or in some cases by twos on wards of brighter girls in an institution for feebleminded children. Preliminary observation had given some indication that such an environment was mentally stimulating for children two to three years of age. As a correlary aim, it seemed pertinent to study a contrast group of dull-normal and normal children of somewhat similar ages residing over a period of time in a relatively nonstimulating orphanage environment.

ORIGIN OF THE STUDY

This research project was the outgrowth of a clinical surprise. Two children under a year and a half, in residence at the state orphanage, gave unmistakable evidence of marked mental retardation. Kuhlmann-Binet intelligence tests were given both children. C. D.,[2] thirteen months of age at time of examination, obtained an I.Q. of 46, and B. D.,[3] at sixteen months, scored an I.Q. of 35. Qualitative observations of the examiner substantiated a classification of imbecile level of mental retardation. In the case of B. D., the examiner felt that the child's actual level was perhaps slightly higher, but not to exceed ten points or an I.Q. level of 45. As check tests for further corroboration, the Iowa Tests for Young Children were used. Mental ages of approximately six and seven months respectively were obtained.

Obviously a classification of feeblemindedness would not be justified if based on results of intelligence tests alone, particularly at these young ages. However, behavioral reactions in conjunction with the examinations of the pediatrician, and observations by the superintendent of nurses relative to activity or lack of activity of these children in the nursery in contrast with other children, gave ample substantiation for a classification of marked

---

[2] Designated as Case 5 in Table 1.
[3] Designated as Case 8 in Table 2.

mental retardation. C. D., at thirteen months, was making no attempts to stand, even with assistance. She could not pull herself to an upright position with the aid of crib or chair, nor did she display much manipulative activity with blocks or play materials. Spontaneous vocalization also was lacking. B. D., at sixteen months, was not vocalizing, was unable to walk with help and made relatively no responses to play materials in the nursery.

There were no indications of physiological or organic defects. Birth histories were negative, both children being full term normal delivery with no indications of birth injury or glandular dysfunction. Social histories were not flattering. Both children were illegitimate. In the case of C. D., the mother had been adjudged feebleminded and a legal guardian was appointed. Although the mother claimed to have finished the eighth grade at sixteen years, the social workers felt that she was very retarded and probably had had a difficult time in school. A Stanford-Binet (1916 revision) intelligence test given at the University Hospital showed a mental age of nine years and an I.Q. of 56. She had always been healthy. Her father was a miner, had been unable to learn in school and had deserted his family. Little is known of the father of the child, although it was reported that he had gone to high school.

B. D.'s mother was an inmate in a state hospital, diagnosed as psychosis with mental deficiency. She was slow to sit up, walk and talk, and went only to the second grade in school. The maternal grandfather drank to excess and his brother died in a state hospital of general paralysis of the insane. One maternal great aunt died of epilepsy. B. D.'s father is unknown; the mother named an inebriate formerly released from the state hospital.

Accordingly, these two children were recommended for transfer to the school for feebleminded.[4] We quote from the recommendations for transfer as follows: C. D.: "Diagnosis of mental ability: Mental deficiency of imbecile level, which will probably continue with an increase in age. Prognosis: Poor. With this deficiency in mental development, C. D. will be unable to make her way outside the care and protection offered by an institution for feebleminded children. Her relatives are not in a position to give her the continuous care she will need." Diagnosis and prognosis on B. D. were similar to the one just quoted.

Following this recommendation, the children were committed to the school for feebleminded. They were placed on a ward of older girls, ranging in age from eighteen to fifty years and in mental age from five to nine years.

Six months after transfer, the psychologist visiting the wards of the institution was surprised to notice the apparently remarkable development of these children. Accordingly, they were re-examined on the Kuhlmann-Binet,

---

[4] These two children were transferred to the state school at Woodward. All other children in the experimental group were sent to the state school at Glenwood.

C. D. obtaining an I.Q. of 77 and B. D. an I.Q. of 87. Twelve months later they were tested again with I.Q.s of 100 and 88, respectively. Tests were again given when the children were forty months and forty-three months of age, respectively, with I.Q.s of 95 and 93.

In the meantime, inquiries were made as to reasons for this unusual development. Their "home" or ward environment was studied. It was observed that the attendants on the ward had taken a great fancy to the "babies." They were essentially the only pre-school children on the ward, other than a few hopeless bed patients with physiological defects. The attendants would take these two children with them on their days off, giving them car rides and taking them down town to the stores. Toys, picture books and play materials were purchased by these admiring adults. The older, brighter girls on the wards were also very much attached to the children and would play with them during most of the waking hours. Thus it can be seen that this environment turned out to be stimulating to these preschool children of low initial mental level.

Following these last examinations, it was felt that the stimulation value of this particular kind of an environment had been pretty well exhausted. If the resulting level of intelligence was to be maintained a shift to a more normal environment seemed essential. Furthermore, since the children were then well within the range of normal intelligence, there ceased to be any justification for keeping them in an institution for the feebleminded. Accordingly, they were transferred back to the orphanage, and from there placed in rather average adoptive homes, their ages then being three years six months and three years eight months. After approximately fifteen months in the foster homes, the children were again examined, this time using the Stanford-Binet. I.Q.s of 94 and 93 were obtained. From the evidence obtained, there is every indication that they will continue to classify as normal individuals as they increase in age. Accordingly, legal adoption has been completed in both cases.

From these startling preliminary findings, several questions were presented. Observations of similarly retarded children comparable in ages, remaining in an orphanage nursery, showed continued lack of mental development. In such a situation, the retarded child with numbers of other children of higher intelligence but of the same age seemed to make no gain in rate of mental growth. Also, since there was a ratio of only one or two adults to twelve or eighteen children, adult contacts were at a minimum and limited largely to physical care. Obviously, the retarded child could not be placed directly in an adoptive home as there could be no marked assurance that later development would be normal. Boarding home care to permit further evaluation and observation of development would, of course, be a logical solution of such a problem. However, the code of Iowa provides only for institutional care or placement in free or adoptive homes. Consequently, there seemed to be only one alternative, and that a rather fantastic one; namely, to transfer mentally retarded children in the orphanage nursery, one to two years of age, to an institution for feebleminded in order to make them normal. In view of the earlier preliminary findings, it was hoped that possibly 50 per cent of the cases might show at least some improvement. With cases not showing improvement, the transfer would be proper, and they could remain in that environment permanently. The suggestion was presented to the Board of Control, and although received with doubts and misgivings, was approved. It was decided that children so transferred would not be technically committed to the institution for feebleminded, but would rather be guests in residence at the school for feebleminded and would continue to appear on the orphanage population list. In other words, they would simply be temporarily hospitalized for therapeutic treatment. In this way there would not be the stigma of commitment to the school for feebleminded appearing on the case histories. Each case was to be evaluated from time to time. If and when improvement failed to ensue, final commitment was to be consummated.

SUBJECTS

Experimental Group

Accordingly, from time to time, retarded children from the Iowa Soldiers' Orphans' Home at Davenport were sent to the Iowa Institution for Feebleminded Children at Glenwood. The experimental group includes all children so transferred who were under three years of age at time of transfer, a total of thirteen. The tabulation on the following page shows sex, chronological age at time of examination before transfer, Kuhlmann-Binet mental age and I.Q., and chronological age at time of transfer.

The mean chronological age at time of transfer was 19.4 months, median 17.1 months, with a range from 7.1 to 35.9 months. Range of I.Q.s was from 35 to 89 with a mean of 64.3 and a median of 65.0. In eleven of the thirteen cases, additional tests had been given shortly before or in conjunction with the tests reported above. These were either repeated Kuhlmann-Binet examinations or Iowa Tests for Young Children. Such tests gave further corroboration of classification of marked mental retardation.

That such retardation was real and observable was substantiated by the reports of the pediatrician and the nurse in charge, indicating lack of development.[5] The orphanage policy is to place children and infants in adoptive

---

[5] The writers are indebted to Dr. M. D. Ott, pediatrician, and Miss Sadie LeFevre, superintendent of nurses, Iowa Soldiers' Orphans' Home, for these observations and reports.

Examination Prior to Transfer

Case	Sex	Chronological age, months	Mental age, months	I.Q.	Chronological age, months, at transfer
1 .....M		7.0	6.0	89	7.1
2 .....F		12.7	7.2	57	13.1
3 .....F		12.7	10.8	85	13.3
4 .....F		14.7	10.8	73	15.0
5 .....F		13.4	6.0	46	15.2
6 .....F		15.5	12.0	77	15.6
7 .....F		16.6	10.8	65	17.1
8 .....F		16.6	6.0	35	18.4
9 .....F		21.8	13.2	61	22.0
10 .....M		23.3	16.8	72	23.4
11 .....M		25.7	19.2	75	27.4
12 .....F		27.9	18.0	65	28.4
13 .....F		30.0	10.8	36	35.9

homes as soon as possible. All children in this group were considered unsuitable for adoption because of mental retardation. In Case 1, although the I.Q. was 89, it was felt that actual retardation was much greater. At seven months this child could scarcely hold his head up without support. There was little general bodily activity as compared with other infants the same age. In Case 3, at twelve months, there was very little activity and sitting up without support was very unsteady. She could not pull herself to a standing position and did not creep. Case 11 was not only retarded, but showed perseverative patterns of behavior, particularly rocking back and forth incessantly. Cases 5, 8 and 13 were classified at the imbecile level. Descriptions of Cases 5 and 8 have been given under the origin of the study. Case 13, the oldest child in the group, showed perhaps the greatest amount of retardation. She was committed to the orphanage at twenty-eight months of age and came from a home where extreme neglect was typical. At thirty months of age she was unable to stand alone, could not walk with help and required support when sitting in a chair.

Following transfer to the school for feebleminded, examinations by the superintendent and other members of the medical staff further corroborated the reports from the orphanage as to the marked degree of mental retardation.

Contrast Group

This group did not exist as a designated group until the close of the experimental period. These children were simply examined as individuals from time to time along with the other children in the orphanage as routine procedure. It was only after the data on the experimental group had been analyzed that the decision was made to study a group of children remaining in the orphanage for contrast purposes. Children were included who (a) had had initial intelligence tests under two years of age, (b) were still in residence in the orphanage at approximately four years of age, and (c) were in the control group of the orphanage preschool study (5), or (d) had not attended preschool. The study of the orphanage preschool referred to included two groups of children matched in chronological age, mental age, I.Q. and length of residence in the institution. The one group had the advantages of the more stimulating environment of preschool attendance, while the control group experienced the less stimulating environment of cottage life. Since the purpose of the contrast group for the present study was to include children in a relatively nonstimulating environment, children who had attended preschool could not be included. Such limitations, however, did not constitute a selective factor as far as the make-up of the children was concerned. A total of twelve children met these requirements and have been designated as the contrast group in the present study.

The following tabulation shows sex, chronological age at time of first examination, Kuhlmann-Binet mental age and I.Q.:

Case	Sex	Chronological age, months	Mental age, months	I.Q.
14 ......F		11.9	11.0	91
15 ......F		13.0	12.0	92
16 ......F		13.6	9.6	71
17 ......M		13.8	13.2	96
18 ......M		14.5	14.4	99
19 ......M		15.2	13.2	87
20 ......M		17.3	14.0	81
21 ......M		17.5	18.0	103
22 ......M		18.3	18.0	98
23 ......F		20.2	18.0	89
24 ......M		21.5	10.6	50
25 ......M		21.8	18.0	83

The mean chronological age at time of first examination was 16.6 months with a median at 16.3 months. The range was from 11.9 months to 21.8 months. The mean I.Q. for the group was 86.7 (median 90.0). With the exception of two cases (16 and 24) the children had I.Q.s ranging from 81 to 103.

Reasons for earlier nonplacement in adoptive homes were in general for those other than mental retardation. In fact, nine were, or had been, considered normal as far as mental development was concerned. Five children were withheld from placement simply because of a poor family history. Two were held because of improper commitment, two because of luetic condition and one because of mental retardation.

Birth Histories of the Groups

In the examination of the birth histories of the two groups, no marked discrepancies were observed. In the experimental group, eight children were full term with normal delivery. Prematurity occurred in three cases (4, 7 and 9). Case 7, two months premature, spent the first two months in an incubator. The other two cases did not require special care. One case, 11, was delivered by Cesarean section. The remaining case, 13, was not admitted to the orphanage until twenty-eight months of age. No birth history was available.

The children of the contrast group present similar birth histories. Eight of this group were full term babies with normal labor. One, Case 23, was premature and delivered by breach extraction. Case 17 was delivered by low forceps at full term. As a result of difficult labor, he presented early symptoms of intracranial hemorrhage. There were periods of cyanosis and clonic convulsions, and feedings were taken poorly. At the end of a week, however, the cyanosis had diminished and there were no longer convulsions. By the end of fifteen days, the child appeared normal. Case 24 was admitted at fourteen months with no birth history available.

These data have been presented in summary form in the following tabulation:

Information Con-cerning Births[6]	Experimental group	Contrast group
Birth injuries		1
Pathological labor ...	2	3
Prematurity	3	1
Normal delivery	8	8
Unknown	1	1

Medical Histories

In the evaluation of the medical histories of both the experimental and contrast groups, little of significance was found in the relationship between illnesses and rate of mental growth. In the experimental group, one child, Case 9, had congenital syphilis, but immediate antiluetic treatment following birth was adequate and serology was negative during the experimental period. In the contrast group, two children, Cases 14 and 16, were luetic, but Case 16

---

[6] A given case may appear in more than one category.

responded to early antiluetic treatment and all serology has been negative during the period of the study. However, in Case 14, a question may be raised as to the contributing effects of persistent syphilis. Blood Wassermann and Kahn were negative at nine months of age, but examination at thirty months revealed four plus Wassermann and Kahn. Treatment was again instituted, and at forty-six months both blood and spinal fluid serology were negative. Case 14, on admission to the orphanage, had enlarged spleen and liver, a tentative diagnosis of Gaucher's disease being made. This did not seriously affect the activity of the child during the course of the study.

Considering all children of both groups, they have had various upper respiratory infections, occasional contagious diseases, mild eczemas, but nothing more severe than the ordinary child of preschool age would have in the average home.

Family Backgrounds

Social histories revealed that the children of both experimental and contrast groups came from homes of low social, economic, occupational, and intellectual levels. The family background is comparable to that reported by Skeels and Fillmore (4) in their study of the mental development of children from underprivileged homes and Skodak's study (6) of children in foster homes placed at ages two to five. The backgrounds of the children in the two groups were comparable.

Mothers

Information relating to education was available for eleven of the thirteen mothers in the experimental group and ten of the twelve mothers in the contrast group. The mean grade completed by mothers of children in the experimental group was 7.8 with a median at grade eight. Only two had any high school work, one having completed the eleventh grade and one the tenth grade (Cases 3 and 6). In one case, it was doubtful if the second grade had been completed (Case 8). Two (Cases 1 and 5) had dropped out of the eighth grade at the age of sixteen.

In the contrast group, the mean grade completed was 7.3 with a median at 7.5. One mother (Case 19) had completed high school and one had an equivalent of ninth grade education.

Occupational history of mothers, available on seven of the mothers in the experimental group and nine of the contrast group, included mainly housework, either in the homes of parents or working out as domestics. In only one instance was there a higher level indicated (Case 24 of the contrast group) in which the mother had been a telephone operator and had done general office work.

Intelligence tests[7] had been obtained on five of the mothers in the experimental group and nine of the mothers in the contrast group. The mean I.Q. for mothers of the experimental group was 70.4, with a median at 66. One additional mother, although not tested, was considered feebleminded and had gone only as far as the second grade. Four mothers had I.Q.s below 70, and one classified as normal with an I.Q. of 100.

Of the nine mothers in the contrast group, only two had I.Q.s above 70, one being 79 and the other 84. The others ranged from 36 to 66. The mean I.Q. was 63, with a median at 62.

Fathers

Little information was available on the fathers, in fact in many cases paternity was doubtful. Ten of the children in each group were illegitimate. In the experimental group, information relating to education was available on only four fathers. Two had completed the eighth grade, one completed high school, and one had gone to high school but how far was not known. Occupational status was indicated on only three of the fathers; one was a traveling salesman, one a printer, and one a farm hand.

In the contrast group, educational information was available on four. One had completed high school and one was considered talented in music (Case 24). Two had completed eighth grade, (Cases 15 and 18), and one the sixth grade (Case 21). Occupational information was known on eight of the fathers. Three were day laborers, two were farm hands, one worked on the railroad section, one was a farm renter, and one was in a C.C.C. camp.

A qualitative analysis of social histories seems to justify the conclusion that within these educational and occupational classifications of true parents, the individuals represent the lower levels in such groups. Most of these fathers and mothers dropped out of school because of having reached their limits of achievement, and in no sense of the word represent the averages of their grade placements. The same may be said with reference to occupational status.

DESCRIPTION OF THE ENVIRONMENTS

Experimental Group

Children in this group were transferred from the orphanage nursery to the school for feebleminded, and placed on the wards with older, brigher girls.

---

[7] Stanford-Binet (1916) intelligence tests. Most of these were given by psychologists either at the Psychopathic Hospital or the University Hospital of the University of Iowa. Maximum chronological age used was sixteen years.

Wards in the girls' school division were used. This included a large cottage of eight wards with a matron and an assistant matron in charge and one attendant for each ward. There are approximately thirty patients on each ward, including girls ranging in ages from eighteen to fifty years. On two wards (wards 2 and 3) are girls of the higher levels, mental ages from nine to twelve years. On two other wards (wards 4 and 5) the mental levels are from seven to ten years, and on another ward (ward 7) the mental ages are from five to eight.

With the exception of ward 7, there were few if any younger children on the wards aside from the experimental children. In some cases, there were one or two other young children on the ward, usually a mongol or a spastic paralysis case. In general, one, or at the most two, children in the experimental group were placed on a given ward.

The attendants and the older girls became very fond of the child placed on the ward and took great pride in its achievement. In fact, there was considerable competition between wards to see which one would have their "baby" walking or talking first. The girls would spend a great deal of time with the children, teaching them to walk, talk, play with toys and play materials, and in the training of habits.

Most of the clothing for these children was made by the older girls. The girls were so fond of the children that they would actually spend their small earnings and allowances to buy them special foods, toys, picture books, and materials for clothing. Similarly attendants gave of their time, money, and affection, and during their free hours frequently took the children on excursions, car rides, and trips. In addition, it was the policy of the matron in charge of the girls' school division to single out certain of these children who she felt were in need of special individualization, and permit these children to spend a portion of time each day visiting her office. This furnished new experiences including being singled out and given special attention and affection, new play materials, additonal language stimulation, and contacts with other office callers.

An indication of the interest in these children was shown by the fact that a baby show was held for one of the Fourth of July celebrations. Each ward made a float upon which its "baby" rode, dressed in costume. Prizes were awarded for the winning baby, most attractive costume, and best float.

The spacious living rooms of the wards furnished ample room for indoor play and activity. Whenever weather permitted, the children spent some time each day on the playground, supervised by one or more of the other girls. In this situation, they had contacts with other children of similar ages. Outdoor play equipment included tricycles, swings, slides, sand box, etc.

In addition to the opportunities afforded on the wards, the children attended the school kindergarten. They were sent to school as soon as they could walk. Toddlers remained for only half of the morning, whereas those of four and five years of age were in kindergarten the entire morning. Activities carried on in the kindergarten were more in the nature of a preschool than the more formal type of kindergarten.

As a part of the school program, the children each morning attended fifteen minute chapel exercises, including group singing and music by the orchestra. The children also attended the dances, school programs, moving pictures, and Sunday chapel services.

In considering this enriched environment from a dynamic point of view, it must be pointed out that in the case of almost every child, some one adult (older girl or attendant) would become particularly attached to a given child and would figuratively "adopt" him. As a consequence there would develop a rather intense adult-child relationship with the other adult contacts being somewhat more marginal. This meant that such a child had some one person with whom he was identified and who was particularly interested in him and his achievement. It was felt that this constituted an important aspect of the environmental impact on the child.

Contrast Group

The environment of the children in the contrast group is considered to be rather representative of the average orphanage. The outstanding feature is the profound lack of mental stimulation or experiences usually associated with the life of a young child in the ordinary home.

Up to the age of two years, the children were in the nursery of the hospital. This was limited to a rather small play room with additional dormitory rooms of two to five beds each. The children were cared for by two nurses with some additional assistance by one or two girls of ten to fifteen years of age. The children had good physical and medical care, but little can be said beyond this. Contacts with adults were largely limited to feeding, bathing, dressing, and toilet details. It can readily be seen that with the large number of children per adult, little time was available for anything aside from the routines of physical care. The girls who assisted the nurses accepted the work as a necessary evil and, in general, took little personal interest in the children as individuals. Few play materials were available and little attention was given to the teaching of play techniques. The children were seldom out of the nursery room except for short walks or short periods of time out of doors for fresh air.

At two years of age these children were graduated to the cottages. A rather complete description of "cottage" life is reported in the study by Skeels, Updegraff, Wellman, and Williams (5) on *A Study of Environmental Stimulation: An Orphanage Preschool Project,* from which the following excerpts are taken:

"Overcrowding of living facilities was characteristic. Too many children had to be accommodated in the available space and there were too few adults to guide them. . . . Thirty to thirty-five children of the same sex under six years of age lived in a "cottage" in charge of one matron and three or four entirely untrained and often reluctant girls of thirteen to fifteen years of age. The waking and sleeping hours of these children were spent (except during meal times and a little time on a grass plot) in an average sized room (approximately fifteen feet square), a sun porch of similar size, a cloak room, . . . and a single dormitory. The latter was occupied only during sleeping hours. . . . The meals for all children in the orphanage were served in a central building in a single large dining room. . . .

"The duties falling to the lot of a matron were not only those involved in the care of the children but those related to clothing and cottage maintenance, in other words, cleaning, mending, and so forth. . . . With so much responsibility centered on one adult, the result was a necessary regimentation. The children sat down, stood up, and did many things in rows and in unison. They spent considerable time sitting on chairs, for in addition to the number of children and the matron's limited time, there was the misfortune of inadequate equipment. . . .

"No child had any property which belonged exclusively to him, except, perhaps, his tooth brush. Even his clothing, including shoes, was selected and put on him according to size. . . ." (pp. 10–11.)

From this it may be seen what a remarkable contrast there was between the environment of the experimental transfer group and the contrast group. Such a radical shift in environment as was experienced by each of the children in the experimental group would scarcely occur in an unselected sampling of children in their own homes more than two or three times in a thousand cases.

Following the completion of these research studies on preschool children, the orphanage has made radical changes in the program for the preschool child. Number of children per cottage has been reduced, thus alleviating to a great extent the overcrowded conditions. Each cottage now has two matrons with additional domestic service. The preschool has been made an integral part of the school system with all children of preschool age in attendance. With the assistance of the state emergency nursery school program a preschool program has been set up for the children in the nursery under two years of age. A trained teacher, in addition to the regular nursing staff, spends full time with the infants providing a more enriched play and educational program.

MENTAL DEVELOPMENT
OF CHILDREN IN EXPERIMENTAL AND CONTRAST GROUPS

The mental development of individual children in the experimental group is presented in Table 1. As the standard measure of intelligence the 1922

Kuhlmann Revision of the Binet was used, excepting in the cases of two or three tests on children who were four years of age or more where the Stanford-Binet (1916) was used. All examinations were made by trained and experienced psychologists. Test one was the measure of intelligence just prior to transfer. Tests two, three, and last test, were given at subsequent intervals of time following transfer. "Last test" is the test at the end of the experimental period, and represents the second, third, or fourth test, depending on the number of tests available at representative time intervals on a given child.

Similar data showing the mental growth of the individual children in the contrast group are presented in Table 2. In the column marked "last test" is given the test on each child at the end of the period of study. This was either the third or fourth test, depending upon the number of available tests at representative time intervals on each child.

Mean, median, and standard deviation comparisons of mental growth from "first" to "last test" for experimental and contrast groups are presented in Table 3. Mean I.Q. at time of transfer was 64.3 with a median at 65. The average gain in intelligence quotient for the experimental group during the course of the experiment was 27.5 points with a median of 23. The mean I.Q. on "last" test was 91.8 with a median at 93. The difference between "first" and "last tests" yielded a critical ratio (Fisher's t) of 6.3 or practical certainty of a true difference. Every child showed a gain, the range being from 7 points to 58 points. Three children made gains of 45 points or more, and all but two children gained more than 15 points (Table 1).

The average chronological age at time of transfer was 19.4 months with a range from 7.1 months to 35.9 months, the median being 17.1 months. Length of the experimental period was from 5.7 months to 52.1 months with a mean of 18.9 months and a median of 14.5 months. The length of the experimental period was not a constant for all children, but depended upon the rate of development of the individual child. As soon as a child showed normal mental development as measured by intelligence tests and substantiated by qualitative observations, the experimental period was considered completed; the child's visit at the school for feebleminded was terminated; and he was placed in an adoptive home or returned to the orphanage.

The mental growth pattern for children of the contrast group is quite the opposite from that of the experimental group. The mean I.Q. on "first" examination was 86.7, whereas on the "last" test it was 60.5, showing an average loss of 26.2 points. The critical ratio (Fisher's t) was 6.1. The median I.Q. on "first" test was 90 and on "last" test 60, with a median of individual losses of 32.5 points (Table 3). With the exception of one child who gained two points in I.Q. from first to last test, all children showed losses, the range being from −8 points to −45 points. Ten of the twelve children lost 15 or more points in I.Q. (Table 2).

Table 1. Mental development of individual children in experimental group as measured by Kuhlmann-Binet intelligence tests before and after transfer

Case number*	Before transfer		Chronological age, months, at transfer	After transfer								Length of experimental period, months	Change in I.Q., first to last test
	Test 1			Test									
				2		3		Last					
	Chronological age, months	I.Q.		Chronological age, months	I.Q.	Chronological age, months	I.Q.	Chronological age, months	I.Q.				
1	7.0	89	7.1	12.8	113			12.8	113			5.7	+24
2	12.7	57	13.3	20.5	94	29.4	83	36.8	77			23.7	+20
3	12.7	85	13.3	25.2	107			25.2	107			11.9	+22
4	14.7	73	15.0	23.1	100			23.1	100			8.1	+27
5	13.4	46	15.2	21.7	77	32.9	100	40.0	95**			24.8	+49
6	15.5	77	15.6	21.3	96	30.1	100	30.1	100			14.5	+23
7	16.6	65	17.1	27.5	104			27.5	104			10.4	+39
8	16.6	35	18.4	24.8	87	36.0	88	43.0	93			24.6	+58
9	21.8	61	22.0	34.3	80			34.3	80			12.3	+19
10	23.3	72	23.4	29.1	88	37.9	71	45.4	79			22.0	+7
11	25.7	75	27.4	42.5	78	51.0	82**	51.0	82**			23.6	+7
12	27.9	65	28.4	40.4	82			40.4	82			12.0	+17
13	30.0	36	35.9	51.7	70	81.0	74**	89.0	81**			52.1	+45

*Arranged according to age at time of transfer from youngest to oldest.
**Stanford-Binet I.Q.

Table 2. Mental development of individual children in contrast group as measured by repeated Kuhlmann-Binet intelligence tests over a period of two and one-half years

Case number*	Test 1 Chronological age, months	Test 1 I.Q.	Test 2 Chronological age, months	Test 2 I.Q.	Test 3 Chronological age, months	Test 3 I.Q.	Last Chronological age, months	Last I.Q.	Length of experimental period, months	Change in I.Q., first to last test
14	11.9	91	24.8	73	37.5	65	55.0	62	43.1	−29
15	13.0	92	20.1	54	38.3	56	38.3	56	25.3	−36
16	13.6	71	20.6	76	40.9	56	40.9	56	27.3	−15
17	13.8	96	37.2	58	53.2	54	53.2	54	39.4	−42
18	14.5	99	21.6	67	41.9	54	41.9	54	27.4	−45
19	15.2	87	22.5	80	35.5	74	44.5	67	29.3	−20
20	17.3	81	43.0	77	52.9	83**	52.9	83**	35.6	+ 2
21	17.5	103	26.8	72	38.0	63	50.3	60	32.8	−43
22	18.3	98	24.8	93	30.7	80	39.7	61	21.4	−37
23	20.2	89	27.0	71	39.4	66	48.4	71	28.2	−18
24	21.5	50	34.9	57	51.6	42	51.6	42	30.1	− 8
25	21.8	83	28.7	75	37.8	63	50.1	60	28.3	−23

*Arranged according to age at time of transfer from youngest to oldest.
**Stanford-Binet I.Q.

Table 3. Mean, median, and standard deviation comparisons of mental growth from first to last test for experimental and contrast groups

Measure	Chronological age, months	Mental age, months	I.Q.	Chronological age, months	Chronological age, months	Mental age, months	I.Q.	Length of experimental period, months	Change in I.Q., first to last test
	Before Transfer			Transfer	After Transfer				
Experimental group (13 children)									
Mean	18.3	11.4	64.3	19.4	38.4	33.9	91.8	18.9	+27.5
Standard deviation	6.6	4.2	16.4	7.4	17.6	13	11.5	11.6	15
Median	16.6	10.8	65.0	17.1	36.8	30.0	93.0	14.5	+23
	First Test			Transfer	Last Test				
Contrast group (12 children)									
Mean	16.6	14.2	86.7		47.2	28.7	60.5	30.7	−26.2
Standard deviation	2.9	2.9	14.3		5.9	6.4	9.7	5.8	14.1
Median	16.3	13.6	90.0		49.3	29.3	60.0	28.8	−32.5

Mean comparisons of mental growth from "first" to "last test" for experimental and contrast groups are shown graphically in Figures 1 and 2. Since the first examinations on children of the experimental group were made about one month before transfer, the unbroken line has been drawn horizontally from chronological age at time of first test to the time of transfer. In Figure 1, since some children in the experimental group had only two tests, the same I.Q. would appear in the second and "last" tests landmarks on the graph. Accordingly, in Figure 2, these have been separated. The unbroken line represents the gain in intelligence from time of transfer to second test and includes all thirteen children. The broken line shows the rate of mental growth for six children having three tests reported and indicates the rate of growth from time of transfer to second test and from second test to third test. Since all children in the contrast group had at least three tests, such a division was unnecessary.

From Figures 1 and 2 and Table 1 it will be seen that as far as central tendencies are concerned, the greatest gain for children in the experimental group was made during the first ten months of the experimental period. Similarly, in Figures 1 and 2 and Table 2, the greatest loss for children in the contrast group was during the first year with a somewhat lower rate of loss during the second and third years.

In the following tabulation children in the experimental group have been arranged in the order of gains from the greatest to the least; children in the contrast group have been arranged in the order of losses from the greatest to the least.

There is a tendency for children in the experimental group initially at the lower levels to make the greater gains. The three children classifying at the imbecile level on first examination made gains of 58, 49 and 45 points I. Q. Also greatest losses in the contrast group were associated with the highest initial levels. Six children with original I.Q.s above 90 lost from 29 to 45 points in I.Q. While this shift may be partially due to regression, there must be other factors operating to bring about such a large and consistent change.

These results, although more marked, are comparable to the findings reported in the orphanage preschool study of Skeels, Updegraff, Wellman, and Williams (5). In that study, children of the preschool group initially at the lower levels made the greatest gains following a period of preschool attendance, and children in the control group originally at the higher levels showed the greatest losses.

There appears to be a marked lack of relationship between mental growth patterns and factors pertaining to the family histories of the children. Numbers of cases are too small to permit statistical treatment of the data. Comparisons are therefore on a more general inspectional basis. In the experimental group, children whose mothers were classified as feebleminded

Case	Changes in I.Q. first to last test	Chronological age, months first test	I.Q. first test
		Experimental group	
8 . . . .+58		16.6	35
5 . . . .+49		13.4	46
13 . . . .+45		30.0	36
7 . . . .+39		16.6	65
4 . . . .+27		14.7	73
1 . . . .+24		7.0	89
6 . . . .+23		15.5	77
3 . . . .+22		12.7	85
2 . . . .+20		12.7	57
9 . . . .+19		21.8	61
12 . . . .+17		27.9	65
10 . . . .+ 7		23.3	72
11 . . . .+ 7		25.7	75

Case	Changes in I.Q. first to last test	Chronological age, months first test	I.Q. first test
		Contrast group	
18 . . . .−45		14.5	99
21 . . . .−43		17.5	103
17 . . . .−42		13.8	96
22 . . . .−37		18.3	98
15 . . . .−36		13.0	92
14 . . . .−29		11.9	91
25 . . . .−23		21.8	83
19 . . . .−20		15.2	87
23 . . . .−18		20.2	89
16 . . . .−15		13.6	71
24 . . . .− 8		21.5	50
20 . . . .+ 2		17.3	81

showed as marked gains as children whose mothers were at a higher mental level. The greatest gain in intelligence (58 points I.Q.) was made by Case 8 whose mother was known to be feebleminded and had only gone as far as the second grade in school.

In the contrast group, the only child who failed to show loss in rate of mental growth (Case 20) from "first" to "last" test was the son of a mother with an I.Q. of 36. Case 24, the most retarded child in the group on first examination with an I. Q. of 50, had a rather flattering family history. His father had graduated from high school and was talented in music. His mother was an eighth grade graduate and had gone to evening business school. She had been a telephone operator and had done general office work.

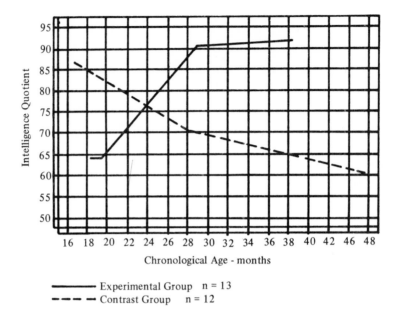

Figure 1. Mean comparisons of mental growth from first to last test for experimental and contrast groups.

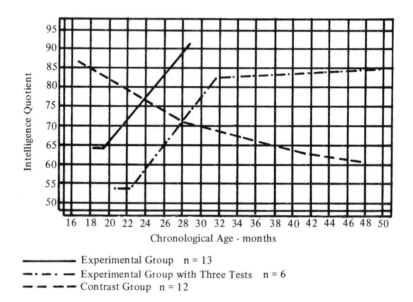

Figure 2. Mean comparisons of mental growth from first to last test for experimental and contrast groups, showing experimental group having three tests.

That the gains in intelligence evidenced by the children of the experimental group were true gains and not due to an artifice in testing seems validated. Practice effects could not have been a contributing factor to these gains as the children in the contrast group, who showed continual losses in I.Q., actually had more tests than children in the experimental group. Improvement was noted independently by members of the medical staff, attendants and matrons, school teachers, and even the older girls on the wards. Teachers are required to submit written reports to the principal at the end of each semester on all children enrolled in classes. Repeated reference is made in these reports to the marked improvement of these children in the experimental group. The following excerpts are taken from such reports: Case 12 after one year preschool or kindergarten: "Well behaved, interested. Joins group for simple games and rhythms. From my observation she apparently possesses about average intelligence for a child her age." Later report: "Very great improvement. Has good vocabulary and muscular coordination. Takes directions readily and can be depended upon. A good leader in games. Does fair handwork." Case 3, after one year: "Very quiet. Has shown a very great improvement this year. Has a fair vocabulary and will take part in games when asked." (This child, two years of age, was one of the youngest in the group.) Case 9, after one year: "Has improved a good deal. Enjoys games and rhythms. Is speaking quite a little. Very attentive."

A close bond of love and affection between a given child and one or two adults assuming a very personal parental role appears to be a dynamic factor of great importance. In evaluating these relationships, nine of the thirteen children in the experimental group were favored with such a relationship. The four other children tended to be less individualized and their adult relationships were more of a general nature involving more adults, the bonds of relationship being less intense with a given individual adult. It seems significant to note that the children favored with the more intense personal contacts made greater gains than those considered as being limited to the more general contacts. The nine children in the "personal" group made gains in I.Q. ranging from 17 to 58 points with an average of 33.8 points gain. The four children in the more general contact group made average gains of 14 points. Two children made gains of only 7 points, one 19 points and one 20 points.

Two children (Cases 10 and 11) showed little progress on ward 7 over a period of a year and a half. This ward differed materially from the other wards in that there were from eight to twelve children of younger ages (three to eight years), and the older girls were of a lower mental level. The attendant on the ward was especially fine with young children, but, of course, was unable to give as much individual attention as was possible on other wards because of the large number of young children. At this time it was feared that these two children would continue to be hopelessly retarded. However, they were subsequently placed as singletons on wards with brighter girls, and after a period of six months with more individualization they showed marked gains in intelligence.

The possibility of "coaching" on test items may be ruled out as a factor. Adults and older girls working with the children were not in any way familiar with the tests used or when they would be administered. Results in terms of I.Q.s were never given out; the only reports made were qualitative ones indicating the general improvement of the child.

As has been indicated, all thirteen children in the experimental group were considered unsuitable for adoption because of mental deficiency. Following the experimental period, seven of these children have been placed in adoptive homes. Of the remaining six, five are considered well within the range of normality and were returned to the orphanage. Only one child (I.Q. 77) will continue in residence at the school for feebleminded for further observation as to subsequent mental development.

Of the children in adoptive homes, four have been examined following one year's residence in the foster home. These are Cases 1, 5, 7, and 8. Final I.Q.s are respectively as follows: 117, 94, 97 and 93. Three of the five children returned to the orphanage have been given an additional test following "last test" reported in Table 2. These are Cases 3, 10, and 11 with subsequent I.Q.s of 115, 84 and 85.

Accordingly, on a basis of last test reported, of the thirteen children two now classify as above average in intelligence with I.Q.s of 117 and 115; five have I.Q.s between 90 and 100; five at the 80 to 90 level and only one child with an I.Q. below 80. No child is now considered to be feebleminded.

In an evaluation of the contrasting mental growth patterns of children in the two groups, one is impressed by the marked relationship between rate of mental growth and the nature of the environmental impact. In the case of the contrast group, the psychological prescription was apparently inadequate as to kinds of ingredients, amounts, and relative proportions. Accordingly, the children became increasingly emaciated in mental growth as time went on.

Conversely, when the psychological prescription was radically changed, the children in the experimental group already retarded at the time of transfer showed marked improvement and either achieved or approached normal mental development after a period of time. The environment of the experimental group apparently included a more adequate prescription as relating to the kinds and proportions of ingredients needed by children of these young ages for normal mental development. It must not be inferred that the environment of the experimental group represented an optimum prescription. Perhaps even greater improvement would have resulted had there been greater facilities and more adequate knowledge of proportioning the ingredients operative in producing optimal mental growth. No instructions were given as to what should or should not be done with the children when they were placed on the wards. This was largely a matter of chance. The general prescription, however, did include certain unmeasured quantitative and qualitative ingredients such as love and affection by one or more interested adults; a wealth of play materials and ample space and opportunity for play with supervision and direction; varied experiences such as preschool or kindergarten attendance and opportunity to be in group gatherings; and a number of other diversified experiences associated with the opportunities afforded a child in a rather adequate home situation. This rather general prescription proved to be conducive to increase in rate of mental development.

With more adequate knowledge as to the correct proportioning of such ingredients in relation to the specific inadequacies or gaps in the developmental pattern of a given child, possibly even more marked mental improvement could have been brought about.

That such increase in rate of mental development may be brought about at older ages through provision of a more adequate psychological prescription is suggested in the studies of Kerhart (3) at the Wayne County Training School. He found that boys of fifteen to eighteen years of age showed increase in rate of mental growth following environmental changes pointed toward alleviation of the development gaps or inadequacies.

It therefore appears that there is an added challenge in the education of the so-called "functional" feebleminded, that is, those not evidencing physiological deficiencies or organic diseases. Not only should the educational program of a school for feebleminded include the teaching of skills at the individual's mental level, but it should be so individualized as to provide for the specific developmental needs of a given child with the strong possibility that the level of mental capacity can be materially augmented.

SUMMARY

This study attempts to determine the effect on mental growth of a radical shift from one institutional environment to another which provided superior stimulation. The experimental group included thirteen mentally retarded orphanage children from one to two years of age, placed singly or by twos on wards with brighter older girls. This environment was stimulating and had many adult contacts. The mean I.Q. of the group at time of transfer was 64.3. As a contrast group twelve average and dull normal children (mean I.Q. 86.7) in an orphanage nursery were studied. Few adult contacts were afforded with limited opportunities for play and development.

Results and conclusions are as follows:

1. Over a period of two years the mean level of intelligence of the experimental group increased markedly while that of the contrast group showed an

equivalent decrease. The experimental group made an average gain of 27.5 points while the contrast group showed a mean loss of 26.2 points.

2. Critical ratios (t's) based on differences between first and last tests for experimental and contrast groups were 6.3 and 6.1 respectively.

3. A change from mental retardation to normal intelligence in children of preschool age is possible in the absence of organic disease or physiological deficiency by providing a more adequate psychological prescription.

4. Conversely, children of normal intelligence may become mentally retarded to such a degree as to be classifiable as feebleminded under the continued adverse influence of a relatively nonstimulating environment.

5. An intimate and close relationship between the child and an interested adult seems to be a factor of importance in the mental development of young children.

6. In a child placing program if children are to be withheld from placement in adoptive homes pending further observation of mental development, it is imperative that careful consideration be given to the type of environment in which they are to be held.

7. The possibility of increasing the mental capacity of "functionally" feebleminded children should be considered as an essential objective in setting up an individualized treatment and educational program in a school for feebleminded.

REFERENCES

1. Binet, Alfred: Les idées modernes sur les enfants. Paris: Ernest Flamarion, 1911. P. 346. Cited from Stoddard, George D.: The I. Q.: Its Ups and Downs. Educ. Rec., 1939, 20, 44-57. (Supplement for January.)
2. Fillmore, Eva A.: Iowa tests for young children. Univ. Iowa Stud., Stud. in Child Welfare, 1936, 11, No. 4, p. 58.
3. Kephart, Newell C.: The effect of a highly specialized institutional program upon the I. Q. in high grade mentally deficient boys. Unpublished study, Wayne County Training School, Northville, Michigan.
4. Skeels, Harold M., and Fillmore, Eva A.: The mental development of children from underprivileged homes. Ped. Sem. and J. Genet. Psychol., 1937, 50, 427-439.
5. Skeels, Harold M., Updegraff, Ruth, Wellman, Beth L., and Williams, Harold M.: A study of environmental stimulation: An orphanage preschool project. Univ. Iowas Stud., Stud. in Child Welfare, 1938, 15, No. 4, p. 190.
6. Skodak, Marie: Children in foster homes: A study of mental development. Univ. Iowas Stud., Stud. in Child Welfare, 1939, 16, No. 1, p. 155.

THE
RELATION OF
SOCIAL
COMPETENCE
TO
SOCIAL
ADJUSTMENT

Edgar A. Doll

Doll's development of techniques for assessing social, emotional, and personality factors represents a further attack upon the I.Q. as the sole criterion for diagnosis and classification of the total individual.

In orienting this presentation to the theme of this conference, "Education for Social and Vocational Adjustment," the argument will be concerned principally with (*a*) the concept of adjustment, and (*b*) the measurement of social competence. We shall think of adjustment as the behavioral expression of the individual's balance between proficiencies and disabilities, needs and frustrations, aspirations and conflicts. We shall not be immediately concerned with the work-methods employed in such problem-solving situations as a means of achieving behavioral balance, but rather with the end results or the psychosocial homeostasis between the individual and his environment. We shall here be only lightly concerned with the measurement of those aptitudes and attitudes which determine the direction and strength of the opposing tendencies involved in the balance of forces between the psychobiological propensities of the individual in relation to the urgencies of his environmental stresses.

The measurement of human attributes has progressed at a rapid and effective pace during the past half-century. The measurement of the social stresses which overtax or capitalize these attributes has been appreciably less successful. This imbalance in the field of measurement is largely due to the greater susceptibility to measurement on the part of individual attributes as compared with the environmental stresses. It is in part due to a professional bias on the part of psychologists toward measurement, and the more limited interest in measurement on the part of sociologists regarding social forces. There is need for coordination in the two fields of effort rather than independent exploitation of either.

The imbalance is further aggravated by the tendency of psychological and educational measurement to be directed toward particular aptitudes (or disabilities) with insufficient consideration of the individual as a whole. This leads to incomplete evaluation of the interrelation of one aspect to another of the total individuality.

More recently we have seen increasing emphasis on the need for relational measurement with respect to holistic, global, or molar assets in their integrative patterns or gestalts as against their discrete, isolated, or molecular fractionation. Encouraging progress is, however, being made in the direction of evaluation of the total personality in respect to both its common elements and its unique patterns with reference to individual psychobiological needs on the one hand and its personal-social purposes on the other.

With such premises in mind we may more clearly conceive of social adjustment as the behavioral reflection of the integration, malintegration, or disintegration of behavioral tendencies in reaction to social situations. We see,

Reprinted from *The Educational Record Supplement,* January, 1948, by permission of Mrs. E. A. Doll and the American Council on Education.

then, the individual achieving psychosocial homeostasis at minimum or optimum level as a balance of forces, whether conceived as a mechanical system or as an ego-determined outcome. Such social adjustment may be inadequate, irrational, unrealistic, undesirable, unconventional, or simply socially objectionable. This we call maladjustment. Or the balance in behavior may be considered adequate, rational, realistic, desirable, conventional, or simply socially commendable. Since individual psychology has been heavily concerned with human deficit rather than human asset, we have no antonym for maladjustment. May I suggest that we call it "bonadjustment." What is important here is that adjustment may be either good or bad, optimum or minimum, adequate or inadequate. Consequently, it behooves us to promote full expressive capitalization of assets as well as remedial correction of deficits. Education has far too long been concerned with bolstering deficiency rather than with fostering talent. There is a marked bias toward deficits in the field of measurement; not that assets are not measured, but rather that their significance is undercapitalized.

In dealing with the problem of social and vocational adjustment, education has notoriously ignored certain major biological, psychological, and social principles in relation of learning as adjustment to learning as achievement. As a result of almost bigoted devotion to the tacit assumption that only that is learned which is formally taught, we have relied too much on subject-oriented instruction and not enough on pupil-oriented growth and experience. If education is to adapt classroom instruction to child growth and development, it must have more regard for both the direction and the timing of instruction. The great scandals in education are teaching too early or too late, too little or too much, too easy or too difficult, with overemphasis on the acquisition of knowledge and underemphasis on self-reliance in the pursuit of knowledge. Our curriculums must be revised in stages, content, and method to the realistic levels of personality maturation and the related selectivity of motivation and experience.

The first of these principles is biological. This involves awareness of the growth and development of the individual as a maturing organism. This principle reveals that birds *grow* into flying, and that children *grow* into walking. *Learning* to fly or to walk presupposes such growth (and development). We need not *teach* ducks to swim, and we do not suceed in teaching chickens to swim. Morphological propensities determine these possibilities. The successive stages of growth and maturation are reflected in progressive patterns of behavior. Whether we consider these as instinctive patterns or growth patterns of behavior, the fact is that they reflect definite footsteps and milestones in the normal processes of growth and development. Social adjustment, whether minimum or maximum, whether "mal" or "bon," is consequently first related to the degree of growth or development (maturation) reflected in the particular individual in relation to his most appropriate norm.

A second principle is that of environmental selectivity. Individual growth and development are obviously modified by personal-social experience in the world of things, people, and ideas. The adjustment of the maturing organism to environmental experience is itself maturational since the organism exercises a selective relation to its environment. The conditioned consequences of such relation reflect this continuing impact of the developing organism to a universe of manifold opportunities.

A third principle is apparent in the aspirational aspects of psychobiological and psychosocial dynamic motivation. *What* the child learns reflects what he *wishes* to learn. Here his personality needs, purposes, desires, and frustrations reflect an interplay of maturational aptitude with environmental inspiration. And here the problem of adjustment is one of the relation of aspiration to aptitude, of wish to reality, of purpose to practicability. Such aspiration may reveal urge from within or pressure from without. Here we encounter expressive striving whether derived from self-projective "needs" or from the aspirations of the parent for the child or the teacher for the pupil. It is particularly in this realm of projective aspiration that fertile opportunities for maladjustment as well as bonadjustment occur. The substitutive projection of adult needs or purposes toward the child may overtax, undertax, or otherwise interfere with the child's own level of aspiration in relation to his maturational aptitudes and environmental selectivity.

Adjustment, then, is seen as dependent upon the degree and kind of coordination or harmony obtaining among these various relationships. This we commonly refer to as "the behavioral reflection of personality integration." We see it reflected in emotional immaturity where reality and wish are out of balance, where desire and aptitude are discordant, or where mature capacity coupled with immature aspiration results in low degree of environmental capitalization. Our concept of adjustment must, therefore, be related to this global or comprehensive relation of individual attributes to environmental opportunities. Our point of view should be positive as well as negative, expressive as well as corrective, and focused toward the capitalization of talent rather than the subsidizing of defect or deficiency.

But it is difficult to pursue this molar concept of adjustment in the field of measurement beyond fairly definite limits. The holistic individual not only may, but also actually must, be considered with respect to the elements which contribute to his aggregated individuality and the social moments which modify its behavioral manifestations in the social scene. This results in the fragmentation of measurement directed toward particular aptitudes, attitudes, or attributes and the assessment of their relative contribution to the integrated whole. In such particular measurement much progress is evident. But we have not yet made much practical progress in the quantitative synthesis of such details. Consequently we must continue to rely on the *art* of personality evaluation until its science is further advanced. How many and which of the numerous and diverse details of total personality study can be encompassed, for example, within the technique of the regression equation?

Some of these distinctive aspects of the personality appear to be more potent than others in the over-all evaluation of adjustment. For example, intelligence, however inadequately conceptualized at present, appears to reflect the most important single aspect of the personality, or at least to command its most general emphasis. Obviously, the effective use of intelligence may be reduced or disturbed by other personality attributes such as emotional repression or perverted motivation. Yet it is precisely such interferences with the normal expression of intelligence that yield the largest single returns in the present systems of either group or clinical measurements.

When we search outside the field of intelligence for any single over-all measurement of personal adequacy, we find little to rely upon in the area of human measurement. This lack is significantly reduced by the Vineland Social Maturity Scale[1] which seeks to quantify the evaluation of social competence as a global aspect of individual maturation at successive age levels. This instrument provides a first means for the measurement of social self-sufficiency in terms of overt social performances. This is expressed as effective accomplishment of the level of aspiration in relation to the complex of personal attributes and social urges. Such an instrument provides a point of departure or of orientation in all casework and is a point of reference for the measurement of specific aspects of total individuality. This device deliberately avoids the measurement of specific aptitudes or disabilities, but seeks instead to assess their relational efficacy. It avoids the specific influence of environmental opportunity by endeavoring to deal with those aspects of social adequacy which are common to all environments. In so far as it fails to do this, it poses modes of specific environmental expression which may be used as points of reference for the evaluation of other environments.

For example, in the course of maturation the child reaches a stage where he feeds himself. Whether he eats with his fingers, with chopsticks, or with a table-fork may be an environmental convention. Whether the relative difficulties of such conventional modes of achievement are equal or different can readily be determined by investigation. And similarly for other details of social adequacy.

---

[1] Edgar A. Doll, *Vineland Social Maturity Scale* (Minneapolis: Educational Test Bureau, 1946).

In all environments the infant is initially dependent on others; but as he grows and develops, he achieves progressive independence; and as an adult he assumes responsibility for the welfare of others. In other words, in the process of growing up he passes through successive stages of dependency, self-sufficiency, and personal-social group and domestic responsibility. His social adequacy, therefore, is individual, parental, and communal. We have, then, an over-all measure of social competence to which the problem of social adjustment may be referred, but without direct identification. That is, the individual, whether relatively socially competent or incompetent, may be maladjusted or bonadjusted according to the social approbation attaching to the expression of such competence. The misdirection or perversion of social competence poses moral issues with which the concept of adjustment may or may not be properly concerned. Indeed, it is this question of moral values with which the world expects education to be increasingly concerned since the misdirection of talent is far more dangerous socially than the misdirection of deficiency. Thus, the competent criminal is more dangerous than the incompetent, and the misguided leader more of a social menace than the misguided follower. And society loses rather than gains from the offender's adequacy because of his perverted purposes.

In constructing such a scale for the measurement of social competence, the immediate task was one of reducing general observations of social adequacy to conceptual principles and these in turn to some form of expression susceptible to measurement. This was accomplished by reducing the over-all concept to specific categorical modes of performance. Two approaches were employed, first, a categorical analysis into such major areas of adequacy as self-help, locomotion, communication, occupation, and socialization; and, secondly, the formulation of definitive stages of maturational progression of performances within these categories. The endeavor further required the avoidance of specific aptitudes and attitudes in favor of their composite integration. Consequently, such specific qualities as intelligence, skill, emotionality, and the like as primary abilities were avoided in favor of their combined effects as compounded behavior. Thus, the ability to dress one's self at successive levels of complexity was taken as the end result of multiple aptitudes, no one of which was given specific weight, but, rather, their end result expressed as functional success or failure. These performances were further considered as overtly expressed habitual performances rather than as native capacities for achieving such performances. What the individual habitually *does* rather than what he is capable of doing became the criterion.

We need not here consider the detailed construction of this scale nor the evidence established with respect to its practicability, validity, reliability, and other proper concerns of measurement techniques. These details have been elsewhere published in some detail and will soon be published in a more comprehensive and elaborate book exposition. Assuming these requirements as reasonably satisfied, and conceding the preliminary state of the investigation, one may assert with some confidence that this scale is reasonably adequate for the purposes intended (with due regard for the likelihood of improvement). What here concerns us more immediately is the universal uses of such an instrument for the evaluation of social competence as a precondition of social adjustment and as a means for interpreting the component variables which may be directly assessed by other presently available methods of measurement. For the most part the shortcomings of the scale are those common to most systems of human measurement, and there is a reasonable presumption that these disadvantages may be overcome in time and with further effort. More important for present purposes is the unique advantage afforded by this instrument, since it is the only means presently available in which the presence of the person examined is not required. This feature alone adds merit to the scale and serves to outweigh many of its present limitations. While the scale in its present form is obviously not culture free, it provides a standardization within a defined culture which may be used as a point of reference for appraising the effects of other cultures. Moreover, standard modifications of the technique permit the evaluation of potential social competence in the face of significant mental, physical, and social handicaps. This is accomplished by the devices of "double-scoring" and "no opportunity scoring" which permit appraising the individual as he might be if certain personal or environment deficits were not present. It also affords an estimate of optimum achievement if the variable components are maximally capitalized.

It may fairly be said that this scale marks a new departure in the field of measurement in the direction of versatility, since the uses to which this scale may be put are both more varied and more practicable than is true of other measuring instruments. In the book formulation of the method soon to be published, eight major areas of usefulness are specifically expounded. Within these eight areas no less than thirty-eight distinctive uses have been outlined.

The opening sentence in Itard's first report on the "Wild Boy of Aveyron" closes with these words, "It is only in the heart of society that man can attain the pre-eminent position which is his natural destiny." Education is clearly concerned with facilitating the accomplishment of this natural social destiny. It would seem that measurement in education is, therefore, pre-eminently concerned with the assessment of social competence and the relation of social competence to social adjustment. If education is to be socially oriented as to its origins, its objectives, its content, timing, direction, and methods, then the measurement of social adequacy is of paramount concern.

The major argument of the presentation may then be briefly summarized in the following propositions:

1.   Social adjustment cannot be adequately evaluated independently of social competence.

2.   The measurement of social competence affords a measurement of the holistic personality in terms of social purpose or meaning.

3.   Such measurement provides a point of departure or an orientation for the assessment of the more specific aspects of personality with reference to the particular components involved in the attainment of social competence.

4.   The measurement of social competence in relation to its component attributes affords an estimate of the degree of their capitalization as minimum or optimum.

5.   The over-all concept, related principles, and progressive stages of social maturation are a paramount concern in the formulation of educational objectives, curriculums, and procedures.

6.   The moral values implicit in the measurement of social competence are of the utmost concern to education from the standpoint of national and world progress.

FOLLOW-UP STUDIES OF 92 MALE AND 131 FEMALE PATIENTS WHO WERE DISCHARGED FROM THE NEWARK STATE SCHOOL IN 1946

Isaac N. Wolfson

By the 1950's the follow-up study had become a familiar research report in the mental retardation literature. The results were almost unanimously favorable, and institutional discharge policy was beginning to reflect this finding.

In 1951 the ideas was conceived to investigate the adjustment of our former patients following a five year discharge period.* This represented a group of 92 males and 131 females, who were discharged in 1946, after a residence in the community for two years or longer on convalescent care program under supervision of our social service department. It was felt important to learn what adjustment these people made while they were back in society on their own. This study became of added interest and importance at the time, as shortly after it was initiated an incident of unpremeditated murder was committed by a former patient of a mental hospital on a total stranger, and an accusing finger was pointed at the psychiatrists, who allegedly were careless in discharging dangerous patients into the community.

The study extended to 1954, thus increasing the follow-up period to 7 or 8 years after discharge. This represents a contact with male patients for an average period of 15 years and with female patients for an average period of 18 years. We were able to trace 89, or 96.5 per cent, of the boys and 119, or 90 per cent, of the girls.

The study consists of a review of the patients' histories and the data on the adjustment during the 7 or 8 year period following discharge. This data was collected through correspondence with members of the family, former employers, and various social agencies who may have had contact with our former patients. Some of the information has been obtained through personal interview by staff members of our social service department with members of the family or other social agencies.

As the study progressed, we became aware of the incompleteness and inadequacy of some of the records. In some case histories the description of the parents and home environment was so scant that it could be of little value. Rarely did a record contain information on the developmental history of the patient's personality. In the majority of cases the reasons for admission were given as general statements without specific or documentary data. The progress notes during their residence in the institution in many cases were meager and uninformative.

The follow-up data through correspondence or visits by our social workers was limited mostly to general statements about economic and social adjustment of the patients, shedding very little light on psychological or emotional adjustment, except by an occasional implication. In spite of these

---

*This paper was presented at the Annual Meeting of the American Association on Mental Deficiency in Detroit on May 28, 1955.

American Journal of Mental Deficiency, 1956, 61(1): 224–238. Reprinted by permission of Dr. Wolfson and the American Association on Mental Deficiency.
    Dr. Wolfson was director of the Newark State School from 1950 until 1956. He currently resides in Monsey, New York.

frustrating limitations, sufficient interesting and pertinent data became available to make it worthwhile to report our findings.

Many things which we learned from the longitudinal study of these cases histories cannot be reported here because of the time element. Therefore, we are limiting ourselves to some general facts and observations.

As we studied the records of our cases, we found it more and more difficult to group them statistically, as each case represented an individual picture with unique features which did not lend itself in its entirety to fit into a generalized group. Appreciating the limitation of statistical classification of clinical material, and with this reservation, we attempted to group the cases on the basis of some similarities of the general features.

The 92 discharged male patients were divided into four groups:

I. Five were discharged because they did not belong in an institution for mentally retarded; 4 were discharged after a short residence here as psychotic, 1 with an I.Q. of 88 as not mentally defective.

II. Ten boys were discharged on demand of parents after a short residence here, but were subsequently returned to the institution and are still here; 9 require custodial care because of their severe degree of retardation and instability. One school boy returned because of poor home conditions.

III. Eighteen boys who were dependent and required supervision were discharged and are remaining with their families, adjusting well. Many of these boys resided in the institution less than one year when they were removed by their parents. This group represents 7 retarded patients who require custodial care, 6 physically handicapped, 2 school age boys and 3 young adults with mild retardation who are still not self-supporting; but are adjusting under family care and supervision. Many of these 18 boys come from more stable families than the families of the next group to be discussed.

IV. This group consists of 59 discharged male patients, most of whom were mildly retarded and could be expected to take their place in society. They represent three types of adjustment:

1. Thirty-six made a continuously good or satisfactory social adjustment. The levels of adjustment, however, were sufficiently different to permit division of this group into two classes labeled as "A" and "B."

The "A" class comprised 17 boys who appeared to have made an adjustment on a higher plane. They were more independent and were adjusting without supervision. Nine of these are married and have 1 or 2 children; 3 are maintaining homes and supporting other members of their family; 2 are assisting in support of one or the other parent; 14 of the boys have been steadily employed since they left the institution; and 1 is serving his second enlistment in the Army. The occupations of these boys were as follows: 4 were working on the railroad; 9 in various factories; 2 worked in hospitals as orderlies; 1 as superintendent of a building; and 1 as clerk in a G.L.F. store.

The "B" class comprised 19 boys. Although they also had made a continuous adjustment since separation from the school, their employment and social adjustment appeared to be on a somewhat lower level. A number of them are living with members of their family and are apparently dependent on their emotional support and supervision. Of this group 3 are married—2 to defective girls, and their marital adjustment has not been satisfactory. Nine live with both or one parent, or other relatives; 4 live on the farms where they work; 2 live alone on a rather low social and economic level; 1, who had a rather unstable work record, is now confined to a tuberculosis sanitarium. The occupations of these boys consisted of: 1 worked on a railroad; 4 on a farm; 2 dishwashers; 1 a clerk in a grocery store; 1 employed in a bowling alley; 1 in a laundry; the occupation of 7 was not specified.

2. The adjustment of 10 patients was not continuous. During some phase of their residence in the community they became involved in difficulties which required their temporary return to this institution or a temporary confinement in a correctional institution.

One boy, at the age of 23, during an emotional episode following his mother's death, was arraigned in January, 1950, for endangering the morals of two boys, 6 and 10 years of age. He was returned to the Newark State School in April, 1950, and remained here until October, 1953. At the present time, he lives at the home of a married sister, is making a good social adjustment and is gainfully employed.

One man, at the age of 33 years, was arrested in 1950 for an alleged attempt at sex play with a young niece and nephew. He was returned to Newark State School for 1½ years. He now lives with his mother, requires some supervision and has seasonal employment.

One boy, in 1947 at the age of 18 years, spent six months in jail for sodomy. This boy now lives at home with his parents, temporarily unemployed.

Two boys, after escaping from the institution in 1946, stole a horse from a stable in a nearby community. One, who was 18 years of age, spent 4½ years in an institution for defective delinquents. He was paroled in November, 1950, but was returned in February, 1953, for violation of parole. In September, 1954, he was discharged from that institution, which reports: "Improved tremendously during his period of confinement. Now works with a line crew for an electric company; services satisfactory. Normal satisfactory adjustment in free society." The other, a 17 year old boy, spent a year in a vocational institution for delinquents. After his release he worked steadily for 4 years adjusting well until he was killed in an accident.

One boy, at the age of 24 years, spent 5 years, from 1946 to 1951, in an institution for defective delinquents charged with sodomy. Since then he has been married for 3 years and is gainfully employed.

One boy, 21 years of age, spent 1 year, from 1948 to 1949, in an institution for defective delinquents for stealing a purse from a woman in a park. This boy is now serving a second enlistment in the Army.

One boy, at 17 years, spent 3½ years, from 1947 to 1950, in an institution for defective delinquents as a wayward minor. He is now in the Army.

One spent 2 years, from 1951 to 1953, in an institution for defective delinquents, being admitted at the age of 19 as a youthful offender. This boy was returned to the same institution in November, 1954, for taking a pick-up truck from his employer without permission.

One boy, in 1947 at the age of 22, stole a car and was charged with grand larceny. He was sentenced to prison where he died in August, 1951.

Of these 10 boys, 3 were discharged on demand of the family against advice of the institution, and 3 after they escaped from the institution.

Of the four who presented sex problems, 2 apparently had a single episode of misconduct as there is no record of their tendency to abnormal sex behavior prior to their admission or during their residence in the institution. One was alleged to have endangered morals of small children, but there was no definite evidence or proof of this; while 1 boy, who was discharged on demand of the family against advice, had been a serious behavior problem since childhood and in recent years has had considerable psychiatric treatment.

3. Ten showed serious personality disorders. Eight of these eventually developed a mental illness which resulted in their confinement in a mental hospital.

One patient after nine months' hospitalization returned home. He now lives with his family. He is apparently adjusting satisfactorily and has seasonal employment. One patient died after drinking turpentine during an acute psychotic episode; whether this was accidental or with suicidal intent was not determined. Five are still in the institution for mentally ill. One escaped from a state hospital, is now at home, but is not well mentally. The diagnosis of 7 cases was schizophrenia; 1 undetermined.

Of the remaining two, one was suffering with a serious personality disorder, characterized chiefly by a tendency to transvestitism. Since his separation from the school he was able to keep a position as an orderly in the same hospital for 9 years until he was dismissed in December, 1950, because he was found reverting to his old habits. Nothing is known about this man after that period. One man, who is now about 53 years old, has spent a great deal of his life in state schools. Of late he has been living in the community on a rather low dependent level.

Three patients could not be located after their discharge, therefore, their adjustment is unknown.

It was found difficult to group the home situation of the 59 mildly retarded patients into specific categories because of the many variable factors involved. For example, even when considering such apparently definite category as broken homes, this was found to have a limited meaning unless many other factors were to be correlated, such as which parent was absent from the home, the reason the home was broken, the age of the patient when the home was broken, and child-parent relationship. With the limited data at hand the homes could be described only in general terms. With a few exceptions the patients came from low income families, many broken homes, and retarded, inadequate or unstable parents with one or more mentally defective or delinquent siblings. Our data does not indicate any direct relationship of the home situation to the final adjustment of the patient—there does not appear to be much difference in the homes of the various adjustment level groups as described above.

The only striking difference in the review of the homes is the fact that of the 36 boys who made a continuous adjustment, 14 resided in orphanages or foster homes prior to their admission in contrast to only 2 of the 23 in the other groups.

There did not appear to be any significant relationship of the ages of admission, the length of residence in the institution and psychometric ratings to the type of adjustment made by the boys after discharge, as indicated by the chart.

There appears to be, however, definite correlation between the adjustment in the community and the circumstances under which the patients left the institution. Of the 36 patients in the continuous adjustment group, 3 patients escaped, were not located and subsequently discharged; 10 were placed on employment convalescent care by the institution; and 23 were permitted to go on home convalescent care to some member of their family. Of the other 23 patients, 10 escaped and were subsequently discharged; 6 were removed from the institution by their parents against advice; 2 were placed on employment convalescent care; and 5 were permitted to go home. That is, 33 of 36 patients of group 1 were released from the institution and subsequently discharged under a planned program, while only 7 out of 23 of groups 2 and 3 were discharged with approval of the institution and 16 were discharged against advice.

When we attempted to analyze the reasons for admission of the boys and the girls to the school, we realized that in many cases the reasons given were actually the precipitating factors. The maladjustment which led to the boys' or girls' admissions were end results of personality conflicts environmentally conditioned. Again, because of limited data and confining ourselves to the purpose of this paper, we have not attempted to analyze these conflicts, but rather are reporting the material as it appears in the admission record. Of the

Table 1. Male

A—Good continuous adjustment
B—Satisfactory continuous adjustment
C—Temporary misconduct
D—Serious maladjustment or personality disorder

Ages on admission in years

A		9	11	12	13 13 13	14 14 14	15 15	16 16 16	17						
B	7	8 8		11 11 11 11	12	13 13 13		15 15 15	16 16	18	24	42			
C		9 9 9	10			13 14 15	15	16	18 18						
D		8 8		11 11	12 12			16 16 16	19 20 22	37					

Residence here in yrs. A 4m 1–3 2–1 2–7 3–7 3–7 4–5 5–3 5–6 5–9 6–4 6–7 7–7 8–2 8–3 11–10 12

B	10m	1–1	1–5	2–3	3–2	3–7 3–8 3–9								11	11–9	12–3	13–3
C	2m 6m	1–1	1–5		3–3	3–9	5–7	6–7		8–9					11–9		
D	1–1 8m	1–4	1–8	2–2 2–9			5–2	6–2 6–10		8 8–1	10–1				12–5		
I.Q.																	
A	41	47	49	51	52 53		57		60 60	63	64 64	71 69 74	75 79				
B	39 41 43 46	48 48		52 52 52 53 52 53 54		58 60		62 66		75 78							
C	36	49		53 54	57	59 60	68 71		81								
D	39 43	48	51	52 53	56	59 61	66	70	74 77								

17 boys in the "A" class, 7 were admitted for training only, no behavior disorder appeared in their record; 2 presented sex problems; 5 boys came with a history of stealing, taking money from home and defiance of supervision; and, 3 patients presented neurotic symptoms.

Of the 19 boys in the "B" class, 10 were admitted essentially for training, 7 for stealing and defiance of supervision. One boy was admitted at the age of 23, after being arrested for annoying a young woman; 1 showed neurotic symptoms.

Of the 23 boys in the second and third groups, 6 were admitted for training only; 11 presented various types of maladjustment, such as stealing, public mischief, poor social adjustment; 5 presented sex problems; 1 was a pyromaniac.

The 131 discharged female patients were divided into three groups.

I. Four were discharged because they did not belong in an institution for mentally retarded, 3 were psychotic and 1 not mentally retarded.

II. Twenty-eight dependent patients were discharged on request of parents or relatives. This group consisted of 8 physically handicapped, 18 severely retarded, 2 unstable and unable to be self-supporting. Five of the severely retarded were returned to the institution and 23 remained at home.

III. Ninety-nine of the discharged were mildly retarded who were expected to take their place in society. They have shown three types of adjustment.

1. Seventy-two made a continuous good or satisfactory adjustment in the community.

Again, on a rather impressionistic basis these 72 patients were divided into two classes, "A" and "B," based on the apparent differences in the level and stability of their adjustment. In the "A" class, those who adjusted on a higher plane, there were 38 patients. Twenty-nine of these have married after their discharge; 3 continue to work in the same place since separation from the institution; 5 live with their families, but are self-supporting; 1 lives by herself and has had continuous employment since discharge.

In the "B" class, those who adjusted on a somewhat lower plane than the "A" class, there were 34 patients. Fifteen of these have married since discharge; 3 are back with their husbands; 7 live with their families and are self-supporting; 5 live alone and have had continuous employment since discharge. Two have married, but left their husbands and live alone and are self-supporting; 1 is divorced and remarried; and, 1 lives with a man to whom she is not married.

It should be stated that the adjustment of some of the female patients from the time of their admission until their final separation was not continuous. A number of them were placed out in colonies, on employment convalescent care or home convalescent care, but failed to adjust and had to be returned for further training or stabilization before they finally had a satisfactory period of convalescent care adjustment and were subsequently discharged.

2. Eight after making a temporary satisfactory adjustment were returned to the institution—1 had three illegitimate children during the discharge period, therefore, was returned to the institution in April, 1952; 1 married after discharge, but was readmitted July, 1950 on petition of her husband because she neglected their three children and was allegedly promiscuous; 2 were returned to the institution because of out-of-wedlock pregnancies; 1 was returned because of ill health; 2 because of death of the interested relative; 1 became emotionally unstable and some time after return to this institution was certified to a State institution as mentally ill.

3. Seven remaining in the community were not making a satisfactory adjustment—4 presented a sex problem (3 of these had a residence in a correctional institution since discharge from this school) and 3 neglected their children, left their husbands and live with men out-of-wedlock on a rather low social plane.

Twelve could not be located after discharge, therefore, their adjustment is unknown.

As noted by the chart, there appears to be a difference in the ages of admission between "A" and "B" groups. In the "A" group 29 out of 38, or 76 per cent, of the patients were admitted at 17 years of age or younger. While in the "B" group 26 out of 34, or 76 per cent, were admitted after the age of 17. Although the small number of patients considered and the rather equivocal basis for the grouping into the two levels of adjustment do not permit definite statistical conclusions, it does appear that the younger age of admission was related to a higher level of adjustment in the community.

The length of residence in the institution and psychometric ratings do not appear to be related to the adjustment after discharge.

The story with the mildly retarded female patients was somewhat different as to the reason for their admission than the males. Although the majority of them came from similar poor home environments, sex problems in one form or another were one of the major reasons for their admission, in addition to simple retardation, neglect by parents and behavior problems at home. Specifically, 5 were admitted because of incest relations with their father or brothers, 24 as sexually promiscuous, 17 because they had one or more out-of-wedlock children, 8 were admitted in pregnant condition, 10 married women with families were admitted because they were unable to take proper care of their family, 35 had a history of other social problems or neurotic symptoms.

It is interesting to note that 13 girls in the "A" group and 2 girls in the "B" group resided in orphanages or foster homes prior to their admission, while all in the other groups came from their homes.

Table 2. Female

A – Continuous good adjustment
B – Satisfactory continuous adjustment
C – Temporary misconduct
D – Serious maladjustment or personality disorder

Age in
Age in
years

	6	7	12	13	14	15	16	17	18	19	20	21	22	23	24	25	26	32	33	34	35	39
						15																
						15																
						15	16															
						15	16															
						15	16															
						15	16															
						15	16	17														
			12			15	16	17								24						
			12			15	16	17			20					24						
A	6	7	12	13	14	15	16	17			20			23	24	25	26				35	

	6	7	12	13	14	15	16	17	18	19	20	21	22	23	24	25	26	32	33	34	35	39
										19												
										19												
										19												
									18	19												
									18	19												
						15				20												
			12	13		15	16	17			20		22		23	24		32				
B			12	13	14	15	16	17	18		20	21	22		23	24	25	26	32	33	34	35	39
					14	15	16	17														
								17														

Table 2 (cont.)

C & D

C & D	12 13	14 15 16	17	19	20	22	26
Unknown	11	15 16				24	
	11 12	14 15 16		19		24 25	42

Residence to discharge

A			7	8			13			
			7	8		12	13			
		3	7	8		12	13		24	
		3 4	7	8		12	13 14		22 24	
	2 3 4 5 6	7	8	9 10	12	13 14	20		30	
B				9 10						
	3	6		9 10		13	15			
	3	6		9 10	12	13		21		
	2 3	6	7	9 1011	12	13 14 15 16	21	28	43	
		6		11						
C & D 1m 3m		6		11						
		6	7	11 12	14	16 17	38			

Table 2. cont.

Table 2. cont.

A—Continuous good adjustment
B—Satisfactory continuous adjustment
C—Temporary misconduct
D—Serious maladjustment or personality disorder

I.Q.	Unknown	6	7 8	8	9 10 11	13	24
A 41	46 48 50 53 48 50 53 49 50 54	57 57 57 58 59 59	60 60 61 61	62 63 63 63	65 65 66 67 71 69 71 69 71	73 73 74 76 77	82
B 44	50 46 50 46 50 44 47 50 53 44 47 50 53	50 50 56 57 57 59	60	62 64 64 64 64	66 67 67 69 71 69 71	72 73	77 79	84
C & D 38 43 44	46 43 44 49	59	60 61 61	64 64	65 68		79 79	
Unknown	46	52 53		63 63	65 65 68 68	76		80

The home conditions of the girls were essentially the same as in the case of the boys. Where specific data was available, in the "A" class fathers were described as: 5 dead, 9 alcoholic, 4 psychotic, 2 deserted their families, 2 were abusive, 5 arrested and sent to jail, 5 were retarded, 2 indulged in incest with patient or other siblings, 1 was a semi-invalid and only 3 were stable. The mothers were described as: 5 dead, 12 defective, 4 promiscuous, 1 alcoholic, 5 neurotic, 1 in jail and 5 were stable. In the "B" group: 7 fathers were dead, 4 alcoholic, 2 psychotic, 3 were in jail, 1 indulged in incest relations with patient or other siblings, 7 were unstable, 3 defective and 2 deserted their families. Of the mothers there were: 5 dead, 8 defective, 1 psychotic, 2 promiscuous, 2 were in jail, 1 was emotionally unstable, and only 2 were stable. The family situation of the third group was quite similar to the above.

The collective data on separate phases of the patients' lives, such as family background, pre-admission history, and adjustment in the community as presented tells very little about the personality deviation or dynamics in the process of adjustment of an individual patient. It would be much more informative and meaningful if one could even briefly relate all the data available as it applies to each case. Because of limitation of time such a report is not possible. To illustrate this point, however, it was decided to report a few representative cases of the better adjusted group.

#5 FB

Family History Father died of tuberculosis when patient was six months old. Mother was described as a coarse, ill-tempered woman who had been reported to have lived with more than one man since the death of her husband. The home was extremely poor, dirty and located in the slum area of the community. After the father died the mother lived with a man whom she later married. Two sisters were removed from the home because the stepfather had sex relations with them.

The boy was sent to Newark State School at 13 years and 9 months of age because of irregular school attendance and undesirable home situation. On admission psychometric showed a rate of 64. He adjusted well in our school, was friendly, a good worker and a member of the Boy Scout Troop. At 19 he was placed on employment on a farm, but returned in a month because he did not like farming, "and was lazy and shiftless on the job." In 1943 at the age of 21 he was allowed to go on a week's vacation to his grandmother. During that period he found a job on the railroad, and, therefore, was allowed to remain at home. He has continued on the same job since then, working in the shops and supplying on the section gang. He is considered a steady and responsible worker, saved money, dressed well. He helped his mother financially and after she died he returned home, paid up all of her bills, renovated the home, put in a telephone and has taken complete responsibility for the care of his two younger step-sisters.

#40 AK

Family History   Father was foreign born. He had been arrested many times for assaulting his wife. He finally left home the same year the patient was born. Mother was committed to a State hospital in 1930 and from there was transferred to Newark State School.

Patient was placed in an orphanage at the age of 9. He remained there for 5 years when he was certified to Newark State School in 1936 at the age of 14, because he was unable to learn, "was a menace in the orphanage," and needed supervision. On admission his psychometric rating showed an I.Q. of 71. He adjusted well in the institution; did well in academic classes; was an honor scout; and was a good worker. In March of 1944 at the age of 22 he was placed to work on a farm, but six weeks later he was returned as being unsuitable for farm work. In a few days he was placed on employment in a hospital in a nearby community to run an elevator and help on the ambulance. During his employment at this hospital he was described as neat, clean, pleasant, well liked by doctors and nurses. He was said to have made an excellent adjustment and was considered one of the most valuable employees there. He continued working at this hospital until 1949 when he obtained a job as a house superintendent of a public building where he was considered a reliable and dependable employee. He is now married and has two children.

#52 EMCK

Family History   Patient was born out-of-wedlock, abandoned by his mother and grew up in an orphanage. He was admitted to Newark State School at 11½ years because "he was retarded and was unable to learn in special class for defectives and is chronic enuretic." On admission his psychometric rating showed an I.Q. of 57. Although he was described as mischievous and playful, he adjusted well and made satisfactory progress in school and occupational therapy classes. He was a Boy Scout. At the age of 18 he was placed to work in a hospital in a nearby community and was reported to be one of the finest boys they had working there. He has been employed on different jobs so that in any emergency he would be able to take anyone's place. To manage his enuresis he secured a night urinal bag. This helped him to control his habits so that he did not wet for weeks. During his employment he kept in close contact by corresponding with one of the school employees in whose department he worked while here. In 1948 he secured a license as a practical nurse. He later served two years in the Army. He is now employed in an industrial plant and the Chief Nurse in the hospital where he worked, who still has contact with him, writes that she is extremely proud of his adjustment. "He is handsome, has a car and is saving money."

#108

Family History   Parents of foreign extraction, illiterate (but allegedly respectable people). They adhered strictly to the rigid principles of the old country. When the patient was 7 years old it was noted that she had difficulty in learning. At 11 she was placed in a special class. At 14 the principal of the school began noting her undue interest in boys. In December, 1938, the father filed a petition charging his 14-year-old daughter as being ungovernable in that she refused to obey and remained away from home late at night and more recently was away from home for 3 days. On her return a medical examination revealed that she had had sex experience. In January, 1939, the girl was placed in the shelter where she was described as untruthful, made several attempts to run away, showed undue interest in men working on the premises. Therefore, in May of 1939 she was admitted to Newark State School at the age of 15.

On admission her I.Q. was 71. She was described as boisterous, unduly fond of boys, at times defiant, but generally well liked. On interview she stated that she felt that she had never received affection from her parents, she was never kissed by them. Her father drank periodically to excess and when intoxicated was cruel to the mother and children. When he was sober he was interested in his children. She adjusted well at the institution and after a period of training of about 3 years she was placed in a colony and then on employment convalescent care in her home town. She was well liked by her understanding employer, who treated her very kindly and had taken her on trips with the family. About a year later she obtained a job in a factory and has continued in the same job. During this time she bought a small house for her parents and is supporting them. In 1952 she married "a respectable citizen and conducts herself with dignity" (according to a report from her former employer).

DISCUSSION

This study raises several questions.

1. As one studies these case histories one wonders how the contemporary theory which emphasizes the importance of early parent-child relationships and wholesome family situation on development of personality applies in these cases. Why is it that such a large percentage of boys and girls with glaringly adverse family background grow up to be stable and responsible people? Could it be that there are also important constitutional elements in the personality of the individual about which we know very little and rarely consider, which allow these people to withstand many of the exigencies of life and still make a satisfactory adjustment after a period of maturation?

2. Are we justified in labeling as mental defective some of these economically independent and socially stable individuals? Perhaps the entire concept of mental deficiency should be redefined.

3. Is it true that limited intellectual endowment "means proportionately lesser judgment, lesser imaginative powers, lesser emotional and volitional control," as postulated by some authorities? Or is this concept of the personality of mentally retarded based on traditional notions carried over from the past and is due for re-evaluation through research?

4. Considering the fact that many of these men and women after discharge have managed their lives quite well primarily by their own resources, this study does not support the view expressed by some authorities that these people need continuous supervision in order to adjust in the community. However, the apparent support some of these patients receive from their employers appears to be significant. It was quite revealing to learn of the lasting, wholesome relationships which were established and, in some cases, carried on for some time after the patients left their employers. It was primarily from the reports of the former employers that we obtained an occasional implication as to the psychological and emotional adjustment of some of our patients by such comments as "married a fine boy, has two lovely children, they built a nice home," "married, they both work in the same place, they have a nice home and are very happy," "married, has one child, is prosperous and happy," et cetera.

5. The value of the records of institutional mentally retarded for clinical research is self-evident. The limited information which was found in the records of Newark State School is not a reflection on the overburdened few social workers and physicians of the institution, who were responsible for these records, but is an indictment of the society at large for neglecting the field of mental deficiency and failing to provide the institutions with needed personnel and to offer facilities and stimulus for research.

6. The statement that there does not appear to be any significant relationship between the psychometric rating and the level of adjustment perhaps needs some elucidation.

It is true that most of the psychometric ratings recorded were those given on admission and by different psychologists and may not have been a true evaluation of the intellectual endowment of the patients. Even if we assume that the ratings were valid at the time, they do not necessarily represent the psychometric rating of the patients after discharge. Those of us who have had an opportunity to review psychometric ratings of large numbers of patients repeated several times in the course of years are aware of the considerable fluctuation in the ratings. A recent study of a small group of patients by our psychologist, who had an opportunity to retest some of the boys and girls some time after they left the institution, revealed in many cases a considerable change upward from the rating on admission.

The fact, however, that some of the patients with higher I.Q.'s are found in different adjustment level groups and the well known fact that some of the boys and girls with higher psychometric ratings still reside in institutions, validate our general postulate that within certain limits the psychometric rating in itself is not a significant factor in determining the potentials of future adjustment of institutionalized mentally retarded boys or girls. Other psychological tests and psychiatric evaluations appear to be more important in predicting future adjustment of these patients.

7. Some comment should be made on the possible role the institutionalization played in the later adjustment of these men and women. It is not necessary to emphasize here the shortage of professional personnel and the authoritarian atmosphere which prevailed in many institutions for mentally retarded 10 or 15 years ago and, unfortunately, still may exist in some of the institutions. This atmosphere is based primarily on strict conformity to the rules and punishment for infraction of these rules without much regard to the underlying causes of misbehavior and emotional needs of the individual boy or girl. Therefore, one cannot claim that any specific therapeutic procedures were associated with the institutional residence. However, it can be stated that apparently the sheltered, orderly life of an institution, the education and training program geared in tempo and scope to the capacity of the patients, and perhaps some emotional support received by an individual boy or girl from some person in authority have helped the inherently stable individuals to pass through the turbulent stage of adolescence, away from untoward environmental influences and frustrating excessive demands, and reach a certain degree of maturity to be able to face the world again.

The adult patients apparently benefited by being removed from excessive responsibilities which they were unable to carry because of their limited endowment and lack of economic and social facilities. After a period of residence in the institution and a planned program with more modest demands, these patients were able to return to the community and make a satisfactory adjustment.

This study could not have been completed without assistance of a person who could devote full time to extracting the pertinent data from the records, locating patients, and collecting the follow-up material. Our original plan to carry out the study with assistance of some of the social workers on the staff, for self-evident reasons, began to bog down until the services of a full-time assistant could be secured, with the aid of a grant provided by the New York State Department of Mental Hygiene.

In conclusion we wish to emphasize that this is a very limited study confined to one New York State institution, serving the 19 western counties of the state. The period of adjustment study was that of relative prosperity and full employment. It is our feeling that other similar studies may help us in learning more about our patients and, therefore, plan for better institutional care and post-institutional follow up and develop community resources to provide a richer and fuller life for these people.

CONCLUSIONS

1. In 1946, 92 males and 131 females were discharged from Newark State School.

2. In 1954, seven to eight years after discharge, we were able to locate 89 males and 119 females in a follow-up study of their adjustment since discharge.

3. Of the 92 males 5 were discharged shortly after admission—4 psychotic, 1 not mentally defective. Ten, discharged on request of parents, were returned to the institution; 9 were severely retarded requiring custodial care.

4. Eighteen of dependents who required care and supervision still remain at home and are adjusting well.

5. Of 59 mildly retarded, 36 have made a continuous satisfactory social and economic adjustment in the community.

6. The adjustment of 10 boys was not continuous. During some phase of their residence in the community they became involved in difficulties which required their temporary return to this institution or a temporary confinement in a correctional institution. Ten failed to adjust; 8 became psychotic, 1 had a serious personality disorder, and 1, a markedly inadequate individual, is economically dependent. Three boys could not be located.

7. Whereas the males were admitted either for training or because of behavior disorders such as stealing, vandalism or defiance of authority, the majority of the females were admitted as a sex problem of one form or another.

8. Of the 131 girls, 4 were discharged shortly after admission—3 psychotic, 1 not mentally defective. Twenty-eight discharged were dependent, requiring care and supervision; 5 of these (markedly retarded) returned to the institution.

9. Of 99 mildly retarded, 72 have made a continuous satisfactory social and economic adjustment. Eight after making a temporary satisfactory adjustment returned to the institution. Four as sex problems; 1 because of emotional instability, she later developed a psychosis and had to be confined to a State hospital; 3 became dependent. Seven females remaining in the community were not making a satisfactory adjustment. Four presented sex problems and 3 made poor social adjustment. Twelve could not be located.

SUMMARY
AND
CONCLUSIONS

Ebert L. Miller

The follow-up study became more sophisticated with the use of normal control groups and more precise criteria of community functioning. Baller's 1935 study of children leaving "Opportunity Rooms" in Lincoln, Nebraska public schools was one of the most comprehensive surveys. Baller's original subjects were followed into midlife by Charles (1953) and Miller (1965).

A. PURPOSE OF THE STUDY

The purpose of this study was to investigate the present social and intellectual status of a low-intelligence group previously studied by Baller (1935) and by Charles (1951). In essence, the study was intended to continue the longitudinal study with special emphasis on midlife adjustment.

B. LITERATURE DEALING WITH MENTAL DEFICIENCY

The reviewer of the literature on mental deficiency suggests that definitions or terminologies are clear only as operationally defined by the investigator in a particular study. The social adjustment of mentally deficient persons presents a hopeful picture, but only within the framework of realistic goals and adequate education for individuals. Adjustment of subnormal persons over the age of 40 years has been largely a matter of prognostication. This study was undertaken to supplant this lack of information with some research evidence.

C. SUBJECTS OF THE STUDY

In 1935, Baller conducted a follow-up study of 206 subjects who had previously been judged mentally defective. These individuals were matched on the basis of sex, nationality, and age with a control group with I.Q.s of 100 to 120 on the Terman Group Test of Mental Ability. The Baller study was followed by one conducted by Charles in 1951, with special emphasis on retest information. He located 151 of the original subnormal subjects.

The present study contains information concerning 146 of the original subjects and 120 of the original control subjects. At the time of this study, the mean age of the subnormal group was 53 years and the mean age of the control group was 50 years.

D. PLAN AND PROCEDURE OF THE STUDY

It was the plan of this research to investigate and present data about the following matters:

Miller, E. L. Ability and social adjustment at midlife of persons judged mentally deficient. *Genetic Psychology Monographs*, 1965, 72: 139–198. Reprinted by permission of the author and Genetic Psychology Monographs.

Dr. Miller is a professor at Ball State University in Muncie, Indiana.

1. Personal Adjustment

Characteristics of the subjects were investigated in relation to location, physical health, institutionalized, marital status, family characteristics, occupation, economic status, law conformity, citizenship participation, and social activities.

2. Retest Information

All available and consenting members of the Charles sample were retested with the Wechsler-Bellevue Intelligence Scale. The data were analyzed for all retested subjects, institutionalized retested subjects, and noninstitutionalized retested subjects.

The procedure was to locate, interview and, if appropriate, retest the subjects. Records of public-relief agencies, courts, and the public schools were searched for pertinent information. The original records of Baller's and Charles' studies, together with public directories, provided leads to enable the investigator to locate the subjects. The state hospitals for "insane" and "feeble-minded" were visited and provided data on some subjects.

E. FINDINGS

1. Personal Adjustment

One hundred forty-six of the original subnormal group and 120 of the original control subjects were located. About 41 per cent of the subnormal subjects and 35 per cent of the control subjects located were still in Lincoln. The trend away from Lincoln (noted in the earlier studies) was maintained, but a larger per cent of the controls have moved from Lincoln and from the state during the midlife period. The percentage comparison shows approximately a two-to-one ratio of control subjects over subnormal subjects living in other states. The mortality rate of the subnormal subjects is twice that of the control subjects. This is considerably less than the seven-to-one ratio reported by Baller in 1935. The death ratio of two males to one female is less than expected during this 11-year midlife period when compared to vital-statistics expectations for persons of the same age range. The subnormal subjects have been much more susceptible to major illnesses and accidents than have the control subjects. For all individuals studied, the male subnormal subjects were the main victims of major accidents reported.

There has been a steady decline in the per cent of subnormal subjects confined to institutions. During the 11 years since Charles study, only one person has been recommitted to a mental hospital and no subject has been initially committed to an institution. All four subjects who are still inmates at the Beatrice State Home are severely handicapped physically, as well as testing low individual intelligence tests. The prognosis that the subnormal individuals in later adult life tend to gravitate to the institutions has not proved true in this study.

More than 80 percent of the surviving subjects are or have been married. Divorce reflects an area of serious lack of adjustment for the subnormal group—almost 22 per cent of them have been divorced. By comparison, about 10 per cent of the controls have been divorced. The per cent of subnormal subjects married showed a progressive gain from 1935 to 1951 and a drop of less than two percentage points from 1951 to 1962. The per cent of subnormal subjects divorced showed a progressive gain from 1935 to 1951 and from 1951 to 1962.

Exactly 70 per cent of the subnormal subjects and slightly more than 81 per cent of the control subjects have children. The average number of children was 2.02 for the subnormal subjects and 1.97 for the control subjects. Families with five or more children comprise 13.3 per cent of the married subnormal group, while such families comprise only 5.2 per cent of the married control group. The subnormal group has a larger percentage of families with no children than either the control group or the averages in the census information.

All but 22.1 per cent of the subnormal subjects were employed. Of those employed, 80.2 per cent had been employed in the same job three or more years. This represents a gain from 20 per cent in 1935 and from 47.7 per cent in 1951. The midlife period occupationally seems to be a much more stable period than the earlier periods reported. Many of the occupations for the subnormal subjects represent a high level of accomplishment for retarded persons, but none are on a professional level. The control subjects have occupations that indicate a much higher level of training or education and generally a much higher level of financial and prestige gains. The highest ranking occupations for subnormal subjects were one small business manager, one accountant, and three self-employed (each a small business employing only the subject).

Only 16.19 per cent of the surviving subnormal subjects had received any relief help during the 11-year midlife period. The sharp drop from the previous studies in the per cent requiring relief aid reflects an increase in economic stability during this period, despite any part that the selective function of death or the better economic times may have played. Over 96 per cent of the control subjects were self-supporting, as compared with almost 68 per cent of the subnormal subjects. However, this 68 per cent represents an increase from about 36 per cent in 1951. The economic stability of the subnormal subjects has improved over previous standings, but was markedly below the standing of the control subjects.

Twenty of the 60 Lincoln subnormal subjects had committed a total of 56 traffic and 12 civil offenses. Nineteen of the 42 control subjects had committed a total of 38 traffic offenses. One male subnormal accounted for eight (67 per cent) of the civil offenses and nineteen (34 per cent) of the traffic violations charged to his group. None of the subjects had committed a crime of major proportion. Drunkenness accounted for 10 of the 12 civil offenses.

Almost one-half of the subnormal subjects reported that they voted regularly, although most of them were very poorly informed on current governmental affairs. Two female subnormals reported belonging to PTA when their children were in school and no other subnormal subject reported belonging to or participating in a social-service organization or project.

Slightly over one-half of the subnormal subjects are members of a church. However, only 20 per cent belonged to any social club or group and only about 46 per cent had a hobby or regular recreational pursuit. Most hobbies and recreational pursuits reported were of a solitary nature. Television was a regular activity of a large majority of the subnormal subjects.

2. Retest Information

The 15 available subjects of the retest sample of Charles study were retested during the fall of 1961 with the Wechsler-Bellevue Intelligence Scale. Examination of the 1950 and 1961 Wechsler I.Q. scores indicated that mean gains in favor of the 1961 retest had been made on the verbal scale, performance scale, and full scale for the total group tested, the institutionalized group, and the noninstitutionalized group. The 1961 mean full-scale I.Q. score was 81.60 for the total group, 65.00 for the institutionalized group, and 85.78 for the noninstitutionalized group.

A technique for calculating differences between two means-correlated samples was used to determine if the observed mean gains were statistically significant. The t values derived show that full-scale and verbal-scale mean scores for the total group and the noninstitutionalized group were statistically significant. The t values for the performance scale means and for all the mean-score values of the institutionalized group were nonsignificant.

An analysis of the mean weighted scores using the same technique, t test-correlated sample, revealed that none of the mean-score differences on any of the scales for any of the groups was statistically significant.

The results of the analysis indicated that these subjects enjoy a higher relative intellectual standing in relation to the standardization group than they did 11 years ago. They have not, however, increased or decreased their capacity to function on the test to any significant degree.

On the basis of the most recent tests, the noninstitutionalized group would best be designated (according to Wechsler's classification) as functioning near or within the "dull-normal" range of intelligence. The institutionalized group could best be described as functioning near the lower level of the borderline classification of intelligence.

F. FINAL APPRAISAL

The evidence contained in this study shows the surviving subnormal subjects to be a more stable group and capable of better functioning intellectually, physically, and socially (with the exception of divorce rate) than they were previously. As a group, they have continued to fare much better than could have been predicted or possibly even hoped for. When compared only with past periods of their life, this 11-year midlife period has been relatively a stable and generally favorable one for them. Economic and social conditions during this period may well have had a significant influence on this adjustment.

However, the optimistic picture presented must be qualified in at least two respects. First, the social and public-service participation of this group is so limited as to suggest that these subjects verge on being (at best) social inferiors and in some cases virtual social outcasts. Due to some undefinable combination of internal and external circumstances, they have failed to participate in social-service organizations and social clubs. The implications for education concerning social and service participation and social tolerance should be evident.

Secondly, the comparisons between the subnormal group and the control group show that occupationally, economically, and physically the controls have fared much better. Although this superiority of the control group is not surprising it does emphasize concern about the subnormal subjects when one considers automation and other modern technological developments. The most successful subnormal subjects in the study have held the same job over a long period of time with only minor modifications in job responsibility. While this particular subnormal group has done surprisingly well, one cannot help but be concerned about such persons in the years to come.

A further conclusion of this study is that one measure, such as an intelligence-test score, cannot alone adequately describe a person as mentally deficient, retarded, or otherwise handicapped. Even a classification using several criteria seems to group individuals wrongly fairly often. This should not be construed as an argument for *not* classifying mentally retarded persons, but only as an appeal for more accurate and reliable measurement and subsequent classification. Multiple-dimensional classification schemes, such as those of Sloan and Birch (52), Katz (33), and DiMichael (17), might possibly have excluded many of the subjects from the original designation of mentally deficient.

The longitudinal inquiry begun by Baller, continued by Charles, and followed up in the present study provides evidence of the importance of considering the individuality of persons regardless of classification. Herein perhaps lies the most important implication of the study as a whole. Environmental factors, physical capacities, and human interactions affect the exceptionally complex intellectual growth and functioning of a person. The data in this longitudinal inquiry indicate that each of the subnormal subjects has had a unique combination of influences affecting his intellectual growth and social adjustment. In order to understand and to help such persons, all of these influences must be considered. Finally, to understand better the subnormal individual, one should see him as a unique person interacting in his perceptual environment and should avoid thinking of him as one of a mass within a single classification.

SECTION TEN

The 1960's and 1970's

We had been through two global wars and the Korean Police Action. The cry for individual freedom and opportunity was never stronger. On college campuses the apathy of the 1950's was replaced by the unrest and turmoil of the 1960's, crystalized by the growing escalation in Viet Nam. The innocence of panty raids at Cornell and "rowbottom" at Penn was lost at Columbia and Kent State. The civil rights movement of protest marches and boycotts and "we shall overcome" erupted to the horrors of Selma, Newark, and Watts. Women had their Gloria Steinem, Chicanos their Caesar Chavez, and consumers their Ralph Nader. The deprived and the oppressed and those who saw themselves that way also gained in militancy.

And mentally retarded citizens finally found their spokesmen and advocates. It was an era of the banding together of parent groups through the National Association for Retarded Children and immense pressures for reversing the trend of institutionalization, improving institutions, and expansion of public school services for the mentally retarded. For the first time, public concern and consciousness were directed toward providing the mentally retarded citizen with the opportunities for life, liberty, and the pursuit of happiness, available to ordinary citizens. Several major legal decisions, designed to safeguard basic human rights of the mentally retarded individual, have applied established constitutional principles such as due process, equal protection under the law, and protection from cruel and unusual punishment.

In 1970 to 1971 a federal court in Alabama (*Wyatt v. Stickney*) supported the plaintiff's contention that residents in the state's two mental hospitals and one institution for the mentally retarded were receiving inadequate treatment or habilitation, and that this represented a violation of their constitutional rights. The court declared habilitation services to be inadequate and ordered improvements in the institutions, reduction in the institutional populations, and return of many of the institutional residents to appropriate community habilitation settings.

A similar case, which is still pending in New York State (New York State *Association for Retarded Children v. Rockefeller*), granted interim relief by calling for improved conditions and programs at Willowbrook State School.

Recent rulings have been applied to the practice of using mentally retarded residents of institutions as unpaid workers to maintain these facilities. In the state of Washington, the attorney general expressed the opinion that such practices, labeled institutional peonage, constitute involuntary servitude and are, therefore, a violation of the Thirteenth Amendment. A federal district court (*Sauder v. Brennan*) ordered the Department of Labor to enforce minimum wage benefits of the Fair Labor Standards Act for working residents in institutions. In New York State, the plaintiff in *Dale v. New York*, who had been released from an institution, sued the state for sixteen years of back wages with interest. While the case is still pending, it is clear that institutions will be forced to modify previous policies of using institutional residents for work activities.

There has also been concern about the violation of the rights of retarded citizens who are brought before the court as defendants. Commitment to an institution for persons considered incompetent may, in effect, constitute a life sentence, imposed without a trial. The United States Supreme Court in *Jackson v. Indiana* recently ruled such sentencing to be an unconstitutional denial of the right to due process.

In 1971, a federal district court (*Pennsylvania Association for Retarded Children v. Commonwealth of Pennsylvania*) issued a consent decree that Pennsylvania's public schools could no longer exclude children from a free public education because they were mentally retarded. In addition, a child could not be transferred from a regular class to a special class, or vice versa, without notification of the parents and provision of an opportunity for an independent reassessment and a formal hearing. In *Mills v. D.C. Board of Education,* a federal court ruled that appropriate public education must be available to every child.

Such fundamental personal rights as marriage, voting, and procreation are still denied many mentally retarded citizens. About forty states deny the mentally retarded person the right to marry. In *Skinner v. Oklahoma,* the Supreme Court ruled that involuntary sterilization, by parents or guardians, infringes on the fundamental right of man to procreate.

Acknowledgment of the injustices which still exist is found in the proliferation of legal advocacy groups for the mentally retarded. The 1973 "Conference on the Mentally Retarded Citizen and the Law" supported the principle of equal rights for all citizens. In 1967, the International League of Societies for the Mentally Handicapped issued a "Declaration of General and Special Rights of the Mentally Retarded." A "Rights of Mentally Retarded Persons," published as an official policy statement of the American Association on Mental Deficiency, includes specific rights to exert freedom of choice in making decisions; to live in the least restrictive environment; to gainful employment and fair pay; to be part of a family; to marry and have a family;

to be free to move without deprivation of liberty by institutionalization; to speak openly, maintain privacy, practice a religion and to interact with peers; and to receive publicly supported education, vocational training, and habilitative programs.

Nirje's (1969) formulation of the principle of normalization was a further attempt to state concretely those areas in which the mentally handicapped should be provided their full rights and benefits as citizens. The principle since has been adopted for standards for residential facilities by the Joint Commission of Accreditation of Hospitals (1971). The cry for deinstitutionalization became deafening as experts re-examined the role of institutions as service suppliers and traced the growth of "dehumanization." Enormous strides were taken to apply vocational rehabilitation and social learning models within institutions (Clark, Kivitz, and Rosen, 1964), and the parole system of the 1940's was replaced by the halfway house, group home, and transitional programs leading to independent community living.

Along with the new optimisim, research also flourished. Congress opened the flood gates of financial support through the Department of Health, Education, and Welfare, stimulating and directing efforts in areas where it seemed necessary.

A new federal act for vocational rehabilitation in 1943 (Public Law 113) included provision for the mentally handicapped so that, for the first time, the mentally retarded and mentally ill were eligible for vocational rehabilitation services. The newly established Office of Vocational Rehabilitation was designed to channel disabled workers into war production and essential industry and to enable the disabled to prepare for employment in peacetime pursuits.

The Vocational Rehabilitation Amendments of 1954 (Public Law 565) were aimed at assisting the states in rehabilitating physically and mentally handicapped individuals so that they might prepare for and engage in remunerative employment. In addition to increasing federal funds to service handicapped people, the new laws provided for the development of rehabilition facilities and the training of professional personnel to staff these facilities. The acts were again amended in 1965. Besides providing substantial increases in federal spending, services were extended to people with "socially handicapping conditions."

The vocational rehabilitation movement continued to grow in the 1960's when, in 1967, the Department of Health, Education, and Welfare was reorganized and the Social and Rehabilitation Service was established and placed under the leadership of Mary Switzer. The Vocational Rehabilitation Amendments of 1968 again increased financial support to the states and provided for state construction of work adjustment centers for physically and mentally handicapped and those termed "disadvantaged," by age, education, ethnic, cultural, or other factors detrimental to employment.

In 1963, Congress passed Public Law 88-164 authorizing the construction for the University Affiliated Facilities to provide a full range of in-patient and out-patient services to the mentally retarded, and by 1969 nineteen such programs had been funded and approximately thirty universities were involved in program development.

Perhaps the most significant research thrust has been an open attack upon the influence of poverty and sociocultural deprivation in producing mental retardation. Renewed interest was found in familial retardation (Zigler, 1967). As Doll (1964) predicted, attempts are now being expended in differentiating "defect, deficiency and mere backwardness." Scientists are attempting to tease out the effects of under-nutrition, exposure to lead in paints frequently found in the slums, poor pre-natal care, and drugs ingested during pregnancy. In 1962, the discovery of techniques for studying the virus in the laboratory marked the beginning of intensive rubella research efforts. The rubella epidemic in Australia in 1941 led to the observation of the "rubella baby," a syndrome characterized by mental retardation, deafness, congenital heart disease and growth defects. The tragic epidemic in the United States in 1963 to 1964 intensified research efforts with rubella and the etiology of many birth defects. Public programs of prevention of mental retardation were initiated. The most successful efforts have been with wide-scale newborn screening for phenylketonuria and dietary treatment. The search for other inborn metabolic errors continues. Advances in cytogenetic techniques have resulted in the discovery of several types of abnormalities of the sex chromosomes (Court Brown, 1968), some associated with mental retardation.

It is scarcely possible to present a comprehensive picture of behavior research in the 1960's and 1970's. Despite the lack of historical perspective to evaluate properly *recent* events, several trends seem noteworthy.

The concept of adaptive behavior was introduced to deal with the limitations of standard intelligence tests in classifying the retarded (Foster et al., 1966). In 1961, the American Association on Mental Deficiency, in its manual of terminology and classification (Heber, 1961), proposed that the diagnosis of mental retardation must rest upon demonstration of deficiencies along two dimensions: measured intelligence and adaptive behavior. Just as Doll wrestled with the concept of social competence three decades before, psychologists today define adaptive behavior as the success of the individual in adapting to the natural and social demands of his environment. The Adaptive Behavior Scales (Nihira, 1969; Nihira et al., 1969), developed for classification and research purposes, are gaining general acceptance as a supplement to established procedures such as the Vineland Social Maturity Scale. The Adaptive Behavior Scales serve to focus attention on the coping skills of retarded persons, independent of preconceived notions of "potential" derived from measures of their intelligence.

The search for some psychological factor which will differentiate the mentally retarded from "normal" populations has been as intense as the search for neurological, genetic, and biochemical factors. Zigler (1967) has pointed out that theorists have been split into those advocating a "defect" and those espousing a "developmental" orientation. Those taking a defect position attribute learning and performance deficits in mentally retarded persons to some structural or organic deficit. Current theories include those describing mental retardation as an inhibition deficit (Denny, 1964), a defect in cortical satiation processes (Spitz, 1963), or a deficit in short-term memory (Ellis, 1963).

An opposing view attributes learning and performance differences between the mentally retarded and intellectually normal populations, at least to a large extent, to motivational lags stemming from cultural-social phenomena. Those taking a developmental position have focused upon the familial retarded and emphasized the greater failure experiences of this group, their histories of social deprivation, and atypical reinforcer hierarchies which produce retarded behavior (Zigler, 1967; Cromwell, 1963; Bijou, 1966). In a research effort reminiscent of the Iowa studies of the 1930's and 1940's, Heber has reported significant differences in I.Q.s of black children exposed to a full day of special stimulation and teaching programs, as compared with children not provided such programs. The children participating in the program are chosen because they are "high risk" babies; their mothers have low tested I.Q.s. Results such as Heber's seem to give credence to theories stressing the importance of environmental and motivational variables in influencing intellectual development.

Another development during the last decade has been the application of a new technology in the training and education of mentally retarded persons. Behavior modification is a general term applied to the use of many strategies derived from the psychology of learning. The most useful techniques with the mentally retarded have been derived from operant conditioning procedures based primarily on the work of B. F. Skinner (1938, 1953). The general principle, labeled "reinforcement," is based on the finding long known to experimental psychologists that a behavior consistently followed by events which are pleasing or gratifying to the organism will recur. The use of operant conditioning procedures in education, training, and therapy involves the systematic application of reinforcement following behavior considered appropriate, and the withdrawal of reinforcement (extinction) following inappropriate behavior.

Mentally retarded populations have been attractive to psychologists interested in behavior modification because of their limited response repertoire, the relative frequency of severe symptoms such as rumination, self-mutilation, rocking, and other stereotyped behaviors. Many of these behaviors, once considered pathognomonic to mental retardation or autism, have been placed under control by the judicious use of reinforcement regimes. Operant conditioning has been used to teach self-help skills such as feeding, toileting, and dressing (Blackwood, 1962; Bensberg et al., 1965; Dayan, 1964; Giradeau and Spradlin, 1964; Watson, 1968, 1971), language (Bricker and Bricker, 1970; Baer and Sherman, 1964; Lovaas et al., 1966; Roos, 1968), social behavior, and academic skills (Birnbrauer et al., 1965).

The "token economy" first used with adult psychotic populations (Ayllon and Azrin, 1965) has been applied in many cottage programs within residential settings. Although there have been recent criticisms of the use of aversive procedures in operant conditioning programs, in general, the application of behavior modification has been an innovative and effective approach at many schools and institutions.

MOTIVATIONAL DETERMINANTS IN THE PERFORMANCE OF RETARDED CHILDREN

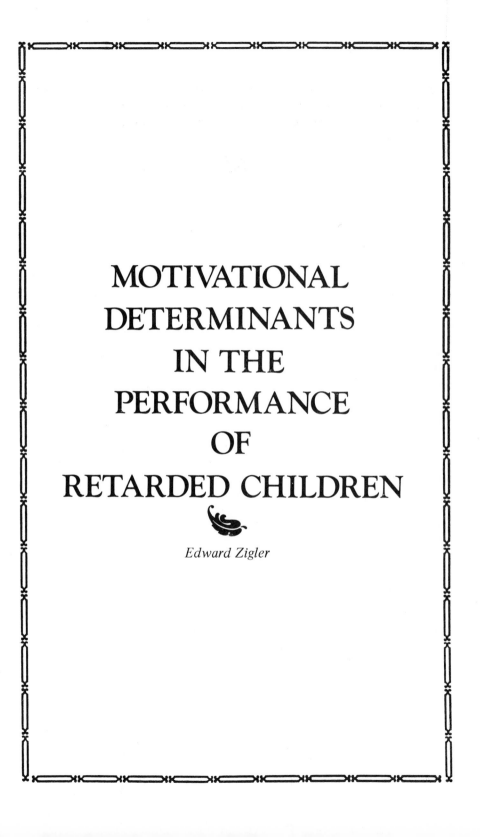

Edward Zigler

In this paper, the studies discussed suggest that many of the behavioral differences between familial retardates and normal children of the same mental age (MA) result from differences in motivation rather than from differences in intellect.

It has long been my view that many of the reported behavioral differences between familial retardates and normal children of the same MA are a product of a variety of differences in the motivational systems of these two types of children rather than being related to the immutable effects of mental retardation itself.* It has become increasingly popular for theoreticians to conceptualize the familial retardate as pursuing not only a slower and more limited course of cognitive development but to be suffering from a variety of specific physiological or quasi-organismic defects as well. Indeed, a plethora of such defects now have been postulated. Thus, we have been informed that the retardates suffer from a relative impermeability of the boundaries between regions in the cognitive structure;[8,9] primary and secondary rigidity caused by subcortical and cortical malformations, respectively;[4] inadequate neural satiation related to brain modifiability or cortical conductivity;[16] impaired attention-directing mechanisms;[22] a relative brevity in the persistence of the stimulus trace;[3] malfunctioning disinhibitory mechanisms;[14] and improper development of the verbal system, resulting in a dissociation between the verbal and motor systems.[10, 11]

Postulating such defects has given rise to what I have referred to as the difference orientation. That is, the retardate is viewed as being inherently "different." This difference orientation receives its most vivid expression in those comparative studies where mental retardates are conceptualized as occupying a position on the phylogenetic scale somewhere between monkeys, on the one hand, and children of average intellect, on the other. It should be noted that in respect to the familial retardate, no "hard" physiological evidence, at least of a convincing type, has been found indicating the presence of any of the defects noted above. Rather, these defects have been postulated on the basis of differences in performance between retardates and normals on some type of experimental task. An implicit assumption in much of this work has been that performance on such tasks is an inexorable product of the cognitive structure or intellectual level. I do not believe this to be the case. Performance on many, if not all experimental tasks is most appropriately

*Presented at the 1965 annual meeting of the American Orthopsychiatric Association, New York, New York. Much of the research reported in this paper was supported by grants from the National Institute of Mental Health, the Social Science Research Council and the Gunnar Dybwad Award of the National Association for Retarded Children.

American Journal of Orthopsychiatry, 1966, 36(5): 848–856. Copyright © 1966 by the American Orthopsychiatric Association, Inc. Reproduced by permission of the author and the American Orthopsychiatric Association.

Dr. Zigler is professor in the department of psychology at Yale University and director of the Child Development Program. He was previously director of the Office of Child Development in the Department of Health, Education, and Welfare.

conceptualized as a multiply determined phenomenon influenced by both cognitive or intellective factors and motivational or emotional factors.

I am, of course, aware that a division between cognitive and emotional factors is in many ways an artificial one. However, in most of our work these two factors have been sufficiently orthogonal for us to demonstrate how each may be independently affecting the child's performance. Motivational differences between normal and retarded children, which are themselves the result of differences in environmental histories, must be ruled out before any difference in performance can be considered prima facie evidence in support of a defect position. Over the years, then, our goal has been to discover the part played by the differences in the experiential histories of normal and familial retarded children in producing the differences in performances so frequently noted in the performance of normals and retardates of the same MA.

Our initial research efforts can be directly traced to perhaps the most influential and widely accepted of the defect positions; namely, the cognitive rigidity formulation of Kurt Lewin[9] and Jacob Kounin.[8] Lewin initially advanced the view that as compared to normal children of the same degree of differentiation, i.e., MA, retardates were characterized by a lessened permeability in the boundaries between cognitive regions. This position was extended somewhat by Kounin, who argued that the degree of permeability in these boundaries was a positive monotonic function of CA. This generated the prediction that with MA held constant, older retardates suffered from greater cognitive rigidity than younger retardates, who in turn were more rigid than normal children. This general prediction was confirmed in a series of experiments in which it was found that retardates as compared to normals of the same MA spent more time on a simple persistence task, showed a lesser amount of transfer effects from task to task and had more difficulty in switching from one concept to another when instructed to do so.

Stevenson and Zigler[17] conducted a study designed to test the validity of the Lewin-Kounin formulation. Moving from the Lewin-Kounin postulate that the boundaries within the life space are more rigid in the feebleminded than in normals, Stevenson and Zigler hypothesized

"... that the solution of a reversal problem would require movement to a new region of the life space and that such movement would be more difficult for the feebleminded subject because of the more rigid boundaries separating the regions of the life space."

Three groups of subjects were used, an older feebleminded group, a younger feebleminded group, and a group of normal children, with the groups being equated on MA. The results indicated a striking equivalence in performance among groups. They did not differ significantly on the number of trials required to learn the initial discrimination problem; the number of correct choices on the reversal problem; the number of subjects in each group who learned the reversal problem; or on the key measure of rigidity employed; namely, the frequency with which subjects of each group made the response on the reversal problem which had been correct for them on the initial discrimination problem.

Stevenson and Zigler[17] conducted a second study in which they employed a more difficult reversal problem. Here again they found no differences between normals and familial retardates of the same MA. In an effort to evaluate the disagreement of their findings with those of Kounin, Stevenson and Zigler advanced a motivational hypothesis to explain Kounin's findings. These investigators noted that in their experiments the subjects were required to learn two successive discriminations with minimal interaction with the experimenter, while in Kounin's tasks the response is made primarily on the basis of instructions. Thus differences in rigid behaviors between normal and feebleminded individuals of the same MA in the instruction-initiated task may be related to differences in the subjects' motivation to comply with instructions rather than to differences in cognitive rigidity. This hypothesis was based on the assumption that institutionalized feebleminded children tend to have been relatively deprived of adult contact and approval and hence have a higher motivation to procure such contact and approval than do normal children. This assumption appears congruent with the view advanced by other investigators that both institutionalized feeble minded and institutionalized normal individuals exhibit an increased desire to interact with adult figures.[2,12,15]

The first test of the motivational hypothesis was contained in a study by Zigler, Hodgden and Stevenson.[27] Employing a number of simple instruction-initiated motor tasks and supportive and nonsupportive reinforcement conditions, Zigler et al. obtained findings confirming their hypothesis that interaction with an adult and adult approval provide a greater reinforcement for the responses of institutionalized feebleminded subjects than they do for those of normal subjects. The study of Zigler et al. thus lent support to the view that the reported differences in the incidence of "rigid" behaviors between normal and feebleminded individuals of the same MA are a function of the greater social deprivation experienced by the feebleminded rather than of their inherent rigidity.

The second test of this position was carried out by Zigler,[24] who employed the following reasoning: if the rigid behaviors found in feebleminded subjects are a result of the social deprivation the subjects have experienced, then within a feebleminded population a relationship should exist between the degree of deprivation and the amount of rigidity manifested. The specific hypothesis tested in this study was:

> "The greater the amount of pre-institutional social deprivation experienced by the feebleminded child, the greater will be his motivation to interact with an adult, making such interaction and any adult approval or sup-

port that accompanies it more reinforcing for his responses than for the responses of a feebleminded child who has experienced a lesser amount of social deprivation."

The procedure employed in this study was that of allowing raters to evaluate the entire pre-institutional history of the child for degree of social deprivation. As predicted, a positive relationship was found between the amount of social deprivation and the time the child would spend playing a socially reinforced but simple and monotonous game. It thus appears that the persistence so frequently encountered in the retardate, rather than being a product of his inherent rigidity, can better be viewed as the behavioral manifestation of his heightened motivation to secure attention and approval. The Zigler study provides direct evidence that this heightened motivation to interact with an attentive adult is related to the sizable amounts of pre-institutional social deprivation typically experienced by the institutionalized familial retardate. The social deprivation hypothesis received further confirmation in subsequent studies[6,25] in which it was generally found that the social deprivation experienced by institutionalized populations, rather than intellectual level, determined how long children would spend on a simple game in order to obtain social reinforcement. Institutionalized children of normal intellect also were found to exhibit the perseverative behavior found in institutionalized retardates of the same MA. On the other hand, noninstitutionalized retardates were found to be no more perseverative than their MA-matched normal controls.

It is now clear that a child's perseveration often may reflect his motivation for social reinforcement and that this motivation is related to the amount of social deprivation experienced. What is not clear at this point is whether this greater social deprivation is to be attributed to institutionalization as such, to the fact that the pre-institutional environment of the institutionalized child is characterized by a relatively great amount of social deprivation, or to some interaction between these two factors.

Especially relevant to the question of the effects of institutionalization on the performance of the retarded are the findings of a recent study by Butterfield and Zigler.[1] Matched groups of mentally retarded children from two institutions which differed markedly in their social climates were compared on a measure of their need for social reinforcement of two types, attention and attention plus verbal approval. Children from the more repressive, depriving institution were found to have a significantly higher motivation to obtain both types of reinforcement.

A recent study by Zigler and Williams[28] has indicated that how an instituion affects a child is determined not only by the nature of the institution, but also by the child's pre-institutional history. After an interval of three years, these investigators retested the children employed by Zigler[24] and discovered that with this increased length of institutionalization, the motivation for social reinforcement of all of the children had increased. However, the increase between the two testings in motivation for social reinforcers was related to the amount of pre-institutional deprivation experienced. Children coming from relatively good homes evidenced a much greater increase in their motivation for social reinforcers than did children coming from more socially deprived homes. It thus appears that the general motivational effects of institutionalization depend on the pre-institutional history of the child, with such institutionalization being more socially depriving for children from relatively good homes than for children who had come from homes characterized by a considerable amount of social deprivation.

Although there is considerable observational and experimental evidence that social deprivation results in a heightened motivation to interact with a supportive adult, it appears to have other effects as well. The nature of these effects is suggested in those observations of the retarded that have noted their fearfulness, wariness or avoidance of strangers, or their suspicion and mistrust.[7,20,21] The experimental work done by Zigler and his associates on the behavior of the institutionalized retarded has indicated that social deprivation results in both a heightened motivation to interact with supportive adults (positive-reaction tendency) as well as a reluctance and wariness to do so (negative-reaction tendency).

The construct of a negative-reaction tendency has been employed to explain certain differences between retardates and normals reported by Kounin, differences that have heretofore been attributed to the greater cognitive rigidity of retarded individuals. As one measure of rigidity, Kounin employed a task in which the subject is instructed to perform a response which he may continue until he wishes to stop; he is then instructed to perform a highly similar response until again satiated. A recurring finding in studies employing such a two-part task [8,23,27] has been that retardates have a much greater tendency than normals to spend more time on task two than on task one. Zigler[23] suggested that this was due to the greater negative-reaction tendency of retarded subjects which was an outgrowth of the more negative encounters that institutionalized retardates experienced at the hands of adults. His reasoning was that the high negative-reaction tendency of retardates was reduced as a result of the pleasant experiences encountered on task one which, in turn, resulted in a longer playing time on task two. Normals tend not to show such a pattern since there is relatively little negative-reaction tendency that can be reduced during task one.

This view was tested in a study[13] in which normal and retarded subjects, matched on MA, were compared on a two-part experimental task similar to those used in the earlier studies. In addition to the basic procedure employed in these studies, three experimental games given under two conditions of reinforcement preceded the two-part criterion task. In a positive reinforcement condition all of the subject's responses met with success, and he was further rewarded with verbal and nonverbal support from the experimenter. It was assumed that this reinforcement condition reduced the subject's negative-reaction tendency. In a negative reinforcement condition all of the subject's responses met with failure, and the experimenter further punished the subject by commenting on his lack of success. It was assumed that this condition increased the negative-reaction tendency. Half of the normals and half of the retardates were given the games in the positive experimental condition, while the other half of each group received the negative condition. All subjects were given the identical two-part criterion task in which they were consistently praised for all responses.

The most striking finding of this study was that, as predicted, both negatively reinforced groups spent more time on Part II than on Part I of the criterion task, while the two groups receiving the positive condition played Part I longer than Part II. The findings of this study offer further validation for the general motivational hypothesis, while also indicating a need for its extension. Future research should be concerned with the isolation of those specific events which give rise to each of these opposing motivational factors, i.e., the desire to interact and the wariness to do so.

A logical conclusion here is that wariness of adults and the tasks that adults present leads to a general attenuation in the retarded child's social effectiveness. Failure of institutionalized retardates on tasks presented by adults is therefore not to be attributed entirely to intellectual factors. The high negative-reaction tendency motivates him toward behaviors, e.g., withdrawal, that reduce the quality of his performance to a level lower than that which one would expect on the basis of his intellectual capacity alone.

Another concept advanced by myself and my colleagues to explain differences in performance between normals and retardates of the same MA is that of the reinforcer hierarchy, i.e., for any individual, reinforcers can be ordered from most to least effective. While the motivational factors noted previously appear capable of explaining many of the normal-retarded differences found by Kounin, they cannot handle parsimoniously Kounin's findings that retardates evidence greater difficulty than do normals in switching from one sorting principle to another following a request to do so. A close examination of Kounin's procedure on his card-sorting task led me to consider the relative "weakness" for retardates of the reinforcer employed by Kounin to motivate children on this task. The only reinforcer obtained by Kounin's subjects for correctly switching concepts was whatever reinforcement inheres in being correct. Being correct is probably more reinforcing for the performance of normal than for retarded children, who may value the interaction with and attention of the experimenter much more than the satisfaction derived from performing the task correctly. The hypothesis being suggested here is that if equally effective reinforcers were dispensed to normals and retardates of the same MA for switching concepts, no differences in the ability to switch would be found. Basic to this proposal is the view that for every child there is a reinforcer hierarchy with the particular position of various reinforcers being determined by the developmental level of the child, the frequency with which the reinforcers have been paired with other reinforcers, and the degree to which the child has been deprived of these reinforcers.

Some recent studies also attest to the feasibility of attributing the differences in performance by normals and retardates on a concept-switching task to such differing reinforcer hierarchies rather than to the greater cognitive rigidity of retardates. Terrell, Durkin, and Wiesley[19] found that middle-class children did better on a discrimination learning task when an intangible rather than a tangible reinforcer was employed, while lower-class children evidenced superior performance in a tangible as opposed to an intangible reinforcement condition. Pertinent here is the fact that institutionalized familial retardates are predominantly drawn from the lowest segment of the lower socioeconomic class.[24] Stevenson and Zigler[17] found that the retarded are no more rigid than normal subjects on a discrimination reversal learning task when tangible reinforcers are given. This body of evidence suggests that not only retardates but lower-class children in general would be inferior to middle-class children when an intangible reinforcer is employed.

These views were tested in a concept-switching experiment conducted by Zigler and DeLabry.[26] This experiment differed from Kounin's in that two conditions of reinforcement were employed. In one condition Kounin's original reinforcer, being right simply for the sake of being right, was used. In a second condition the reinforcer was a tangible reward. Half the subjects in each group received the tangible reinforcer and half received the intangible reinforcer as a reward for switching from one concept in their sorting (either form or color) to the other concept. As predicted, the retarded and normal lower-class children did better in the tangible than in the intangible condition, while the normal middle-class children did somewhat better in the intangible than in the tangible condition. Of central importance here is that when each child was receiving what was for him a highly effective reinforcer, no significant difference in performance was found to be related to either intellectual level or social class.

Another factor frequently noted as a determinant in the performance of the retarded is their high expectancy of failure. This failure expectancy has been viewed as an outgrowth of a lifetime characterized by frequent confrontations with tasks for which the retarded are intellectually ill equipped to deal.

Assuming such a failure set, Stevenson and Zigler[18] tested the hypothesis that retardates would be willing to "settle for" a lower degree of success than would normal children of the same mental age. These investigators employed a simple position discrimination task involving three knobs which the child could push. Only one knob was reinforced, with the degree of reinforcement for the three reinforcement conditions employed being 100 per cent, random 66 per cent, or random 33 per cent. Maximizing behavior on such a task would involve pushing only the reinforced knob on every trial. As might be expected, such maximizing behavior was exhibited by both normal and retarded children (matched on MA), who received 100 per cent reinforcement. As previously had been found with adults, normal children did not evidence maximizing behavior in the two partial reinforcement conditions but tended to match reward probabilities, i.e., the 33 per cent and 66 per cent reinforcement conditions, resulting in the child's selecting the correct knob on a little more than 33 and 66 per cent of the trials, respectively.

Goodnow[5] in an analysis of the determinants of choice behavior of this type, has suggested that one of the conditions influencing whether or not a child will maximize his guesses of the more frequently reinforced stimulus is the level of success a child will accept in the task. Goodnow suggests that maximizing behavior will be found when a child will accept less than 100 per cent success as a good final outcome, while other distributions of choices will be found when a child has an interest in 100 per cent success or in a level of success which is greater than that allowed in the situation.

On the basis of this analysis, it may be hypothesized that different types of behavior will be obtained with children who differ in the degree of success that they have learned to expect. Normal children such as those used by Stevenson and Zigler may be assumed to have learned, on the basis of their everyday experience, to expect a high degree of success. Probability matching rather than maximizing behavior would be predicted for these children. Institutionalized retarded children, however, may be assumed to have learned to expect and to settle for lower degrees of success. These children, therefore, would be predicted to maximize their choices of the reinforced stimulus to a greater degree than would normal children. This, in fact, was what Stevenson and Zigler found. Retardates in both the 33 and 66 per cent reinforcement conditions evidenced more maximizing behavior than did their normal MA controls.

An alternative explanation of the Zigler and Stevenson findings should be noted. It could be argued that the greater tendency of retarded as compared to normal subjects to "stick" with the partially reinforced knob did not reflect the lower expectancy of success of the retarded but rather their greater rigidity. In an effort to further validate the expectancy-of-reinforcement hypothesis, Stevenson and Zigler[18] conducted another experiment involving two groups of normal children performing on the same knob-pressing task. Prior to performing on this task, one group received 33 per cent reinforcement on their responses across three nonlearning games. The other group received 100 per cent reinforcement. Both groups then played the position-discrimination, knob-pressing task under a 66 per cent random reinforcement schedule. As predicted from the expectancy-of-reinforcement hypothesis, the children in the 100 per cent pretraining condition showed a significantly lower frequency of choice to the reinforced knob than did children who had received the 33 per cent pretraining condition. We thus see again that if normal children receive the experimental analogue of the real-life experiences of retardates, they behave in much the same manner as do retardates. The conclusion here again seems to be that certain atypical behavior patterns of retardates are due to certain life experiences rather than to organismic factors which somehow inhere in mental retardation.

In summary, the work outlined in this paper appears to have provided support, in varying degrees, for the following five hypotheses:
1. Institutionalized retarded children tend to have been relatively deprived of adult contact and approval and hence have a higher motivation to secure such contact and approval than do normal children.
2. While retarded children have a higher positive-reaction tendency than do normal children, due to a higher motivation to interact with an approving adult, they also have a higher negative-reaction tendency. This higher negative-reaction tendency is the result of a wariness which stems from the more frequent negative encounters that retarded children experience at the hands of adults.
3. The motive structure of the institutionalized retardate is influenced by an interaction effect between pre-institutional social history and the effect of institutionalization. This effect is made complex by the fact that institutionalization does not constitute a homogeneous psychological variable.
4. The positions of various reinforcers in a reinforcer hierarchy differ as a function of environmental events. Due to environmental differences experienced by institutionalized retarded children, the positions of reinforcers in their reinforcer hierarchy will differ from the positions of the same reinforcers in the reinforcer hierarchy of normal children.
5. Institutionalized retarded children have learned to expect and settle for lower degrees of success than have normal children.

It is my view that the psychological processes underlying each of these hypotheses more often operate in combination with one another than in isolation. This is merely to assert that the behavior of the retarded child on any task is a complex and multiply determined phenomenon. This view stands in opposition to those efforts which have attempted to encompass such behavior by postulating some single inherent deficiency.

REFERENCES

1. Butterfield, E. C., and E. Zigler. 1965. The influence of differing institutional climates on the effectiveness of social reinforcement in the mentally retarded. Amer. J. Ment. Defic. 70: 48–56.
2. Clark, L. P. 1933. The nature and treatment of amentia. Wood, Baltimore.
3. Ellis, N. R. 1963. The stimulus trace and behavioral inadequacy. Handbook of Mental Deficiency. N. R. Ellis, ed. McGraw-Hill, New York. Pp. 134–158.
4. Goldstein, K. 1943. Concerning rigidity. Charact. and Pers. 11: 209–226.
5. Goodnow, J. J. 1955. Determinants of choice distribution in two-choice situations. Amer. J. Psychol. 68: 106–116.
6. Green, C., and E. Zigler. 1962. Social deprivation and the performance of retarded and normal children on a satiation type task. Child Develpm. 33: 499–508.
7. Hirsh, E. A. 1959. The adaptive significance of commonly described behavior of the mentally retarded. Amer. J. Ment. Defic. 63: 639–646.
8. Kounin, J. 1941. Experimental studies of rigidity. I. The measurement of rigidity in normal and feebleminded persons. Charact. and Pers. 9: 251–273.
9. Lewin, K. 1936. A Dynamic Theory of Personality. McGraw-Hill, New York.
10. Luria, A. R. 1956. Problems of higher nervous activity in the normal and non-normal child. Akad. Pedag. Nauk RSFSR, Moscow.
11. O'Connor, N., and B. Hermelin. 1959. Discrimination and reversal learning in imbeciles. J. Abnorm. Soc. Psychol. 59: 409–413.
12. Sarason, S. B. 1953. Psychological Problems in Mental Deficiency (2nd ed.). Harper, New York.
13. Shallenberger, P., and E. Zigler. 1961. Rigidity, negative reaction tendencies, and cosatiation effects in normal and feebleminded children. J. Abnorm. Soc. Psychol. 63: 20–26.
14. Siegel, P., and J. Foshee. 1960. Molar variability in the mentally defective. J. Abnorm. Soc. Psychol. 60: 141–143.
15. Skeels, H. M., R. Updegraff, B. L. Wellman and H. M. Williams. 1938. A study of environmental stimulation: an orphanage preschool project. Univer. Iowa Stud. Child Welf. 15(4).
16. Spitz, H. H. 1963. Field theory in mental deficiency. Handbook of Mental Deficiency. N. R. Ellis, ed. McGraw-Hill, New York. Pp. 11–40.
17. Stevenson, H., and E. Zigler. 1957. Discrimination learning and rigidity in normal and feebleminded individuals. J. Pers. 25: 699–711.
18. Stevenson, H., and E. Zigler. 1958. Probability learning in children. J. Exp. Psychol. 56: 185–192.
19. Terrell, G., Jr., K. Durkin and M. Wiesley. 1959. Social class and the nature of the incentive in discrimination learning. J. Abnorm. Soc. Psychol. 59: 270–272.
20. Wellman, B. L. 1938. Guiding mental development. Childh. Educ. 15: 108–112.
21. Woodward, M. 1960. Early experiences and later social responses of severely subnormal children. British J. Medical Psychol. 33: 123–132.

22. Zeaman, D. 1959. Discrimination learning in retardates. Train. Sch. Bull. 56: 62–67.
23. Zigler, E. 1958. The effect of pre-institutional social deprivation on the performance of feebleminded children. Unpublished doctoral dissertation. University of Texas.
24. Zigler, E. 1961. Social deprivation and rigidity in the performance of feebleminded children. J. Abnorm. Soc. Psychol. 62: 413–421.
25. Zigler, E. 1963. Rigidity and social reinforcement effects in the performance of institutionalized and noninstitutionalized normal and retarded children. J. Pers. 31: 258–269.
26. Zigler, E., and J. DeLabry. 1962. Concept-switching in middle-class, lower-class, and retarded children. J. Abnorm. Soc. Psychol. 65: 267–273.
27. Zigler, E. L., L. Hodgden and H. Stevenson. 1958. The effect of support on the performance of normal and feebleminded children. J. Pers. 26: 106–122.
28. Zigler, E., and J. Williams. 1963. Institutionalization and the effectiveness of social reinforcement: a three-year follow-up study. J. Abnorm. Soc. Psychol. 66: 197–205.

CHANGING
ROLES
OF THE
RESIDENTIAL
INSTITUTION

Philip Roos

The following is the abstract that accompanied the paper. "The response of the residential institution to the impact of recent changes in the field of mental retardation is described in this paper. Changes which have been particularly significant in modifying the institution's roles are outlined. The institution is responding to these changes by evolving services to meet growing needs and by modifying existing programs. The author emphasizes the importance of the institution in the continuum of services to the retarded."

Darwin's observation that living organisms survive only to the extent that they are able to adapt to changing environments is no doubt equally applicable to social agencies and institutions. The residential institution for the retarded is in danger of emulating the dinosaur if it does not undergo adaptive modifications in response to the rapid changes occurring in the field of mental retardation. The first part of this paper summarizes some of these changes which are having greatest impact on the institution. The second part of the paper describes the institution's adaptive responses to its changing environment.

THE CHANGING ENVIRONMENT

The pall of pessimism which enveloped the field of mental retardation during the early decades of the present century is being replaced by growing optimism. The pendulum is rapidly swinging from skepticism and hopelessness to enthusiasm and hopefulness. This changing attitude reflects encouraging scientific advances in a number of fields. Probably of primary significance is the abandonment of the concept of the "constancy of the I.Q." The traditional concept of irreversibility and of ingrained genetic limitations is being replaced by a much more flexible model, reflecting the empirical evidence which emphasizes the potency of the environment in modifying intellectual functioning (McCandless, 1964). Mental retardation no longer needs to be considered an "irreversible condition," but may be approached as a potentially modifiable syndrome.

Significant advances in prevention of specific forms of mental retardation through medical intervention have fostered considerable enthusiasm regarding possible treatment and prophylaxis. Although effective discoveries have been limited to an extremely small fraction of the retarded population, these "breakthroughs" tend to be interpreted as precursors of vastly more extensive advances. Success in cases of phenylketonuria and galactosemia, and in hydrocephaly and craniostenosis, emphasizes that early intervention *can* prevent severe intellectual impairment. Discoveries of the possible effects of prenatal maternal infections and malnutrition and of obstetrical difficulties further underline the growing emphasis on prevention.

Recent applications of principles derived from the behavioral sciences to training the retarded are demonstrating that significant progress can be made,

Mental Retardation, 1966, 4(2): 4–6. Reprinted by permission of the author and the American Association on Mental Deficiency.

Dr. Roos was formerly superintendent of the Austin (Texas) State School. Currently he is executive director of the National Association for Retarded Citizens.

even with the profoundly retarded (Ellis, 1963; Dayan, 1964; Roos, 1965). Derivatives of operant conditioning procedures are proving to be potent tools for modifying types of behavior considered for many years to be unmodifiable. As one result of these advances, the term "sub-trainable" is being abandoned, and workers in the field of mental retardation are being challenged to train retardates of all levels.

A second potent factor in the institutional environment was highlighted by the establishment of the National Association for Retarded Children in 1950. It is estimated that roughly one-tenth of our population is directly affected by mental retardation. It is not surprising, therefore, that parent groups have exerted considerable influence, and that recent years have witnessed encouraging changes—both in state and federal programs—resulting from their efforts. The basic concern of these groups has been for improved excellence of services to the retarded. They have demanded that training and habilitation replace custodial maintenance. Increased pressures can be anticipated from these interested groups as a function of growing awareness of new treatment and training techniques on the one hand, and as a function of social changes, on the other. Automation and urbanization are making it increasingly difficult for individuals of impaired intellectual functioning to maintain self-sufficiency in our society, necessitating expanded and improved specialized services (Goldstein, 1964).

A third factor exerting pressure toward institutional change entails shifts within the composition of the institution's resident population. There is general recognition of an increase in the proportion of severely and profoundly retarded institutionalized cases. At least three variables are operating to foster this trend: (1) a decrease in birth and infant mortality, (2) an increase in the life span of the profoundly and severely retarded, and (3) increased availability of community services for the mildly and moderately retarded. Within the mildly retarded segment of the institutionalized population, an increase in the proportion of the emotionally disturbed and the socially disruptive is becoming evident. It appears that the socially adjusted mildly retarded individual is increasingly able to remain in the community, whereas the mildly retarded whose behavior is socially unacceptable is selectively being referred to the institution.

As a corollary to these changes, a corresponding decrease in that segment of the institutional population which has been relied upon to help operate the institution is being noted. The decrease in resident helpers is being reflected by greater demands on the time of the paid institutional staff. The over-all effect of this gradual change in resident population is that the institution is being required to handle cases necessitating more intense management with a decreased manpower supply.

ADAPTIVE RESPONSES

The institution is responding adaptively to the environmental pressures described above. The impact of growing needs in the area of mental retardation is leading to exciting developments in institutional programs.

Assimilation of the Institution into the Community

Institutions are typically actively seeking avenues for reaching into communities and for serving community needs. As a product of increased public acceptance of the retarded, communities are becoming less concerned with keeping the institution at a "safe distance," and they are inviting the institution into the community. The basic result of this rapprochement is that the institution is rapidly assuming a key role in the broad continuum of services becoming available to the retarded. Rather than remaining an agency distinct and separate from community programs, the institution is assuming a prominent part in community programs.

Custodial care and hospitalization are no longer the primary purposes of the institution. The majority of institutional residents are not ill, and hence do not require hospitalization. Many residents have the potentials for community living, so that the appropriate goal of institutionalization of these retardates is habilitation through behavior modification rather than custodial care. Consequently, temporary placement is replacing indefinite institutionalization for many of those referred to the institution. Many institutions are placing increasing stress on accelerated placement programs, including nursing home placements of older retardates and discharge of young adults to the expanding community sheltered workshops.

Institutions are rapidly evolving multiple programs aimed at (1) supplementing community resources, (2) facilitating transition from institutional to community living, and/or (3) preventing or minimizing institutionalization by providing alternate services. Such programs include diagnostic and evaluation clinics, day care centers, sheltered workshops, vocational rehabilitation programs, trial placements, day work, and foster home programs.

Bridging the traditional gap between institution and community is being facilitated by three important developments:

(1) Volunteers are being enlisted in ever-growing numbers to render direct services to the institution. They are increasingly being assimilated into treatment teams, where they function as extensions of the regular institution staff (Roos, 1964).

(2) Professional members of institutional staffs are offering consultation to agencies, private practitioners, and others in communities. Frequently the

institution has the highest concentration of professional talent within an extensive geographical area and serves as a manpower resource for surrounding communities.

(3) Institutions are placing greater emphasis on involving parents of the retarded in treatment planning. Prevention or reduction in the length of institutionalization is being fostered through pre-admission parent counseling. Parents are being invited to participate in training programs within the institution to equip them to handle their retarded children more effectively (Roos, 1965). Pre- and post-discharge parent counseling are becoming recognized as essential facets of habilitation efforts.

Inservice Training Programs

Concern with improving the excellence of institutional services is being reflected by the energetic expansion of inservice tranining programs. In general, these programs have been aimed primarily at the caretaker personnel, although they have not been limited to this group. The Southern Region Education Board Attendant Training Project (Bensberg, Barnett & Hurder, 1964) and the Inservice Training Program funded by the National Institute of Mental Health have been potent catalysts in up-grading attendant level staff through inservice training. Training programs are being expanded to include such special groups as supervisory personnel, resident helpers and volunteers. Pre-employment training programs are being instituted in some settings.

Demonstration Programs

No longer satisfied with a "good custodial program," institutions are developing specialized demonstration projects. Many institutions are still seriously impaired in development of training and treatment programs by insufficient funds. The personnel-to-resident ratio is usually considerably below that recommended by the AAMD project on technical planning (Scheerenberger, 1965). The typical approach to this frustrating situation has been the development of one or more demonstration projects for the purpose of establishing the effectiveness of special techniques and procedures. The significant benefit to the retardates selected for these special projects may be less important than the impact of the programs on the institution. It is generally anticipated that such circumscribed programs will benefit the entire institution by fostering staff acceptance of new attitudes and techniques and by validating requests for additional appropriations. The federally sponsored Hospital Improvement Projects have contributed heavily to the development of demonstration projects.

Development of such programs is being facilitated in some institutions through subdivision into relatively small administrative subunits. The primary advantage claimed for this unit system is the fostering of greater individual care and training. The trend toward replacing large multi-purpose facilities by smaller specialized institutions also reflects this concern for improved programming.

Research

Frustrated by the serious limitations of knowledge in the area of mental retardation, institutions are placing increasing emphasis on programs of research. It is becoming increasingly apparent that many significant research questions can be answered most meaningfully within the institutional setting. Previous artificial barriers between applied and basic research are gradually being broken down. Consequently, a number of institutions are developing full time research staffs. Others are evolving cooperative projects with neighboring universities, medical schools and research centers. Institutional administrators are finding that research not only adds to knowledge, but that it contributes significantly to care and treatment programs by helping to evaluate and refine treatment and training techniques. Research programs also foster recruitment and retention of professional staff.

Changing Role of the Professional

The serious professional manpower shortage in the area of mental retardation is leading to significant changes in the role of the professional. Available evidence suggests that the current rate of training professionals for the field of mental retardation will not satisfy the growing need (President's Panel on Mental Retardation, 1962). It is becoming increasingly apparent that professionals are unable—and probably will continue to be unable—to give direct service to the majority of the institutionalized retarded. As a result, there has been a gradual abandonment of the one-to-one therapeutic model. The traditional therapist-patient treatment situation is being relinquished as being neither practical nor particularly effective. Professionals are beginning to function primarily as consultants, teachers, trainers and supervisors.

Greater reliance is being placed on subprofessional staff, on volunteers and even on parents for implementation of training programs. The psychiatrist, the social worker and the psychologist, in particular, are modifying their professional roles to meet effectively the reality demands of the changing institutional situation.

CONCLUSION

In summary, the demarcation between the residential institution and the community is rapidly fading. Institutions are evolving specialized demonstration programs aimed at meeting newly created needs, developing improved methods of training and care, and demonstrating the effectiveness of known techniques. The scope of services offered by institutions is expanding dramatically to meet community needs. Professionals are abandoning traditional roles in favor of training and supervising subprofessionals in the implementation of treatment and training programs. Institutions are obviously in a stage of rapid metamorphosis. Evidence to date suggests that they are effectively adapting to changes, and that they will become the nucleus for a broad spectrum of services for the mentally retarded.

Until considerably more progress is made in the understanding and treatment of mental retardation, it appears the residential institution will continue to serve an important function in providing a relatively controlled situation allowing maximal environmental manipulation. For many retardates, such a situation seems to be the most effective approach to behavior modification. Although it is becoming unfashionable to refer to isolation of the retarded, it is nonetheless still very realistic to recognize that the institution furnishes a refuge for those retardates whose behavior is grossly unacceptable to society. Families will continue to institutionalize the profoundly retarded to escape from the trauma of their presence in the home.

A final word of caution regarding the potential dangers of over-optimism seems warranted. That significant gains have been made is obvious. However, serious disappointments will follow if our progress generates unrealistic expectations. We must guard against promising too much. Even our most effective training programs will not make the behavior of all retardates acceptable to society. It is probable that for years to come the profoundly and severely retarded members of our society will be unable to adjust satisfactorily for a prolonged period of time to an extra-institutional environment.

REFERENCES

Bensberg, G. J., Barnett, C. D., & Hurder, W. P. Training of Attendant Personnel in Residential Facilities for the Mentally Retarded. *Mental Retardation,* 1964, 2, 144–151.

Dayan, M. Toilet Training Retarded Children in a State Residential Institution. *American Journal of Mental Deficiency,* 1964, 2, 116–117.

Ellis, N. R. Toilet Training the Severely Defective Patient: An S-R Reinforcement Analysis. *American Journal of Mental Deficiency,* 1963, 68, 98–103.

Goldstein, H. Social and Occupational Adjustment. In *Mental Retardation, A Review of Research,* Stevens, H. & Heber, R. Chicago and London: The University of Chicago Press, 1964.

McCandless, B. R. Relation of Environmental Factors to Intellectual Functioning. In *Mental Retardation, A Review of Research,* Stevens, H. & Heber, R. Chicago and London: The University of Chicago Press, 1964.

President's Panel on Mental Retardation. *A Proposed Program for National Action to Combat Mental Retardation.* Washington, D. C.: Superintendent of Documents, U. S. Government Printing Office, 1962.

Roos, P. Mental Retardation—A Challenge to Volunteers. Paper presented at the 1964 Annual Mental Hospital Institute of the American Psychiatric Association, Dallas, Texas.

Roos, P. Development of an Intensive Habit-Training Unit at Austin State School. *Mental Retardation,* 1965, **3,** 12—15.

Scheerenberger, R. C. A Current Census of State Institutions for the Mentally Retarded. *Mental Retardation,* 1965, **3,** 4—6.

THE
IMPORTANCE OF
PREVENTION
IN
MENTAL
RETARDATION

Gunnar Dybwad

The paper is a call to action for planning, service delivery, and legislation along a broad spectrum of preventative measures.

In addressing myself to the topic "The Importance of Prevention in Mental Retardation," I would like to highlight certain considerations which merit the attention of our Association. Some of them, indeed, should be dealt with as urgent issues of policy. In subsequent meetings during this Convention, some of our colleagues will present specific substantive issues which relate to the prevention of mental retardation, but today I shall focus primarily on policy and strategies.

In 1962, Leon Eisenberg challenged the American Orthopsychiatric Association (in his paper "Preventive Psychiatry—If Not Now, When?") to concern itself with contemporary social issues which relate significantly to any large scale effort at prevention. His provocative question, "If not now, when?" is one which certainly confronts us, but a second question must also be raised—"If so, how?"

This much-quoted statement from the work of the President's Panel on Mental Retardation, "If only we would apply what we know, we could prevent fifty per cent of mental retardation," brings to mind what Kingsley Davis said in a paper entitled "The Perilous Promise of Behavioral Science":

> "Given the great promise that social science holds out for solving our problems, one is puzzled by what appears to be a mocking reality. I have observed, for example, that solutions to social problems tend to have three characteristics: First, they are extremely simple, especially compared to technological solutions. Second, they are foolproof—that is, if they were applied, they would solve the problem. Third, they are not being applied."

As long as we consider prevention to be just a state of mind, something fine and sacred like the Fourth of July, to be celebrated rather than pursued, we have hardly laid a basis for effective action. Prevention permeates everything we do; everything we do allows us to include preventive aspects. Prevention thus must be a concern whenever we are discussing delivery of services. Prevention requires large scale planning, but it also requires strategy to weave individual efforts into a logical and effective network. Dr. Richard Masland said in 1958, "One cannot escape the conclusion that progress in the program for prevention of mental retardation will take place by small advances along a broad front." Our strategy, therefore, must deal with both the coordinative aspects of prevention and the preventive aspects of coordination. Thus, Phenylketonuria (PKU) screening must be related to the availability of the PKU diet (something that proved to be quite a serious problem in one State), and case findings must be related to the availability of diagnostic

Mental Retardation, 1969, 7(2): 3–6. Reprinted by permission of the author and the American Association on Mental Deficiency.

Dr. Dybwad is professor of human development at the Florence Heller Graduate School for Advanced Studies in Social Welfare, Brandeis University.

facilities. Daignosis must initiate follow-through action, which in turn must be linked to evaluative procedures.

When one reviews the array of reports emanating from the national effort at statewide mental retardation planning, one finds frequent emphasis on the need for coordination, but very little emphasis on actual coordinative strategies, both intra-departmentally and inter-departmentally. This urgent problem must be solved.

The report of the Task Force on Prevention of the President's Panel on Mental Retardation stressed that it is not enough to have preventive tools available. A considerable amount of education, directed at personal motivation toward their acceptance and use, is a necessity.

In recent years there has been considerable discussion on the point that a preventive service, such as a prenatal clinic, must not only be available, but must also be accessible from the viewpoint of the potential recipient (a viewpoint which may differ considerably from that of those involved in the rendering of the service). Continuing failure in some of the preventive services offered has led more recently to the recognition that acceptance of the service by the prospective recipients is of equal importance. This involves both the understanding of the service and the willingness to use it.

The recent conference on "Assessing the Effectiveness of Child Health Services" indicates that we have underestimated the amount of effort that must go into effecting the changes which usually precede preventive services. The conference also suggests that we take longer periods of time to deal with the deep-seated habits of people. This is an area in which very little research has been done. Past efforts addressed themselves to groups which require large scale preventive efforts, namely those with socioeconomic and cultural deprivation. These efforts met with limited success. Unless we become more skillful in this area, the effectiveness of crucial preventive efforts will be severely curtailed.

In fact, not only in order to limit more effectively and sensibly the tasks which we would set for ourselves within the field of mental retardation, but also in order to clarify our relationships with official agencies and their functional and statutory responsibilities, it appears ever more urgent that we arrive at a clearer picture of the line of demarcation between the field of mental retardation, on the one hand, and the broader field of socioeconomic and cultural deprivation, on the other. It may seem superfluous to emphasize that not all mild mental retardation is associated with socioeconomic and cultural deprivation, yet broad generalizations recently encountered in the literature and at conferences suggest that there *is* a need for reemphasis. Of widely greater quantitative significance, of course, is the fact that, among the disadvantaged, those who would be considered mentally retarded constitute a distinct minority.

The monograph "The Prevention of Disability in Mental Disorders," published by the Subcommittee on Tertiary Prevention of the American Public Health Association (and applying to both the field of mental retardation and that of mental illness), raises serious questions about the too liberal use of diagnostic labels. In this connection, it might be of interest to the members of the American Association on Mental Deficiency that, while two recent advisory groups to the Mental Health Unit of the World Health Organization endorsed the 1959 AAMD classification in principle, they took very strong exception to the term and concept "borderline mental retardation," since they considered this to be an intrusion into a general area which was characterized much more adequately by the previous term and concept of "borderline intelligence." The considerations of these two committees of the World Health Organization's Mental Health Unit were similar to those put forth by the APHA Subcommittee, in focusing on the deleterious social and psychological effect of being referred to as mentally retarded, albeit "borderline." Obviously, this also raises important questions about strategy and about the respective areas of primary responsibilities of various public services. The result will undoubtedly be a confrontation between those who see a primary need for the establishment of logically "clean" systems of classification, and those who feel that the profession cannot be oblivious to the social aspects of any classification scheme it may develop. We are dealing here with a broad area of concern, which has recently been illuminated by Robert B. Edgerton in his work "The Cloak of Competence—Stigma in the Lives of the Mentally Retarded."

The new emphasis on preventive efforts in the area of cultural and socioeconomic deprivation brings up a point impinging on the strategies of AAMD as a professional organization. Since the Association, through its membership, is becoming more and more involved in broader issues such as prenatal care, enrichment of early life experience, urban renewal, housing, the poverty program, etc., it must relate itself organizationally to the various governmental and voluntary agencies which function primarily in these areas. AAMD must also be ready to enter into temporary and ad hoc alliances with groups of this nature, to make sure that the professional concerns of the field of mental retardation are properly represented in deliberations and in program development. This will involve reciprocal relationships with those organizations, as well as a farsighted, broadly oriented leadership for the Association. This implies commitment to more extensive, more active participation in the social issues of the day.

The field of education is one professional group to which AAMD relates well. James Gallagher, the distinguished head of the Office of Education's Bureau of Education for the Handicapped, stated at a conference last year that, of all the prevailing myths about education, one of the most pervasive and most harmful is the belief that there is a specific locality where education takes place. This locality, he added, is often marked off by four brick walls and called a school, an institution, or a university. It is fair to say that this myth and the resulting functional patterns of education have been responsible in the past for a somewhat limited interplay of AAMD with its counterparts in the field of education, such as the Council for Exceptional Children, the National Education Association, and the Office of Education's Bureau of Education for the Handicapped.

However, now that there is such an insistent focus on the preventive aspects of early educational intervention with the infant and pre-school child in disadvantaged families, now that it has been amply demonstrated that with moderately, severely, or even profoundly retarded individuals, the potential for educational intervention is far greater than had previously been assumed, our Association must help to establish a sound basis for close collaboration and interchange with these public and nongovernmental educational organizations. We must take an active part in the shaping of new programs and their legislative and fiscal bases. Again, I would like to quote from Dr. Gallagher: "The school of the future for ages three to six will provide a real opportunity for intensive remedial work (with the moderately retarded child) with the view toward eventual transfer of the exceptional child to the regular programs, an often sought but rarely achieved goal." In other words, we find here a clear determination to reshape educational programs so that, for a large number of children, they can constitute a truly preventive service from the point of view of mental retardation. We should also refer to the program which Dr. Kugel and his associates developed in Iowa City ten years ago, a comprehensive educational program directed not only at retarded children, but also at their disadvantaged parents. New legislative provisions on the Federal level provide room for a variety of combinations of federally supported programs. If our Association is to play a significant role in the prevention of mental retardation, we must be fully aware of these statutory possibilities. We must relate ourselves to the respective governmental agencies on the Federal level. In order to work our strategies, we must cooperate with the other professional groups involved.

When I first accepted the invitation to contribute my thoughts on the importance of prevention to this evening's program, it had been my intention to focus on an area which, in my opinion, has been seriously neglected, that is, secondary prevention through the extension of a broad spectrum of services to the retarded infant, the very young retarded child, and their families. Although this matter is of particular interest to me, conversations with colleagues from various parts of the country convinced me to change the tenor and substance of my remarks. I now feel that it is essential that, in this first session of our Annual Meeting, a clear note of alarm be sounded with regard to recent developments in Washington, developments which have resulted not only in a sharp decrease of funds available for mental retardation services, training and applied research, but also in the discontinuation of essential and promising new programs and the demoralization of our colleagues working in the Federal establishment.

It is not my intention to accuse anyone. As a matter of fact, the situation can largely be attributed to a lack of definitive information regarding these changes, the reasons behind them, and the great uncertainty concerning future developments which may indicate additional far-reaching changes. The facts on hand clearly demonstrate that the mental retardation "honeymoon" is over—and that we now find ourselves without some of the necessities for establishing and maintaining our household.

It takes years to effectively establish new services, to organize a qualified staff, to develop procedures in collaboration with other departments and agencies at the Federal level, and, more importantly, with the agencies and departments, public and private, throughout the United States. Long before the gains initiated by President Kennedy's efforts have been consolidated, we are suffering from cutbacks which have totally severed parts of the program. The consequences for the development of services are serious enough, but, as was pointed out earlier in this presentation, effective programs of prevention are much harder and require much more time to develop; therefore, the present crisis is devastating to the area on which our Program Committee has decided to focus.

The situation to which I allude is multifaceted and complicated. It leads us into such a network of statutory and budgetary provisions, administrative assignment of responsibilities, personnel policies, administrative allocation of funds, etc., that I know of no one except Dr. Elizabeth Boggs who could present a coherent picture of the total situation. Let me give you an example: For the purpose of consolidating all rehabilitation activities, the Mental Retardation Division was transferred out of the Public Health Service into the newly established Social and Rehabilitation Service. However, funds absolutely essential to the maintenance of the Mental Retardation Division stayed behind in the Public Health Service. One can only surmise that there is no possibility of replacing these funds. In any event, some of the Division's programs are at a standstill.

From the point of view of overall preventive efforts, the removal of the Mental Retardation Division from the Public Health Service (PHS) operating programs (as contrasted with the research-oriented activities of the National Institutes of Health) has left us in a grotesque situation—there is no unit or person in the Public Health Service complex responsible for the field of mental retardation. Altogether this flight of PHS from responsibility to the field of mental retardation contrasts ironically with the vociferous insistence of organized medicine that it must claim primary responsibility for this field.

More specifically, even though the records of the Social Security Administration in HEW clearly show that mental retardation is a major cause of life-long disability, the component in the Public Health Service concerned with prevention of chronic disease and disability sees, to judge from its testimony before Congress, no relationship between disability and retardation. Nothing in these remarks should in any way detract from the tremendous contribution which the Children's Bureau has made to the public health aspects of the prevention of mental retardation, through its maternal and child health programs, but the very nature of the Children's Bureau limits its program development.

Legislation introduced in 1963 initiated a most significant program providing for the establishment of mental retardation research centers and university-affliated mental retardation training centers. Most of these programs are still in the earliest stages of development; some of them are now facing acute deprivation. We must keep in mind that preventive efforts, because of their inherent delayed effect, require exceptional long-range planning and consistency. Therefore, stability and continuity are of particular importance. For this reason, as far as we as a professional organization are concerned, the plans of both the Association's activities and our own individual professional projects have been greatly hampered by the fact that much of this Federal reorganization has come as a surprise, with a minimum of professionally helpful interpretation and a large hidden agenda. No one has explained why the functional reorganization and changes in fiscal support of the programs had to be accomplished under such extraordinary circumstances.

There is no intention here to suggest that we should dispute the responsibility and right to decision inherent in the executive department of our Government, or arrogate any of these prerogatives. As a professional organization, however, we have a right to be heard; we should have the right to receive intelligible, meaningful information. It is, therefore, most appropriate, at this crucial stage, that we ask ourselves whether we are ready to meet the problems facing the field of mental retardation in this country.

I hope you will allow me, as a member of 28 years' standing, to state that I see a need for vigorous reorganization and reorientation of our Association so that we can live up to these new responsibilities, if indeed our members agree that they are properly within the realm of our goals and activities.

The record will show that, in past years, whatever contacts our Association has had with the Federal establishment have been on a highly selective basis. We have failed to be involved in the broad spectrum of agency programs and legislative considerations impinging on our field. To do so now will mean the allocation of manpower and of financial resources; it will mean the active involvement of our regional organizations and, last but not least, a readiness of the individual members to assist when and where their particular talents, knowledge or personal connections are needed for the common good.

I am indebted to one of the Far Eastern students at our University for the perceptive comment that, in the Western countries of liberal academic persuasion, the prevailing value pattern discourages efforts in the direction of radical change, and that national planning is not taken as a serious alteration to current modes of thought. The Comprehensive Mental Retardation State Plans are a good example of this. Without detracting from the many contributions they have made toward betterment of services to the retarded, they are essentially conservative and cautious with regard to change.

I hope that during the next week we shall hear some new and far-reaching proposals for preventive action in the field of mental retardation. Unless we are prepared to accept them as no more than academic exercises, we must accept, and constructively reply to, the challenge of preparing ourselves to meet this new crisis in our chosen field of endeavor.

> ". . . whatever difference there is between the mentally retarded and other children, there is one respect in which they are all the same—they can be taught, they can be helped, they can lead normal lives, contributing to the society instead of burdening it—if we will it.
>
> If we are prepared to accept responsibility for these children to work with them—not to what we think is the limit of *their* abilities, but to the limit of *our* abilities—they can be helped."
>
> *Robert F. Kennedy*
> Address to the Rhode Island
> Association for Retarded Children
> April 24, 1965

PURGATORY

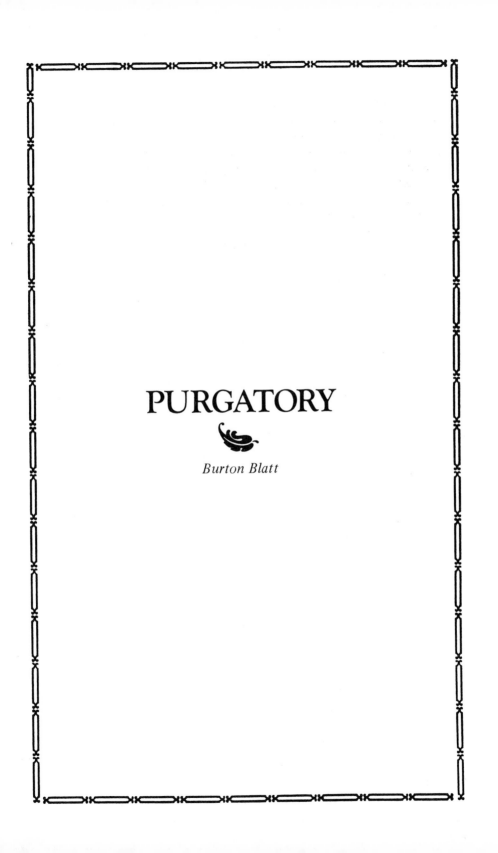

Burton Blatt

Blatt's photographic essay of pictures taken with a hidden camera on the wards of several state institutions aroused a storm of criticism. Charges of bias were leveled by those who felt he had neglected to depict more positive aspects of programs at such institutions. Later investigations and exposés of similar conditions at many facilities for the retarded served to arouse public indignation. Blatt's report was a step toward radical reform in the quality of care and service provided within public and private institutions for the mentally handicapped.

"All hope abandon, ye who enter here."–Dante.

With a good deal of anxiety, I waited for the white-uniformed attendant to respond to my knocking and unlock the door to Hell.[1] And in America, we have our own special Inferno. I was a visitor there during the Christmas season, 1965, while studying five state institutions for the mentally retarded, located in four Eastern states.

As I awaited entrance to the above-mentioned building, which was a residential dormitory, my anxiety belied the ostensible situation. In the 18 years that I had been professionally active in the field of mental retardation, I had been to scores of institutions. I had served on numerous commissions to evaluate or advise such institutions. In fact, the building I was about to enter–and which terrified me now–was no stranger to me. Over the years, and for one reason or another, I had found it necessary to visit this building, never giving it any particular thought; one might say I had visited it thoughtlessly.

However, my fears were not the neurotic outcroppings of an unhinged mind. I had a great deal to be worried about and, during the few moments I waited for entrance to this dormitory, my thoughts flashed back to those antecedents that brought me here. In the early fall of 1965, Senator Robert Kennedy visited several of his state's institutions for the mentally retarded. His reactions were widely published in our various news media, shocking millions of Americans as well as infuriating scores of public officeholders and professional persons responsible for the care and treatment of the mentally retarded. Most of the laymen with whom I discussed his visits reacted to the Senator's disclosures with incredulity. For it is difficult for "uninvolved" people to believe that, in our country, and at this time, human beings are being treated less humanely and under more deplorable conditions than are animals. A number of the "involved" citizenry, i.e., those who legislate and budget for institutions for the mentally retarded and those who administer them, were infuriated because the Senator reported only the worst of what he had seen, not mentioning the worthwhile programs that he undoubtedly was

---

[1] This work is part of a chapter of the author's forthcoming book, *Exodus From Pandemmia.* It was written during the summer of 1966 for *Look.* As a result of the severe space limitations, a very modest fraction eventually appeared in that magazine. The author believes that his work represents a more complete discussion of his story *Christmas in Purgatory* as it pertains to the so-called back wards.

Changing Patterns in Residential Services for the Mentally Retarded. Washington, D.C.: President's Committee on Mental Retardation, 1961, chapter 3. Reprinted with permission of the author.

Dr. Blatt is director of the Division of Special Education and Rehabilitation at Syracuse University.

shown. Further, this latter group was severely critical of the Senator for taking "whirlwind" tours and, in the light of just a few hours of observation, damning entire institutions and philosophies.

During the time of these visits, I was a participant in a research project at The Seaside, a State of Connecticut regional center for the mentally retarded. The superintendent of The Seaside, Fred Finn, and I spent a considerable amount of time discussing, in particular, the debate between Senator Kennedy and New York Governor Nelson Rockefeller. We concluded the following: it does not require a scientific background or a great deal of observation to determine that one has entered the "land of the living dead"; it does not require too imaginative a mind or too sensitive a nose to realize that one has stumbled onto a dung hill, whether or not, as Cervantes wrote, it is covered with a piece of tapestry when a procession (of distinguished visitors) goes by; it is quite irrelevant how well the rest of an institution's program is being fulfilled if one is concerned with that part of it which is terrifying. No amount of rationalization can mitigate that which, to many of us, is cruel and inhumane treatment.

It is true that a short visit to the back wards (the hidden, publicly unvisited living quarters) of an institution for the mentally retarded will not provide, even for the most astute observer, any clear notion of the causes of the problems observed, the complexities of dealing with them, or ways to correct them. It is not difficult to believe that Senator Kennedy could not fully comprehend the subtleties, the tenuous relationships, the grossness of budgetary inequities, the long history of political machinations, the extraordinary difficulty in providing care for severely mentally retarded patients, the unavailability of highly trained professional leaders, and the near-impossibility in recruiting dedicated attendants and ward personnel. Further, I do not believe the conditions Senator Kennedy claimed to have observed were due to evil people. As Seymour Sarason, Professor of Psychology at Yale University, wrote in the preface to our book (*Christmas in Purgatory: A Photographic Essay on Mental Retardation.* Boston: Allyn and Bacon, 1967), these conditions are " . . . not due to evil or incompetent or cruel people but rather to a conception of human potential and an attitude toward innovation which when applied to the mentally defective, result in a self-fulfilling prophecy. That is, if one thinks that defective children are almost beyond help, one acts toward them in ways which then confirm one's assumptions."

However, regardless of their antecedents, I believe, as well as do thousands of others who have been associated with institutions for the mentally retarded, that what Senator Kennedy reported he saw he very likely did see. In fact, I know personally of few institutions for the mentally retarded in the United States that are completely free of dirt and filth, odors, naked patients groveling in their own feces, children in restraints and in locked cells, horribly crowded dormitories, and understaffed and wrongly staffed facilities.

After a good deal of thought, I decided to follow through on what then seemed, and what eventually became, a bizarre venture. One of my friends, Fred Kaplan, is a professional photographer. On Thanksgiving Day, 1965, I presented the following plan to him. We were to arrange to meet with each of several key administrative persons in a variety of public institutions for the mentally retarded. If we gained an individual's cooperation, we would be taken on a "tour" of the back wards and those parts of the institution that he was *most* ashamed of. On the "tour" Fred Kaplan would take pictures of what we observed, utilizing a hidden camera attached to his belt.

Through the efforts of courageous and humanitarian colleagues, including two superintendents who put their reputations and professional positions in jeopardy, we were able to visit the darkest corridors and vestibules that humanity provides for its "journey to purgatory," and, without being detected by ward personnel and professional staff, Fred Kaplan was able to take hundreds of photographs.

Our photographs were not always the clearest. On the other hand, it required a truly creative photographer to be able to take these pictures, "from the hip" so to speak, unable to use special lighting, not permitted to focus or set shutter speeds, with a small camera concealed in multitudes of clothing and surrounded by innumerable "eyes" of patients as well as of staff. Although our pictures cannot even begin to capture the total and overwhelming horror we saw, smelled, and felt, they represent a side of America that has rarely, if ever, been shown to the general public and is little understood by most of the rest of us.

I do not believe it is necessary to disclose the names of the institutions we visited. First, to reveal those names is assuredly an invitation to the dismissal of those who arranged for us to photograph their deepest and most embarrassing "secrets." However, involved is not only a matter of promises made to altruistic people but avoidance of the impression that the problems now exposed are local rather than national ones. I am completely convinced that in numerous other institutions across America I can observe similar conditions—some, I am sure, even more frightening.

Had I known what I would actually be getting myself into and had I known what abnormal pressures would subsequently be exerted upon me as a result of this story and my efforts to bring it before the American people, I might have turned away from that first dormitory entrance as I was, finally, being admitted; and I might have fled to the shelter and protection of my academic "ivory tower" to ruminate on the injustices prevailing in society. Although I did not expect this to be a pleasurable study, I was in no way prepared for the degradation and despair I encountered, experiences which caused me to develop a chronic sorrow, one that will not abate until the American people are aware of—and do something about—the treatment of certain mentally retarded human beings in our state institutions.

As I entered this dormitory, housing severely mentally retarded adolescents and adults, I was still reminiscing about Senator Kennedy, Governor Rockefeller, and our fateful Thanksgiving dinner until, almost immediately after I passed the threshold, an overwhelming stench enveloped me. It was the sickening, suffocating smell of feces and urine, decay, dirt and filth, of such strength as to hang in the air and, I thought then and am still not dissuaded, solid enough to be cut or shoveled away. But, as things turned out, the odors were among the gentlest assaults on my sensibilities. I was soon to learn about the decaying humanity that caused them. This story—my purgatory in black and white—which, ironically, was conceived of and written on the 700th anniversary of the birth of Dante, represents my composite impressions of what I consider to be the prevailing conditions of certain sectors of most institutions for the mentally retarded in this country. It is in the hope of calling attention to the desperate needs of these institutions, and thereby, paving the way for upgrading all institutions for the mentally retarded in all dimensions of their responsibilities that this study was undertaken and this story written.

Several things strike a visitor to most institutions for the mentally retarded upon his arrival on the institution grounds. Sometimes there are fences, once in a while with barbed wire. Very frequently the buildings impress him with their sheer massiveness and impenetrability. I have observed bars on windows and locks—many locks—on inside as well as outside doors. As I entered the dormitories and other buildings, I was impressed with the functional superiority of the new building but, on the other hand, with the gross neglect in many of the older ones. I have observed gaping holes in ceilings of such vital areas as the main kitchen. In toilets, I frequently saw urinals ripped out, sinks broken, and toilet bowls backed up. In every institution I visited, with the exception of The Seaside, I found incredible overcrowding. Beds are so arranged—side by side and head to head—that it is impossible, in some dormitories, to cross parts of the rooms without actually walking over beds; oftentimes the beds are without pillows. I have seen mattresses so sagged by the weight of the bodies that they were scraping the floor.

Before I go further, it would be well to point out a crucial factor giving rise to the overcrowdedness, the disrepair of older buildings, the excessive need for locks and heavy doors, and the enormity of buildings and the numbers of patients assigned to dormitories. About 200,000 adults and children currently reside in public institutions for the retarded in this country, at a cost of about $500,000,000 a year in operating expense alone. At first glance, this appears to be a great deal of money and, to the unknowing laymen, is cause for comfort, i.e., the mentally retarded have finally received their due. However, simple arithmetic tells us that $500,000,000 divided by 200,000 amounts to $2,500 a year, or about $48 per week or $7 per day. This is about one-eighth the amount spent for a day's general hospital care. Four states spent less than $4 per day in 1966. In some checking that I have done recently, I learned that in our better zoos, the larger animals require a higher per capita expenditure.

The average per capita daily cost for maintaining a retarded resident in each of the four institutions I described was, at that time, less than $7, in one case less than $5. In contrast, The Seaside, a new regional center for the retarded, sponsored by the Connecticut Department of Health and discussed in our aforementioned book *Christmas in Purgatory,* spent $12 daily for care and treatment of each resident. Although it may be true that money corrupts, it may be equally true that its absence is similarly corrupting.

"Inasmuch as ye have done it unto one of the least of these my brethren, ye have done it unto me."—Matthew 25:40.

All of the doors in institutional buildings visited that are used as living quarters for young children, and moderately and severely retarded residents of any age, have locks. These locks are on all outside doors as well as all inside doors. Many of the doors are made of heavy gauge metal or thick wood. All of the locks appear to be formidable, and it is routine, second nature, for attendants to pass from room to room with a key chain in hand unlocking and locking doors en route.

Many dormitories for the severely and moderately retarded ambulatory residents have solitary confinement cells or, what is officially referred to and is jokingly called by many attendants, "therapeutic isolation." "Therapeutic isolation" means solitary confinement—in its most punitive and inhumane form. These cells are usually located on an upper floor, off to the side and away from the casual or official visitor's scrutiny. (Coincidentally, a United States Senator had visited a dormitory at a state institution 3 days prior to one of my visits there. In discussing this with him weeks later, I showed him pictures taken of solitary confinement cells in that dormitory. As one might expect, he had not been shown these cells during his tour and, I believe it possible, he was not absolutely sure that I did not concoct this coincidence to impress upon him the urgency of my mission.) Isolation cells are generally tiny rooms, approximately 7 feet by 7 feet, shielded from the outside with a very heavy metal door having either a fine strong screen or metal bars for observation of the "prisoner." Some cells have mattresses, others blankets, still others bare floors. None that I had seen (and I found these cells in each institution visited) had either a bed, a wash stand, or a toilet. What I did find in one cell was a 13- or 14-year-old boy, nude, in a corner of a starkly bare room, lying on his own urine and feces. The boy had been in solitary confinement for several days for committing an institutional infraction, as I recall, directing abusive language to an attendant. Another child, in another institution, had been in solitary confinement for approximately 5 days for breaking windows. Another had been in isolation, through a long holiday weekend, because he had struck an attendant. Ironically, in the dormitory where this boy was being incarcerated, I saw another young man who had been "sent to bed early" because he had *bitten off* the ear of a patient several hours previously. Apparently, it is infinitely more serious to strike an attendant (and it should not be misunderstood that I condone this) than to bite off the ear of another resident.

In one institution I saw a young man who was glaring at me through the screen of the door in the solitary cell, feces splattered around this opening. He, too, was being punished for breaking an institutional regulation. In this particular dormitory, I had a good opportunity to interview the attendant in charge. I asked him what he needed most in order to better supervise the residents and provide them with a more adequate program. The attendant's major request was for the addition of two more solitary confinement cells, to be built adjacent to the existing two cells that, I was told, were always occupied, around the clock, day in and day out. Unfortunately, I have recent confirmation of the constant use of the solitary cells. Seven months after the above-mentioned incident I revisited this dormitory. Both solitary confinement cells were occupied, and there was a waiting list for other youngsters who were to receive this punishment.

I saw a great deal of restraints used with children. I observed many children whose hands were tied, legs bound, or waists secured. After a good deal of discussion with a number of attendants and supervisors in the four institutions, I was convinced that one of the major reasons for the frequent use of solitary confinement and physical restraints was the extraordinary shortage of staff in practically all of these dormitories. The attendant who requested the construction of two additional solitary confinement cells was, with one assistant, responsible for the supervision of an old multilevel dormitory, housing over a hundred severely retarded ambulatory residents. Almost in desperation he asked me, "What can one do with those patients who do not conform? We must lock them up, or restrain them, or sedate them, or put fear into them." At that point, I did not feel I had a response that would satisfy either him or me. I suffered in silence in much the same way, I imagine, men of conscience suffered upon reading Reil's description in 1803 of institutional problems that were astonishingly similar to those I encountered. He said then,

"We lock these unfortunate creatures in lunatic cells, as if they were criminals. We keep them in chains in forlorn jails . . . where no sympathetic human being can ever bestow them a friendly glance, and we let them rot in their own filth. Their fetters scrape the flesh from their bones, and their wan, hollow faces search for the grave that their wailing and our ignominy conceals from them."

My thoughts went back to that anonymous writer who, in 1795, said:

"A humanitarian is bound to shudder when he discovers the plight of the unfortunate victims of this dreadful affliction; many of them grovel in their own filth on unclean straw that is seldom changed, often stark naked and in chains, in dark, damp dungeons where no breath of fresh air can enter. Under such terrifying conditions, it would be easier for the most rational person to become insane than for a mad man to regain his sanity."

"I sometimes hold it half a sin to put in words the grief I feel."
—Alfred, Lord Tennyson.

In each of the dormitories for severely retarded residents there is what is called, euphemistically, the dayroom or recreation room. The odor in each of these rooms is overpowering, to the degree that after a visit to a dayroom I had to send my clothes to the dry cleaners in order to have the stench removed (and, probably because of psychological reactions, whose odor I continued to smell months later whenever I wore certain clothes). The physical facilities often contributed to the visual horror as well as to the odor. Floors are sometimes made of wood and, as a result, excretions are rubbed into the cracks, thus providing a permanent aroma. Most dayrooms have a series of bleacherlike benches on which sit denuded residents, jammed together, without purposeful activity or communication or any kind of interaction. In each dayroom is an attendant or two, whose main function seems to be to "stand around" and, on occasion, hose down the floor, "driving" excretions into a sewer conveniently located in the center of the room.

I was invited into female as well as male dayrooms, in spite of the supervisor's knowledge that I, a male visitor, would be observing denuded females. In one such dormitory, with an overwhelming odor, I noticed feces on the wooden ceilings, and on the patients as well as the floors.

Early in the evening, sometimes at 5 o'clock, patients are put to bed. This is to equalize the workload among the different shifts. During the day, I saw many patients lying on their beds, apparently for long periods of time. This was their activity. During these observations, I thought a good deal about the perennial cry for attendants and volunteer workers who are more sympathetic and understanding of institutionalized retarded residents. One of the things I realized was that attendants might be sympathetic, might interact more with patients, if institutional administrators made deliberate attempts to make patients cosmetically more appealing. For example, adult male residents should shave, or be shaven, more than once or twice a week. Dentures should be provided for any patient who needs them. It seems plausible to believe that it is much more possible to make residents more attractive and, therefore, more interesting to attendants than it is to attempt to convince attendants that they should enjoy the spectacle of unwashed, unkempt, odoriferous, toothless old men and women.

"My friends forsake me like a memory lost."—John Clare.

The living quarters for older men and women were, for the most part, gloomy and sterile. There were rows and rows of benches on which sat countless human beings, in silent rooms, waiting for dinner call or bedtime. I saw resident after resident in "institutional garb." Sometimes, the women wore shrouds—inside out. I heard a good deal of laughter but saw little cheer. There were few things to be cheerful about. A great many of the men and women looked depressed and acted depressed. Even the television sets, in several of the dayrooms, appeared to be co-conspirators in a crusade for gloom. These sets were not in working order, although, ironically, the residents continued to sit on their benches, in neat rows, looking at the blank tubes. I observed adult residents during recreation playing Ring-Around-The-Rosy. Others, in the vocational training center, were playing Jacks. These were not always severely retarded patients. However, one got the feeling very quickly that this is the way they were being forced to behave. Or, as Hungerford said, ". . . in an institution there is always tomorrow so that he who starts out a student ends up, by default, an inmate." Lastly, I viewed old women and very young girls in the same dormitories and old men and young boys as comrades in the dayroom. In the "normal" world, there is something appealing, even touching, about such friendships; in the institution, there is something opportunistic, sinister, and ludicrous.

"Suffer the little children. . ."

The children's dormitories depressed me the most. Here, cribs were placed, as in the other dormitories, side by side and head to head. Very young children, one and two years of age, were lying in cribs without contact with any adult, without playthings, without apparent stimulation. In one dormitory that had over 100 infants and was connected to nine other dormitories that totalled 1000 infants, I experienced my deepest sadness. As I entered, I heard a muffled calling, "Come, come play with me. Touch me." I walked to the door. On the other side were 40 or more unkempt infants crawling around a bare floor in a bare room. One of the children had managed to squeeze his hand under the doorway and push his face through the side of the latched door and was crying for attention. His moan begged me for some kind of human interaction.

In other dayrooms I saw groups of 20 or 30 very young children lying, rocking, sleeping, sitting—alone. Each of these rooms was without doors or adult human contact, although each had desperate-looking adult attendants "standing by."

During my visit to the institution, I was told about the development of a new research center on the institutional grounds. The assistant superintendent mentioned to me that the "materials" for the research center would come from the institution and this center would require the addition of approximately 30 or 40 "items." I was quite confused by this statement and, as a result of some verbal fumbling and embarrassment, I finally did understand what was being said to me. At that institution, and apparently at others in that state, patients are called "material" and personnel are called "items." It was so difficult not to believe that this assistant superintendent was either "pulling my leg" or using some idiosyncratic jargon that during my subsequent visits to dormitories in that institution I asked the attending physicians, "How many 'items' do you have in this building? How much 'material' do you have?" To my amazement, they knew exactly what I was asking for and gave me the numbers immediately.

In another dormitory, I was taken on a tour by the chief physician, who was anxious to show me a child who had a very rare condition. The doctor explained to me that, aside from the child's dwarfism and misshapen body, one of the primary methods for diagnosing this condition is the deep guttural voice. In order to demonstrate this, he pinched the child. The child did not make any sound. He pinched her again, and again—harder and still harder. Finally, he insured her response with a pinch that turned into a gouge and caused the child to scream, in obvious pain.

In some of the children's dormitories I observed "nursery programs." What surprised me most was their scarcity and, unfortunately, the primitiveness of those in operation. Therefore, I was not unprepared to see several children with severe head lacerations. I was told these were the "head bangers." Head banging is another condition that some people think is inevitable when confronted with young, severely mentally retarded children. I challenge this. I have reason to believe that head banging can be drastically reduced in an environment where children have other things to do. Alice Metzner once said, "There are only two things wrong with most special education for the mentally handicapped, it isn't special, and it isn't education." From my observation of the "nursery programs" conducted at the state schools visited, I would have to agree with the second part of Miss

Metzner's complaint. The special education I observed at the state schools bore no resemblance to what I would consider to be "education." But, it was special. It was a collection of the most depressing "learning" environments I have ever had the misfortune to witness. But, as Hungerford also said, "Time buries the mistakes of many school programs."

"One may find his religion in the clinical setting." – Albert T. Murphy.

I have learned a great deal during my visits to these institutions. I have learned about the treatment of the severely mentally retarded, and all young children, who are institutionalized. But, essentially, and possibly most importantly, I have learned something about the dominating factor that influences man in his treatment of other human beings. And this is a concept that is worth striving to understand. No doubt the reader of this piece has asked himself several times, "Why do attendants and supervisors treat mentally retarded patients the way this author presents the situation to be?" It is probably imcomprehensible to you to believe that such conditions exist. Because of my years in observing these affairs, I may have been a little further along the way in rationalizing and, to my shame, accepting them. That is to say, I knew with certainty that these conditions existed. However, I was about as puzzled as anyone else in explaining why we permit them to continue. Now I may have a glimmer of enlightenment that I want to share with you.

It has always intrigued me to think about why antivivisectionists are so passionate in their beliefs concerning the use of animals for scientific experimentation. To me, animals have always been creatures to enjoy, to act kindly toward, and not to inflict any unnecessary punishment on. I believe this is they way most thoughtful human beings view the animal kingdom. I think of myself as a reasonable man. I have no interest—in fact I have revulsion—in inflicting unnecessary pain on any creature. However, I would be less than candid if I did not admit that stories about carefully controlled, and apparently necessary, animal experimentation never offend me. Further, I have never really lost any sleep or had any sustained grief in hearing about or observing cruelty to animals. I do not enjoy such spectacles. On the other hand, I have never been motivated enough to directly intervene to prevent them. However, there are people, some of our closest friends, who cry real tears and display deep emotions when confronted with cruelty to animals. During this study I began to understand, finally, why antivivisectionists are the way they are and why I am so different. Further, I began to understand how human beings can be treated so dispassionately and cruelly in institutions. Antivivisectionists must conceive of animals in ways other people conceive of human beings. If you look at the antivivisectionists in this light, it is not difficult to understand their anguish in observing inhuman behavior to animals. On the other hand, certain human beings have been taught or trained—or this is part of their nature—to conceive of other human beings in ways that most of us think of animals. If this is so, it is not difficult to understand why, and how, institutional attendants and their supervisors can treat the mentally retarded in the ways they do. It is not that these attendants are cruel or incompetent people—although, all too often, they are—but they have come to believe, for various reasons, that those in their charge are not really human. The words that are used in institutions describing certain mentally retarded residents give substance to my notion. When one views a group of human beings in an official kind of way as "material," an increased per capita expenditure for resident care and additional staff is not sufficient alone to bring about the massive changes in institutional treatment that are necessary. The use of such terms as "basket case," "vegetable," and others too offensive to record here indicates that the basic problem to be surmounted before state institutions for the mentally retarded will change substantially lies in the realm of our conception about human behavior and its amenability to change. Or, as Sarason has said: ". . . When one looks over the history of man the most distinguishing characteristic of his development is the degree to which man has underestimated the potentialities of men." Whatever ways we implement a program to reconstruct the philosophy and practices of institutions for the mentally retarded, our most forceful thrust must be in our attempts to reconceptualize our understanding of the nature and prerogatives of man. More important than the desperately needed increased per capita expenditure for institutional care, more important than the obvious necessity to reduce the size of institutions, more important than the alleviation of the now hopeless crowdedness of most institutions, is the necessity for infusing a fundamental belief among all who work with the mentally retarded that each of these individuals is equally human, not equally intellectually able, not equally physically appealing, but equally human beings. Carl Sandburg stated this much more eloquently than I could: "There is only one man in the world: and his name is ALL MEN."

AFTERTHOUGHTS

It is many months since I have visited the institutions described here. During that time I have shown and discussed this story with a formidable, very heterogeneous but carefully selected, number of individuals. Their backgrounds range from those in very high public office to undergraduate college students preparing as special class teachers. The sentiments of the aforementioned individuals, and others too numerous to mention, convinced me that this story must be brought to the American people as speedily as possible. In discussing this work with my colleagues, I have been able to resolve some of my anxieties insofar as the possible adverse consequences of publication of this story. Further, I have been able to finally conceptualize a plan (presented later in this monograph) that might correct those antecedent conditions that led to the horror I observed.

The major questions that dictated caution and painful deliberation before a thoughtful answer could be found concerned themselves with whether or not this work represented an invasion of privacy of certain individuals, on the one hand, and whether the general public has a right to be protected from the knowledge of degradation, on the other. Insofar as the first matter, invasion of privacy, is concerned, I must question privacy on moral grounds. I believe that the so-called privacy of the back wards of these institutions contributes to suffering, for outsiders do not know the conditions within these buildings and, therefore, do little or nothing to promote improvements. When privacy contributes to suffering, it loses its significance as a cherished privilege. For those who could so reason, I do not believe that there would be many in the institutions who would object to my exposure of these frightening conditions if such exposure offered some possibility for a better life and chance for the residents. Lastly, as I discussed this issue with a number of people, I began to wonder whose privacies were being protected, institutionalized residents or the rest of us?

This leads to the second consideration. Do people have a right to know, whether they request this knowledge or not, the unvarnished nature of human activity? In order to avoid hysterical reactions to this study, I have deliberately shied away from comparisons of what I have seen with what took place in another country, with other kinds of human beings, toward the solution of other problems. I do not want to, in any way, leave the impression that what goes on in American state institutions for the mentally retarded is, by administrative design, barbaric, inhumane, or callous. However, I see certain obvious major problems, not the least being the general public's unawareness of conditions in our back wards.

The American people have the *right to know*. In spite of what we wish to know, in spite of the pain that knowing may bring to us, we have the right to be informed about any serious conditions that affect the human condition. There is a maturity that comes to a people when it no longer needs the protection of ignorance and, thus, of ignoring what needs to be attended to. Only very young children, with their fantasies, or sick adults, with theirs, believe that ignoring a problem can make it go away.

POSTSCRIPT

One thousand copies of *Christmas in Purgatory* were published and distributed during the summer of 1966, without cost, to prominent legislators, commissioners of mental health, university professors, and leaders of the parent movement in mental retardation. It is not necessary here to discuss the flood of extraordinarily encouraging mail and calls I have received in response to this first edition of our book. It may be instructive to mention some of the negative, or otherwise puzzling, comments and hectoring that came to me.

One well-intentioned clergyman believes that I exhibited bad taste in reproducing photographs of nude men and women. An acquaintance in our field thinks of our work as a fake, the immoral use of a concealed camera comparing the atypical worst I had seen with "posed pictures" theatrically staged at The Seaside. A wise and beloved Commissioner of Mental Health asked me whether these conditions exist in his state's institutions. (How can I tell him about something he, as the principal responsible officer, should be aware of—and doing something about?) In another state that I have deep feeling for, a legislator who has championed mental health legislation circulated copies of *Christmas in Purgatory*, in the vain hope that it would help in the passage of social welfare legislation. He received scant support from his own party, who did not want the "opposition governor" to gain stature through such legislation in this an election year. The bill appeared doomed for many weeks, but subsequently passed, owing, I have been informed, in some part to the influence of our book.

I have just finished rereading C. P. Snow's two great essays on "The Two Cultures and the Scientific Revolution," in which he presents compelling arguments for viewing with alarm the completely separate paths trod by literary intellectuals and scientists. After reflecting on Snow's thoughts, one would have to be slow indeed not to realize the threat posed to society when two powerful cultures cannot or do not communicate and are often working at what appear to be cross purposes. However, there is another, far greater, danger to society!

For better and worse, the literary and artistic crowd and the scientists both have secure and powerful roles in our civilization. Will there ever be a day for the "literal" humanist? Is it the fate of mankind—for this is his history—to deny our human relatedness and the goodness that can come from it? We have *all* been, in our time, strangers in the land of Egypt and, consequently, must not willfully wrong any stranger—for he is our brother.

Albert Camus wrote, "Again and again there comes a time in history when the man who cares to say that two and two make four is punished with death." I have written the truth, as plainly and as simply as I see it—not for money or fame, for there has been very little of either connected with this assignment and there has been a good deal of grief. I would be surprised if this work changes radically the nature of institutions. My current depression will not permit such grand thoughts. On the other hand, as Camus wrote further, "Perhaps we can't stop the world from being one in which children are tortured but we can reduce the number of tortured children."

In spite of those who protest this presentation, there will be no turning back; the truth can no longer be concealed. Some good must come from all this pain and anguish to so many institutionalized residents and their families. Once seeds are sown, one only has to wait for the crop to harvest. It has also been said that, when the bellman is dead, the wind will toll the bell.

So hurry, wind! Or revive yourselves, noble bellringers.

THE
NORMALIZATION
PRINCIPLE
AND
ITS HUMAN
MANAGEMENT
IMPLICATIONS

Bengt Nirje

The author provides a set of guidelines to allow the mentally retarded the full range of opportunities, experiences, rights, and privileges available to non-handicapped citizens.

THE NORMALIZATION PRINCIPLE

In an earlier section of this book I have described some observations and reactions upon visiting public institutions in the United States. I will not attempt to describe the theoretical perspective from which my reactions to my observations stem.

My entire approach to the management of the retarded, and deviant persons generally, is based on the "normalization" principle. This principle refers to a cluster of ideas, methods, and experiences expressed in practical work for the mentally retarded in the Scandinavian countries, as well as in some other parts of the world. The normalization principle underlies demands for standards, facilities, and programs for the retarded as expressed by the Scandinavian parent movement. The papers by Scandinavian contributors Bank-Mikkelsen and Grunewald in this monograph provide specific descriptions of functioning programs which incorporate normalization principles.

To discuss human endeavors to create wholesome programs, facilities, and life conditions for other human beings in terms of one unifying principle might seem preposterous, especially when the mentally retarded are involved, a group which is characterized by wide variations in age, degree of handicap, complicating physical and emotional disorders, social backgrounds, and educational and personality profiles. Nevertheless, in the Scandinavian countries, a general principle which expresses the aims, attitudes, and norms implied in quality work for and with the mentally retarded has been found of value. As expressed by N. E. Bank-Mikkelsen of Denmark, this principle is given in the formula "to let the mentally retarded obtain an existence as close to the normal as possible." Thus, as I see it, the normalization principle means making available to the mentally retarded patterns and conditions of everyday life which are as close as possible to the norms and patterns of the mainstream of society.

This principle should be applied to all the retarded, regardless whether mildly or profoundly retarded, or whether living in the homes of their parents or in group homes with other retarded. The principle is useful in every society, with all age groups, and adaptable to social changes and individual developments. Consequently, it should serve as a guide for medical, educational, psychological, social, and political work in this field, and decisions and actions made according to the principle should turn out more often right than wrong. Some of the many facets and implications of the normalization principle are discussed below.

Changing Patterns in Residential Services for the Mentally Retarded. Washington, D.C.: President's Committee on Mental Retardation, 1969, chapter 7. Reprinted with permission of the author.

Dr. Nirje presently works with the Ministry of Community and Social Services, Ontario, Canada.

1. Normalization means a normal rhythm of day for the retarded. It means getting out of bed and getting dressed even when you are profoundly retarded and physically disabled. It means eating under normal circumstances: sometimes, during the span of the day, you may eat in large groups, but mostly eating is a family situation which implies rest, harmony, and satisfaction. A normal daily rhythm also means not having to go to bed earlier than your peers because you are mentally retarded, not earlier than your younger sisters and brothers, or not too early because of lack of personnel. Facilities must also give consideration to the individual's need for a personal rhythm, allowing him to break away occasionally from the routine of the group.

2. The normalization principle also implies a normal routine of life. Most people live in one place, work or attend school somewhere else, and have leisure-time activities in a variety of places. Consequently, it is wrong when a retarded person, for example, has his training classes, his structured therapies, and his recreation activities in the same building that serves also as his "home." Of course, even when vocational activities are conducted in a special building, it is not satisfactory if this consists only of a few hours of low-motivated activities for a few days a week. Activation of the mentally retarded, which is all-important, must convey the experience that the daily work routine has vigor and meaning and, consequently, fills a proper part of the day. The afterwork satisfactions of leisure-time activities, whether they are for pure relaxation and fun or have more personal, educational implications, may sometimes take place in institutional or special settings, but for habilitational purposes, use should also be made of the facilities of the regular society, thus lending these activities realism. With wider experiences and proper social training, the retarded thus will be able to use the normal leisure-time facilities of his society on his own, and also learn to cope with unprepared, unstructured situations without panicking (Avedon, 1967; Chigier, 1967; Nirje, 1967).

3. Normalization means to experience the normal rhythm of the year, with holidays and family days of personal significance. Most people change their life situations and refresh their bodies and minds at least once a year by going on vacation. In Scandinavia, travel, including travel abroad, has proved meaningful and valuable even for the severely and profoundly retarded.

4. Normalization also means an opportunity to undergo normal developmental experiences of the life cycle:

a) Children should have available warmth of atmosphere, rich sensory stimulation and surroundings, and settings of proper proportions. Handicapped individuals especially need to be fed with stimuli which will nourish knowledge and abilities. In cases where a retarded child cannot live with his own family, this aspect is of special importance. In normal society, small children live in a world especially structured for them, guided and taught by a few significant adults. In child-care homes, turnover of personnel should be minimal, thus offering the children basic security and opportunities for identification of the stand-in parents. These essential demands have proved almost impossible to realize in large heterogeneous institutions, where one is confronted with the specific attitudes of the personnel and the adult retarded. It is therefore completely wrong to let mentally retarded children live in the same institutions as retarded adults.

b.) Youths of school age in normal society also live in a world specifically structured for them. Childhood is a highly developmental period of great importance for learning about one's own personal abilities and potentialities, for obtaining understanding of oneself, and for building self-confidence that can serve as a sound basis for life after the school years. It is also a period during which social experiences outside the classroom are very important for personal stimulation and development. Youngsters and adolescents of school age who are retarded should therefore never live in a confined setting together with mentally retarded adults, because the young people's socialization and impressions of life should be gained as much as possible through contacts with normal rather than a deviant society.

c.) For the mentally retarded, growing from adolescence into adulthood is often a longer, more painful, and more uncertain process than for others. Their image of themselves often becomes warped and confused. They are not always accepted, treated, and respected as adults. Here, the attitudes expressed toward them by others are of utmost importance, whether these others are parents, relatives, or institution personnel. Thus, like everybody else, the retarded should experience the coming of adulthood through marked changes in the settings and circumstances of their lives. Just as it is normal for children to live with their parents, so it is normal for adults to move away from home and start a life of their own, as independently as possible. Therefore, it is wrong for mentally retarded adults to live on the same premises as children and youngsters, because this serves as a constant reminder that they are different from other adults, and that they are as dependent as children. Training programs for retarded young adults should assist them to become as competent and independent in their personal daily routine as possible, and to develop social skills which will enable them to take part in the regular community life as much as they can.

d.) The period of old age, when work is no longer possible or feasible, consists for most people of contacts with the familiar settings and acquaintances that have given life so much of its content and meaning. Therefore, alternate living facilities for the aged retarded should be arranged close to the place where they have spent their adult periods of life, in case they cannot remain in that very place.

5. The normalization principle also means that the choices, wishes, and

desires of the mentally retarded themselves have to be taken into consideration as nearly as possible, and respected. In May 1968 a conference was
arranged for mentally retarded young adults, IQs about 35-70, from eight
cities in Sweden. In this conference, these young men and women, 18-30
years old, discussed vocational training and their leisure-time and vacation
problems. They wanted a stronger voice in their own leisure-time programs,
student clubs, and labor union participation. They objected to being included
in activities with children below the age of 15 or 16, and to being in too large
and too heterogeneous groups. In discussing group study tours and group
vacation trips, they stressed their demand to be only in small homogeneous
groups. They found communication in large groups unsuitable, as it is more
difficult to hear and understand what is being communicated. Obviously,
they had too often had the normal tourist experience of moving in herds.

6. Normalization also means living in a bisexual world. Accordingly, facilities should provide for male and female staff members. When it comes to the
integration of retarded boys and girls or men and women, the 1967 Stockholm Symposium on "Legislative Aspects of Mental Retardation" of the
International League of Societies for the Mentally Handicapped[1] came to the
following conclusion:

> "Being fully mindful of the need to preserve the necessary safeguards
> in the relations between mentally retarded men and women, the members
> of the Symposium are of the opinion that the dangers involved here have
> been greatly exaggerated in the past. This has often resulted in the
> unfortunate segregation of the sexes in an unnatural way and has mili-
> tated against their interests and proper development.
>
> "Accordingly, the Symposium strongly advocates the mixing of the
> sexes in a manner as free as is commensurate with normal restraints, not
> only in day centers and workshops, but also in leisure time activities.
>
> "Experience in some countries indicates the advantage of mixing men
> and women in hostels and other residential facilities in such a way as is
> approximate to normal life."

Mixing of the sexes according to the normal patterns of everyday society
results in better behavior and atmosphere, as more motivations are added.
And the mildly retarded sometimes suffer in a loneliness that has no sense,
and as others, they may be better off married.

7. A prerequisite to letting the retarded obtain an existence as close to
normal as possible is to apply normal economic standards. This implies both
giving the retarded those basic financial privileges available to others, through
common social legislation, as well as any other compensating economic

---

[1] The League is an international federation of associations of parents of the mentally
retarded. The symposium, published by the League, summarizes basic principles upon
which practices in the field of mental retardation should be based. These principles were
derived from a definition of the rights of the mentally retarded.

security measures that may be applicable. This includes child allowances, personal pensions, old age allowances, or minimum wages. Of these allowances, the larger part may be used for board and lodging, but a normal amount of pocket money for the individual's private use should be given regularly, both to assist in realistic social training and to help foster independent choices. Work that is done in competitive employment, in sheltered workshops, or within institutions should be paid for according to its relative worth.

8. An important part of the normalization principle implies that the standards of the physical facilities, e.g., hospitals, schools, group homes and hostels, and boarding homes, should be the same as those regularly applied in society to the same kind of facilities for ordinary citizens. Application of these standards to facilities of various types implies a number of important specifics:

a.) It means that the sizes of facilities should conform to what is normal and human in society. Especially, it should be kept in mind that a facility for the retarded should never be intended for a larger number of persons than the surrounding neighborhood readily assimilates in its regular everyday community life.

b.) It further implies that in planning the location of these facilities, they should never be placed in isolated settings merely because they are intended for the mentally retarded. With normal locations and normal sizes, facilities for the mentally retarded will give their residents better opportunities for successful integration.

SOME BENEFITS OF THE NORMALIZATION PROCESS

All the above-mentioned facets of the normalization principle make a normalization of the life situation of individual retardates quite feasible: the normalization process can aid many in achieving complete independence and social integration; a great number will be helped in developing relative independence though they may always need various kinds of assistance to various degrees; even the relatively few who are severely or profoundly retarded, or who are afflicted with complicating medical, psychological, or social handicaps will, no matter how dependent they may be, have life conditions, facilities, and services that follow the normal patterns of society.

For the retarded child, adolescent, and young adult, almost every situation has pedagogical implications, possibilities, and values. Just as the right of education is important for every citizen, so it is important for the mentally retarded to have a right to equal opportunities for education, training, and development.

Development of various abilities always has bearings on the development of the whole person. Development of the retarded therefore places particularly heavy responsibilities on persons in charge of the life conditions of the retarded. Mental retardation as a handicap creates especially high frustrations and hurdles for the individual, thereby making it even more urgent to assist and stimulate the retarded in the building up of his self-confidence.

Through stimulating and rich experiences, he can experience himself as an active agent while sensory deprivation imposes a further handicap. To develop a feeling of personal identity is an essential growth factor, and thus the experience of being nameless and anonymous is dangerous and damaging. The self-image of the retarded must be built on letting him experience his personal abilities; thus experience of rejection and disregard creates confusion, stress, and unhappiness.

To develop self-regard, the retarded person must learn how he can succeed through his efforts to cope and thereby to obtain experiences of responsibility. Thus, a too sheltered and barren environment which does not allow for personal activities too often leads to experiences of failure and of being without status and value. The development of a feeling of personal dignity can determine the degree of self-control established, while the experience of lack of regard from others is threatening and corroding.

All these factors coincide decisively when the retardate in his development comes to the state of accepting himself as an adult and as a responsible person with a realistic self-confidence. These points are the more important, as becoming adult for the mentally retarded also means coming to terms with his own awareness of being mentally retarded (Cobb, 1966).

As almost every situation for the mentally retarded has a pedagogical significance and often is related to his slow building up of a self-concept, it is essential that the mentally retarded should be offered appropriate facilities, which assist his educational processes and development and which make it possible for him to experience himself as becoming adult in his own eyes and in the eyes of others. This is a basic requirement for helping his life development come as close to the normal as possible.

Large institutions and the conditions we can observe in their back wards can never offer facilities of the kind and quality that are essential. In the large wards, the rhythm of the day reduces the retarded to an object in an empty, machinelike atmosphere. The normal rhythm of daily routines of occupation, leisure, and personal life is emasculated to surrogate activities, not integrated with a meaningful personal existence. The normal rhythm of the year is mostly dwarfed through the experience of monotonous confinement. The development of individuality is helplessly mutilated and crushed in a life in herds.

Application of normalization principles has profound implications not only to the retarded but also to the public, to those who work with the retarded, and to the parents of the retarded.

When residential facilities for mentally retarded children are constructed, located, operated, and interpreted as homes for children; when special schools for the mentally retarded are integrated into regular schools or are looked upon as no more than schools for children and youth; and when group homes and hostels for the adult retarded are looked upon mainly as homes for adults; then such direct and normal experiences will result in a normalization of society's attitudes toward the retarded. Isolation and segregation foster ignorance and prejudice, whereas integration and normalization of smaller groups of mentally retarded improve regular human relations and understanding, and generally are a prerequisite for the social integration of the individual.

Normalizing a mental retardation setting also normalizes the working conditions of the personnel. Workers perceive the retardate, his role, and their own roles in entirely different ways. In turn, the workers themselves are perceived differently by society. They enjoy a higher status and gain in self-respect. Almost always, an increase in work efficiency and effectiveness is one of the results.

Application of normalization principles also can serve to normalize the parents' situation. When residential centers, group homes, and schools of normal standards, sizes, and locations are available, as well as day centers and workshops, the parents of the retarded can choose placements according to the individual needs of the retarded person and the needs of the family. Their choice of placement can be accomplished freely and with an easier mind, rather than being an anguished and forced choice between the horrible and the impossible.

The closer persons in the decision-making bodies of society come to the mentally retarded, the more likely they are to render decisions resulting in appropriate and efficient programs. It may be sobering to many Americans that in Sweden, programs based on normalization principles are not dreams but actual realities brought about by the decisions of "hard-headed" penny-pinching county council appropriation committees. For those who are interested in how normalization principles have been embodied in Swedish legislation, details are provided in the Appendix.

REFERENCES

Avedon, E. M. Therapeutic recreation service and mentally retarded adolescents. Paper presented at the symposium on *The Adolescent Retardate*,

First Congress of the International Association for the Scientific Study of Mental Deficiency, Montpellier, France, 12-20 September 1967. Published by the Israel Association for Rehabilitation of the Mentally Handicapped (AKIM). Pp. 9-11.

Chigier, E. The use of group dynamics in the rehabilitation of severely retarded adolescents in an institution in Israel. Paper presented at the symposium of *The Adolescent Retardate*, First Congress of the International Association for the Scientific Study of Mental Deficiency, Montpellier, France, 12-20 September 1967. Published by the Israel Association for Rehabilitation of the Mentally Handicapped (AKIM). Pp. 1-4.

Cobb, H. V. The attitude of the retarded person towards himself. In International League of Societies for the Mentally Handicapped. *Stress on families of the mentally handicapped*. Brussels: ILSMH, 1967. Pp. 62-74.

International League of Societies for the Mentally Handicapped. *Legislative aspects of mental retardation*. Stockholm: ILSMH, 1967.

Nirje, B. Integrational Know-how: Swedish programs in social training. Paper presented at the Symposium on *The Adolescent Retardate*, First Congress of the International Association for the Scientific Study of Mental Deficiency, Montpellier, France, 12-20 September 1967. Published by the Israel Association for Rehabilitation of the Mentally Handicapped (AKIM). Pp. 5-8.

APPENDIX

The Normalization Principle in Swedish Law

The normalization principle has grown out of Scandinavian experiences in the field, both from mistakes and errors of the past as well as from planning and development of new and better programs. The new Swedish law on mental retardation, effective as of July 1, 1968, can be seen as an expression of the normalization principle. This "law about provisions and services for the mentally retarded," dated December 15, 1967, is printed in the Swedish Code of Statutes 1967 (Svensk Författningssamling), No. 940, published on January 31, 1968. The Law can be viewed as a Bill of Rights for the mentally retarded, being based on what their rights are believed to be. It provides for a wider range of services, and stresses that these services should be given to each retarded person according to his personal needs.

The new law is more comprehensive than the previous one of 1954, and covers a wider range of community services for the mentally retarded. It not only reflects developments which have actually taken place but also shows a new line of thought concerning what county councils must do to bring about radically improved conditions. Some sections of the law are summarized, discussed, and interpreted below.

Section 1: "This law concerns those who, due to retardation in their mental development, need special care and services from the community for their education, training, and integration in the community."

If there is a need for the provisions listed in the law, there is also a right to receive them. Through this general wording, it is possible to provide borderline cases, for instance, former wrongly placed students of remedial classes for slow learners, in the regular school system with the services they may need.

Mental retardation is not necessarily seen as a life-long condition. If, for instance, it is possible for a person to manage without the care and services of the community after special school and training for daily living, this person is no longer considered mentally retarded.

The previous law dealt mainly with the institutions the county councils had to establish. The new law has sections on both residential services and nonresidential services such as education and training. These provisions do not exclude but are complementary to one another.

Section 4: "Residential institutions, special hospitals, day centers for children, and occupational centers shall be provided for the care of the mentally retarded, and there shall be special residential institutions for those mentally retarded who need care in residential institutions with special arrangements.

"Mentally retarded who need care according to this law, but who do not need care in an institution as referred to above in the first section, shall be provided with care in their own homes."

Thus, mentally retarded who live with their parents shall have access to day centers for children, or occupational centers for adults, with the care, training, and therapy being equal to the standards of good residential care institutions. The county councils have so far concentrated on various residential facilities, but a great deal has to be accomplished in Sweden in order to surpass, for instance, England in the matter of developing and extending nonresidential service facilities.

The right to be provided with services at home—involving one or several persons who visit the home regularly to give care and provide training or occupational activities—will, of course, serve as an additional spur to the county councils to invest in day centers and occupational centers.

Section 4 has been written so that parents, so far as possible, will be free to choose between different services and be able to decide on either care within or outside the home, according to the estimated needs of the mentally retarded and the family circumstances.

Section 5 contains one of the great new features of the law:

Section 5: "Accommodation in other private homes, boarding homes or student hostels shall be provided for those mentally retarded who cannot stay in their own homes but who do not need to live in a residential care institution or a special hospital."

Those who do not need to live in residential institutions should not. It is just as normal for an adult to live as independently as possible as it is for a child to live with his parents. Thus, society has to provide other accommodations as close to normal as possible. This rule is of special interest to older parents whose retarded children have grown up and can manage without too much supervision. In the future, there will be boarding homes not only for those working on the open market but also for those working in sheltered workshops or occupational centers who can manage without the more extensive care provided by a modern residential institution.

All the mentally retarded below school age have a right to preschool training. At age seven, compulsory school starts and includes both "educable" programs for the mildly and some of the moderately retarded children (I.Q.s between about 45 and 70) and "trainable" programs for most of the moderately and some of the severely retarded (I.Q.s between about 25 and 50). Education is to be given for 10 years, followed by compulsory vocational school attendance up to age 21, which can be prolonged to age 23 in certain instances. Relevant sections of the law follow:

Section 24: "Special school attendance is compulsory for mentally retarded who can profit from education, but who are unable to participate in educational training within the general education scheme.

"Such compulsory education starts from the autumn term of the calendar year when he will be seven years old, and lasts as long as he needs training, although not longer than up to and including the spring term of the calendar year when he will be 21. However, if there are exceptional reasons, this compulsory education may be prolonged up to and including the spring term of the calendar year when he will be 23."

Section 3: "School education is provided for the mentally retarded in special schools, where they also shall receive personal and medical care as needed. Special schooling includes preschool, provision for the educable and trainable, vocational training, or several of these.

"Separate classes or schools shall be provided for those mentally retarded who are able to attend special education but have difficulties in adjusting to the activities of the school, or who need special arrangements for their education. Mentally retarded who are unable to participate in the regular work of the special school, due to motor difficulties, sensory handicaps, long periods of illness, or similar circumstances, shall be provided with educational forms specially adjusted to them."

It should be noted that compulsory education, i.e., the right to receive special school education, includes children residing in institutions and special hospitals.

Preschool education prior to the age of 7 is defined as a right of the child, but not compulsory to him. All mentally retarded children who can make use of preschool training have a right to receive it, regardless if they might later be compelled to attend special school or not. Early training is fundamental for mentally retarded children, and the county councils are counted upon to work actively in tracing these children.

The education given in educable programs (I.Q.s 45-70) as well as in trainable programs (I.Q.s 25-50) is intended for the ages 7-17. A new provision here concerns trainable programs intended for children who are unable to participate in educable programs, but who can make use of practical education and social training.

The right to attend school, as well as compulsory school duty, will in this way finally be implemented for those children who have, until now, been referred to "practical" classes or day centers, or who have not received any education and training at all. As a consequence of this rule, trainable programs will also be established at residential institutions for children. In other words, the law has made mandatory what is considered "trainable" education in the United States.

The autumn term of 1968 will then mean compulsory school for a larger number of retarded children and youths between ages 7 and 20 who previously did not receive any education and training at all. The county councils have a big task here. To begin with, a number of provisional measures must, of course, be approved by the authorities, but the essential fact is that there is a compulsory school duty in force from July 1, 1968. As far as the enforcement is concerned, the law, in Section 2, states: "The county council communities shall provide the mentally retarded residing within the county council community with education, care and other services made mandatory by this law, insofar as someone else does not provide for it." Section 6 states that "the activities of the county council community shall be administered in accordance with this law by a Board for the provisions for the mentally retarded. A committee which handles other administrative tasks of the county council community may be appointed to such a board." "Such Boards of provisions for the mentally retarded shall include appointments of a head of special schools, a head of care facilities, and a head physician."

Section 8 decrees that "the county council community shall draw up a plan for organizing provisions and services for the mentally retarded. This plan shall include the facilities needed for the mentally retarded." The plan shall be authorized by the King or by an authority appointed by the King. In accordance with Section 13, the Board of Education and the Board of Health and Social Welfare are the authorities responsible for the supervision of the actual implementation of the activities in accordance with the law.

Section 16 contains a summary of the tasks of the Boards for provisions:

Section 16: "The Board for the provisions and services for the mentally retarded shall:

> work towards the attainment of the provisions needed by the mentally retarded residing within the county council community;
>
> plan and coordinate the activities of the county council community according to the law, and work towards the satisfactory development of the law;
>
> administer the facilities for the retarded which are under their management and other activities for them which are managed by the county council community, if not otherwise governed according to the second, third, and fourth paragraph of Section 6;
>
> take charge of the local supervision of other facilities for the retarded according to the more detailed instructions given by the King;
>
> bring before the county councils those proposals which concern provisions for the retarded as they are found to be needed."

This "energy section" of the law aims at actively engaging the Board for provisions and services for the benefit of all retarded in need of the provisions ensured to them by this law. A prerequisite for this is the dissemination of information, and active cooperation with child care centers, agencies working with the mental hygiene of children and youths, district physicians, district nurses, children's hospitals and child clinics, Swedish parents' association for the retarded, etc. The Boards for provisions shall also be responsible for the development of services in a satisfactory manner, as, for instance, the supply and training of personnel, and the application of new methods and practices in the training of the retarded and their integration into the community.

The old painful system of registration is eliminated; the new procedure will be to register at the residential institution or special hospital of residence or in the school attended. In the rest of all cases, only the Boards for provisions will only keep a record of all known mentally retarded and will there make a notice of the different kinds of provisions supplied in each special case.

While the Swedish law offers a basis for the creation of decentralized, differentiated, specialized smaller institutions, hostels, and boarding homes for the retarded, some conditions still exist in Sweden that are not consistent with the normalization principle. For example, there are still about half a dozen institutions for more than 400 persons, the largest having as many as 740 residents. These institutions, as well as some in the 200–400 range, are institutions for heterogeneous age groups from early childhood to senescence, and two of them still even have special schools on the grounds. (All the other 25 special boarding schools have independent locations.)

More than half of the mentally retarded living in institutions in Sweden do so in facilities built after 1954, when a special law on mental retardation services was enacted. These newer institutions usually provide single and double bedrooms, and occasionally 4-bed rooms. Most of the older institutions have been modernized and rearranged according to modern standards. However, there still are a few deplorable regional institutions in Sweden where the retarded have to live as many as 10 to a room, with large, inadequate dayrooms which serve as many as 25 or 30 persons. These institutions are satisfying neither to the retarded nor to the Swedish parents— nor, for that matter, to the authorities.

There are also institutions which, even with modern communications, remain isolated from the mainstream of community life. One of the main conclusions of the previously mentioned Stockholm Symposium was "that facilities for retarded persons should not be situated in remote or secluded areas, which preclude the essential contact between them and the community and which would prevent their complete integration in society."

With regard to residential accommodations, the following conclusion was reached:

"The Symposium recommends that each country should determine and proclaim the desirable standards of accommodation for mentally retarded persons having regard to the following considerations:
1. that the structure of each facility planned should take into account the special needs of mentally retarded persons;
2. that facilities should not be sited in isolation, nor planned in such a manner that the mentally retarded persons for whom they are intended, would be deprived of normal contacts with the community;
3. that while there are differences of opinion as to the optimum size of multi-purpose complexes, such as residential centers which incorporate education, training and treatment functions, there is general agreement:
a.) that it is much more difficult to fulfill the rehabilitation programme in all its aspects in a big institution than in a relatively smaller one;
b.) that the living, dining and recreational units of such complexes should be small, with living accommodation for numbers not exceeding some 15 to 20 persons;
c.) that, on the other hand, there is a necessity to determine a minimum size for each facility, commensurate with its purpose and special needs;
"It has been the experience, at least in the Scandinavian countries that large institutions tend to counteract the social integration of the mentally retarded person and militate against his individual needs for education and training and that, further in the relationship between effect and cost, the smaller unit is preferable and more economical in the final analysis."

The Symposium also stressed the necessity to ensure implementation and concluded:

"Each country should formulate and put into effect that system of control best suited to its governmental structure, in order to exercise supervision of the implementation of legal measures regarding the care, education, training and employment of retarded persons. The aims of such control should be: (*a*) to ensure that full coverage is provided for the retarded population, and that every retarded person regardless of his personal means or those of his parents or guardians is provided with the facilities which he needs; (*b*) to ensure that the standards of facilities provided are adequate and that all services conform to the standards promulgated."

Both our service structures and our service concepts must continually evolve. It is hoped that Swedish provisions will improve further so as to be fully consistent with the Stockholm and normalization principles. It is further hoped that by that time, there will be even more advanced principles to challenge us.

COMMUNITY
ADJUSTMENT
OF
INSTITUTIONALIZED
RETARDATES

Gerald R. Clark, Marvin S. Kivitz,
Marvin Rosen, and Earl A. Wilkie

This paper was the initial report of the adjustment of a group of Elwyn Institute residents discharged to independent living and competitive work situations in the community. From 1964 to 1968, this study was supported in part by Federal Research and Demonstration Grant funds from the Vocational Rehabilitation Administration (Project No. RD-1275-P). The favorable adjustment of subjects studied in this project was an important factor in helping to change a traditionally custodial institution into one emphasizing vocational and social rehabilitation programs. Elwyn has served as a model for other institutions and the follow-up study has been continued over a ten-year period. Elwyn Institute was the recipient of the Gold Medal Award of the American Psychiatric Association in 1972, for innovative programming in vocational training and rehabilitation that has "prepared hundreds of mentally handicapped people to live and work in the community."

In 1964 Elwyn Institute undertook a special project to demonstrate the feasibility of preparing institutionalized orphans and abandoned mentally retarded adults for independent community living. It was hoped that systematic study and feedback would enable the staff to continually improve their understanding and to modify the program to increase its effectiveness. Encouraged by the results of the Monyhull Program in England (Gunzburg, 1960), a broad range of rehabilitation services were developed.

A. THREE ARE SEVEN MAJOR PHASES IN THIS TRANSITIONAL PROGRAM. THESE INCLUDE:

1. Preliminary Appraisal

All subjects are given a comprehensive battery of psychological tests that cover a wide spectrum of psychological variables and include measures that other studies have reported as predictors of vocational and social adjustment. A special assessment feature measures functioning in nine practical areas such as monetary knowledge, measurement, time concepts, job application scale, telephone, and transportation knowledge.

2. Adult Education

This includes training in social and academic skills considered essential for independent living.

3. Pre-industrial Experience

This phase is designed to provide training in proper work habits and attitudes and to provide exposure to a wide range of trades that are suitable for the

Presented at the First Congress of the International Association for the Scientific Study of Mental Deficiency, Montpellier, France, September 18, 1967.

Dr. Clark has served as superintendent and president of Elwyn Institute since 1960. He was Pennsylvania Physician of the Year in 1969, and recipient of the United States Physicians Award in 1970. In addition to his responsibilities at Elwyn Institute, Dr. Clark is senior physician at Children's Hospital of Philadelphia and professor of psychiatry and pediatrics at the University of Pennsylvania. Dr. Kivitz is a clinical psychologist who has been director of education and training at Elwyn Institute since 1961. He is also consultant to the Delaware Country Association for Retarded Children and the United States Office of Education. He serves as vice president of the American Association on Mental Deficiency for the Vocational Rehabilitation Division and is consulting editor to the American Journal on Mental Deficiency. Dr. Rosen has been director of psychology at Elwyn Institute since 1963. He was research coordinator of the follow-up investigation described in this paper. Mr. Wilkie has been an essential member of the rehabilitation teams at Elwyn Institute since 1961. He is currently director of education and principal of Elwyn's work-study program.

mentally retarded. A sheltered workshop, which exists as part of the institution, is also utilized (Clark et al, 1963).

4. Vocational Program

This consists of 15 trade training courses in unskilled or semi-skilled occupations suitable for the retarded and licensed by the State of Pennsylvania.

5. Community Work—Halfway House Program

After completing trade training, the student is assisted in obtaining community employment. While working full time in the community, he continues to reside in special facilities at Elwyn Institute. He is given increasing freedom and responsibility, while supported by counseling and adjustment training.

6. Community Placement

After successfully completing the community work program, students are aided in obtaining suitable housing and employment before discharge from the institution. At the time of this report 72 persons have been discharged to independent community living.

7. Follow-up and Continuing Contact

All graduates are seen at least twice a year in their homes. Formal rating procedures are conducted at six-month intervals during the first year and annually thereafter. They cover a broad range of topics such as personal information, housing and possessions, economic characteristics, social characteristics, vocational characteristics, attitudes and self-perception, and rater estimates of overall adjustment.

B. DATA ANALYSIS AND PRELIMINARY RESULTS

1. The Graduate Population

The 72 subjects in the community are predominately male (81%). Racially, the group is 90% Caucasian and 10% Negro. Subjects were either orphaned or had families who were inadequate, incapacitated, or unwilling to accept the individual after discharge from Elwyn.

The majority had originally been referred to Elwyn as children from public agencies, orphanages, or other institutions and were enrolled as state-supported students. Their average age at admission was twelve years. None of the subjects was diagnosed upon admission as having severe emotional disturbance or psychosis. However, almost the entire group were admitted with diagnoses of feeble-mindedness, most in the "Moron" category. Their average I.Q., upon admission, was 63.9, but the range was as low as 41. Terms such as "Moral Defective" were frequently applied to those who presented management or behavior problems. Guarded prognosis and recommendation of life-long institutionalization appear in over 80% of their records.

At the time of their discharge, the average age of the subjects was twenty-eight. The average length of institutionalization was 15 years, ranging from 3 to 49 years. The average IQ was 72.6. All had severe education deficits; the majority were functioning below a fourth grade reading level. Nine of the subjects had gross physical anomaly (such as atrophied arm, hunchback, or microcephaly). Sixty-five graduate subjects now reside in Pennsylvania, five have moved to other states and are still being followed, two have been inducted into military service.

2. Preliminary Data Analysis

Repeated interviews and ratings of the same subjects yearly permit study of the process of community adjustment as a function of time since leaving the institution. Although the results obtained to date have, of necessity, utilized relatively small numbers because of the time sequence analyses, statistical trends already seem to be developing. These are summarized by vocational, economic, and social characteristics and as related to earlier institutional adjustment.

a) Vocational Characteristics. All but two of the 72 discharged subjects have worked steadily since discharge or worked until they became housewives. Their jobs are primarily in unskilled or semi-skilled occupations in personal, food, or building services. The complete listing of their occupations corresponds roughly with those described in other studies as suitable for the retarded (Strickland, 1964). Their median gross annual income after one year, ten months (median) in the community is $2,867, as compared with $3,391 for the United States population as a whole (1963). Their earnings correspond to that of the lowest third of the population according to published census information but are higher than the limits of poverty income defined by the Economic Report of the President (1967). Seventy-two percent of the group at the time of interview were earning higher salaries than their initial salaries after discharge.

Twenty-five percent of the group had experienced some period of unemployment since leaving the institution. None of these had been unemployed long enough to require unemployment compensation during this time. While initial positions had been obtained through the institution, job changes were usually effected by the individual's own efforts through newspaper want ads, friends, or the State Employment Security Office, using methods learned in Adult Education Classes in the institution. Subjects tended to stay in the same general type of occupation as their initial job placement and these corresponded to the area of their institutional training in 80% of the cases studied. Less than one-quarter of the subjects had made more than one job change in the one-to-two-year period of independent living.

The Minnesota Employment Satisfaction Scale (Carlson, 1962) was used to provide information about the worker's general job satisfaction and his attitudes toward various aspects of his employment situation. Analysis thus far indicates that differences between the Elwyn subjects and a Minnesota handicapped (non-retarded) group are not significant. However, Elwyn subjects were less satisfied than a Minnesota group of normal (non-handicapped) controls. Highest satisfaction scores occurred with measures reflecting satisfaction with the supervision they receive on the job, with their co-workers, and with their working conditions. Lowest satisfaction scores occurred on measures dealing with their earnings and their social positions in their companies. The group was also almost unanimous in selecting compensation as the most important job characteristic, a finding which is in direct contrast with trends reported for normal workers who usually rate security as most important (Viteles, 1953; Vroom, 1964).

b) Economic characteristics. Sixty-eight percent of the group live in rented apartments; the median rent paid per month is approximately $60. All the units are at least adequately furnished with items necessary for comfortable living. The most commonly owned appliances are radios and television sets. About 85% of the group have active bank accounts, with a general trend of decreasing savings since leaving the institution, due to the purchase of furniture and clothing. About one-third of the group have purchased second-hand automobiles, and about three-quarters have some form of life insurance, either through their jobs or by individual policies.

c) Social Adjustment. None of the subjects in the community have required re-institutionalization. Twenty-six percent of the group have married since returning to the community. Most of these have married persons who are also previously Elwyn graduates. Six of the married couples have had children; a seventh couple is also expecting a child. All of the children appear to be receiving appropriate pediatric care; thus far, none has been diagnosed as mentally retarded. Only one person has experienced serious legal difficulty. He was charged with rape, but the case was dropped when it was revealed that the incident involved mutal compliance. The subject obtained legal counsel from the Legal Aid Society through methods taught in the Adult Education

Program. One female gave birth to an illegitimate child. She was helped by a Welfare Agency, eventually married the natural father, and is caring for the child.

As a group, the subjects are doing an adequate job in handling housekeeping, personal hygiene, health, and medical care, money and financial care, transportation, and everyday decision-making. When asked to indicate problem areas in personal management, more than half the sample studied reported difficulties in budgeting finances, saving money, controlling their temper, and using profanity. Subjects expressed a high degree of satisfaction with their living arrangements and their neighbors.

Ratings of psychiatric symptomatology based on the Katz Adjustment Scale (Katz and Lyerly, 1963) revealed few reported problem areas. These were limited to such things as "Feels lonely," Feels restless," "Gets nervous or upset." Thus far, no graduate has required psychiatric help.

Subjects spend their leisure time watching TV, going to the movies, or visiting and entertaining friends. Approximately 50% of the subjects report that they attend church services sporadically; approximately one-third are church members. Several subjects expressed a desire to become church members, but were shy about doing so. Arrangements were made through the Council of Churches to introduce discharged persons who so desired to congregations of their choice.

d) Measures of Institutional Functioning. Test re-test reliability was determined for the Scale of Employability, the Work Evaluation Scale, and the Global Rating Scale for periods of six months and one year. As initially planned, these ratings were performed by service-oriented work supervisors, who varied greatly as to degree of sophistication and cooperation. Because job assignments frequently changed from one rating to another, and because there was a high turnover of work supervisors, the second rating was often performed by a different person than the original rater. Under these circumstances, reliabilities of the scales were relatively high when the same rater was involved and were poor when different raters were used. Because of these considerations, Training Coordinators, who are responsible for job assignments within the institution, were used as raters. These persons are more stable in job tenure, more aware of research needs, and are familiar with the students. Ratings are based on interviews with the job supervisors and on-the-job observations of the students. Inter-rater reliabilities of these ratings have proven to be high.

Intercorrelations between the Work Evaluation Scale and the Scale of Employability were high on the same rating occasion and both correlated highly with a Global Rating question ("What are this person's chances for leaving Elwyn to live and work in the community?"). Correlations between both work evaluation scales and the Interpersonal Scale, completed by house-parents, were low, suggesting that two separate dimensions of institutional functioning were being rated.

3. Discussion and Evaluation

Since the inception of the project, 72 persons have returned to independent community living. Despite prolonged institutionalization up to 49 years, physical deformities and handicaps, I.Q. as low as 48, and severe educational deficits as low as first grade level, none of these persons have thus far had to be re-institutionalized. In addition to humanitarian considerations and the contribution to society these graduates are making, a tremendous financial saving has already been realized. At Elwyn's current tuition rate of $3,600 per year, the 72 graduates represent a savings to the taxpayer of approximately $260,000 for each year they remain out of the institution.

Students experiencing difficulty after discharge usually have problems of social adjustment rather than inadequacies in job performance. For example, a female graduate entrusted all her savings to her boyfriend who then deserted her; a male graduate was fired from his department store position for a minor shoplifting offense. Despite such problems, subjects were usually able to cope with the situation without intervention of the institution. They have thus far displayed ability to handle legal matters, unemployment, housing, driving, and marriage.

In addition to providing services to the subject population, the project has been of value to non-orphaned retarded within the institution who now have improved rehabilitation services available to them. Many parents who were formerly unwilling to accept their children in their homes have had a marked attitude change as a result of seeing them perform successfully in the Community Work Program. Thus, eight subjects initially considered abandoned at the beginning of the program were omitted for statistical purposes of the research when their families demonstrated a willingness to accept them back in the home.

Because Elwyn's program is multi-phased and has been in existence a relatively brief time, it is difficult to pinpoint the specific factors that contribute most to the favorable outcomes obtained. One major factor is undoubtedly the gradual transition process and continuing evaluation during every phase of the program. For example, the Community Work Program allows a trial period of six months to one year of on-the-job experience in the community, while the individual still resides within the institution. During this time a student may be withdrawn if his performance is unsatisfactory. In this case, an individual is provided with remedial training geared to his specific deficits and is often given a second and third trial. Of 114 persons entering the

Community Work Program over the first three years of the project, twenty-six persons were withdrawn for vocational or social inadequacies. After remediation training, ten of these subsequently re-entered the program and are now discharged, and five are reinstated in the Community Work Program. Elevan others are still receiving remediation training. Seventy-two subjects have graduated and 31 are still residing at Elwyn. Thus, there is a success ratio for the Community Work Placement of approximately 89%.

Thus far, the success of these individuals in remaining out of the institution supports the conclusion that this type of program can be applied to the traditionally custodial institution with a high expectation of success.

REFERENCES

Carlson, R. E., Davis, R. V., England, G. W., and Lofquist, L. H. The measurement of employment satisfaction. *Minnesota studies in vocational rehabilitation:* XIII, University of Minnesota, 1962, Bulletin No. 35.

Clark, G. R., Kivitz, M. S., and Landon, H. J. New vistas in rehabilitation of the mentally retarded. *Pennsylvania Psychiatric Quarterly,* Fall, 1963.

Economic Report of the President. U. S. Government Printing Office, 1967.

Gunzburg, H. C. *Social rehabilitation of the mentally retarded.* London: Bailliere, Tindall & Cox, 1960.

Katz, M. M. and Lyerly, S. B. Methods for measuring adjustment and social behavior in the community: 1. Rationale, description, discriminative validity and scale development. *Psychological Reports,* Monograph Supplement, 4-13, 1963.

Strickland, C. G. Job training placement for retarded youth. *Exceptional Children,* 1964, 31, 83-86.

Viteles, M. S. *Motivation and morale in industry.* New York: Norton, 1935, 302-306.

Vroom, V. H. *Work and Motivation.* New York: Wiley, 1964.

EVALUATION
OF
OPERANT
CONDITIONING
WITH
INSTITUTIONALIZED
RETARDED
CHILDREN

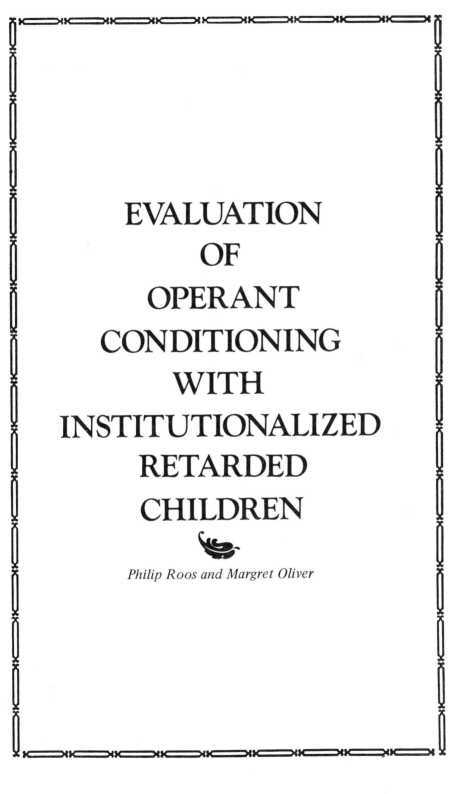

Philip Roos and Margret Oliver

The following is the abstract that accompanied the paper. "The effectiveness of operant conditioning procedures implemented by attendants was evaluated by comparing the progress of three groups of severely and profoundly retarded institutionalized young children. In addition to the experimental and control groups, a placebo group, which received classroom-type training, was included. The results indicated significantly greater improvement in the group trained by operant conditioning."

Reports of the application of operant conditioning procedures to mentally retarded subjects have appeared with increasing frequency during recent years (Watson, 1967). Particular emphasis has been placed on development of self-help skills in severely and profoundly retarded institutionalized children (Bensberg, Colwell, and Cassel, 1965; Giles and Wolf, 1966; Gorton and Hollis, 1965; Kimbrell, Luckey, Bartuto, and Love, 1967; Roos, 1965; Watson, 1966). Reports have generally been encouraging, but there has been a general paucity of objective, controlled studies. Most reports have described changes in research subjects without reference to comparison groups. Since operant conditioning programs have typically been accompanied by marked interest in the "experimental ward" as well as significant enrichment in staffing, it becomes difficult to attribute observed changes to the operant conditioning procedures as opposed to the demonstrated Hawthorne effect and the impact of improved staff-resident ratios (Blackwood, 1962). The study by Kimbrell et al. (1967) did include a control group, but since the group received no special attention or treatment, it did not control effectively for the Hawthorne or the placebo effects.

This study[1] was conducted to test the hypothesis that profoundly and severely retarded children would show greater improvement in self-help skills when trained by operant conditioning procedures than when trained by more traditional procedures or than when receiving no special training. By including a group which received a great deal of attention as well as a special training program ("placebo group"), this investigation permitted a more rigid evaluation of operant conditioning procedures than those reported to date.

METHOD

Subjects

Children were assigned to the 30-bed operant conditioning unit (E group) when they met the following criteria: (a) age between 6 and 12 years, (b) functioning at Level IV of Adaptive Behavior (Heber, 1961), (c) ambulatory, (d) some ability to use hands for manipulation of objects, (e) ability to chew and swallow, (f) at least a minimal degree of vision and hearing, and (g) "good

[1] Appreciation is expressed to James Hawker of Lamar State College of Technology for valuable assistance in the statistical treatment of the data.

American Journal of Mental Deficiency, 1969, 74(3): 325–330. Reprinted by permission of the author and the American Association on Mental Deficiency.
    Dr. Roos is executive director of the National Association for Retarded Citizens. Margret Oliver was the principal of the Austin State School, Austin, Texas.

average health" (i.e., absence of incapacitating physical conditions as judged by a physician). Control subjects included all residents on two 36-bed units judged to be equivalent in resident composition and physical facilities to the E group (in fact, the physical plant was considerably newer and better equipped than the building housing the E group). Residents on each of these two units were randomly assigned to the placebo group (P group) and to the control group (C group).

At the completion of the first year of the program, attrition had reduced the original sample so that 20 subjects remained in the E group (9 boys and 11 girls, mean social quotient (S.Q.) = 16.35, mean age = 9.64 years), 22 subjects remained in the P group (16 boys and 6 girls, mean S.Q. = 34.41, mean age = 6.64 years), and 12 subjects remained in the C group (9 boys and 3 girls, mean S.Q. = 26.42, mean age = 7.28 years). The relatively large attrition rate can be explained as the result of frequent transfers from Austin State School to other state institutions, since Austin State is the admission center for three other facilities. Transfers to other instituitions were based on the geographical residence of the children's parents and/or the suitability of vacancies in other institutions. There did not appear to be any systematic bias in the production of attrition. The total group size for each of the units remained relatively constant throughout the study since discharged residents were replaced rapidly, but of the 102 children residing on the three research units, only 54 were included in the study as having been in the program a full year.

Procedure

The operant conditioning program was implemented by attendants who had participated in a preliminary training workshop. Consultation was available from psychologists, nurses, and members of the inservice training department throughout the study. Weekly staff meetings were held for all attendants on the morning and afternoon shifts to discuss individual children and general training problems.

The E group was divided into four subgroups, each of which was assigned to a specific attendant who was responsible for the training and supervision of all children in her subgroup. All attendants serving a given subgroup wore a distinctively colored apron to facilitate the children's identification of "their" attendant. In general, four attendants were available during the morning and afternoon shifts, but only two were present during the night shift. Detailed schedules were developed outlining ward activities for each of the three shifts. Each child was scheduled for two individual training sessions daily, each lasting from 5 to 15 minutes. In addition, all children participated in group training activities, such as toileting and feeding, and were included in recreational activities, such as marching, taking walks, and using a wading pool. Each child averaged between 3 and 4 hours per day in training activities, but only 10 to 20 minutes of this time was spent in individual training.

Attempts were made to modify the environment to facilitate training. For example, swivel spoons and spoons with adhesive bands were used with some children, bathroom doors were color-coded (pink for girls and blue for boys), color-coded feeding tables were designed so that eight children could be easily monitored by one attendant (who sat in a chair equipped with coasters in the center of two semicircular tables), loose fitting clothing with large head holes and sleeves were used, mirrors were installed in the dayroom, etc.

The training program has been described elsewhere (Roos, 1965), and details of the specific procedures are available (Patterson and Overbeck, 1968). Training was based on positive reinforcement, using both primary and social reinforcers. The specific reinforcers were selected by the attendants to meet the needs of individual children. Primary reinforcement was always paired with social praise, and in some cases was replaced by social praise. Desserts were withheld from some meals (noncontingently) to enhance the desirability of some reinforcers. Play with a favorite toy, access to a wading pool, play outside, and other desired activities were also used selectively as reinforcers. Elimination of undesired behavior was attempted through extinction and judicious use of a "time-out" procedure, i.e., removing the subject from the opportunity to obtain reinforcement when the undesirable behavior occurs (Hamilton, Stephens, and Allen, 1966). Aversive conditioning was not used.

Complex behaviors, such as dressing, were developed using the principle of successive approximation and chaining (Watson, 1967). Behavior was brought under stimulus control by consistently using the same simple commands and distinctive gestures to obtain specific behaviors.

Primary emphasis was placed on development of self-help skills. Patterson and Overbeck (1968) have described the procedures used in detail. Toilet training and self-dressing skills were developed using the general approach described by Bensberg et al. (1965). Self-feeding procedures generally followed those reported by Gorton and Hollis (1965). Attempts were also made to develop socially desirable behaviors (e.g., self-grooming, social play, interaction with adults) and, in a few cases, to develop simple language.

The program developed for the P group was based on current theory and practice in special education. The objectives of the training were similar to the objectives for the E group, including development of self-help skills, refining motor control, development of social skills, and development of communication. Two teachers, experienced in teaching trainable mental retardates, were assigned to the project. Curricula were developed by the teachers in collaboration with the principal, and were based on the works of Frostig and Horne (1964), Kephart (1960), Gaston (1956), Fitzgerald (1949), Strauss and Lehtinen (1947), and Montessori (1912). Music activities were an important part of the program (Gaston, 1956). Classes were held from 8:30 a.m. until 3:15 p.m. in a well-equipped classroom located on the dormitory. At the outset of the program, subjects were assigned to groups of two or three, meeting 5 days per week for 30 minutes each day. Classes were gradually increased in size and duration, so that by the end of the program one class included 10 students meeting for 1½ hours each day of the week (one class of 2 still met for 30 minutes five times a week). Periodic meetings were held between teachers and attendants, and the latter were familiarized with training goals and procedures and were encouraged to apply them in daily work with the children.

The C group was housed in the same living units as the P group, i.e., roughly half of the children on each of the two dormitories were in the P group and half were in the C group. With the exception of the systematic classroom program, both groups participated in the same activities. The program included, principally, recreational activities, musical activities, and training efforts by attendants aimed at developing self-help and social skills. The attendants' training efforts were not systemized, but rather, were representative of the types of endeavors traditionally found on most living units of the institution. Although no rigid schedule was followed, approximately 3 to 4 hours per day were devoted to these activities.

All subjects were rated on the Pinecrest Modification of the Vineland Social Maturity Scale (Pinecrest, 1963) prior to the onset of the program, after approximately six months, and finally, after completion of one year in the program. This scale was standardized at Pinecrest State School on a population of young, profoundly and severely retarded, institutionalized residents. Ratings were completed both by the attendants assigned to the morning shift and independently by attendants assigned to the afternoon shift. Subjects in the P group were also rated by their classroom teachers.

Methods of Analysis

Ratings were analyzed using a repeated-measures analysis of variance to test for significant main effects and interactions. In those cases where an overall significant effect was found, Turkey's Q technique (Snedecor, 1956, pp. 251–253) was used to test for significance of differences among group means.

RESULTS AND DISCUSSION

The data were first analyzed by a 2 × 3 × 3 repeated-measures factorial design (Shifts × Groups × Rating Sessions). This analysis revealed that ratings made by the morning shift were consistently higher than those made by the afternoon shift. Reliability of these ratings was indicated by lack of a significant Group × Shift interaction and lack of a significant Group × Shift × Time interaction. Further evidence of rater reliability was obtained by noting close agreement between attendant and teacher ratings of the P subjects. A comparison of teacher and attendant ratings yielded an F ratio less than 1.00. Correlations between ratings were high and statistically significant (+.85). In view of these findings, further analyses were based on the ratings of the morning shift. Analyses based on the afternoon shift ratings yielded essentially identical results and are therefore not reported here.

A summary of the Vineland total scores for each of the groups at the time of each of the rating sessions is presented in Table I.

Table II presents a 3 × 3 repeated-measures analysis of variance of the data. It is apparent that there were no significant overall differences among the three groups ($F = 1.51$, $df = 2/108$, $p < .05$), but that the ratings increased significantly over sessions ($F = 12.50$, $df = 2/102$, $p < .01$). Of particular importance is the finding that the rate of increase varied for the three groups as indicated by the significant Session × Group interaction ($F = 4.66$, $df = 4/102$, $p < .01$).

In order to determine significant group differences at each rating session, analyses were conducted on each individual rating session, as summarized in Table III. These data indicate significant group differences for rating sessions 1 and 2, but not for session 3. Figure 1 depicts the relationship of group means at each rating session. Tukey's Q technique was used to determine the significance of differences among group means. The results of these analyses were as follows: (a) During session 1, the P and C groups did not differ, the E and C groups did not differ, but the P group was significantly higher than the

Table I. Means and standard deviations of Vineland scores of the three groups over three sessions

Group	N	Vineland scores			
		Session 1	Session 2	Session 3	Gain scores sessions 1–3
Experimental	20				
mean		38.50	59.95	58.90	20.40
standard deviation		10.82	17.01	14.18	11.99
Placebo	22				
mean		52.45	54.68	59.41	6.96
standard deviation		15.46	13.95	19.56	17.91
Control	12				
mean		42.25	41.92	53.00	7.75
standard deviation		21.34	14.84	16.93	14.35

Table II. Analysis of variance of Vineland scores

Source	Degrees of freedom	Mean square	F
Between subjects	(53)		
groups (G)	2	900.53	1.51
error (b)	51	579.70	
Within subjects	(108)		
sessions (S)	2	2,056.22	12.50**
S X G	4	766.91	4.66**
error (w)	102	164.53	
Total	161		

**$p<.01$.

E group. (*b*) During session 2, the E and P groups did not differ, but both were significantly higher than the C group. (*c*) During session 3, the groups did not differ.

These analyses suggest that the E group showed much greater improvement than did either of the other two groups. Hence a further analysis was done on the gain scores from rating session 1 to session 3 (the mean gains for each group are presented in Table I). This analysis, presented in Table IV, revealed that the groups did differ significantly in amount of gain ($F = 4.76$, $df = 2/51, p < .05$). Tukey's Q technique further indicated that the amount of gain of the E group (mean = 20.40) was significantly greater than the gain of the P (mean = 6.96) and C (mean = 7.17) groups, and that the latter two groups did not differ significantly. These analyses clearly indicate significantly greater improvement in the E group than in the other two groups.

Figure 1 suggests that the greatest gains by the E group were made during the first 6 months, and a slight decrease is noted during the remainder of the study. This finding suggests the possibility that operant conditioning proce-

Table III. Summary of analysis of variance for individual rating sessions

Source	Degrees of freedom	Session 1 Mean square	F	Session 2 Mean square	F	Session 3 Mean square	F
Between	2	1,021.48	4.50*	1,234.07	5.24**	178.82	< 1.00
Within	51	226.90		235.42		294.22	

*$p < .05$.
**$p < .01$.

Table IV. Analysis of variance of gain scores

Source	Degrees of freedom	Mean square	F
Between	2	1,093.67	4.76*
Within	51	230.00	

*$p < .05$.

dures with the profoundly retarded lead to rather rapid (and often dramatic) gains, followed by a "tapering off" period. Further data are needed to determine whether this finding can be validly generalized and whether the tapering noted in this study is a temporary plateau or a more permanent leveling off. Since the scale used has 97 items of graduated increasing difficulty, the effect is obviously not the function of restriction imposed by the testing instrument.

Another finding of interest is the initial decline noted in the C group, followed by improvement during the second part of the program. Although housed with the P group and participating in all ward activities, it is possible that these children initially received less attention by the attendants, or— more probably—that they perceived themselves as "neglected" since they did not "get to go to class" as did their peers in the P group. Again this finding needs replication to warrant generalization, but it suggests the possibility of what might be termed a "negative placebo effect"; that is, some decrement in

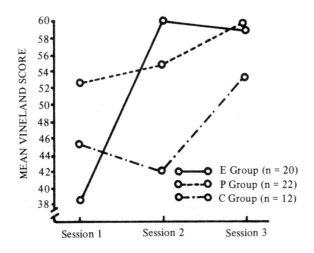

Figure 1. Mean total score during each rating session.

behavior associated with the C subjects' self-perception as being "neglected" relative to the E subjects with whom they are in contact.

SUMMARY

This study compared the improvement in self-help skills of three groups of severely and profoundly retarded institutionalized children. Using the Pine-crest Modification of the Vineland Social Maturity Scale, subjects were rated at the start of the program, after six months, and at the end of a year. The group trained by operant conditioning procedures showed significantly greater improvement than either a control group or a placebo group receiving classroom-type training.

P. R.
420 Lexington Avenue
New York, N.Y. 10017

REFERENCES

Bensberg, G. J., Colwell, C. N., & Cassel, R. H. Teaching the profoundly retarded self-help activities by behavior shaping techniques. *American Journal of Mental Deficiency,* 1965, 69, 674-679.

Blackwood, R. O. Operant conditioning as a method of training the mentally retarded. Unpublished doctoral dissertation, Ohio State University, 1962.

Fitzgerald, E. *Straight language for the deaf.* Washington: Volta Bureau, 1949.

Frostig, M., & Horne, D. *The Frostig program for the development of visual perception.* Chicago: Follett, 1964.

Gaston, E. T. (Ed.). *Music therapy.* Lawrence, Kan.: National Association for Music Therapy, 1956.

Giles, D. K., & Wolf, M. M. Toilet training insititutionalized, severe re-tardates: An application of operant behavior modification techniques. *American Journal of Mental Deficiency,* 1966, 70, 766-780.

Gorton, C. E., & Hollis, J. H. Redesigning a cottage unit for better program-ming and research for the severely retarded. *Mental Retardation,* 1965, 3, 16-21.

Hamilton, J. W., Stephens, L., & Allen, P. The management of aggressive behavior with retarded persons. Paper presented at American Association on Mental Deficiency, Chicago, May 1966.

Heber, R. A manual on terminology and classification in mental retardation. (2nd ed.) *American Journal of Mental Deficiency,* 1961 (Monogr. Suppl.).

Kephart, N. C. *The slow-learner in the classroom.* Columbus: Charles E. Merrill, 1960.

Kimbrell, D. L., Luckey, R. E., Barbuto, P. F., & Love, J. G. Operation dry pants: An intensive habit-training program for severely and profoundly retarded. *Mental Retardation,* 1967, 6, 32-36.

Montessori, M. *The Montessori method.* Philadelphia: F. A. Stokes, 1912.

Patterson, E. G., & Overbeck, D. B. *Behavior shaping.* Austin: Austin State School, 1968.

Pinecrest Modification of the Vineland Social Maturity Scale. Pineville, La.: Pinecrest State School, 1963.

Roos, P. Development of an intensive habit-training unit at Austin State School. *Mental Retardation,* 1965, 3, 12-15.

Snedecor, G. W. *Statistical methods.* (5th ed.) Ames: Iowa State College Press, 1956. Pp. 251-253.

Strauss, A. A., & Lehtinen, L. E. *Psychopathology and education of the brain-injured child.* New York: Grune & Stratton, 1947.

Watson, L. S., Jr. Application of operant conditioning techniques to institutionalized severely and profoundly retarded children. *Mental Retardation Abstract,* 1967, 4(1), 1–18.

Watson, L. S., Jr. Application of behavior-shaping devices to training severely and profoundly mentally retarded children in an institutional setting. Paper presented at Midwestern Psychological Association, Chicago, May 1966.

WILL THERE
ALWAYS BE
AN INSTITUTION?
I: THE IMPACT
OF
EPIDEMIOLOGICAL
TRENDS

Wolf Wolfensberger

The following is the abstract that accompanied the paper. "In this two-part series of articles, it is predicted that institutions will be phased out because of five trends: development of nonresidential community services; new conceptualizations of and attitudes toward residential services; increased usage of individual rather than group residential placements; provision of small, specialized group residences; and a decline in the incidence and prevalence of severe and profound retardation due to reduction in the birthrate of high risk groups, improvement of health services for the population generally and for high risk groups specifically, increased practice of abortion, general environmental betterment, and early childhood education. In this (first) part, the impact of the predicted epidemiological trends upon residential services is discussed."

Recently, I ventured 20 predictions about the future of residential services in mental retardation (Wolfensberger, 1969d). Several of these predictions implied that the traditional institution would gradually fade away. The rationales for this prediction as well as certain related ones were enumerated and briefly discussed, but space limitations prevented more extensive elaboration of these points. Herewith, I will explore these points further, but first it is necessary to ask a very basic question.[1]

WHAT IS AN INSTITUTION?

Both the 5000-place institution as well as the 5-place hostel are residential services; what makes us apt to label one as an institution, and the other one as something else? Obviously, definitions are arbitrary. We are free to define institutions in such a way as to reflect the typical citizen's opinion of what an institution is; we can impose an arbitrary definition that is more scientific or technical; or we can combine elements of both approaches.

Goffman (1961) rendered a brilliant analysis of what he called "total institutions" which he defined ultimately in terms of the barriers which exist between it and the outside, especially the barriers to departure. I suspect that even without awareness of this definition, most citizens today would similarly define an institution largely on the basis of features that emphasize separateness from the community mainstream. Yet, as attractive and useful as this definition has proven to be, I feel that such a barrier is merely a common rather than essential feature of an establishment that might be defined as a total institution, and that appears to typify our traditional mental retardation institutions. It seems to me that ultimately, an even more useful definition would be based on the *deindividualization* that permeates the atmosphere of a residential community. More of the features commonly associated with an institution appear to be corollaries of deindividualization rather than of separation from the "outside." Such corollary features include the following:

1. *An environment that aims at a low common denominator among its residents.* For instance, because a few or occasional residents may be unstable

---

[1] The help of Dr. Warren Pearse in furnishing some of the population data is gratefully acknowledged. I thank Drs. Robert Kugel and Richard Kurtz for contributory critiques of earlier drafts.

Mental Retardation, 1971, 9(5): 14–20. Reprinted by permission of the author and the American Association on Mental Deficiency.

Dr. Wolfensberger is currently visiting scholar at York University, Ontario, Canada.

or destructive, *all* residents may be subjected to an environment that appears necessary and/or appropriate to the few or occasional ones. We are all familiar with the locked doors, heavy-duty construction and furnishings, and socio-behavioral surveillance, structure, and restrictions imposed on a group for the sake of a few of its members. The fact that deindividualization can be a more significant feature than confinement is apparent from the fact that physical restraints, even when used, are usually quite unnecessary and often ineffective in maintaining separateness and confinement.

2. *Congregation of persons into residential groups larger than those typically found in the community.* In American society, the most typical grouping residing together in the community is the nuclear family, which rarely exceeds six to eight members.

3. *Reduced autonomy of residents, and increased regimentation*, including mass movements and mass action on the part of the residents, and regimentation of their routine. Again, a surprising amount of regimentation can be attained even when there is no physical and even few social barriers to departure. The voluntary deindividualization, regimentation, and separateness of monasteries is a good example.

4. Ordinary citizens sleep, study, work, and play in separate contexts and settings, and tend to interact with different fellow citizens in each setting; in institutions, these *settings tend to be physically fixed under one roof or on one contiguous campus*, and sometimes programmatically unified in terms of environmental and supervisory structures. Also, the same group of persons tends to interact with each other in each such setting, resulting in an inward-directedness. Again, these features greatly reduce opportunities for individualization.

Thus, when I distinguish between institutions and other group residences in the subsequent discussion, the term institution refers to a deindividualizing residence in which retarded persons are congregated in numbers distinctly larger than might be found in a large family; in which they are highly regimented; in which the physical or social environment aims at a low common denominator; and in which all or most of the transactions of daily life are carried out under one roof, on one campus, or in a largely segregated fashion.

INSTITUTIONS WILL "FADE AWAY"

Both the desirability of the disappearance of the institution as well as the realism of such a prediction are controversial, and one can readily hear the argument that goes something like this: "Go ahead, start your hostels, dump the aged retarded into nursing homes, expand your community services—but when you are all done, you will still need the institution."

Some workers in the field resent the drift toward a new model because of their commitments to the past model, and because of a very understandable human rigidity. Others are free of such essentially irrational "hang-ups," and on an intellectual level see programmatic and social benefits in patching up or salvaging the old model. For instance, they may believe that the very isolation (social or physical) of institutions serves a societal purpose by permitting society to separate itself in a relatively humane fashion from those it has rejected and discarded; that there is no other, better, or more economical alternative for the care of the profoundly retarded or multiply handicapped; or that the present institutions represent too great an investment to be discarded. Yet other workers see little merit in the old model, but while some labor optimistically for new models, some are pessimistic in regard to constructive changes; even as they support new trends in residential services, they believe that the traditional institution will still be with us for a long time, and perhaps forever.

My proposal is that institutions as I have defined them *should* and *will* disappear. The *should* implies a value judgment on the part of myself and many "young Turks" (both old and young) in the field. The *will*, however, implies a prediction on the scientific-empirical level. It is predicated on certain socio-cultural-political-fiscal realities. I propose that four trends and one phenomenon will combine to slowly evaporate the institution. The four trends are: a lowering in the incidence and prevalence of the severely and multiply damaged;[2] increasing provision of residential alternatives; increasing provision of nonresidential community services; and a change in the ideology and conceptualization of services. The one phenomenon is the largely unrecognized fact that present institutions are not as good an investment as they are widely believed to be. Each of these points will be elaborated below.

THE INCIDENCE AND PREVALENCE OF MENTAL RETARDATION, AND IMPLICATIONS TO RESIDENTIAL DEMAND

Research on the epidemiology of mental retardation is voluminous. While this work has yielded some consistent findings, it has also left some problems unsolved, and perhaps unsolvable. One perennial problem of epidemiology has been: what is the incidence and prevalence of mental retardation? Ever

---

[2] Incidence refers to the occurrence of new cases; prevalence to the ratio of cases in a population. The reader should recall that incidence and prevalence may not be highly related. For instance, a high incidence coupled with a high death rate may result in a low prevalence.

since this question has been asked, workers in the field have been apt to seek "the" answer. For instance, studies that are in agreement with each other are greeted with satisfaction; studies that disagree with each other are viewed as problematic.

The search for "the" answer appears to rest on an assumption—often unconscious and implicit rather than explicitly stated—that retardation is a static phenomenon with invariable input and output events and channels. This posture is difficult to understand unless one assumes that it rests on the presumption that retardation is largely due to hereditary causes which should be relatively stable over time and space. Most epidemiologists and other workers in the field would reject such a presumption while yet continuing to assume a posture consistent with it.

Many diseases show vast fluctuations over time, space, cultures, and subcultures. So do many social phenomena such as marriages, births, divorces, crime, wealth, etc. If we truly believe that mental retardation can result from a large number of interactions of a large number of psycho-bio-socio-medical phenomena, then why should even large variations in incidence and prevalence surprise us? To the contrary, absence of such variations should surprise us.

It would thus appear that the perennial search for *the* incidence and *the* prevalence of retardation constitutes an attempt to solve a pseudo-problem of our own making. Instead, we should be concerned with the conditions under which incidence and prevalence vary, and with the ways in which causative mechanisms can and do interact.

At present, the prevalence of retardation in the United States is relatively high, especially if the operational definition of the American Association on Mental Deficiency (Heber, 1959) is adopted. Even aside from this particular definition, a high prevalence is to be expected on *a priori* grounds. Perhaps in no other country of the world are typical cultural expectations for complex behavior as high as in ours; and yet, probably in no other advanced nation is severe deprivation of resources and opportunities as common. The interaction of these two phenomena probably explains why our prevalence of mental retardation appears to be one of the highest among advanced nations.

On the one hand, the demands for complex behavior can be expected to continue to increase, and therefore to make for an increase in the overall incidence of mental retardation; but on the other hand, there are many changes, events, and trends which are likely to reduce the incidence of retardation, and particularly so of severe and profound retardation. Thus, the question is which of the two effects is larger and most relevant to residential needs. Let us first review the factors that appear to reduce the rate of retardation.

CONTINUING REDUCTION
IN BIRTHRATE AMONG HIGH RISK GROUPS

It is a well-recognized phenomenon that as nations advance economically, their birthrates decline (e.g., Berelson and Steiner, 1964; Statistical Office of the United Nations, 1969; Department of Economic and Social Affairs, 1965). In the United States, this trend has also been evident, although some irregularities which are believed to be due to wars and depressions have occurred (Kiser, Grabill, and Campbell, 1968). Generally, rates have declined since 1800 (Okun, 1958; Yasuba, 1961), and sharply so since about 1955 (e.g., United States Bureau of the Census, 1969). Much of this continuing recent decline can be attributed to the introduction of new contraceptive means and techniques, and increasing acceptance of the practice of contraception generally.

The decline in birthrate should mean a decline in the relative number of damaged infants generally. However, of even more significance should be the decline in the birthrate of certain "high risk" groups which have been particularly apt to produce impaired offspring. Among these groups have been the poor and disadvantaged (and consequently a large proportion of the noncaucasoid population); very young and older women; mothers in poor health, with numerous previous pregnancies, and with a history of reproductive problems; and unmarried women. Impaired children from such groups appear to have accounted for a disproportionate number of our institutional residents.

In the past, it was assumed (with only limited documentation) that mild retardation was especially prevalent among lower socio-economic groups, while more severe retardation was relatively equally distributed across all socio-economic strata. Today, we do not only know that poverty is one of the major correlates of retardation generally, but with perspicacious hindsight we can now recognize that we should have expected all along that factors making for *severe* impairment should be especially prevalent among the poor and disadvantaged (e.g., Hurley, 1969; Kosa, Antonovsky, and Zola, 1969; Mooring, 1968; President's Committee, 1969). Some high risk groups (e.g., the poor, the disadvantaged, and the noncaucasian) have also had much higher birthrates than more favored "middle Americans." However, while in the past the birthrates of high risk groups have not fallen either as rapidly or as low as that of middle Americans (e.g., Kiser, Grabill, and Campbell, 1968), the gap will probably narrow rather rapidly.

For instance, a study of tentative Omaha data found that if Omaha birth rates are examined by census tracts grouped according to average family income, the most affluent tracts in which birthrates were already very low showed *no* further decline in rates between 1960 and 1967; in the second quartile tracts, rates declined by 17%; in the third by 24%; and in the fourth by 37%. Within the Negro ghetto, some census tracts showed a decline of 63%. The overall non-white birthrate dropped from 47.3 per thousand in 1957 to 26.5 (equivalent to 44%), while the white rate dropped from 27.4 to 17.5, or only about 16% (*Omaha World Herald*, June 11, 1969).

Another high risk group is that of unmarried mothers. From Sweden (Karl Grunewald, personal communication) comes a finding that had been unforeseen though quite expectable, i.e., that increased practice of contraception by the unmarried had had a sizeable effect in reducing the relative incidence of impaired infants from this source.

The implication of these phenomena and trends are that we can expect substantial declines in birth rates among high risk groups even after the birth-rate of middle Americans levels off; and in turn, this means a substantial reduction in the relative number of impaired infants.

PREVENTIVE HEALTH SERVICES TO HIGH-RISK GROUPS

Not only is the birthrate of high-risk groups relevant to our discussion, but also the health of and health-related services to such groups. One index of the health of a population group that is relevant to severe impairment is neonatal and infant mortality. Such mortality, prematurity, and high risk status are highly related to each other as well as to infant damage and to the incidence and prevalence of severe and multiply damaged children.

Neonatal and infant mortality rates in the United States have dropped steadily since 1915 (Shapiro, Schlesinger, and Nesbitt, 1968; United States Department of Health, Education, and Welfare, 1969). However, two phenomena stand out.

1. Relative to other nations, the United States has been falling behind, and for 1966, there were 22 nations reported to have had lower infant mortality rates (Statistical Office of the United Nations, 1968). While some artifacts may be involved, the data are probably correct for at least twelve of these countries. Tentative data for 1967 (Statistical Office of the United Nations, 1969) suggest that the list had grown to at least thirteen nations, and the rates of Scandinavian countries (e.g., 12.9, 13.3, and 14.2 per 1000 births, and thus 60–70% of U.S. rates) points the way to a minimal goal that *can* be achieved.[3]

---

[3] These and other data were the most recent ones I could obtain at the time the paper was submitted. They are slightly outdated because of publication lag.

2. Infant mortality rates differ greatly between various population groups in this country. They tend to be very low in advantaged, and very high in disadvantaged groups. For instance, white-nonwhite differences have been near 100% for years (United States Department of Health, Education, and Welfare, 1969), and another example from Omaha is very informative. In Omaha, as in most urban centers of the United States, residential areas of wealth and of poverty are clearly defined and differentiated. In recent years, the infant mortality rates in some of the wealthier residential areas have been less than a third of the national average, while in certain census tracts in the poverty and Negro areas, they have been over three times the national average. In other words, the chances that an infant in a poor family would die were occasionally ten times higher than that of infants of privileged backgrounds. Again, the current rates for advantaged population segments can be viewed as *minimal* targets that can be achieved for the entire population.

Figures cited above have profound implications to the incidence and prevalence of severe and multiply damaged children. Now, that Omaha poverty areas are beginning to receive extensive services for handicapped children, the prevalence of damaged children from disadvantaged backgrounds is beginning to become visible for the first time, and appears to be staggering. With some variation, the Omaha situation is repeated across the nation.

Another index of great relevance here is the rate of maternal death associated with childbirth. This rate, of course, had declined phenomenally over the years (e.g., Shapiro, Schlesinger, and Nesbitt, 1968; United States Department of Health, Education, and Welfare, 1969). In 1915–1919, the overall rate was 728 per 100,000 live births; by 1967, the rate was down to 28, and still declining. However, while in 1915–1919, noncaucasians had a rate that was 179% higher than that of causasians. The difference between these rates increased dramatically as the maternal death rates for caucasians dropped much faster than that of noncaucasians. By 1957, the difference was 430%, and in 1967, it was still 356%. Once more, such data demonstrate dramatically the progress we can, must, and will make, and the tremendous unrealized preventive vistas that still lie before us. These vistas, we should note, do not even involve new discoveries, new drugs, new surgeries, etc.; *they involve no more than applying what we know and have the means of doing right now!*

Fortunately, the last few years have seen extensive improvements in the health care of high risk groups. For instance, mother-child centers, maternal and child health programs, and children and youth programs have served the poor, unwed mothers, and other special risk groups. Such services undoubtedly will be expanded further.

However, health services are not enough, since social and health factors interrelate in intimate but ill-understood patterns. Therefore, it is comforting to know that the socio-cultural factors which can obviate health services are also improving. In time, the effects of these combined trends should be expressed in a significant reduction in the incidence of severe retardation and multiple handicaps.

INCREASED LEGALIZATION AND PRACTICE OF ABORTION

Although the practice of abortion involves complex questions of morality—even to an extent contraception never did—there is every reason to believe that in the future, high-risk women who do conceive (perhaps because of contraceptive failure) will have relatively ready access to abortion. There are strong grounds for predicting that within a generation, abortions may be performed as readily in the United States as in countries with highly liberalized abortion laws, such as Japan, although probably not as widely. In Japan, abortion is utilized as an equivalent to contraception, while it is to be expected that in this country, effective contraception will be practiced so universally that abortion will be employed mostly for other reasons.

A significant proportion of severely and multiply damaged infants are products of hereditary, genetic, and intrauterine damage. In many cases, the presence of such damage can be suspected and increasingly even confirmed prenatally. As the practice of abortion in high-risk pregnancies becomes widely accepted, we can expect a very significant decline in the birth of damaged infants. In fact, in order to fully visualize future trends, we must recall that infants with prenatal abnormalities make up a large proportion of the visibly, severely damaged, such as we now encounter in our present institutions, and in community programs for the severely retarded.

IMPROVEMENT OF HEALTH AND PREVENTIVE SERVICES GENERALLY

It is to be expected that health services generally will improve, and that some preventive measures will have special relevance to the reduction of severe impairment. Significant recent advances in the latter category include rubella and measles vaccination, and Rh desensitization. Other noteworthy developments are: improved and increased genetic counseling, prenatal diagnosis of fetal abnormalities, prenatal exchange transfusions, and numerous improvements in early postnatal management. Many advances, though of relatively minor effect upon retardation by themselves, do add up. Better standards for drugs, improved auto safety, and better control over X-ray usage and sources are a few examples. Many other preventive improvements can be reasonably expected.

GENERAL ENVIRONMENTAL BETTERMENT

Adverse environmental factors interact with each other and with yet other factors in a number of ways which have implications to the incidence and prevalence of mental retardation. However, many of these adverse conditions appear to yield to increased material prosperity and progressive social enlightenment. Poverty, and the culture of poverty, are perhaps the two conditions which both have extensive implications to retardation, and which also appear to be on the decline.

That poverty is a significant factor is readily apparent in the indices which accompany poverty in this country, such as poor medical care and nutrition. However, much more subtle, but perhaps even more significant than poverty itself, is what has been called the "culture of poverty" (Lewis, 1959). When a poor, expectant mother does not have the money for a baby-sitter or for bus or taxi fare to go for a prenatal examination, then her poverty may contribute to the birth of a damaged child; when she has a baby-sitter, and gets free transportation, but fails to go for her examination because of low motivation or superstitious beliefs, then we may say that her risk is higher because of her cultural ways which are associated with poverty. When she is too poor to nourish herself or her children properly, her poverty may well result in stunted and damaged children; when she has enough money for food, but serves mostly starchy foods and ill-balanced meals, her culture rather than poverty may cause ill effects.

Although we still have a shameful amount and distribution of poverty, not only the proportion but even the number of the poor has declined steadily and substantially in the 1960s, and it has done so in almost all segments of the poor population (e.g., National Advisory Commission on Civil Disorders, 1968; United States Bureau of the Census, 1969; United States Department of Labor, 1969). For instance, between 1960 and 1967, the number of poor persons had declined from 38.9 to 26.1 million overall, and from 10.7 to 8.4 million among noncaucasians (United States Bureau of the Census, 1969). Particularly encouraging is the fact that employment gains made by Negroes have been even larger than those made by caucasians (e.g., National Advisory Commission on Civil Disorders, 1968; United States Department of Labor, 1969). This trend appears to hold up even at this time of recession.

While the culture of poverty may linger long after poverty itself has ended, we can still expect a significant long-range decline in both proportion and number of mothers and infants who are at risk because of poverty and its culture. This, of course, should express itself in a reduced incidence of retardation.

EARLY CHILDHOOD EDUCATION

Growing acceptance of the fact that man is most shapable early in life has led to a number of trends, six of which will be mentioned because of their relevance:

1. *The private early education movement*, manifested in the explosive growth of private Montessori schools, kindergartens, and similar establishments. Many such schools have accepted retarded youngsters.

2. *Operation Headstart*, intended to reduce the shock of school entry for disadvantaged youngsters. Appropriately, goals have been raised to actually prevent scholastic and mental retardation, and accordingly, Headstart has expanded from a three-month summer program to a one-year and even longer program for many children.

3. *Lowering of school entrance age for many types of handicapped children*. For instance, until recently, severely retarded children in Nebraska public schools had to be eight years old; today, they are accepted at age six, and some are accepted as early as age three.

4. *Mandatory education for the severely retarded*. Formerly, lack of mandatory provision meant that the child might have received no education until his teens, if ever; now, he will be exposed to intensive shaping in his more plastic early years. To cite Nebraska again: education for the severely retarded was mandated as late as 1967, and was not effectively implemented until 1969. In a few years, all states will mandate and implement such education.

5. *A new emphasis on enabling mothers on welfare as well as others to work, which is resulting in a rapid growth of day care centers*. Since standards for these day care centers are being tightened, one can increasingly refer to them with justification as *developmental* day care centers. They may well be the transition to universal school entry at an earlier age.

6. *Increased provision of kindergarten programs in the public schools*. Here, we see movement from no provision to permissive to mandatory services; from half-day to full-day programs; and from one-year to two- and even three-year programs.

A recent government report (Nehrt and Hurd, 1969) showed that 8% of three-year-olds, 23% of four-year-olds, and 66% of five-year-olds were enrolled in pre-primary programs of a developmental nature. Although these figures are probably much larger than most citizens would suspect, they are still too small. There can be little doubt that we will and indeed should lower our age for universal public education. Within one generation, we shall probably see first grade entry at ages three and four, and some kind of developmental program for two-year-olds.

One major implication of these trends to mental retardation is clear. Early education will contribute substantially to a reduction in the prevalence of mental retardation, both by reducing the incidence of retardation that results from environmental deprivation, and by reversing such retardation in many instances. However, the effect is likely to be most marked in the reduction of mild retardation. Its greatest impact upon demand for residential places is not likely to come from this reduction, but from the belief and hope that early education offers to parents of the more severely retarded.

CONCLUSION

For years, writers in the field have called for more and better preventive efforts and measures. However, medically oriented workers have had a "hang-up" on the inborn errors of metabolism. Because here, an apparently success-ful paradigm had been established in what was otherwise a sea of pessimism, the paradigm was glorified out of all proportion. However, the pay-off to this paradigm so far has been negligible, while the ongoing and relatively rapid implementation of the vastly more significant near-eradication of measles and rubella, for instance, was not well foreseen. Even the much more readily foreseeable reduction in the incidence of retardation due to contraception was virtually unforeseen, and is probably not fully grasped even today. The effects of liberalized abortion have long been predicted, but their impact on programs for the multiply impaired and more severely retarded are probably also not fully grasped.

In attempting to assess the meaning of the various trends traced and predicted above, one may conclude that in mental retardation, the medical advances will be manifested most spectacularly by a reduction in the inci-dence of the more severely retarded and multiply handicapped. Social and educational prevention will probably have its most spectacular effects in mild retardation. That there should be such an equivalence (medical prevention of the severely retarded versus socio-educational prevention of the mildly re-tarded) is not new. What is new is that we now can predict with confidence that these effects will be strongly manifested in the future. The medical effects will probably be manifested much sooner and stronger and, indeed, are already in evidence; however, the socio-educational ones will have greater significance to our society.

For a long time, a common conjecture has been that there was a kind of balance between the number of infants saved by medical advances from damage, and those damaged but saved by the same or other advances from death. We have no way of knowing how true this conjecture was, but today, I believe that circumstantial evidence weights the scales strongly in favor of infants saved from damage over those damaged ones saved from death.[4]

The predicted trends toward lowered incidence and prevalence of damaged children could be reversed by an unforeseen disaster, equivalent to the Thalidomide tragedy or the rubella epidemic. However, even the impact of such disasters upon the prevalence of retardation is very likely to be blunted by the increased practice of abortion.

While the incidence of damaged infants will probably decline considerably, the prevalence of the aged retarded is apt to increase. At present, the life expectancy of severely and multiply damaged children and adults still appears to be well below that of the population as a whole. This gap can be expected to be narrowed, which will result in a higher prevalence of such individuals of advanced age. Also, the effects of the preventive measures mentioned can be expected to be offset in part by the increasing complexity of our society, and the greater likelihood that increased behavioral demands will make many persons retarded. However, persons who will pass into the retarded zone because of such social changes will be considered mildly retarded. Even if their number should outweigh the number of those whose retardation is prevented or reversed, they are not likely to contribute significantly to the demand for residential places. Instead, they are likely to increase the demand for certain community services, particularly special education, vocational training, and personal guidance.

In evaluating the likely effects of preventive measures upon residential demand, it is important to consider two points.

1. *In all likelihood, there is a high correlation between the severity of impairment, and the degree to which residential demand is met.* In other words, among the most impaired, the demand for residential places is probably much more completely met now than among the more moderately impaired. For instance, as medical improvements prolonged life, and as institutions modified their admission criteria, the rate of admission of more severely retarded persons to public institutions began to increase in about 1945 (e.g., Goldstein, 1959). However, the annual institutional movement reports of the United States Department of Health, Education, and Welfare

---

[4]Grunewald (1969) discusses several of the above points in regard to the Swedish scene. In a personal communication (October, 1970), he also felt that the data coming in now indicate a definitely lowered incidence of profound retardation in the 0–5 age group.

suggest that in approximately 1958, such admissions reached a peak and have declined gradually, at least through 1967, which is the last year for which complete data were accessible to me as this article was written.

2. *Over the years, as attitudes changed, there has also been a change in what constitutes a reasonable demand for residential placement.* Only now are we about to agree that a newborn infant should not be placed merely because he has Down's Syndrome. Only fifteen years ago, even a minor community problem was enough to institutionalize a mildly retarded person.

From the above it appears to follow that even though a specific preventive measure may prevent many more cases of mild than of severe impairment, it is exactly this latter effect which would have the more significant implication to residential provisions. Even modest preventive successes may have noticeable effects upon the demand for residential places, and the demand should decline most and first for the more severely impaired, and then "work its way" upward.

One might think that a survey of studies of waiting lists for institutions would be of assistance in clarifying this situation, but as noted in a recent review (Wolfensberger and Halliday, 1970), such studies suffer from a number of artifacts which appear to render their conclusions irrelevant to the issue.

In sum, a number of current and predictable trends appear to make for a lower incidence of severe retardation. Prevalence of severe retardation is likely to decline for children, remain more stable for mature adults, and perhaps increase for the aged. While a possible increase in the prevalence of mild retardation will have little effect on residential service demand, the trends in severe retardation imply a significant reduction of such demand for children. There is apt to be an increase in demand for such services for the aged severely retarded, but such a demand can be met largely through generic residences for the aged.

The concluding article in this two-part series discusses the impact that the newly developing service model in mental retardation will have upon institutions.

REFERENCES

Berelson, B., and G. A. Steiner, 1964. *Human behavior: An inventory of scientific findings.* New York: Harcourt, Brace & World.

Department of Economic and Social Affairs. 1965. *Population bulletin of the United Nations: Conditions and trends of fertility in the world* (No. 7–1963). New York: United Nations.

Goffman, E. 1961. *Asylums.* Garden City, N. Y.: Anchor.

Goldstein, H. 1959. Population trends in U. S. public institutions for the mentally deficient. *American Journal of Mental Deficiency* 63:599–604.

Grunewald, K. 1969. *The mentally retarded in Sweden*. Stockholm: The Swedish Institute.

Heber, R. 1959. A manual on terminology and classification in mental retardation. *American Journal of Mental Deficiency* 64(2). Monograph Supplement.

Hurley, R. L. 1969. *Poverty and mental retardation: A causal relationship*. New York: Random House.

Kosa, J.; Antonovsky, A.; and Zola, I. K., eds. *Poverty and health: A sociological analysis*. Cambridge, Mass.: Harvard University Press.

Kiser, C. V.; Grabill, W. H.; and Campbell, A. A. 1968. *Trends and variations in fertility in the United States*. Cambridge, Mass.: Harvard University Press.

Lewis, O. 1959. *Five families: Mexican case studies in the culture of poverty*. New York: Basic Books.

Mooring, I. 1968. *The planning and implementation of comprehensive services for the mentally retarded in Los Angeles County*. Los Angeles, Calif.: Mental Retardation Services Board.

National Advisory Commission on Civil Disorders. 1968. *Report of the National Advisory Commission on Civil Disorders*. Washington, D. C.: U. S. Government Printing Office.

Nehrt, R. C., and G. E. Hurd, 1969. *Preprimary enrollment of children under six: October 1968*. Washington, D. C.: U. S. Government Printing Office.

President's Committee on Mental Retardation. 1969. *MR69: The edge of change*. Washington: U. S. Government Printing Office.

Okun, B. 1958. *Trends in birth rates in the United States since 1870*. The Johns Hopkins University Studies in Historical and Political Science, Series 76, No. 1. Baltimore: Johns Hopkins Press.

Shapiro, S.; Schlesinger, E. R.; and Nesbitt, R. E. L., Jr. 1968. *Infant, perinatal, maternal, and childhood mortality in the United States*. Cambridge, Mass.: Harvard University Press.

Statistical Office of the United Nations, Department of Economic and Social Affairs. 1968. *Demographic yearbook: 1967*. New York: United Nations.
_____. 1969. *Statistical yearbook: 1968*. New York: United Nations.

United States Bureau of the Census. 1969. *Statistical abstract of the United States: 1969*. 90th ed. Washington, D. C.: U. S. Government Printing Office.

United States Department of Labor. 1969. *Manpower report of the President: A report on manpower requirements, resources, utilization, and training*. Washington: U. S. Government Printing Office.

United States Department of Health, Education, and Welfare. 1969. *Vital statistics of the United States: 1967, mortality*. Vol. 2, Part A. Washington, D. C.: U. S. Government Printing Office.

Wolfensberger, W. December 1969. Twenty predictions about the future of residential services in mental retardation. *Mental Retardation* 7(6):51–54.

Wolfensberger, W., and Halliday, R. 1970. Socio-ecological variables associated with institutionalization of retardates. *Journal of Mental Deficiency Research* 14:1–15.

Yasuba, Y. 1962. *Birthrates of the white population in the United States, 1800–1860*. The Johns Hopkins University Studies in Historical and Political Science, Series 79, No. 2. Baltimore: Johns Hopkins Press.

WILL THERE ALWAYS BE AN INSTITUTION? II: THE IMPACT OF NEW SERVICE MODELS

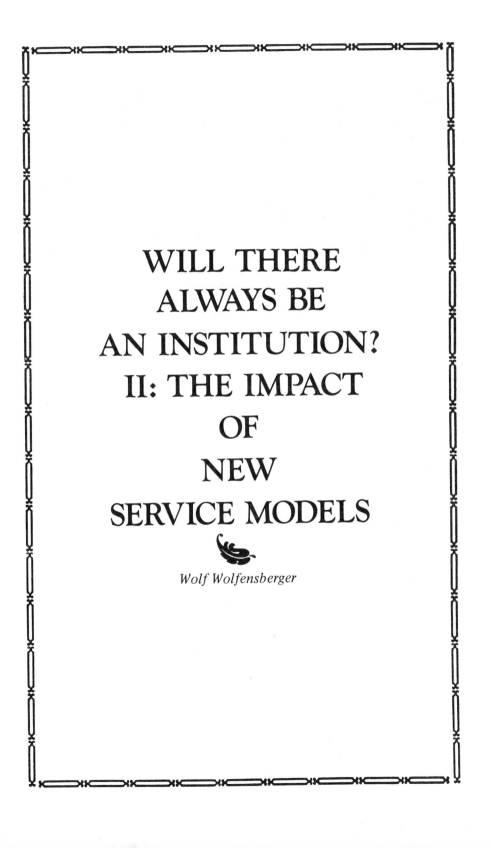

Wolf Wolfensberger

The following is the abstract that accompanied the paper. "In this two-part series of articles, it is predicted that institutions will be phased out because of five trends: development of nonresidential community services; new conceptualizations of and attitudes toward residential services; increased usage of individual rather than group residential placements; provision of small, specialized group residences; and a decline in the incidence and prevalence of severe and profound retardation due to reduction in the birthrate of high risk groups, improvement of health services for the population generally and for high risk groups specifically, increased practice of abortion, general environmental betterment, and early childhood education. In this (second) part, the impact of the developing new service model upon the institution is discussed."

Residential alternatives to institutions can be divided into group and individual residences, both to be discussed below.

GROUP RESIDENCES

A major new model of group residential services involves small residential units which, in most cases, are of family size and employ live-in houseparents. These units would be highly specialized in terms of their mission, their clientele, and their manpower structure. They would be administratively, physically, and socially integrated into the community, and located in all the population centers of their states.

The group residences of this new model lack the features which I earlier defined as archetypal of institutions. Thus, the new model involves small groups, extensive autonomy on the part of residents, a high expectancy for normalized behavior, and a separation of functions such as sleeping, learning, working, treatment, and playing. Thus, the new model is highly individualized and individualizing. It has been described in enough detail elsewhere (e.g., Dunn, 1969; Dybwad, 1969; Governor's Citizens' Committee, 1968; Menolascino, Clark, and Wolfensberger, 1968, 1970; Wolfensberger, 1969a) so as not to need extensive recapitulation here. However, certain other options for individual residence do.

INDIVIDUAL RESIDENCES

In the past, removal of a retarded person from his home was almost automatically equated with group placement, and group placement was generally equated with and tantamount to life-long group residence. For instance, the state often imposed the life-long total service of the institution as a solution to a short-term situational family crisis. While it was difficult to gain admittance to an institution, it was often even more difficult to gain release from it. Rarely was an attempt made to arrange individual rather than group placement. Yet, at least three forms of individual placement suggest themselves: boarding, foster, and adoptive placement.

The term "boarding" can have multiple meanings, some of them equivalent to fostering. I propose to use the term to refer to (a) temporary individual (rather than group) placement of a *child* who has a home which continues to function as the primary and legal residence; and (b) any

Mental Retardation, 1971, 9(6):31–38. Reprinted by permission of the author and the American Association on Mental Deficiency.

individual placement of an *adult* into a family setting where he receives room and board, regardless of the likely duration of the arrangement. In both cases, it is assumed that the family providing boarding receives remuneration, and it is obvious that boarding can be for adults what fostering is for children. The term "family care" is sometimes used to refer to both foster- and boarding-type arrangements.

Boarding placements, especially for adults, were common prior to the advent of institutions. During the alarmist period (ca. 1890–1925), boarding was ruled out by attitudes (Wolfensberger, 1969c); between 1925 and the recent past, it was ruled out by ignorance and the lack of legal and fiscal frameworks. Today, it is ruled out only by rigidity of our service structures.

Yet, boarding placement is a creative and very normalizing alternative to the hospital placement of an adult who is in vocational training or in sheltered or competitive work. In rural areas, it is of particular promise regardless of the boarder's age. For instance, in sparsely populated areas, local services may not be feasible even in the service system of tomorrrow. Special classes, workshops, etc., may have to be placed into regional population centers which are beyond commuting distance of much of the surrounding population. One solution, of course, is the establishment of hostels, including some that operate only for five days a week. Such hostels, for example, have been established in several population centers of rural Nebraska, and serve severely retarded children who live with houseparents and who attend special classes during the day.

However, even more creative than five-day hostels is the provision of five-day boarding arrangements. Again, such boarding situations with individual families have been set up in at least eleven Nebraska towns. This arrangement has several advantages: a one-to-one relationship; a more normalizing atmosphere; economy; reduction of the hostel staffing problem; and a solution to the problems of finding buildings that meet the stringent fire codes for group living.

I predict that once the advantages of boarding arrangements have been recognized, and once resistance to novel service options has been overcome, this provision will play a role in reducing demand not only for institutional but also for other types of group residences.

Foster (exclusive of group foster placements, which are really more like hostels) and adoptive placements constitute additional types of individual residential placement. Again, such placements were often ruled out because of peculiar attitudes and practices that prevailed and largely still prevail in the relevant agencies. Such attitudes often demanded that prospective substitute parents be paragons of parenthood—better yet than the typical parent in the community—motivated only by idealism and unmoved by material incentives.

Thus, it came about that foster homes were ridiculously underpaid, and that numerous children were placed into no-love high-cost institutions rather than into medium-love medium-cost foster homes, even though a workable legal-fiscal and even administrative structure existed.

In addition, there prevailed an attitude that retarded children *should* not be adopted. For instance, in Iowa, infant testing had its upswing primarily in order to prevent adoption of children who were retarded (Crissey, 1970).

Finally, an almost universal agency dogma was that citizens would not accept a retarded child for foster or adoptive placement. Today, we can only wonder to what degree this agency dogma was an agency myth. What we do know is that prophecies can be self-fulfilling. Obviously, an agency worker who "knows" that retarded children cannot be placed is not going to seek such placements and support them with vigor and inspiration, if at all, and is therefore not likely to make many successful placements, if any.[1]

In Omaha (Nebraska), we wanted to find foster homes for eight mongoloid infants who had been transferred from the institution to a ward at the College of Medicine for a research project. With the agencies emitting the customary owl hoots, a young nurse and a social work student were told to go out and do the job. These two people employed unorthodox means such as a mobilization of the news media, and within two months, every child had a foster home (Kugel, 1970). Three years later, seven children are still placed; had they been free for adoption, several would have been adopted by their foster parents. (The eighth child lives in a hostel.) Similar reports of the feasibility of foster placements are beginning to trickle in from other sources (e.g., Chambers, 1970).

The realization is slowly growing that removing a retarded child from his home need not be tantamount to institutional or even group placement. Foster, adoptive, and boarding placements are virtually unmined resources of potentially major proportion. However, to actualize these resources, it may be necessary to provide more vigorous programmatic and more realistic financial backup than has been customary in the past. Thus, the fees for fostering a retarded child should be increased substantially—at the same time as certain standards for foster homes are raised and others lowered. Subsidized adoption (now enacted at least in Illinois and Nebraska) should be made permissible in all states. To both foster and adoptive parents, a continuum of services should be made available. Particularly, specific child develop-

---

[1] Franklin's (1969a, 1969b, 1969c) documentation of successful adoptive placements of children with even severe medical conditions is highly relevant. Also, today, we should move toward subsidized adoption (e.g., Wheeler, 1969) as another powerful option, especially with handicapped children whose upbringing may be very expensive.

ment guidance and assistance should be offered in order to assist the parent surrogates in surmounting the crises of the family life cycle.

One day these things will be done, and institutions will be prevented from admitting any child that can be fostered or adopted. Such developments will not only reduce the demand for group residential places rather directly, but also indirectly: parents who now seek and obtain institutional placement inappropriately will refrain from seeking such placement if they know that another family, probably in the same town, will accept their child as their own.

CONCLUSION

I can see no reason why small, specialized living units (mostly hostels) cannot accommodate all of the persons now in institutions.[2] In turn, I believe that many persons who could be well served in hostels will be served even better in individual placements. Thus, we should experience not only a shift of places from institutions to other group residences, but also a decline in the demand for any type of group residence.

Furthermore, any feature of a residential service that is normalizing will increase the likelihood that the resident will either return to his family, move to a more advanced form of residence (e.g., from hostel to apartment or boarding), or be fully habilitated. Therefore, the more normalizing atmosphere and practices of small group residences, the use of community instead of segregated resources, the maintenance of family ties because of close physical proximity, the use of five-day instead of seven-day, and nine-month instead of twelve-month residences, will all combine so as to reduce the need for life-long residence, and increase the movement from group to individual residence.

In addition, the open-endedness of the flow into and out of the various types of residences, and the increased availability of residential services specifically geared to genuine short-term crisis relief for the family (e.g., "vacation homes," "respite centers," or "crisis assistance units" as proposed and described in Governor's Citizens' Committee, 1968) are apt to further reduce the need for long-term or even life-long residences. Those individuals in group placements that are of a long-term nature are more apt to spend days, weekends, and holidays at home. This, in turn, will open space for the

---

[2] The references cited earlier explain how even the more severely impaired can be served in small units.

short-term admission of others for purposes of family relief, thus further reducing the need for long-term placements.

In sum, there are many features associated with the envisioned new residential model which will tend to diminish the need for residential places of any kind.

NONRESIDENTIAL COMMUNITY SERVICES

General Considerations

Nonresidential community provisions will serve those who have been placed into group and individual residences in the community, as well as those domiciled with their families or on their own. However, whether such services will reduce the demand for residential placement has been controversial.

On the surface, one would certainly think that many residential placements of the past would have been prevented by the provision of alternative services. Yet it is a fact that this assertion has not been very well documented to date. One reason for this failure is the shifting interrelationship among the following: amount and type of residential placement as reflected in applications and waiting lists; real demand; actual admissions when residential places are offered; the nature of a service area and its population; and changes in the conceptualization of and attitudes toward retardation and both residential and nonresidential services. Also, service areas with good or plentiful services tend to attract families who move there from elsewhere, thus creating a demand not inherent in the original population base. As in our conceptualization of the prevalence of retardation, we must give up our search for "the" service demand which, once satisfied, remains stable. The service demand must be conceptualized as differing between localities, and as changing over time.

It appears reasonable to think that some services will have greater impact upon residential demand than others. Thus, services that relieve a major share of those family stresses which are particularly burdensome should be most effective in reducing this demand. Yet it is exactly this type of service which we have not done very much about. For instance, very few young retarded children are receiving (or receiving adequate) developmental day care. In many states, the severely retarded of school age are still excluded from school. We have only begun to meet the need for vocational services for adults. And sustained, wise family guidance is almost impossible to obtain, although it is the key to adaptive and full use of all other services.

A striking example of what the introduction of even a modest service system can do is the recent events in Nebraska. Until about 1967, there were hardly any community service provisions in the entire state; the state institution had a population of over 2,300; and the need for additional "beds" seemed endless. Then, within a brief period of incredibly intense planning, campaigning, legislating, funding, and service development, community provisions expanded greatly. Perhaps of greatest impact was the passage of a mandatory education act for the severely retarded, and the establishment of county-funded service systems in the two largest population centers of the State. Almost immediately, the number of residents at the institution dropped. By early 1971, it was down 34% (by 700) and to its lowest level in over thirty years. The remarkable thing is that the new services alone probably do not account for this drop; instead, two other factors appear to be decisive: for the first time, parents could hold realistic hope for the future; and professionals and agencies now apply more stringent standards on what they consider appropriate reasons, sites, and facilities for placement. Thus, despite the once hopeless-appearing demand for institutional and other group residential places, there are now grounds for believing that the need for such places, at least among the younger age groups, can be cut drastically. And all this in less than three years!

At this point, I want to focus upon one particular type of service option which I believe will be of some impact upon residential demand in the future: family subsidy.

Family Subsidy

A foster placement is a form of family subsidy: a family is paid to raise somebody else's child who presents special problems. Only socio-political attitudes have prevented us from generalizing this option to include families who raise their own very special child.

These attitudes have cost us dearly. The cost of life-long institutional residence has been estimated to be between $100,000 and $300,000. A small fraction of this sum applied to family subsidy may often suffice to keep a child at home. In many cases, this sum may amount to no more than a few hundred dollars a year.

For instance, there are many cases where institutional placement is sought because of the stresses created by the fact that the mother is overworked. Here, a family subsidy might permit the purchase of a washer, a dryer, a dishwasher, and the hiring of a housekeeper for a half-day a week. In other cases, living quarters may be too cramped or inappropriate to accommodate a hyperactive child. Here, a subsidy might permit a move to more spacious quarters, the addition of a room, installation of a yard fence, and/or the purchase of some gross motor play equipment. In yet other instances, the direct or indirect cost of special treatment may threaten to impoverish a family. Subsidy here might pay for such treatment, for special gadgets, special clothing, cab fare to community services, etc.

Family subsidy is one of the most efficient service options. It already exists in some indirect forms as when certain treatment expenses of poor and dependent persons are paid by various public programs. The sociopolitical climate is now such as to permit expansion of this option, and the formulation of some direct forms of subsidy. These forms should be applied not merely to the poor, but also to those middle class families who are apt to seek residential placement for their child because of conditions which might be alleviated by modest, perhaps even short-term, expenditure of money. I predict that the family subsidy option will become an accepted provision that will contribute to the lowered demand for removal of a child from his home.

Conceptualization of Services

The demand for and use of services is profoundly affected by prevailing ideologies which are based on facts, attitudes, traditions, politics, and other factors. For instance, during the alarmist period arose the ideology that all the retarded should be institutionalized. I remember that even during my training as a clinical psychologist in the mid-1950s, it was common and appropriate to write in a psychological report: "This person is mentally deficient and *therefore* should be institutionalized."

Today, we are more advanced in some respects, but we still adhere to objectionable and confused ideologies regarding residential placement. For instance, the literature extols the subjectivity of the placement decision, as if there were no principles that could be applied, or as if decision theory were not relevant to this problem. Thus, we can see extreme inconsistency: on the one hand, our residences are crowded and our waiting lists long; on the other hand, we keep admitting many persons inappropriately. Yet, it appears that specific principles for placement can be evolved (Wolfensberger, 1967), and that decision theory can be utilized (Wolfensberger, 1969b).

Failure to apply decision theory and systems management principles results in an almost universal failure to distinguish between the process and the mission of a service. For instance, we may say that a family needs counseling, that a child should be in a special class, that an adult should be in a hostel, etc., when we mean that the family should be prevented from making an inappropriate placement, that the child needs to be shaped, and that the adult needs to live away from home. Because we equate goal and process, we never stop to explore alternative processes and means, and therefore we fail both in the creative development of new service options, and in the application of cost-yield rationales. This issue is rather complex, and can only be mentioned here; it is elaborated at greater length elsewhere (Wolfensberger, 1969a).

A corollary of our present ideological confusion is the strong but inappropriate ideology prevalent today that parents have a right to decide whether to keep a retarded child or whether to divest themselves of it. The literature is replete with this implication, or with explicit statements that "the placement decision is the parents'."

In our society, it is assumed that when couples contract to procreate, they assume a heavy burden of personal responsibility for their offspring. Society makes very few exceptions from this expectation. One exception is the parent who, in effect, did not contract (i.e., the unwed mother). Here society sanctions her choice of keeping or discarding her offspring. Otherwise, such a choice is virtually never sanctioned, and only under extreme conditions—unless the child is retarded. Then, a child can be discarded even if it is only mildly retarded, or even if the parents have both the personal and financial resources for discharging customary parental responsibilities. For instance, when we permit (as we do) an upward mobile young couple to discard its mongoloid infant, we are saying in effect: "The mere fact that you find your responsibility distasteful and bothersome suffices for you to divest yourself thereof, and for us to spend $100,000 to $300,000 in assuming this burden for you." Such an ideology is difficult to understand, unless one makes the assumption that it is based on the dehumanizing interpretations of retardation of the past (Wolfensberger, 1969c). This then makes it clear: the retarded individual is not a human being, or human child, but a chattel and therefore discardable. That this is so is further underlined by the fact that parents can divest themselves of their retarded child not only physically, but also legally and emotionally. In most of our states, placement has transferred not only custodianship but even guardianship to the state. To this day, there are no measures for censure of parents for breaking all contact with the child, and even for moving out of the state and ceasing payments.

I have discussed this issue and its implications elsewhere (Wolfensberger, 1969b; see also Dybwad, 1969). We need to reconceptualize the parental right as being one of seeking divestiture of the child but not necessarily of implementing it. At least where public funds are involved, society (through its representatives), and not the parents, must be conceptualized as making the ultimate decision on whether a parental demand for divestiture should be met.

We have every reason to believe that one other ideology will change: societal tolerance of dehumanizing practices. Perhaps not since the days of the American Revolution has concern over individual rights been as strong and widespread in the United States as today. In all areas of our society, practices once considered normative are now rejected as objectionable on constitutional and moral grounds. We have witnessed the manifestation of this trend in retardation, where the retarded share a new acceptance with other deviant groups. Increasingly, the man on the street perceives the retarded as humans, as citizens, and as capable of change and growth. Increasingly, therefore, he will reject not only the more grossly dehumanizing features of our current institutions, but even the more subtle ones. Consumers, in the new spirit of the consumer rights revolution, will file suit against such practices where they continue, and will win these suits. As in mental health, suits for appropriate services, if filed, will also win, and even a vastly improved institution is apt to fail the future standards for appropriate services. Citizens will demand, and get, the new service system of which the group residential component will consist of small, community-integrated units.

Finally, society's tolerance for deviance appears to be increasing considerably, and because of the high interrelationship between societal tolerance for different types of deviance (Wolfensberger, 1969c), community tolerance for the retarded should increase. This, in turn, is apt to lower residential demand, both by resulting in greater community acceptance of retarded persons' deviant behavior, and by making such behavior more tolerable to the family.

In conclusion, I predict that we shall adopt new ideologies as well as systems management and decision theory principles into our service system of the future, that this will result in the evolution and/or implementation of new service options, and that these developments will reduce not only institutional placements, but also the need for other group residence places.

Our Institutional Investment

The dogma that we cannot afford to scrap our institutional system because of financial reasons is almost universally accepted. I submit that this dogma is a myth.

According to the President's Committee (1968), the average age of institutional buildings is 44 years; some are 100 years old; many are in a state of decay; at least 50% are functionally inadequate; and renovation is often economically unjustifiable because it would be cheaper or little more expensive to tear down and rebuild.

In Nebraska, an architectural-engineering survey of the Beatrice State Home (Henningson, Durham, & Richardson, Inc., with Davis & Wilson, Inc., 1968) disclosed that five buildings housing 460 residents were condemnable, and some had been condemned years ago; buildings housing another 325 residents could be renovated as service buildings only; and nine buildings housing 1,528 residents could be renovated to accommodate 684 occupants. Only one building, just erected, was usable "as is." Applying contemporary group residence standards, the entire institution, then housing 2,313 residents, was judged fit for only 822 after extensive renovation estimated to cost an average of $5,800 per bed.

A similar architectural-engineering survey was conducted in Colorado (Division of Mental Retardation, 1968). Even though many buildings and even entire institutional modules were relatively new, much of the same situation prevailed, or even worse: of 32 residential buildings in three institutions housing 3,918 retarded persons, 16 structures with 2,360 occupants were either condemned, condemnable, or programmatically unsuitable as well as unprofitable to renovate as residences. Another six buildings (including some very new ones) with 878 residents required considerable renovations in order to accommodate a maximum of 574 beds. Yet another eight buildings with 640 residents were judged renovatable for short-term occupancy only, and only for 480 persons. Only two buildings with 40 residents were usable "as is," and for their current number of occupants. In other words, in their present conditions, the three institutions with their combined 3,918 occupants were judged fit for 40 occupants; after renovation, they were to be fit for 1,054 residents for 10 years at most; and after that, for only 574 persons at the most, at a renovation cost of almost $4,800 per space.

Undoubtedly, the situation in Nebraska and Colorado is repeated in many, probably most, states, and the implications are clear: if we apply prevailing community health, welfare, fire, hospital, child residence, nursing home, and other group living standards to our state institutions, and if we adopted a rule that no building requiring renovation should be renovated if such renovation costs more than 60% of replacement cost, then perhaps 75% of our entire state institution system would be out of business.

Confronted with such a reality, and the need to create living space for those that would be displaced by the application of needed, common, and basic group living standards, one can choose from a number of options to be discussed below.

New Construction on the Grounds of Old Institutions

Given the chance for new construction, it would be foolish to construct at inappropriate locations, to enlarge already large congregations of deviant individuals, or to perpetuate such large congregations which violate all aspects of the principle of normalization. Therefore, new residential construction on the sites of old institutions is not defensible on rational and programmatic grounds.

Construction of New Institutions

If we truly believe in the normalization principle, and if we wish to give the model of dispersed small group residences a chance, we must oppose the building of further institutions until the demand and need for small residences have been met. New institutions—even regional centers which are normally only small institutions—will be major obstacles in the development of the new residential model.

Utilization of Institutions Discarded by Others

We are all familiar with the mental hospital, the VA hospital, the general hospital, the tuberculosis sanatorium, the prison, the orphanage, and now even the monastery or convent that is discarded by its former users, and converted for the retarded. Often, such arrangements merely create "instant old" institutions. Only occasionally should such facilities be used, and even then they should be labeled as compromises, rather than glorified. Temporary compromises may be defensible if the facility is small, located in a population center, and does not require extensive remodeling. Too often, we spend more money putting these monstrosities to use than it would cost us to develop hostels—but the rigidity of tradition is so terribly hard to overcome!
rigidity of tradition is so terribly hard to overcome!

New Construction of Noninstitutional Group Residences in the Community

Extensive construction of community group residences will undoubtedly be needed. However, it is almost impossible under existing codes to construct such buildings without making them institutional in appearance. The moment retarded persons are mentioned to an architect or building inspector, a mental shutter clicks shut. Even architects who are not bound by fiscal restraints, and who pride themselves on their skill to design a building on the basis of its function described to them by others, will design institutional features that go even beyond those required by the building codes.

I was deeply impressed to observe this phenomenon even in the almost incredibly normalizing hostels of the Swedish service system. Most homes used as hostels were indistinguishable from ordinary homes, but purpose-built hostels often had a slight institutional flavor. Even in an apartment that was designed for the retarded in the construction of a new apartment house for ordinary citizens, "heavy duty" features were added by the architect—and quite unnecessarily so, as the personnnel acknowledged.

I have a phrase for this, and maybe it says more than volumes of technical discussion: "You mention retardation, and they just can't let things be."

Another remarkable fact is that data are now coming in from all over the country, indicating that construction of a new institutional place costs up to $40,000 each. Even at that level of costs, we still end up with large, dehumanizing buildings which are part of an inappropriately large congregation of deviant persons, usually at an inappropriate location. In contrast, residential space even in the upper-middle and lower-upper class neighborhoods of our cities may cost no more than $3,500–5,000 per person, if we think in terms of groups of large family size. This contrast between the high cost of dehumanization and the low cost of normalization is almost beyond belief.

Utilization of Existing Community Buildings

New construction not only devours massive blocks of capital funds, but does so all at once and in a highly visible fashion. This explains in part why legislatures do not appropriate adequate operating costs once they have approved capital costs. In our Douglas County (population 400,000) plan in Nebraska, we therefore adopted a cardinal principle: money for services, not for buildings. Accordingly, we rent or lease if we can, buy on occasion, and build only if we must, after all alternatives are exhausted.

Obviously, one major advantage of leasing or renting is that capital costs can be both "hidden" as operating costs, and spread out over time, in both cases in the form of lease or rent expenses. This appeals to many powers-that-be, such as county commissioners and state legislators. It also opens the way to get residences going on establishment-type grants when no capital funds are available.

Utilization of existing buildings has three other advantages. First, existing buildings can be selected so as to be normalizing in terms of design and location. The codes may permit the use of an existing building that does not have the institutional features that would be required in new buildings. Also, existing buildings in normalizing surroundings are common, while available building sites are less commonly found in areas which are clearly normalizing. Second, existing buildings can be acquired and put into use relatively quickly; the delay between initially planning and finally utilizing a new building may be as much as five years. Third, a building that is rented, leased, or even bought can be abandoned or sold within a reasonable period, and the service can move as our ideology demands, or as the neighborhood or the population changes. In contrast, a new building erected with public funds and owned by a public agency is quasi-permanent. It is an obstacle to change of any kind.

Conclusion

On programmatic, ideological, and fiscal grounds, the present institutional system is essentially unsalvagable. Indeed, I believe that it is the duty of every institution's superintendent to do all he can to phase out his institution, and to encourage the new residential and service model. Among the residential alternatives, the use of existing community housing is optimal, although new construction in the community is often necessary. Provisional use of institutions discarded by others is to be viewed as a tempoary desperation compromise at best. Construction of new institutions, and of new buildings at old institutions, should be categorically prohibited, and Federal agencies and even law should prevent the use of Federal funds for such purposes.

The argument is sometimes raised that increased provision of nonresidential services will not necessarily reduce residential demand, and high residential rates from nations with extensive community provisions are occasionally cited in support. In rebuttal, I submit that such data are the results of cultural differences, and of different strategies which we should not and/or need not emulate. For instance, one of the major reasons why Denmark and Sweden have a relatively high rate of residential provision can be a lesson to us: residential placement for children is not strongly discouraged, and residential placement for adults is actually encouraged (e.g., Nirje, 1969). While community provisions are steadily increasing, I cannot see where Danish—and to some degree Swedish—service ideology places high emphasis on a vigorous policy of attempting to maintain the retarded person with his family.

In contrast, in the United States, maintenance of the retarded person in the home has not merely been advocated because of scarcity of alternatives, but also because of a different set of historical and socio-cultural attitudes and values. Such values can be expected to endure even when our service provisions are greatly improved. Thus, it appears safe to predict that the demand for residential places in this country should decline if the prevalence of severe retardation can be reduced, if needed community services are provided, and if these services are provided in conjunction with vigorous and sustained family guidance which emphasizes home maintenance of retarded children.

CONCLUDING SUMMARY

At the 1969 National Conference on Residential Care in Houston (National Association for Retarded Children, 1969), a sentiment of state program coordinators was summarized as follows: "I hope that we can recognize the fact that institutions are with us, they are going to continue to be with us and we had better accept the fact that this is one facet in a total program for the retarded" (p. 19).

Obviously, my conclusion differs sharply: institutions will *not* always be with us. Some of the newer ones will take a long time dying, and will be visited by our students as historical curiosities. In some states, there will be regional centers with built-in residential components, but these will be transitory (and inappropriate) in the rapid move toward small, specialized, dispersed, homelike units which are physically and socially intimately integrated into the community.

Not only will the institution fade away, but the need for any type of group residence will decline, except perhaps for the aged retarded who, however, can be served in regular community homes for the aged. We may find that the need for places in group residences specifically for the retarded will be less than half what it is now, i.e., perhaps .3 to .5 instead of about 1 per thousand populations.

Some nations, such as Denmark and Sweden, have a much lower prevalence of mental retardation than the United States, and yet have a residential rate which is as high and higher, and still considered inadequate.[3] While this fact should make us cautious in relating the need for residential places to the prevalence of mental retardation, as long as we take into account other factors which determine residential needs, at a given point in time and location, there is bound to be a causal relationship between the prevalence of retardation on the one hand, and the need for residential places on the other.

REFERENCES

Bank-Mikkelsen, N. E. 1968. Services for mentally retarded children in Denmark. *Children* 15:198–200.

Chambers, D. E. 1970. Willingness to adopt atypical children. *Child Welfare* 49:275–79.

Crissey, M. S. 1970. Harold Manville Skeels. *American Journal of Mental Deficiency* 75:1–3.

Division of Mental Retardation. 1968. *A new program plan for the mentally retarded.* Denver: Colorado State Department of Institutions.

Dunn, L. K. 1967. Small special-purpose residential facilities for the retarded. In *Changing patterns in residential services for the mentally retarded,* eds. R. Kugel and W. Wolfensberger, pp. 213–26. Washington, D.C.: President's Committee on Mental Retardation.

Dybwad, G. 1969. Action implications, U. S. A. today. In *Changing patterns*

---

[3] For Swedish prevalence and residential data, see Grunewald (1969). A rate of 2 per 1000 population is projected for 1974. Prevalence data on Denmark are available from various Danish sources; of special interest is an apparently unpublished translation of a paper by E. Berg, entitled "The Frequency of Mental Retardation in Denmark," and furnished to the author by the Danish National Service for the Mentally Retarded. Residential rates for Denmark are quoted by Bank-Mikkelsen (1968) as about 9000 per 4.8 million, or roughly 1.9 per 1,000 population. Both figures correspond to about double our own rates (Public Health Service, 1969).

in residential services for the mentally retarded, eds. R. Kugel and W. Wolfensberger, pp. 383–428. Washington, D.C.: President's Committee on Mental Retardation.

Franklin, D. S. 1969a. The adoption of children with medical conditions: Part I. Process and outcome. *Child Welfare* 48:459–67.

———. 1969b. The adoption of children with medical conditions: Part II. The families today. *Child Welfare* 48:533–39.

———. 1969c. The adoption of children with medical conditions: Part III. Discussion and Conclusions. *Child Welfare* 48:595–601.

Governor's Citizens' Committee on Mental Retardation. 1968. *The report of the Nebraska Citizens' Study Committee on Mental Retardation.* Vol. 2. Lincoln, Nebr.: State Department of Public Institutions.

Grunewald, K. 1969. A rural county in Sweden: Malmöhus County. In *Changing patterns in residential services for the mentally retarded,* eds. R. Kugel and W. Wolfensberger, pp. 255–87. Washington, D.C.: President's Committee on Mental Retardation.

Henningson, Durham, & Richardson, Inc., with Davis, & Wilson, Inc., 1968. *State of Nebraska program implementation, facilities evaluation, mental health-mental retardation,* Vol. 2. Omaha, Nebr.: (Published by the authors).

Menolascino, F.; Clark, R. L.; and Wolfensberger, W., eds. 1968. *The initiation and development of a comprehensive, county-wide system of services for the mentally retarded of Douglas County.* 2nd ed., Vol. 1. Omaha, Nebr.: Greater Omaha Association for Retarded Children.

———. 1970. *The initiation and development of a comprehensive, county-wide system of services for the mentally retarded of Douglas County.* Vol. 2. Omaha, Nebr.: Greater Omaha Association for Retarded Children.

National Association for Retarded Children. 1969. *Final Report of the National Conference on Residential Care (Houston, Texas, July 22–23, 1969)* New York: NARC.

Nirje, B. 1969. The normalization principle and its human management implications. In *Changing patterns of residential services for the mentally retarded,* eds. R. Kugel and W. Wolfensberger, pp. 179–95. Washington, D.C.: President's Committee on Mental Retardation.

President's Committee on Mental Retardation. 1968. MR68: *The edge of change.* Washington: U.S. Government Printing Office.

Public Health Service, National Institute of Mental Health. 1969. Provisional patient movement and administrative data: Public institutions for the mentally retarded in the United States July 1, 1967–June 30, 1968. In U.S. Department of Health, Education, and Welfare, *Mental health statistics: Current facility reports.* Washington, D.C.: U.S. Government Printing Office.

Wheeler, K. B. 1969. The use of adoptive subsidies. *Child Welfare* 48:557–59.

Wolfensberger, W. 1967. Counseling the parents of the retarded. In *Mental retardation: Appraisal, education, and rehabilitation,* ed. A. A. Baumeister, pp. 329–400. Chicago: Aldine.

———. 1969a. An attempt to reconceptualize functions of services to the mentally retarded. *Journal of Mental Subnormality* 15:71–78.

———. 1969b. A new approach to decision-making in human management services. In *Changing patterns in residential services for the mentally re-*

tarded, eds. R. Kugel and W. Wolfensberger, pp. 367–81. Washington, D.C.: President's Committee on Mental Retardation.

_____. 1969c. The origin and nature of our institutional models. In *Changing patterns in residential services for the mentally retarded,* eds. R. Kugel and W. Wolfensberger, pp. 59–171. Washington, D.C.: President's Committee on Mental Retardation.

EPILOGUE

It is hazardous, without perspective of time, to interpret recent events or to predict future trends. One guideline is constant. The pendulum swings in both directions.

At the time of this writing, early in 1975, the first hint of reaction to the deinstitutionalization process is evident. Reports of adjustments of moderately and severely retarded persons transferred from institutions to group homes and community facilities have not been uniformly favorable. In an editorial in the *British Journal of Mental Subnormality* (1972), Gunzburg has challenged the indiscriminate use of normalization concepts in group living situations for persons not equipped for independence. He argues that proponents of normalization tend to overlook real deficits in the mentally handicapped where they exist. "Do we perhaps tend to forget that the handicapped are also emotionally immature, unstable, insecure, anxious, inadequte, they they are easily disturbed, tend to vegetate, to collapse in face of difficulties and show little confidence in their admittedly meagre abilities? . . . there is nothing to suggest that sizeable and significant weaknesses in his personality make-up will not still remain after transplanting him to new, more normal, but also more demanding conditions" (p. 64).

Certainly the next decade will see an expansion of community services for the mentally handicapped, with public schools assuming greater responsibility than ever before for education and training. It also seems likely that the large institution, isolated from the community, is going to become obsolete. In its place we may find new facilities prepared to return to the educational goals of Seguin, Howe, Wilbur, and Brown. Such facilities will be necessary to provide long-term services and programs for those who require them as well as adequate preparation programs for those who can be equipped to live in the community.

The arguments continue but the issues appear and reappear like a dèja vu. The same problems remain largely unresolved since 1848: reversibility and remediation, physical vs. environmental determinants, classification and measurement, criteria of adjustment, prediction, segregation and control, genetic factors, potential social threat, prevention, and the safeguarding of basic human rights.

Each generation painfully confronts and somehow copes with the same dilemmas. Previous solutions no longer seem acceptable in retrospect. The challenge remains, as it has always been, to advance our knowledge and understanding of mental retardation, to encourage innovative efforts on behalf of mentally retarded citizens, to distinguish between useful innovations and the clever packaging of older, outworn policies and programs, and to promote human welfare for the mentally handicapped no less than we would for any other group of citizens. Can we be wise enough to benefit from the footsteps of our predecessors, selecting only what is worthy and learning from earlier mistakes? Can we recognize where we have been before, avoiding the blind alleys, and rejecting the false prophets? Mental retardation is not simply going to disappear in the foreseeable future, even if research efforts meet our most fanciful expectations. The attitudes expressed in these volumes are a sensitive index of the fiber of our society over the past century and a half. Perhaps they also hold some previews of our future.

REFERENCES

Ayllon, T. and N. H. Azrin. 1965. The measurement and reinforcement of behavior of psychotics. Journal of the Experimental Analysis of Behavior 8: 357–383.

Baer, D. M. and J. A. Sherman. 1964. Reinforcement control of generalized imitation in young children. Journal of Experimental Child Psychology 1: 37–49.

Bayley, N. 1933. Mental growth during the first three years: A developmental study of sixty-one children by repeated tests. Genetic Psychology Monographs 14: 1–92.

Baller, W. R. 1936. A study of the present social status of a group of adults who, when they were in elementary schools, were classified as mentally deficient. Genetic Psychology Monographs 18: 165–244.

Barr, M. 1904. History. In Mental defectives: Their history, treatment and training. Chap. 2. Blakiston's Sons & Co., Philadelphia.

Bensberg, G. J., C. N. Colwell, and R. H. Cassel. 1965. Teaching the profoundly retarded self-help activities by behavior shaping techniques. American Journal of Mental Deficiency 69: 674–679.

Bijou, S. W. 1966. Functional analysis of retarded development. In N. R. Ellis (ed.), International review of research in mental retardation. Vol. 1. pp. 1–19. Academic Press, New York.

Birch, H. G., and J. D. Gussow. 1970. Disadvantaged children: Health, nutrition, and school failure. Harcourt, Brace, New York.

Birnbrauer, J. S., M. M. Wolf, and J. D. Kidder. 1965. Programmed instruction in the classroom. In L. Ullmann & L. Krasner (eds.), Case studies in behavior modification. Holt, Rinehart & Winston, New York.

Blackwood, R. O. 1962. Operant conditioning as a method of training the mentally retarded. Doctoral dissertation, Ohio State University. University Microfilms, Ann Arbor, Michigan.

Bricker, W. A. and D. D. Bricker. 1970. A program of language training for the severely language handicapped child. Exceptional Children 37: 101–111.

Brockett, L. P. 1956. Idiots and the efforts for their improvement. Barnard's American Journal of Education, May.

Charles, D. C. 1953. Ability and accomplishment of persons earlier judged mentally deficient. Genetic Psychology Monographs 47: 3–71.

Clark, G. R., M. S. Kovitz, and M. Rosen. 1968. A transitional program for institutionalized adult retarded. Project No. 1275P. Vocational Rehabilitation Administration, Department of Health, Education and Welfare, Washington, D. C.

Court-Brown, W. M. 1968. Males with an XYY sex chromosome complement. Journal of Medical Genetics 5: 341.

Crissey, M. S., Harold Manville Skeels. 1970. American Journal of Mental Deficiency 75: 1–3.

Crissey, M. S. 1974. Mental retardation: Past, present, future. Paper presented at 82nd Annual Convention of the American Psychological Association, New Orleans.

Cromwell, R. L. 1963. A social learning approach to mental retardation. In N. R. Ellis (ed.), Handbook of Mental Deficiency, pp. 41–91. McGraw-Hill, New York.

Davies, S. P. 1923. Social control of the feeble-minded: A study of social programs and attitudes in relation to the problems of mental deficiency. The National Committee for Mental Hygiene, New York.

Davies, S. P. 1930. Social control of the mentally deficient. Thomas Y. Crowell, New York.

Dayan, M. 1964. Toilet training retarded children in a state residential institution. Mental Retardation 2: 116–117.

Dennis, W. 1948. Readings in the history of psychology. Appleton-Century-Crofts, New York.

Denny, M. R. 1963. Reserach in learning and performance. In H. A. Stevens and R. Heber (eds.), Mental retardation: A review of research, pp. 134–158. McGraw-Hill, New York.

Dinger, J. C. 1961. Post-school adjustment of former educable retarded pupils. Exceptional Children pp. 353–360.

Doll, E. A. 1964. Yesterday, today and tomorrow. Mental Retardation 2: 203–208.

Doll, E. E. 1962. Historical survey of research and management of mental retardation in the U. S. In E. E. Trapp and P. Himelstein (eds.), Readings on the exceptional child: Research and theory. Appleton-Century-Crofts, New York.

Doll, E. E. 1967. Historical review of mental retardation, 1800-1965. A symposium. American Journal of Mental Deficiency 72: 165–189.

Doll, E. E. 1970. A historical view of the private residential facility in the training and study of the mentally retarded in the United States. Mental Retardation 8: 3–8.

Doll, E. E. 1972. The historical collections of the AAMD. Mental Retardation 10: 16–19.

Down, J. L. H. 1867. Observations on an ethnic classification of idiots. Mental Science 13: 121–128.

Dugdale, R. L. 1877. The Jukes: A study in crime, pauperism, disease and heredity. Putnam's Sons, New York.

Eagle, E. 1967. Prognosis and outcome of community placement of institutionalized retardates. American Journal of Mental Deficiency 72: 232–243.

Ellis, N. R. (Ed.). 1963. Handbook of mental deficiency. McGraw-Hill, New York.

Estabrook, A. H. 1915. The Jukes in 1915. Carnegie Institution of Washington, No. 240.

Fairbanks, R. 1933. The subnormal child: Seventeen years after. Mental Hygiene 17: 177–208.

Fernald, W. E. 1893. The history of the treatment of the feeble-minded. Proceedings of the National Conference on Social Welfare 22: 203–221.

Fernald, W. E. 1924. Thirty years progress in the care of the feeble-minded. Journal of Psycho-Asthenics 29: 206–219.

Foster, R., K. Nihira, and H. Leland. 1966. Measurement of adaptive behavior. American Psychologist 21: 601.

Gall, J. 1808. Introduction au cours de physiologie du cerveau.

Galton, F. 1869. Hereditary genius. London: Macmillan.

Gardner, J. M. 1968. Lightner Witmer: A neglected pioneer. American Journal of Mental Deficiency 72: 719–720.

Giradeau, F. L. and J. E. Spradlin. 1964. Token rewards in a cottage program. Mental Retardation 2: 345–351.

Goddard, H. H. 1907. Psychological work among the feeble-minded. Journal of Psycho-Asthenics 12: 18–30.

Goddard, H. H. 1914. The Kallikak family: A study in the heredity of feeble-mindedness. Macmillan, New York.

Goldstein, H. 1964. Social and occupational adjustment. In H. A. Stevens and R. Heber (eds.), Mental Retardation. University of Chicago Press, Chicago.

Grob, G. N. 1966. The state and the mentally ill. University of North Carolina Press, Chapel Hill.

Grob, G. N. 1966. The state mental hospital in mid-nineteenth century America: A social analysis. American Psychologist 21: 510–523.

Grunberger, R. 1971. The 12-year Reich: A social history of Nazi Germany, 1934–1945. Holt, Rinehart & Winston, New York.

Gunzburg, H. C. 1972. Editorial. The British Journal of Mental Subnormality, 28, Part 2: 63–65.

Haskell, R. H. 1944. Mental deficiency over a hundred years. American Journal of Psychiatry 100: 107–118.

Heber, R. 1961. A manual on terminology and classification in mental retardation. American Journal of Mental Deficiency, Monograph Supplement.

Heber, R., R. Dever, and J. Conry. 1968. The influence of environmental and genetic variables on intellectual development. In H. J. Prehm, L. A. Hamerlynch, and J. E. Crosson (eds.), Behavioral research in mental retardation, pp. 1–23. University of Oregon Press, Eugene, Oregon.

Hitler, A. 1943. Mein Kampf. Houghton Mifflin, Boston.

Ireland, W. W. 1877. On idiocy and imbecility. Churchill, London.

Itard, J. M. G. 1801. De l'education d'un homme savage. Goujon, Paris.

Jensen, A. R. 1969. How much can we boost IQ and scholastic achievement? Harvard Educational Review 39: 1–123.

Joint Commission on Accreditation of Hospitals. 1971. Standards for residential facilities for the mentally retarded. JCAH, Chicago.

Kanner, L. 1967. A history of the care and study of the mentally retarded. Charles C. Thomas, Springfield, Illinois.

Kennedy, R. J. R. 1966. A Connecticut community revisited: A study of the social adjustment of a group of mentally deficient adults in 1948 and 1960. Project No. 655, Office of Vocational Rehabilitation, U. S. Department of Health, Education and Welfare, Washington, D. C.

Lombroso, C. 1911. Crime, its causes and remedies. Translated by H. P. Horton, Little, Brown, Boston.

Lovaas, O. I., J. P. Berberich, B. F. Perloff, and B. Schaeffer. 1966. Acquisition of imitative speech by schizophrenic children. Science 161: 705–707.

Lovaas, O. I., B. Schaeffer, and J. Q. Simmons. 1965. Experimental studies in childhood schizophrenia: Building social behavior in autistic children by use of electric shock. Journal of Experimental Research in Personality 1: 99–109.

Malthus, J. R. 1803. Essay on the principle of population. J. Johnson, London.

McCarver, R. B. and E. M. Craig. Placement of the retarded in the community: Prognosis and outcome. *In* N. R. Ellis (ed.), International Review of Research in Mental Retardation, Volume 7. (In press.)

McCullers, J. C. 1969. G. Stanley Hall's conception of mental development and some indications of its influence on developmental psychology. American Psychologist 24: 1109–1114.

Miller, E. L. 1965. Ability and social adjustment at midlife of persons earlier judged mentally deficient. Genetic Psychology Monographs 72: 139–198.

Murphy, G. 1951. Historical introduction to modern psychology. Harcourt, Brace, New York.

Myerson, A. 1926. Researches in feeblemindedness. Journal of Psycho-Asthenics 31: 203–209.

Nihira, K. 1969. Factorial dimensions of adaptive behavior in adult retardates. American Journal of Mental Deficiency 73: 868–878.

Nihira, K., R. Foster, M. Shelhass, and H. Leland. 1969. Adaptive behavior scales. AAMD, Washington, D. C.

Potter, H. W. 1922. Fourteenth annual report of the board of managers, Letchworth Village. Albany, New York.

Roback, A. A. 1964. History of psychology and psychiatry. The Citadel Press, New York.

Roos, P. 1968. Initiating socialization programs for socially inept adolescents. Mental Retardation 6: 13–17.

Royfe, E. H. 1971. A systems analysis of an historic mental retardation institution: A case study of Elwyn Institute - 1852-1970. Doctoral dissertation, Temple University.

Schwartz, H. 1952. Samuel Gridley Howe as phrenologist. The American Historical Review 57: 644–651.

Schwartz, H. 1956. Samuel Gridley Howe: Social reformer, 1801-1876. Harvard University Press, Cambridge.

Seguin, E. 1843. Hygiene et education des idiots. Balliere, Paris.

Seguin, E. 1870. New facts and remarks concerning idiocy. Wood & Co., New York.

Seguin, E. 1907. Idiocy: And its treatment by the physiological method. Teachers' College, Columbia University Press, New York.

Skeels, H. M. 1966. Adult status of children with contrasting early life experiences. Monographs of the Society for Research in Child Development, 31, No. 3.

Skeels, H. M. and H. B. Dye. 1939. A study of the effects of differential stimulation on mentally retarded children. Proceedings and Addresses of the American Association on Mental Deficiency, 44: 114–136.

Skinner, B. F. 1938. The behavior of organisms: An experimental analysis. Appleton-Century-Crofts, New York.

Skinner, B. F. 1953. Science and human behavior. McMillan, New York.

Sloan, W. 1963. Four score and seven. American Journal of Mental Deficiency 68: II, 6–14.

Spitz, H. H. 1963. Field theory in mental deficiency. *In* N. R. Ellis (ed.), Handbook of Mental Deficiency, pp. 11–40. McGraw-Hill, New York.

Spruzheim, J. G. 1832. Phrenology, or the doctrine of mental phenomena. Marsh, Capen & Lyon, Boston.

Stevens, H. A. 1965. The field is rich . . . and ready for harvest. American Journal of Mental Deficiency 70: 4–15.

Stevens, H. A. and R. Heber, (eds.). 1964. Mental retardation. University of Chicago Press, Chicago.

Talbot, M. E. 1964. Edouard Seguin: A study of an educational approach to the treatment of mentally defective children. Teachers College, New York.

Tizard, J. 1958. Longitudinal and follow-up studies. *In* A. Clarke and A. D. B. Clarke (eds.), Mental deficiency: The changing outlook, pp. 422–449. Methuen, London.

Tyor, P. L. 1972. Segregation or surgery: The mentally retarded in America, 1850–1920. Doctoral dissertation, Northwestern University. University of Microfilms, Ann Arbor, Michigan.

Vail, D. J. 1967. Dehumanization and the institutional career. Charles C Thomas, Springfield, Illinois.

Wallin, J. E. W. 1917. Feeblemindedness and delinquency. Mental Hygiene 1: 585–590.

Wallin, J. E. W. 1955. The odyssey of a psychologist: Pioneering experiences in special education, clinical psychology, and mental hygiene. Wilmington, Delaware: Published by the author.

Wallin, J. E. W. 1956. Mental deficiency: In relation to problems of genesis, social and occupational consequences, utilization, control, and prevention. Journal of Clinical Psychology. Brandon, Vermont.

Watson, L. S., Jr. 1968. Application of behavior-shaping devices to training severely and profoundly mentally retarded children in an institutional setting. Mental Retardation 6: 21–23.

Watson, L. S., Jr., J. M. Gardner, and C. Sanders. 1971. Shaping and maintaining behavior modification skills in staff members in an MR institution: Columbus State Institute Behavior Modification Program. Mental Retardation 9: 39–42.

Watson, R. I. 1956. Lightner Witmer: 1867–1956. American Journal of Psychology 69: 680–682.

White, W. D. and W. Wolfensberger. 1969. The evolution of dehumanization in our institutions. Mental Retardation 7: 5–9.

Windle, C. 1962. Prognosis of mental subnormals. American Journal of Mental Deficiency, Monograph Supplement. 66, No. 5.

Wolf, T. H. 1964. Alfred Binet: A time of crisis. American Psychologist 19: 762–771.

Wortis, J. (ed.), 1969-1974. Mental retardation and developmental disabilities: An annual review. Volume I - VI. Brunner/Mazel, New York.

Zigler, E. 1967. Familial retardation: A continuing dilemma. Science 155: 292–298.

CHRONOLOGY

1743   Péreire instructs deaf mutes.

1794   Pinel appointed director of the Salpêtrière; institutes moral treatment.

1801   Abbe Bonnaterre brings "wild boy of Aveyron" to Jean Marc Gaspard Itard.

1833   Opening of Worcester State Hospital in Massachusetts; Samuel Bayard Woodward, first superintendent; Horace Mann instrumental in its establishment.

1838   Edouard Seguin forms an experimental class at the Salpêtrière in Paris.

1841   Johann Jacob Guggenbuhl establishes the Abendberg, near Berne, Switzerland.

1842   Seguin starts class for idiots at the Bicêtre.

1842   Institution established in Berlin; M. Saegert, director.

1843   Publication of Seguin's *Hygiène et Éducation des Idiots.*

1846   Private institution established at Leipzig by Dr. Kern.

1846   Private school established for idiots at Bath, England.

1846   Appointment of a committee to inquire into the conditions of idiots in the Commonwealth of Massachusetts; Dr. S. G. Howe, chairman.

1848   Samuel Gridley Howe establishes an "experimental school for idiots" at Perkins Institute for the Blind.

1848   Founding of first private school at Barre in Massachusetts by H. B. Wilbur.

1851   H. B. Wilbur organizes New York State Experimental School at Albany; later moves to Syracuse.

1852   Establishment of school in Germantown, Pennsylvania; J. B. Richards, principal; move to Media, Pennsylvania, 1859.

1852   Institution established near Dundee, Scotland, by Sir John and Lady Jane Ogilvy.

1854   Institution at Riag founded by Friedrich Platz.

1855   Day school for trainable imbeciles opens at The Hague, Netherlands.

1855   Small private institution opens in Copenhagen; Pastor Durloo, super-intendent.

1855   Opening of institution of Earlswood, England.

1855   Opening of Edinburgh Institution in Scotland; Dr. David Brodie, director.

1857   Establishment of institution at Columbus, Ohio; Dr. Dorin, Super-intendent.

1858   School opened at Lakeville, Connecticut, by Dr. Henry M. Knight.

1860   State school opened at Frankfort, Kentucky.

1861   Founding of Scottish National Institution for the Education of Imbe-cile Children at Darbert, Stiringshire; Dr. William W. Ireland, super-intendent.

1863   First idiot asylum in Sweden.

1866   John Langdon Haydon Down describes "mongolian type of idiocy."

1866   Publication of Seguin's *Idiocy, and its Treatment by the Physiological Method.*

1869   Opening of the Stewart Institution at Palmerston, Dublin.

1870   An asylum opened in Prague, Czechoslavokia.

1871   First school for retarded in Norway; Dr. Ludvig Dahl, director.

1876   Organization of the Association of Medical Officers of American Institutions for Idiotic and Feeble-Minded Persons, at Elwyn, Pennsyl-vania (Seguin, Kerlin, Brown, Doren, Knight, H. B. Wilbur, C. T. Wilbur).

1876   Small school opened in Jakobstad, Finland, by M. K. Lundberg.

1877   Publication of *On Idiocy and Imbecility* by William Weatherspoon Ireland.

1877   Publication of *The Jukes* by Richard L. Dugdale.

1878   New York State Custodial Asylum opened at Newark.

1881–1887   Warren Tay and Bernard Sachs describe Amaurotic familial idiocy (Tay-Sachs disease).

1887   Stephen Garrison opens private school in Milville, New Jersey, soon followed by Charles Garrison's school at Cranberry and Olin S. Garri-son's at Vineland.

1889   First school for mental defectives established in Italy at Chiavari, by Professor Antonia Gonnelli-Gioni.

1890   Private institution in Japan; Mr. R. Ishii, director.

1892   Menage in Hainault, Belgium, an asylum for idiots and epileptics.

1894   Rome State Custodial Asylum.

1896   First psychological clinic in United States, founded by Lightner Witmer.

1897   Opening of institution for western Pennsylvania at Polk.

1898   Formation of National League for protection of backward children, in Italy. Signorina Montessori active in establishing special schools and adapting Seguin's methods.

1900   Templeton Farm Colony in Massachusetts founded.

1904   Martin Barr publishes *Mental Defectives, Their History, Treatment and Training.*

1905   First appearance of the Binet-Simon intelligence scale.

1912   Henry Goddard publishes *The Kallikak Family.*

1934   Folling describes phenylpyruvic oligophrenia as a metabolic disturbance.

1935   Edgar A. Doll publishes *The Measurement of Social Competence.*

1950   National Association for Retarded Children founded

1958   Congress amends Rehabilitation Act to include mental handicap.

1961   President Kennedy establishes President's Panel on Mental Retardation.

1963   Congress passes Public Law 88-164 for the construction of University Affiliated Facilities.

1967   Declaration of general and special rights of the retarded by International League of Societies for the Mentally Handicapped.

1971   Pennsylvania Right to Education decision.

1971   *Wyatt v. Stickney* decision in Alabama.

INDEX